The Driftless Reader

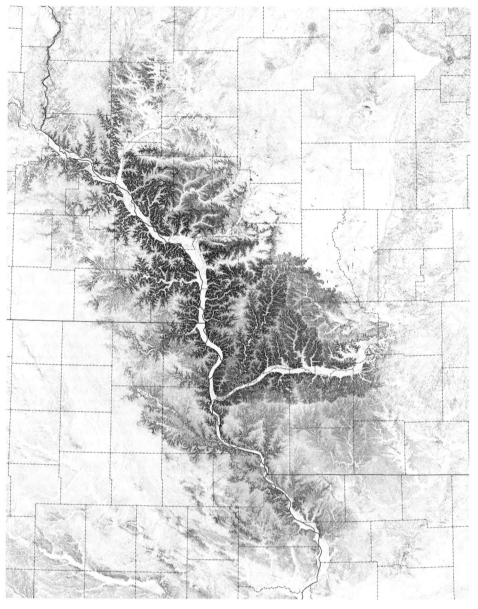

Driftless Slope Map, Joshua Wachtua (2013). The distinctive topography of the Driftless Area inspired Joshua Wachuta to create this digital map to show its contrast to the surrounding region. In the map, the slopes of the Driftless are highlighted, with steeper hillsides shaded more than level land. The major rivers and their floodplains show as flat white channels amid the blufflands. Wachuta grew up on a farm in southwestern Wisconsin and is pursuing graduate studies in history at Loyola University in Chicago.

The Driftless Reader

Edited by

CURT MEINE *and* KEEFE KEELEY

The University of Wisconsin Press

The University of Wisconsin Press
728 State Street, Suite 443
Madison, Wisconsin 53706
uwpress.wisc.edu

3 Henrietta Street, Covent Garden
London WC2E 8LU, United Kingdom
eurospanbookstore.com

Printed in the United States of America

This book may be available in a digital edition.

Library of Congress Cataloging-in-Publication Data
Names: Meine, Curt, editor. | Keeley, Keefe, editor.
Title: The Driftless reader / edited by Curt Meine and Keefe Keeley.
Description: Madison, Wisconsin : The University of Wisconsin Press, [2017] |
Includes bibliographical references and index.
Identifiers: LCCN 2017010429 | ISBN 9780299314804 (cloth : alk. paper)
Subjects: LCSH: Driftless Area—Description and travel.
Classification: LCC F351 .D75 2017 | DDC 977—dc23
LC record available at https://lccn.loc.gov/2017010429

For all those working on behalf of
healthy human and natural communities
in the Driftless Area

A large area in the southwestern portion [of Wisconsin] bears
no evidence of having suffered glaciation, and hence has been
designated the *Driftless Area*.

> —T. C. CHAMBERLIN, *Geology of Wisconsin,*
> *Survey of 1873–1879* (1883)

The land remembers. It says, "I am here. You are part of me."

> —BEN LOGAN, *The Land Remembers* (1975)

I like this place, and this is sacred to me.

> —JIM FUNMAKER, Bear Clan, Ho-Chunk Nation (1994)

Contents

Illustrations

Color plates between pages 152 and 153

Plate 1. "Theoretical Map of Wisconsin during the Second Glacial Epoch," T. C. Chamberlin (1883)

Plate 2. Main bison panel, Geri Schrab (2016)

Plate 3. *Third Buffalo Hiding*, Geri Schrab (2016)

Plate 4. *Black Hawk, Prominent Sac Chief*, George Catlin (1832)

Plate 5. "Bird's Eye View of the City of McGregor and North McGregor, Clayton County, Iowa 1869"

Plate 6. *Boyhood Home of Hamlin Garland*, Hans John Stoltenberg (1937)

Plate 7. *Wisconsin Farm Scene*, John Steuart Curry (1941)

Plate 8. *Residence of Mr. Martin Lutscher. Town Honey Creek. Wis.*, Paul Siefert (c. 1880)

Plate 9. *Milking Time*, Lavern Kammerude (1981)

Plate 10. *Contour Farming*, Jim Klousia (2013)

Plate 11. *Cow Crossing in Grant County*, Kerry G. Hill (2012)

Plate 12. Hmong Pa Dau (c. 1990)

Plate 13. *Syttende Mai 2015*, Lauren Louise Anderson (2015)

Plate 14. Steamboat *J. S.* on the Mississippi River (c. 1900)

Plate 15. *Traffic Serenade*, Paul Bergquist (2012)

Plate 16. *The Remarkable Cow*, John Craig (2016)

Credits

From *A Thousand Pieces of Paradise: Landscape and Property in the Kickapoo Valley* by Lynne Heasley. Copyright © 2005 by the Board of Regents of the University of Wisconsin System. Used with permission of the University of Wisconsin Press.

"Frac Sand Song" by Emmett J. Doyle. Licensed by Creative Commons 2013. Used with permission of the author.

"Driftless Elegy" from *The Earth Avails* by Mark Wunderlich. Copyright © 2013, 2014 by Mark Wunderlich. Used with permission of the Permissions Company, Inc., on behalf of Graywolf Press.

From *The Driftless Zone; or, A Novel Concerning the Selective Outmigration from Small Cities* by Rick Harsch. Copyright © 1997. Used with permission of the author.

From *Driftless* by David Rhodes. Copyright © 2008 by David Rhodes. Used with permission of Milkweed Editions.

"Postville: Iowa's Entry into the Post-Modern" from *Heartland Portrait: Stories from the Rural Midwest* by Robert Wolf. Copyright © 2009 by Free River Press. Used with permission of Free River Press.

"Things I Love About Where I Am" by Kathe Davis. Copyright © 2012 by Kathe Davis. Used with permission of the author.

"Broken Gates" from *Broken Gates* by Ken McCullough. Copyright © 2012 by Ken McCullough. Used with permission of the author.

From *Going Driftless: Life Lessons from the Heartland for Unraveling Times* by Stephen J. Lyons. Copyright © 2015. Used with permission of Rowman & Littlefield Publishing Group.

From *Jerusalem Creek: Journeys into Driftless Country* by Ted Leeson. Copyright © 2002. Used with permission of Rowman & Littlefield Publishing Group.

From *The Driftless Land: Spirit of Place in the Upper Mississippi Valley* by Kevin Koch. Copyright © 2010 by Kevin Koch. Used with permission of the Southeast Missouri State University Press.

Illustrations

Driftless Slope Map, Joshua Wachuta (2013). Used with permission of the artist.

Black Earth Valley, Adolf Johann Hoeffler (1852). Used with permission of the Wisconsin Historical Society, WHS-31174.

Deer head petroglyph (c. 1000). Used with permission of Daniel Seurer.

The Gottschall Head (c. 1000). Used with permission of Beloit College.

"Monument Erected at Wyalusing State Park, Wisconsin, in Memory of the Passenger Pigeon," Hjalmar A. Skuldt (1947). Used with permission of the Dane County Historical Society, Otto Schroeder Records Center.

Badger and Prairie Smoke, Dan Hazlett (2002). Used with permission of the artist.

Untitled wood engraving, Frank Utpatel (1966). Used with permission of Stanton & Lee Publishers.

Devil's Lake Sunrise, John Miller (2012). Used with permission of the artist.

Bird Effigy, Truman Lowe (1997). Used with permission of the artist and the Heard Museum.

The second Fort Crawford (c. 1840). Used with permission of the Wisconsin Historical Society, WHS-5385.

The Mississippi River along Highway 35, Paul Vanderbilt (1962). Used with permission of the Wisconsin Historical Society, WHS-37132.

Cross-section of a Lead Mine, David Dale Owen (1844). Used with permission of the Wisconsin Historical Society, WHS-129204.

Rafting pine on the Upper Mississippi River (c. 1900). Used with permission of the Wisconsin Historical Society, WHS-128731.

Untitled drawing, Lawrence E. Blair (c. 1948). Used with permission of the Wisconsin Historical Society, WHS-128732.

Brisbois Fur Trading Post (c. 1920). Used with permission of the Wisconsin Historical Society, WHS-42458.

Sketch of Mineral Point, Aaron Bohrod (1973). Used with permission of Stanton & Lee Publishers.

Cemetery at Pleasant Ridge (c. 1958). Used with permission of the Wisconsin Historical Society, WHS-2204.

Train from Coon Valley to Viroqua (c. 1919). Image courtesy of Tom Sharrat.

Threshing scene, Frank Feiker (c. 1905). Used with permission of the Wisconsin Historical Society, WHS-31816.

Tobacco weeding, Andrew John Mueller (1968). Used with permission of the Wisconsin Historical Society, WHS-91776.

Before the Heat of the Day, Kathie Wheeler (2010). Used with permission of the artist.

Maiden's Rock, Lake Pepin, Alfred Waud (1874). Used with permission of the Wisconsin Historical Society, WHS-95897.

Swimming in the Mississippi River, Gerhard Gesell (c. 1890). Used with permission of the Wisconsin Historical Society, WHS-2083.

Along the Kickapoo River, Adam Haydock (2014). Used with permission of the photographer.

Erosion in the Black River watershed (1935). Image courtesy of USDA Natural Resources Conservation Service.

Cows at Taliesin #64, Pedro Guerrero (1940). Used with permission of the Pedro E. Guerrero Archive.

Buggy, Carl Homstad (2005). Used with permission of the artist.

Lucy Stone historic marker, Robert Clovis Siemon (2016). Used with permission of the photographer.

Restoration on Shake Rag Street, Mineral Point (c. 1940). Used with permission of the Wisconsin Historical Society, WHS-37981.

A menorah above the meat-processing plant in Postville, Carol Highsmith (2016). Image courtesy of Library of Congress.

La Crosse River, Memorial Park to County Highway J, Michael Lind (2014). Used with permission of the artist.

Farmed Frame, David Wells (2012). Used with permission of the artist and the photographer.

Main bison panel, Geri Schrab (2016). Used with permission of the photographer.

Third Buffalo Hiding, Geri Schrab (2016). Used with permission of the artist.

Black Hawk, Prominent Sac Chief, George Catlin (1832). Image courtesy of the Smithsonian American Art Museum, Gift of Mrs. Joseph Harrison, Jr.

"Bird's Eye View of the City of McGregor and North McGregor, Clayton County, Iowa 1869." Image courtesy of Library of Congress.

Boyhood Home of Hamlin Garland, Hans John Stoltenberg (1937). Used with permission of the Wisconsin Historical Society, WHS-2680.

Wisconsin Farm Scene, John Steuart Curry (1941). Used with permission of the Chazen Museum of Art, University of Wisconsin–Madison, Gift of First National Bank and First Wisconsin Corporation, 1985.319.

Residence of Mr. Martin Lutscher. Town Honey Creek. Wis., Paul Siefert (c. 1880). Used with permission of the Wisconsin Historical Society, WHS-41161.

Milking Time, Lavern Kammerude (1981). Used with permission of the artist's estate.

Contour Farming, Jim Klousia (2013). Used with permission of Edible Madison.

Cow Crossing in Grant County, Kerry G. Hill (2012). Used with permission of the photographer.

Hmong Pa Dau (c. 1990). Used with permission of Luther College Anthropology Lab Ethnographic and Archaeological Collections.

Syttende Mai 2015, Lauren Louise Anderson (2015). Used with permission of the artist.

Steamboat *J. S.* on the Mississippi River (c. 1900). Used with permission of the Wisconsin Historical Society, WHS-5684.

Traffic Serenade, Paul Bergquist (2012). Used with permission of the artist.

The Remarkable Cow, John Craig (2016). Used with permission of the artist.

Preface

Where does here end, and there begin?

During the most recent ice age, massive glaciers repeatedly shouldered their way south across the northern hemisphere. As the climate warmed, the ice giants melted back in retreat. They left behind land flattened and littered with their aftermath: the boulders, gravels, sands, and other sediments collectively termed glacial drift. But an island of odd topography in the Upper Midwest, spared the glacial razing, lacks such drift. It is *driftless*.

Glaciers defined the edges of the Driftless Area. Waterways vein its interior. The Mississippi, Wisconsin, Upper Iowa, Kickapoo, Zumbro, Root, and other rivers flow through the region, each fed by fractal tributaries branching up into their valleys of origin. The Driftless Area includes southwestern Wisconsin and parts of neighboring Minnesota, Iowa, and Illinois. Geologists and other Driftless aficionados recognize different boundaries—areas that were partially covered during earlier episodes of glaciation, that escaped the last "Wisconsinan" phase, that were under pooled waters during the Great Melt.

However defined, the Driftless is overlaid with modern political boundaries. Across those boundary lines, it is distinguished by its layered foundations of sedimentary rock; by its rolling ridgelines, hilltops, and bluff lands; by its dendritic network of waterways; by soils born of bedrock, blown in as loess, and carried in its running waters; by its mix of remnant prairies and savannas, woodlands, forests, and wetlands; by a rich array of wildlife adapted to its variety of wildlands, farms, woods, waters, towns, and cities.

The Driftless is a good place for people. For twelve millennia, plant and animal provisions have sustained its human inhabitants. For several more recent millennia, cultivated crops have thrived as well. Perhaps to honor that abundance, or to mark strategic sites to enjoy it, ancient peoples built earthen mounds in profusion across the Driftless land-scape—conical and linear mounds and effigies in the shapes of various spirits, birds, mammals, and, in some sites, humans. The mounds and other creations—cave-walls adorned with pictographs and petroglyphs, hillside caches of arrowheads and spear points, potsherds and ancient garden beds—link us to the long line of people who have made the Driftless their home.

Across time, the cultural amalgam of the Driftless has included (among others) the Ho-Chunk, Dakota, Ioway, Sauk, Meskwaki (Fox), Kickapoo, Menominee, Ojibwe, and Potawatomi people; Spanish gover-nors, French fur traders, and blackrobe missionaries; British officers, American armies, and Indian agents; naturalists, geologists, and adven-turers; Cornish miners, Norwegian rosemalers, Irish railroad builders, Yankee lumbermen, African American barn builders, barbers, and newspaper editors; Civil War soldiers and widows; German brewers, Polish polka dancers, Czech musicians, and farmers of every national-ity; Dominican sisters, Protestant pastors, Unitarian teachers, Buddhist monks, and Wiccan ministers; and, more recently, hippie entrepre-neurs, homesteader scientists, master cheesemakers, Hmong organic farmers, Amish activists, Guatemalan farm workers, Mexican *mercado* owners, and kosher meat-packing magnates.

No one book can embrace all the stories, histories, and visions of the Driftless Area. This collection aims to give readers access to an essential sample of those voices. We hope that such an introduction can help bridge what the Driftless has been, what it is, and what it is becoming.

Along the way, we may learn more of who *we* have been and are becom-ing. More than just *location*, a place is built of the meanings people find and create there. Perhaps that is what is behind this quirk: a geological term that is coming to define an emerging bioregional identity. The term *driftless* is being attached to distilleries and fly-fishing shops, com-munity radio stations and folk schools, novels and albums, scientific studies and ecological restoration projects. As compellingly poetic as the word is, there are, and have been, other names for this place. It has been called, in parts or in whole, the Coulee Region; the Little Ozarks,

Little Appalachia, Little Norway, and Little Switzerland; the Ocooch Mountains, Bluff Country, Bluff Lands, the Ridge and Valley region, the Uplands, and the Paleozoic Plateau. It has even been designated (quite in earnest) as "the veritable Garden of Eden"; in 1886 the circuit-riding Reverend D. O. Van Slyke self-published a treatise providing evidence that the biblical Paradise was in fact Trempealeau, Wisconsin.

For many, the area has simply been known as "the hills."

Even as we cherish the poetry, diversity, and specificity of these alternatives, for the purposes of this collection we use the term *Driftless*. We consider its geographic scope to include the distinctive topography of nonglaciated uplands, ridges, and valleys formed by flowing water, even though some forms of glacial drift have technically been identified within the region, and we could argue for embracing other areas on its periphery.

Geology provides our foundation for understanding the extent of the place, but from there we step into other modes of understanding. The geological, hydrological, and ecological space becomes personal and cultural through the stories and meanings that it gathers—layered, shaped, grown over, and occasionally exposed, like the strata of Driftless bedrock. Individual experience colors these lenses and layers, so we offer the reader a sense of our own histories with the Driftless.

Keefe Keeley: Near the crown of a certain hillside, an outcropping of limestone has resisted the influences of time. This durable dolomite, stiffened by ancient seashells, overhangs slightly, lending a half-roof shelter to an older, softer face of exposed sandstone below. Standing at this rock face, I see sketches of wind and water, roots and fire, claws and paws, and, most recently, human etchings. There is no sign of ancient art on this sandstone canvas, but here are marks from not so long ago: my first initial plus a first love's, both enclosed within the outline of a valentine heart. A few dates carved elsewhere, some decades old, unsentimentally add to the palimpsest.

Compared with writing on paper, or uploading words into the cloud, this little cliff seems an enduring place to have made a mark, but these rocks, too, are pages of history, turning into eroded stories, myth, and mystery. Sand falls on sand, my feet, oak leaves, and coyote droppings. Maybe the dark scat just seems so plentiful because it stands out against the sandy ground. Or maybe this is a sign the old tricksters like it here too, where primal rock exposes other worlds, seemingly far away—in time, or whatever medium holds stories—but right here.

Sharing the story of my youthful petroglyph feels a bit like sharing this volume. By whose authority do I mark this rock face, or anthologize this place? And what responsibilities come with the territory? Part of the charm of the Driftless is that it feels *undiscovered*. But discovery of an already peopled place is a knotty notion, inescapable in my European and back-to-the-land heritages, and still echoing in contemporary concerns that newcomers with foreign customs and dubious purposes might bring unwelcome changes to the Driftless.

Yet at its most innocent, discovery is personal. As the mural on a wall of my school in the Kickapoo Valley paraphrased Proust: "The real voyage of discovery consists not in seeking new landscapes, but in having new eyes."

Curt Meine: Through absolutely no intent of my own, I have found myself along the margins of long-gone glaciers for as long as I can remember: born along the terminal moraine in western Pennsylvania; raised on recessional ridges bearing the drift of post–WWII Chicago suburban development (i.e., Park *Ridge*, Des *Plaines*, etc.); schooled along the lakes of Madison, just a short bike-ride in from the Johnstown moraine. For a good portion of my adult life I have lived and worked along the edge of the ancient ice, in Sauk County, Wisconsin.

This Driftless landscape holds bits of my memory—deposited like loess on the surface of the subconscious! A childhood excursion to New Glarus, colored sad November grey. A walkabout starting in Bellevue, Iowa. The impression of Grand Dad Bluff while investigating college possibilities in La Crosse. Heading across the Driftless from Mount Horeb to Effigy Mounds National Monument—passing through a gateway of sorts, on my first trip west to the Rockies and California. None of this was informed by geology or ecology or history. None of this was driven by much of anything except restlessness and the winds of circumstance.

But now, here I live, at the east portal of the Driftless, marginally more aware of its anomalous geology, its kaleidoscopic ecology, its deep and complex human history, its problems and its potential. Now I know it to be a place utterly unique, yet utterly like every other place: layered with many pasts, home to an idiosyncratic community of life, burdened and blessed by rich human histories, and seeking its way forward in times of accelerating and unprecedented change. Here in the Driftless we have opportunities to make necessary and valuable connections, both within and beyond its boundaries.

And so to match Proust's words on Keefe's schoolhouse wall, I offer poet Gary Snyder's words from his home in California's Sierra foothills: "If the ground can be our common ground, we can begin to talk to each other (human and non-human) once again."

We knew when we began this project that selecting readings would be both an absorbing and frustrating task. So it has been. We have been delighted to identify Driftless storytellers of all varieties: eminent and obscure, bygone and contemporary, indigenous and outsider, poetic and scientific and historic and hybrids thereof. But we have also been unsettled by that abundance, knowing that we could not include all the noteworthy and interesting voices who have spoken of, from, and about the Driftless. We followed no set formula for making our selections. We have chosen the readings here based on some combination of historic significance, evocative prose, useful insight, vital perspective, breadth of expression, literary genre, and serendipity.

This collection is a mosaic. We have organized the pieces based on how well they portray collectively the character of the region. We hope that unexpected connections and patterns emerge as the different pieces work with and play off each other. The volume is organized in a roughly chronological manner, through sections whose core themes extend from ancient geology to imagined futures. These boundaries too are artificial, but they offer coherence and opportunities for interpretation. And because certain pieces just do not fit well in an imposed outline, we have sometimes placed a reading simply where it feels right. We provide overviews for each section, and brief notes for each reading.

We hope that the selected readings will encourage interested readers to explore more deeply the original texts. We also urge readers to seek out the many others that we could not include here (see Sources and Further Readings). In compiling this collection, we have learned that the literature of the Driftless Area, like its sedimentary bedrock, is extensive, multilayered, and surprising. And while many of our favorite readings appear here, we have had to leave many more hidden under this volume's surface. Further discoveries await any curious reader.

With the choice of images, we faced similar challenges: an abundance of evocative maps, illustrations, paintings, woodcuts, photographs, and other materials; an array of regional artists, known and unknown, historic and contemporary; and not enough space to do them justice or to adequately depict the Driftless. We have chosen a small sample to complement the readings, to tell particular stories, to highlight key events and artists, and to evoke the Driftless.

After all the searching and sorting and selecting and piecing together, what have we discovered in the Driftless landscape? What do these readings and images show? We hope you will make your own discoveries in these pages, but we have been struck by certain qualities, tensions, and even paradoxes that these readings reveal.

The Driftless landscape is almost by definition old, tough, and stable; yet it is fragile and subject to constant (and sometimes disruptive) change.

In its intimate geography, it can be a landscape of comfort and contentment; yet its coulees can also seem narrow and confining.

It has been, throughout its history, a place to come to, to stay, to leave, to return to.

It is a landscape prone to insularity but also to tolerance, acceptance, and celebration.

It has seen painful cultural collisions and surprising assimilations.

It has offered opportunities to resist and opportunities to change. On its ridges and in its valleys, continuity walks with innovation, conservatism abides by progress, and communitarian values coexist with individualistic spirit.

The Driftless Area has also been an important laboratory for working out the relationship between humans and the land. It is neither "pristine" nor wholly humanized. It holds within it the wild and the cultivated.

The Driftless is not unique in displaying such tensions. They can and do arise any place that people inhabit. Yet the confluence of nature and culture in the Driftless is unique, the channels of ecological and social change still shaping the hills.

We have, alas, omitted much here: the Decorah Impact Crater and the Rock Elm Disturbance; the Moscow Fissure and the Lost River Sink; the Wisconsin River when it flowed backwards; sturgeon and paddlefish, rare freshwater mussels and populations of endemic trout; muskroot, northern monkshood, the Iowa Pleistocene snail, and other boreal denizens of algific talus slopes; the Dickeyville grotto and the steampunk creations of Dr. Evermor; Blue Wing in Reedsburg, Father Mazzuchelli in Dubuque, Elisabeth Koren in Decorah, George Edwin Taylor in La Crosse, Hieronim Derdowski in Winona; the mystery of Bogus Bluff and the birth of the Gideon Bible; the nation's first solar village (Soldiers Grove) and largest organic farmer cooperative (based in La Farge); a chorus of voices calling from local newspapers, church bulletins, correspondence, and other ephemeral writings. And obviously much more. Further encounters await.

We hope that these explorations encourage readers within the Driftless Area to value this shared landscape, and to work to protect, regenerate, and sustain its ecological health, its human communities, and its local economies. A literature of this place can help shape its next chapters. In the past the Driftless Area has periodically seen its assets diminished and its people dispossessed. Minerals, soils, waters, fauna, furs, prairies, savannas, and forests have been exploited to excess from beyond, and from within. People have been removed, or have felt forced to remove themselves. But Driftless residents have also pioneered new approaches to land protection and stewardship, community renewal, and economic resilience. Wendell Berry has suggested, "If you don't know where you're from, you'll have a hard time saying where you're going." Knowing this place better may not be sufficient, but it is necessary if we are to create a future not of extraction and depletion but of vitality and self-renewal.

For readers outside the Driftless, or from its fringes, we invite you to enjoy its stories, and perhaps pay a visit. More than that, we hope this collection encourages you to seek out the stories of *your* place and to inhabit *its* literature. We know of comparable "readers" for the Great Lakes, the Great Plains, the Adirondacks, Yellowstone, the Appalachian Trail. But such collections can be compiled for any landscape or region. Why not place-based readers for Lake Michigan and the Upper Peninsula; Gary, Indiana, and the Finger Lakes; the Green Mountains and the coast of Maine; Chesapeake Bay and the Piedmont; Charleston and the

Florida Keys; the Mississippi Delta and the Llano Estacado; the Front Range and the Apache Highlands; the Willamette Valley and Puget Sound; the Palouse and the Black Hills; the Platte River and the Prairie Pothole country?

We can dwell on that which divides us, but we all dwell within landscapes that connect us. By listening deeply to the voices of our diverse places, we may find many ways home and many ways forward.

Acknowledgments

We knew when we embarked on this project that *The Driftless Reader* would come together best by tapping into a large and informal network of Driftless-minded friends, neighbors, and colleagues across the region (and beyond). We are grateful to all the following for their contributions to this volume.

This book has taken us deep into the many layers of the region's landscape, history, literature, and culture. That journey began in many ways in conversations with Jack Holzheuter, whose detailed knowledge of the history of Wisconsin and the Upper Midwest never ceases to inform and amaze. We are similarly indebted to Mark Lefebvre, whose personal and professional insights into Wisconsin's literary heritage guided our work on this project in a dozen different ways.

We are deeply grateful to members of the Ho-Chunk Nation who provided guidance and advice for inclusion of the Nation's voices and stories throughout this volume. Through many conversations and communications, President Wilfred Cleveland, Verna Blackdeer, Paula Cleveland, Michelle Cloud, Rhonda Funmaker, David Greendeer, Chloris Lowe, Truman Lowe, Bill Quackenbush, Samantha Skenadore, Jodee Smith, and Marlon WhiteEagle have offered essential foundations, information, and vision for this collection. *Pi na gigi!*

In the course of exploring and selecting the readings and images for this volume, we paid several visits to colleagues across the Driftless. For their good advice and suggestions, we thank David Faldet, Andy Johnson, Paul Johnson, David Lester, Beth Lynch, Loyal Rue, and Bob Wolf (Decorah); Tom Davis, Dale Easley, Dianne Koch, Kevin Koch, Dana Livingston, Yasmin Rioux, and Jessica Schreyer (Dubuque); Gayle Bull and Dixie Guerrero (Mineral Point); Connie Arzigian (La Crosse); and Tex Hawkins and Ken McCullough (Winona).

For so many other conversations and consultations about Driftless geology, history, landscape, literature, conservation, and culture, we thank Wendy Allen, John Ashley, John Attig, Barb and Jeb Barzen, Dennis Boyer, Eric Carson, Destiny Crider, Homer Daehn, Maryo Gard Ewell, Bill Gartner, Margaret Hipwell, Forest Jahnke, Mary Lloyd Jones, Patricia Kelly, Gigi La Budde, Gail Lamberty, Jamie Lamonde, Jim Leary, Jon Lee, Nicolette Meister, Dan Miller, Donna Neuwirth, Rob Nurre, Jay Salinas, Carl Schlect, Edward Schultz, Tom Sharrat, Sam Skemp, Kat Tigerman, Duke Welter, Michael Whaley, and Bonnie Wideman. Our colleagues in the University of Wisconsin–Madison's Center for Culture, History, and the Environment helped shape the framework for this volume through their commitment to place-based, interdisciplinary, and integrated exploration of landscapes near and far—including the Driftless. And we offer a special word of appreciation for the late and much loved Annie Randall, who demonstrated her deep commitment to community, literature, and storytelling through her founding and proprietorship of the Village Booksmith in Baraboo.

We are most obviously and especially grateful to the storytellers, poets, writers, scientists, and artists whose work is represented in this volume. For those no longer with us, we trust that their spirits, like their words and images, still enliven our Driftless coulees and waterways! We thank all the living contributors whose work is included here: Lauren Louise Anderson, John Attig, Paul Bergquist, Florence Bird, Ernie Boszhart, Lynne Burgess, John Craig, Bill Cronon, Alice D'Alessio, Kathe Davis, Lynne Diebel, Bob Dott, Emmett J. Doyle, Fabu, David Faldet, Rick Harsch, Adam Haydock, Dan Hazlett, Lynn Heasley, Carol Highsmith, Kerry G. Hill, Carl Homstad, E. Barrie Kavasch, Robin Kimmerer, Jim Klousia, Kevin Koch, Ted Leeson, Patty Leow, Michael Lind, Truman Lowe, Stephen J. Lyons, Ken McCullough, Laurie Hovell McMillin, Katherine Mead, John Miller, Brian J. Palik, David Rhodes, Geri Schrab, Lisa A. Schulte, Daniel Seurer, Monika E. Shea, Robert Clovis Siemon, Thomas R. Smith, Stan Temple, James Theler, David Wells, Jacqueline West, Kathie Wheeler, Robert Wolf, Mark Wunderlich, and Catherine Young.

We are grateful to Josh Wachuta for allowing us to use his striking slope map of the Driftless Area in the frontispiece of this volume.

It would be a large task to thank all those who assisted in securing the many permissions required to include the readings and images in this volume. But among these, special thanks indeed to: Danielle Hackett of Arkham House Publishers; Diane Drexler, Andy Kraushaar, and Lisa Marine of the Wisconsin Historical Society; Dikkon Eberhart; the Frank Lloyd Wright Foundation; Dixie Guererro; Hope Heavenrich and Jill Sherry Heavenrich; William Houghton; Buddy Huffaker of the Aldo Leopold Foundation; Mark Lefebvre; Anne McKenna of the University of Wisconsin Press; Ann Sinfield of the Chazen Museum of Art; Buck Kiechel of Kiechel Fine Art; Betty Murphy of the Heard Museum; Edward Kammerude; Michael McDermott of the Black Earth Institute; Charley Preusser of the *Crawford County Independent*; Christine Parkinson-Schakel; Tivoli Gough and Sam Skemp of the USDA Natural Resources Conservation Service; Sheila Oberreuter of the U.S. National Park Service; Andy Stoltman of the Wisconsin Department of Natural Resources; and Wendy Vardaman of *Verse Wisconsin*.

At an early stage in the proposal for this volume, and as the manuscript took shape, this collection benefited tremendously from the objective and critical comments of several reviewers. We are indebted to Lynne Heasley, Tom Vale, Mark Lefebvre, and an anonymous reviewer for their keen comments and suggestions.

Our colleagues at the University of Wisconsin Press were enthusiastic about this book from the outset. Thank you to Andrea Christofferson, Sheila Leary, and Dennis Lloyd for their early support and encouragement; to Gwen Walker for shepherding this project through the proposal and review process; to Sarah Hope Kapp for careful assistance with permissions and manuscript preparation; to Adam Mehring for overseeing copyediting and production; and to Patrick Flynn and Terry Emmrich for bringing the design together.

Our work on the *Driftless Reader* was supported in important ways by two great friends of the Driftless Area. Having studied geology at the University of Wisconsin–Madison, Bob Hallum developed an appreciation the Driftless landscape (especially Iowa County!). Bob's contributions to this project allowed us to include the full array of images included herein. Jay Knight loves books and the Driftless Area and is committed to creative work at the intersection of conservation and the humanities. The support of the Bradshaw-Knight Foundation allowed us to secure the necessary permissions for the selected readings and images. For their timely backing, we are deeply grateful to Bob and Jay.

CM thanks all my colleagues at the Aldo Leopold Foundation, the Center for Humans and Nature, the International Crane Foundation, and the University of Wisconsin–Madison for their support of this project and their commitment to connecting people and land through conservation; Wendell Berry, Paul and Pat Johnson, Robin Kimmerer, Rick Knight, Gary Paul Nabhan, Lauret Savoy, and Gary Snyder for their work, words, and example of bioregional awareness and affection that they have provided for so long; John Day for his wonderfully serendipitous gift of Laura Sherry's *Old Prairie du Chien*; my family, most especially the La Crosse and Winona branches; and Patrice for her encouragement and inspiration.

For the support, latitude, and inspiration they provided, KK thanks Steve Ventura and colleagues at the University of Wisconsin–Madison; everyone at the Savanna Institute; my teachers and librarians; Cedarose, family, and the Driftless community.

As we were completing work on this book, we lost a dear mutual friend in the very heart of the Driftless. Rob Horwich was a dedicated leader who worked creatively, tirelessly, and effectively, in the Driftless and in distant places, to guide communities in cooperative conservation of their home lands. He helped us, and so many others, to see how special a place can be. We hope and trust that this book carries something of his spirit in its pages.

The Driftless inspires and sustains us. This book is a token of our gratitude to this land.

Editors' Note

In editing this volume, we have condensed many of the selected readings. We encourage readers to explore the full, original texts. Many older text sources have been digitized and are available online. For these older writings in particular, we have in most cases chosen to retain the original grammar, spellings, and punctuation. We have made infrequent silent corrections for accuracy and readability. Many of the texts have appeared in multiple editions. In the Sources and Further Readings section at the end of this volume we cite the edition from which the text was derived. Some original texts included footnotes and references. For the sake of easier reading, we have chosen not to retain these. (We have, however, included several explanatory footnotes for obscure or technical terms.) Similarly, some texts were accompanied by maps, illustrations, charts, and other graphics not included here.

I

GEOLOGIC ORIGINS

ANY DWELLER OF THE DRIFTLESS AREA, and even the casual visitor,
recognizes that this place is unlike the rest of the American Midwest. Distinguished by its rugged ridge-and-valley topography,
outcrops of sedimentary rock, sinuous streams, and winding roadways,
the region surprises outsiders who imagine the Midwest to be fundamentally flat and its lines straight. As the Big Ice pushed its way south,
multiple times over the last two-and-a-half million years, it scraped over
what are now Canada and the northern United States, leaving behind its
loads of glacial "drift." In the Driftless Area, however, the preglacial topography survives and the ancient forces of landscape formation are fully
evident: sands and carbonate minerals deposited under primordial seas,
groundwater seeping through the rock strata, surface waters flowing in
channels carved over the eons, river basins scoured and filled by catastrophic floods, soils built of decomposed bedrock and blown in on periglacial winds.

We can imagine the first humans coming into this landscape, trac-
ing their way across northwestern North America along expansive flats,
braided streambeds, and spare moraines recently released from the ice.
We can suppose that they too recognized something different in the
Driftless hills and valleys, something unlike the geographies they and
their ancestors had encountered along their long trek into the continent's
interior. We can wonder what stories, legends, visions, and songs they
found within themselves to explain this Driftless anomaly—and how
some of those narratives survived and evolved to inform the worldviews
of their descendants.

Native peoples marked the landscape. In *The Physical Geography of
Wisconsin* (1932), Lawrence Martin noted that "the Indians . . . actually

1

worshipped an erratic bowlder" at the northwest edge of the Driftless near Newport, Minnesota. Martin quoted Minnesota politician and writer W. H. C. Folsom: "The peculiarity of the painted boulder . . . is that it was a shrine, to which from generation to generation pilgrimages were made, and offerings and sacrifices presented. Its Indian name was 'Eyah Hsah,' or 'Red Rock.' . . . The Indians call the stone also 'Waukan,' or 'mystery.' . . . The Dakotahs say it walked or rolled to its present position, and they point to the path over which it traveled." To the south and east of the red rock, the land was driftless.

Over the last two hundred years, science has provided its own changing story of the Driftless Area. Scientific understanding of the region advanced as the discipline of geology developed. Martin credited geologist William Keating, a member of Major Stephen Long's 1805 expedition into the Upper Mississippi Valley and Minnesota, with providing "the first recognition and understanding of the Driftless Area phenomenon." From the 1830s to the 1860s other explorers and scientists, including Henry Schoolcraft and Increase Lapham, would note the absence of erratic boulders and other drift phenomena in the Driftless Area.

The *explanation* of the Driftless anomaly, however, remained elusive; the past presence and role of continental glaciation was still not understood. The mystery began to lift in the mid-1870s. In 1877 Roland Irving, a professor of geology at the University of Wisconsin, published what Martin regarded as "the first correct explanation of the origin of the Driftless." Irving concluded that the deep basin of Lake Superior and the resistant highlands of adjacent Wisconsin had impeded the advance of the Pleistocene glaciers. At about the same time, T. C. Chamberlin in Wisconsin and Newton Winchell, director of Minnesota's geological and natural history survey, arrived at the same explanation. In part because of its distinctive juxtaposition of Driftless and drift-laden lands, the Upper Midwest had in fact become a globally important region for geological research and discovery.

Getting to Black Earth (2013)

PATRICIA MONAGHAN

Patricia Monaghan (1946–2012) was a poet, writer, teacher, and scholar with interests in Celtic mythology, women's spirituality, and the communion of the arts and sciences. While teaching at DePaul University, she co-founded the Black Earth Institute outside Black Earth, Wisconsin, to encourage writers and artists exploring the connections between justice, spirit, and the earth. Monaghan's reflection on the geological history of the Driftless landscape and the lower Wisconsin River appeared in the Institute's *About Place Journal*.

Start with ocean. A shallow sea, populous
with plankton, and giant fish that feed on it.
Let storms and sunlight flash across the sea.
As bodies die, let them drift down to mud.

Then let there be light. And fire. And heaving:
rock on rock. Let the sea sink. Let it
pour away into other, younger seas.
Let the land rest, damp, exhausted, rich.

Now, let ice appear from north and east
and west. Let it move south to form an isle
of green in a sea of snow. Let this happen over
and over and over for half a million years.

Let low pink quartzite hills hold back the ice.
Let lakes appear beyond, inland seas
with coastlines of blue snow. Let eagles float
above the blue and icy waves, fishing.

Now, catastrophe: Let water break
through ice, drowning sleeping bears still

in their caves, and wolves, and fleeing deer, and mice.
Let a great pathway open on the land

marking the pathway of the flood. Let creeks
and rivers deepen crevices in rock,
and gullies form and soften under wind.
Let oaks take root, and shagbark hickory,

and elderberry, yarrow, bee balm, clover,
big and little bluestem, rattlesnake master,
downy gentian, boneset, dogbane, ragweed,
and thickets of sumac, blackberry, blackcap, rose.

Let black soil deepen over limestone seabed
except where it erupts on crowns of hills.
Then, not long ago, let people come.

Start with ocean. End with Black Earth.

Black Earth Valley, Adolf Johann Hoeffler (1852). This pencil sketch portrays
oak savanna on hillsides surrounding the prairie in Black Earth Valley in the
1850s. Itinerant German artist Adolf Hoeffler's depictions of southern
Wisconsin, especially his careful portrayal of open-grown trees, have been
used along with other works of art, written accounts, and surveyors' records
as benchmarks for understanding Driftless landscape patterns at the onset of
European settlement.

From *Roadside Geology of Wisconsin* (2004)

ROBERT H. DOTT JR. AND JOHN W. ATTIG

Since the 1850s the University of Wisconsin in Madison has served as an important center for the study of geology. Robert Dott retired from the UW–Madison in 1994 after thirty-six years of research and teaching in the university's geology department. John Attig served for thirty-one years with UW–Extension and the Wisconsin Geological and Natural History Survey, retiring in 2012. In *Roadside Geology of Wisconsin*, Dott and Attig provide a general introduction to the recent Pleistocene and more ancient bedrock geology of the Driftless Area.

Ice ages when glaciers expanded to cover large parts of the earth have occurred several times during geological history, some before the continents broke apart and drifted to their present positions. We are living in the most recent of these ice ages. During the last 2.5 million years, glaciers have expanded repeatedly to cover the northern parts of North America. The terms *Quaternary Period* (a geologic term for the last 1.8 million years) and *Ice Age* (a term for a geologic event) are often used interchangeably in describing this most recent of the ice ages even though they are not strictly the same in meaning or time equivalence. Several of the glacier expansions during the last few million years reached the Midwest, covering all or part of northern and eastern Wisconsin and reaching southward to Indiana and Illinois. Only southwestern Wisconsin and adjacent parts of Illinois, Iowa, and Minnesota escaped glaciation. This region is known as the Driftless Area because it lacks glacial deposits, which in the past were collectively called "drift." Glaciers expanded to reach all sides of the Driftless Area at different times during the Quaternary Ice Age but are not known to have surrounded it completely at any one time. . . .

Having escaped the footprint of ice, the Driftless Area has undergone millions of years of landscape evolution by running water, which has given it a very different face from the rest of the state. Natural lakes and wetlands so common in glaciated regions are absent from the Driftless Area except locally on river floodplains. Instead, systems of connected tributaries and larger streams have produced a well-drained, deeply dissected terrain. Outcrops of Paleozoic bedrock are especially abundant and continuous in the bluffs along the Wisconsin and Mississippi Rivers. During the last glaciation, these rivers carried large volumes of meltwater that undercut the bluffs and removed slope deposits.

At various times throughout the last several million years, continental ice sheets have advanced to all sides of the Driftless Area, but never covered it. Why was this area spared? The broad lowlands containing Lake Superior and Lake Michigan deflected the generally southerly flow of ice either toward the east or west of the Driftless Area. In addition, the area is near the southernmost extent of the ice sheets so that the ice was thin enough that even the modestly higher topography of the Driftless Area was enough to limit the ice's further expansion.

The bedrock exposed in the Driftless Area consists primarily of 500- to 440-million-year-old sedimentary strata of late Cambrian and Ordovician time. Small areas of Precambrian rocks appear along several river valleys in the northeastern part of the Western Uplands. At the other extreme, several hills in southwestern Wisconsin have small caps of Silurian strata thought to be as young as 425 million years. These are but small remnants left from the erosion of what must have been a blanket of Silurian and even younger Paleozoic marine strata, which formerly covered the state. At widely scattered localities on ridges in the Driftless Area, there are patches of still-younger gravels believed to be of Cretaceous age, or roughly 100 million years old, but they could be much younger. They are probably remnants of widespread river deposits formed over a long span of time before the present river valleys became established.

The Paleozoic strata appear perfectly flat to the human eye, but in fact they are tilted westward very slightly. Although this tilt is only about one tenth of a degree, it is enough to cause each stratum to decline in elevation ten to twelve feet for every mile traveled in a westward direction. The base of the Cambrian rock exposed at an elevation of 800 feet above sea level at Black River Falls on I-94 is about 600 feet lower at the Mississippi River, fifty miles to the west, where it is only 200 feet above sea level. This means that it lies about 500 feet beneath the land surface, for the river is at an elevation of about 700 feet here. As you travel up and down over the ridges and valleys of the Driftless Area, imagine you are on a roller-coaster traveling back and forth through geologic time; going uphill you move through younger strata, but going downhill you cross older ones.

From *Wisconsin's Foundations* (2004)

Gwen M. Schultz

In this passage from *Wisconsin's Foundations: A Review of the State's Geology and Its Influence on Geography and Human Activity*, Gwen Schultz (1923–2014) highlights the contrast between glaciated and nonglaciated landscapes that the Driftless Area provides. A native of Milwaukee, Schultz was a professor of geography at the University of Wisconsin–Madison and worked with the Wisconsin Geological and Natural History Survey from 1969 to 1986.

We can never really know what might have been, but the difference that exists between glaciated and unglaciated terrain now is striking and significant.

In the Driftless Area we see a highly dissected surface, often hilly and rough. Tall bluffs, rugged cliffs, and rocky ledges are common sights, as are jagged crags and isolated mounds. Bedrock outcrops are far more numerous than in drift-covered areas. The land is well drained by mature streams tapping all areas, so it is virtually a lakeless region. There lakes and ponds are artificially made. Waterfalls and cascades are gone, because glaciation did not upset stream courses, and because over a long period of time obstacles that once existed in those old channels have been worn away.

In the glaciated area, on the other hand, the topography is smoothed and gently rolling, with shallow valleys; and the glacier-built moraines and hills—not overly steep or angular—blend into the flowing contours. Drainage is irregular. Youthful streams run this way and that around uneven rises of drift, meeting obstructions and drops that create rapids, falls or diversions. Lakes, ponds, marshes, and swamps are familiar features.

Soils (other than loess) in the Driftless Area are residual, developed essentially in place from underlying rock, so they bear a close relationship to that rock. But in the glaciated region the residual soils were removed; the cover of imported, heterogeneous rock material was left instead, and from that the present soils have developed, usually bearing little or no direct relationship to the bedrock.

One of the things that makes Wisconsin especially interesting geologically is this side-by-side contrast it offers of heavily glaciated and nonglaciated terrain. Although there are other drift-free "islands" elsewhere, Wisconsin's Driftless Area is particularly impressive because of its large size and its location in a highly developed region. Also, the ice lobes that bypassed it or encroached upon it on all sides were powerful ones. Yet it was never completely surrounded by ice at any one time, or not for long. If it had been it would have lake-bed sediments throughout, which it does not. The known limits of the Driftless Area are not everywhere as precise as they appear on maps, because maps have to be generalized, and because along old-drift borders one cannot clearly discern anymore exactly how far the ice came.

Many a person has come to the Driftless Area to search for evidence that it was glaciated. Some looked but did not find; some thought for a while that they had found "proof," only to have it disproved; some ultimately changed their minds and gave up, or failed to convince others of their "evidence." The Driftless Area has been closely combed for signs of glaciation, and will continue to be, for it presents a challenge. Despite attempts to prove otherwise, this driftless "island" still retains its claim to fame.

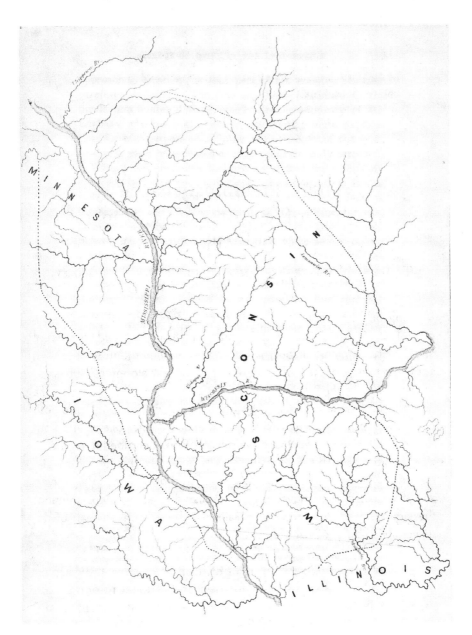

"Diagram of the Region Destitute of Drift and Boulders in Wisconsin, Iowa, and Minnesota," J. D. Whitney (1862). Even as geologists began to study the conspicuous glacial features of the Upper Midwest, they were also drawn to the region by the mineral resources of the lead mining region then booming in the southern portion of the Driftless Area. In his *Report of a Geological Survey of the Upper Mississippi Lead Region*, published in 1862, geologist J. D. Whitney provided the first known map of the "region destitute of drift and boulders." The map was included with Whitney's discussion of the "Surface Geology of the Lead Region."

From "Preliminary Paper on the Driftless Area of the Upper Mississippi Valley" (1885)

T. C. Chamberlin and Rollin D. Salisbury

Building on more than half a century of accumulated scientific knowledge, T. C. (Thomas Chrowder) Chamberlin (1843–1928) and his student and assistant Rollin Salisbury (1858–1922) provided the most thorough summary to date of the Driftless Area's geologic development, published in the *Sixth Annual Report of the United States Geological Survey to the Secretary of the Interior, 1884–1885.* Chamberlin and Salisbury were both sons of southeastern Wisconsin; both attended Beloit College; and both joined the University of Wisconsin in Madison. Chamberlin served as chief geologist for the Wisconsin Geological Survey, director of the glacial division of the U.S. Geological Survey, and president of the University of Wisconsin. He moved on to establish the geology department at the University of Chicago, where Salisbury joined him as dean of the university's school of science.

In the midst of the great mantle of drift that overspreads the Upper Mississippi Basin there lies a drift-barren tract of about 10,000 square miles, the driftless area of Wisconsin and adjoining States. This island in the sea of drift is unique. To find that the crest of an eminence towered above the great mer de glace [sea of ice] would not be remarkable; to find that the summit of a plateau near the border of the drift-covered area lifted itself above the invading ice would create no surprise; but to find a broad tract, lying in the very valley of the great river of the region, overlooked by higher land on different sides, and yet untouched by the glaciation that prevailed all around, very naturally awakens marvel. Strangely enough, the margin of the drift on almost every hand lies on a slope descending toward the driftless district. The drift-bearing ice was stayed in its course, not by some acclivity, not by some great topographic barrier it could not overcome, but by some agency that arrested it in its downward career on the slopes toward the unglaciated basin.

The driftless character of the region has arrested the attention of geologists from the days of [Richard] Owen to our own. . . . [T]he subject is yet a mine of truth largely unworked. The strange story it has been made to tell yields to the stranger story it must yet reveal when all its riddles are solved. We can easily foresee some of the lessons it must teach, though we are unable yet to fully read them. . . .

The driftless region is exceedingly instructive concerning the glacial movements of a very large adjacent territory, and adds much strength to the evidence drawn from striation. The great drift-burdened ice stream, as it moved southwestward from the Canadian heights, was divided and diverted, and the separated currents swept around the area and mingled their burdens below it. Beside these leading phenomena, there are many strange features of a minor character which are displayed in the special movements of the marginal currents around the borders of the region.

In the study of these marginal phenomena the significant fact is developed that there are distinct varieties of drift border. Far from being alike on its several sides, the margin of the driftless region is, in one part, sharply limited by a stout moraine; in another part, it is bordered by a thin sheet of drift which has a definite limit but no marginal aggregation; while, in another part, the drift becomes attenuated to an extreme degree, and the point of its cessation is only determined by careful search for scattered and insignificant pebbles. Over a portion of the drift there is spread a mantle of loess, which stretches out upon the margin of the otherwise driftless region and fades insensibly away. Over other portions, quite in contrast, no such mantle obtains. These varieties of drift border indicate corresponding differences in glacial and aqueous conditions, and these lead on to some of the most pregnant questions that spring from the drift of the interior. . . . So also there are differences in the relative antiquity or freshness of the drift deposits adjoining the driftless area, and thus we are introduced to the fertile question of glacial epochs. . . .

What were the conditions that enabled the driftless area to escape the glaciation that repeatedly intruded itself upon the surrounding country? In the very fact that the glaciation of adjacent regions was repeated, we

have an element of significance. The immunity from drift was mani-
festly not due to some fortuitous condition that chanced to direct the
glacial incursion. The cause was a constant one, influencing each of the
episodes in which the region was threatened by ice. The cause must,
therefore, have been a geographically fixed one. . . . [T]he region is not
a conspicuous elevation, but rather the opposite. Its average altitude is
less than the average altitude of an equal area lying north or west, while
it is not notably different from that east and south. Its driftlessness cannot, therefore, be attributed to its own elevation, unless that elevation
were very different from the present. . . .

[I]f we extend our view and take into consideration the topography of
the whole territory involved, the most important elements of the true
explanation will, we think, be found. In 1877, Professor Winchell called
attention to the fact that the driftless area lies in the lee of the elevated
territory of Northern Wisconsin and Michigan, which, he maintained,
acted as a wedge, forcing the ice aside and so protecting the driftless
region in its rear. In the same year Prof. Irving called attention to the
fact that the great valleys of Lake Superior and Lake Michigan lie in
such a relationship to the driftless area as to tend to divert the glacial
streams to the right and left, and this, in connection with the highlands
lying between the lakes, turned away the ice from the driftless region.
Two years anterior, the senior writer had entertained and expressed to
his associate, Mr. [Moses] Strong, who was then engaged in the inves-
tigation of the lead region lying in the heart of the driftless district, an
opinion respecting the origin of the phenomenon which was closely
similar to that of Professor Irving. . . .

Appeal has already been made to the influence of the highlands
immediately north of the driftless area and to that of the valleys of Lakes
Superior and Michigan, which flank it. To the east of the Lake Michigan
trough lay the capacious valley of Lake Huron, flanked by Georgian Bay.
There is strong evidence that these valleys diverted the glacial streams
southward, in the retiring stages of glaciation at least, and presumably
at all stages. This is shown both by striation and by transportation.
Copper, presumed to come from the Lake Superior region, has been
found in Eastern Michigan and even in Ohio. . . . While it is possible
that both the native copper and . . . quartzites may have had an origin
farther to the eastward, these instances, taken in connection with a
wider class of evidence, leave little room for doubt that the basin of

Lake Huron determined a southerly movement of the ice current, and thereby rendered collateral aid to the Michigan basin in diverting the broad stream east of the unglaciated island.

On the other hand, immediately northwest of Lake Superior, lies a high northeast and southwest trending highland belt, beyond which is a relatively low tract. Farther away is the broad depression through which the Nelson and Churchill Rivers drain a large portion of the northwestern basin. The highest land of this region is said to lie immediately northwest of Lake Superior and trends southwesterly parallel with it. The mer de glace, therefore, flowing southwesterly from the Hudson Bay region found freer passage along the more westerly courses, and this less obstructed flow obviously aided the divergence of the currents to the right. The broad open valleys of the Red River of the North and the James River, aided by the somewhat lower elevation which they probably then had, doubtless led the currents southward through these freer passageways, until they had reached the central latitudes of Nebraska and Iowa. Here the southeasterly slope which seems there to have then obtained, as now, caused them to curve easterly around the driftless region and coalesce with the Lake Michigan stream which had spread itself upon the plains of Illinois.

These collateral agencies of diversion must have greatly relieved the force of the invasion which the immediate barriers of the driftless area encountered, and which, through this and other aid, they were enabled to successfully divert. Meanwhile the meager, unfavored stream that came over the highlands above the area crept slowly down the southerly slope and was met by the wasting winds from the iceless tract. . . .

Diverted by highlands, led away by valleys, consumed by wastage where weak, self-perpetuated where strong, the fingers of the mer de glace closed around the ancient Jardin of the Upper Mississippi Valley, but failed to close upon it.

From "The Pleistocene History of Northeastern Iowa" (1891)

W J McGee

William John Mcgee (1853–1912)—known as "W J"—was born in Farley, Iowa, at the southwestern edge of the Driftless. A self-educated polymath, McGee became an eminent geologist, anthropologist, and ethnologist, serving as director of the U.S. Bureau of American Ethnology and president of the American Association for the Advancement of Science, the American Anthropological Association, and the National Geographic Society. Early in his career, he provided a classic review of the Iowa portion of the Driftless Area.

The most prominent geographic feature of the driftless area is the Mississippi cañon—a steep-sided, flat-bottomed gorge ranging from a mile to seven or eight miles in width, and gradually diminishing in depth southward from nearly 500 feet at the north line of the State to less than 200 feet at the tip of "Cromwell's Nose." Yet, although a veritable rockbound cañon, similar in genesis to that of the Colorado and in depth approaching that of the Hudson, this gorge is not confined between continuous palisades, but rather guarded by lines of isolated or nearly isolated bluffs stretching along either side of the great river like lines of giant sentinels. Sometimes, indeed, the bluffs are closely crowded, and for a score of miles the cliff wall may be broken only by narrow ravines or the constricted gorges of petty streams: but again the interspaces widen and the bluffs contract until the cañon wall, as seen from the river, becomes but a line of isolated buttes, now round-topped, again crowned with a fillet of precipitous rock, and always forest clad on the north slopes but grassed toward the sun. . . .

The tourist who views the cañon walls of the upper Mississippi from the deck of one of the packets plying between St. Louis and St. Paul can

14

not fail to note two distinct aspects in the bluff faces. The prevailing cañon wall is a line of gracefully rounded bluffs whose slopes are either continuous from base to summit or broken by one or more sensibly horizontal ledges of hard rock cropping out now in narrow precipices and again in nearly continuous vertical faces ten to 100 feet high. In Allamakee County the principal outcropping ledge by which the bluff faces are broken is the Oneota dolomite. . . . In the northern part of Clayton County two conspicuous ledges score the face and interrupt the slopes of the rounded river bluffs, the lower representing the Oneota dolomite and the upper the Trenton limestone. . . . [W]hile the gracefully rounded contours of the first aspect of bluff faces continue, and while the eminences diminish in height, the cañon walls are steeper and more rugged south of the Turkey [River] than toward the Oneota [River]; for the Trenton and Galena limestones are more homogeneous and more obdurate than the alternating calcareous and arenaceous beds of the subjacent formations so well developed in the extreme northeastern corner of the State. These rounded bluffs have been subjected to erosion for a long period; they are mature forms. . . .

The reason for the diversity in form of the bluffs overlooking the Mississippi gorge is evident from a casual inspection of the cañon itself, or indeed of the illustrations representing it. The rivers, the valleys, and the hills are all of the autogenetic type, and were evidently fashioned by the progenitors of the present streams during a vast period of constant base-level, perhaps somewhat lower than now; but latterly the base-level has been disturbed, the Father of Waters has silted up his bed, and in his wanderings from side to side has impinged now against this and now against that part of the cañon wall, and so by the process which [G. K.] Gilbert calls "lateral corrasion" has truncated the limiting salients and thereby formed additional material for the further filling of his bed.

Next to that of the Mississippi, the valleys of Oneota and Turkey Rivers are the most conspicuous geographic features of the Driftless area in Iowa; and toward their mouths they are but miniature copies of that of the great river to which they pay tribute. The local relief which they have formed, and which is measured from their waters, also simulates that of the Mississippi. . . .

Southwest of the Turkey, the boundary of the distinctive topography of the driftless area approaches and finally crosses the Niagara escarpment; for, although both ice sheets stretched eastward to that escarpment in this part of the State, their action was feeble and their effect upon the topography insignificant. So the prominent line of cliffs, spurs, and knobs forming the escarpment is a conspicuous feature of the south-western part of the driftless area. Thus the Little Maquoketa and the Tête des Morts rise among rock-bound but rounded hills, as do Village Creek and Snymagil, and like them flow in narrow V-shaped gorges gradually increasing in depth and in the ruggedness of their sides; but half way to its mouth the cañon walls of the Little Maquoketa withdraw, the gorge first becomes U-shaped and then flat-bottomed, and at length its channel deepens into an inner gorge incised into the Galena limestone; and in this inner gorge, which exhibits all of the characteristic features of those of other driftless area rivers, it once found its way directly into the Mississippi. Then the mouth of the stream was just above the present position of Dubuque. But during some ante-Pleistocene shift of the great river the western bluffs were cut away, and the channels, greater and smaller, anastomosed some miles above the original confluence; when the larger stream withdrew, the smaller followed, building a delta plain like that of the Turkey, which has not since been invaded; and the channel between the old confluence and the new is a deep, rock-walled gorge, broad enough for a river, though occupied only by a spring-fed brooklet. This was "la coulée" of Julien Du Buque and his compatriots, and is "The Cooley" of the present; while the course of the brooklet is followed by "Couler" Avenue.

Watch for Fallen Rock (2012)

KATHERINE MEAD

Katherine Mead grew up in Wisconsin, studied geography at the University of Minnesota, and lives in St. Louis, Missouri.

> Cruising the scenic route in Grant County
> Grandpa said he would always love corn
> the vista, he meant, and not the food.
> The hills and waving tassels,

tractors and blood red barns
are the scenes that anchor his nerves.

I replied I felt the same toward trees.
Green, I needed, in my life.
There was silence a moment.
He never plays the radio
when he has passengers.
"You will always love best
where you lived as a child."

We passed by limestone bluffs
Assembled from the carcasses
of billions of sea creatures
living in a geologic era
far removed from this teal Ford Taurus.
Battered yellow signs warn us
"Watch for Fallen Rock"

When we get back to the farm
I will hike the back forty
to the double track that runs
through remnant forest.

I inspect every promising stone
for tiny invertebrates
immortalized in ancient mud,
scallops and miniature corals
reveal themselves after
brushing off the dust.

It's curious, these marine fossils
in the middle of farm country
like finding obsidian in boreal forest
or a Yankee living south of Mason-Dixon.
I am a fallen rock.

"View of Bluff of Galena Limestone, Near Cassville on the Mississippi" (1877). As geologists described and documented the extent of the Driftless Area in the nineteenth century, their scientific reports were often accompanied by detailed renderings of notable formations and the landscapes in which they occurred. This depiction of the bluff face and Mississippi River at Cassville was included in *Geology of Wisconsin, Survey of 1873–1877, Volume II* (1877) as a frontispiece to Part IV by Moses Strong, "Geology and Topography of the Lead Region."

2

ANCIENT PEOPLES

THE STORY OF THE PEOPLING of the Driftless Area over more than twelve millennia is still unfolding as new archeological evidence emerges, enduring oral traditions are passed down, and cultural meanings and relationships are reconsidered. Ojibwe writer and University of Wisconsin–Madison professor Patty Loew writes that the history of Native cultures prior to European contact "encompasses a vast expanse of time. . . . According to the origin stories of most Indian nations in Wisconsin, the tribes have been here 'from the beginning of time.'"

That "vast expanse of time" begins, for archaeologists, with the first material evidence of human presence. Excavations of woolly mammoth and mastodon kill sites indicate that humans found their way to the region soon after the glaciers melted back. Sites in Wisconsin along what was the southernmost extent of the last ice advance have been dated to more than thirteen thousand years before the present—among the earliest confirmed signs of human activity in North America. Scientific work, of course, continues, yielding new findings and further analysis and conjecture—about how people came, how they lived, and how they affected their fellow creatures and landscapes—with findings subject to constant revision and debate.

Early peoples came into a land where life was returning in the aftermath of the ice, a place of tundra and boreal forests; of cold-water swamps, bogs, and open windswept steppe; of not just mammoths and mastodons but a whole wild menagerie of giant beavers, short-faced bears, dire wolves, American lions and cheetahs, saber-tooth cats, horses, camels, bison, and stag moose. Most of these Pleistocene megafauna species would disappear as the climate warmed and the first people, small bands of hunter-gatherers (the Paleoindians), came into and dispersed across

North America. The exact cause-and-effect of the megafaunal extinctions remains a topic of ongoing research and vigorous scientific debate. In the Upper Midwest, the Paleoindian period lasted from 10,000 BC to 7000 BC and is evidenced most conspicuously by the occurrence of distinctive stone spear-points used in pursuit of the abundant game animals.

As the Paleoindian cultures of the Upper Midwest transitioned to Archaic cultures (roughly 7000 BC to 500 BC), which then gave way to Woodland cultures (roughly 500 BC to AD 1200), the human marks on the land became more sophisticated, more extensive, more laden with expressions of mythic power, pragmatic purpose, and social meaning. Fire and hunting, trapping and fishing, foraging and cultivation, mining and trading, and the building of trails, homes, and villages—the activities and features of daily life—occurred across the Driftless. But the most prominent and compelling marks on the landscape, and the ones that make the Driftless unusually rich as a place of ancient human imagination, are those that reveal other dimensions of the spirit: rock art on sandstone walls and in hidden shelters; decorated pottery and other earthenware; arrowheads, tools, and other artifacts; and a globally significant profusion of conical, linear, and effigy-shaped earthen mounds. From these pieces of the ancient past, we reconstruct the story of "the old ones"—and connect it to our own.

Wisconsin Mounds (1963)

Edna Meudt

Several high hills capped by remnant bits of resistant Niagara dolomite rise above the Driftless Area in Wisconsin. Poet, writer, and editor Edna Meudt (1906–1989) reflects here on the cultural memory of these landmark "mounds" (not to be confused with the effigy mounds described elsewhere in this section). Meudt was born on a farm in Wisconsin's Wyoming Valley and lived most of her life in nearby Dodgeville. She published six books of poetry, an autobiography (*The Rose Jar*), and *An Upland Reader*, a series of three anthologies of the literature and lore of southwestern Wisconsin.

Until this scientific age the Mounds
concealed their minerals and ancient caves.
When none but birds flew over nameless graves
and secret trails—even as now—their bounds
triangulated a region of astound-
ing grandeur. Voyageurs came here to brave
a wilderness whose leagues of prairie gave
our cities names . . . When ghostly tribes surround
my hill—an equidistant point between
Sinsinawa, the Platte, and wooded Blue—
I climb the signal rock, imagining scenes
of other times with greedy men who knew
no code. Asylumed here I cling to the green
hill's core, aware of justice overdue.

From *Twelve Millennia:*
Archaeology of the Upper Mississippi
River Valley (2003)

James L. Theler and Robert F. Boszhart

In the ancient past the Driftless Area was a center of human activity; today it is an active center for the study of prehistoric people and their cultures. In the epilogue to their book *Twelve Millennia*, James L. Theler and Robert F. Boszhardt summarize the main periods of the human past in the Driftless. Theler is professor emeritus of archaeology at the University of Wisconsin–La Crosse; Boszhardt is a past president of the Wisconsin Archaeological Society and has worked extensively as an archaeologist in the Upper Mississippi Valley.

Approximately 12,000 years ago the first people laid eyes on the Upper Mississippi River Valley. The landscape at that time would have been hardly recognizable to us. The region would have resembled the sub-arctic, and the people would have seen not only caribou and musk ox but also mastodons and mammoths, relatives of the modern elephant;

Deer head petroglyph, Daniel Seurer (c. 1000). The Driftless Area is rich in
rock art. This deer or elk head is found at a small overhanging rockshelter
that offers signs of habitation as early as two thousand years ago. Ancient
people also carved petroglyphs here that have been interpreted as a wolf, a
bison nursing her calf, deer, elk, eagles, fish, geese, swans, thunderbirds,
and human figures. The parallel lines from the mouth to the interior of the
figure represent a motif in ancient and modern Native American imagery
commonly known as a heartline.

giant ground sloths; 400-pound beavers; and huge buffalo with straight horns. To the first people in this region, these sights were normal, and the people were perfectly adapted to surviving in that environment. They and their ancestors had been living along glacial margins of the last Ice Age for thousands of years, hunting megafauna all the while.

The Upper Mississippi region was, however, new land, and the initial colonists had to find critical reserves, such as supplies of stone for making their weapons and tools. They also had to quickly learn the landscape in order to return to these sources periodically. It must have been an amazing process to wander through this absolute wilderness in a continual pursuit of game and food to forage and yet be able to find the way back to places like Silver Mound. The first people here certainly established landmarks, and the vast outwash gorge of the Mississippi River undoubtedly became a principal locational feature, as it remains today.

Despite the difficulties that the first people must have faced for survival, they were adapted to the cold periglacial environment with its associated wildlife. Living through the climate changes that mark the onset of the Holocene and the concomitant mass extinctions of the megafauna must have been somewhat disconcerting to Paleoindian hunter-gatherers, even though this shift may have occurred over a thousand-year period involving nearly fifty generations. On the other hand, dramatic changes may have been experienced within individual lifetimes. During this transition, people adapted to new environments, first the replacement of the tundra with spruce-fir forests, followed by deciduous forests and later a major expansion of the prairies and eastward migration of buffalo. After people had successfully adapted to these environmental waves, the climate of the Upper Mississippi region shifted once again in the late Holocene, witnessing the retreat of the prairies. Again the inhabitants changed and survived.

The human adaptations to environmental changes are reflected in the archaeological record by technological innovations that archaeologists use to mark the sequence of cultural traditions and stages for this region. The first people, those of the Paleoindian tradition, were bands of Ice Age hunters and gatherers following herds of mammoths and other large game across a tundra-like landscape. Their descendants, the people of the Archaic tradition, hunted deer and elk and gathered nuts and other food in recognizable territories. Late in the Archaic, people began to cultivate simple gardens, and this begat Woodland tradition people, who added pottery to the material culture and marked formal cemeteries with earthen mounds. The Archaic-to-Woodland transition is signaled by wide-ranging trade systems and extensive ritual ceremonialism. The Woodland tradition in the Upper Mississippi Valley experienced a series of fluctuations, ending 1,000 years ago at the time intensive corn agriculture was adopted in the region. This was a period of conflict, and the newly introduced bow and arrow provided a far superior weapon that played a role in the development of the first fortifications. Groups consolidated, tribes were born, and the Upper Mississippian, or Oneota tradition, came into being. These people renewed an interest in hunting bison on the nearby eastern margins of the Plains, and it was the Oneota who were here when the French explored and provided the first written records in the mid-1600s. Despite the incredible and sudden disruption caused by the arrival of Europeans, Native people have survived.

Native people have a long story, and it is rarely told from beginning to end. Indeed, the story has no end but continues in the lives of Native people today and as the archaeological record continues to be explored and deciphered. The story is invariably incomplete. Much has been lost through the natural processes of time, but even more has been lost within the last 150 years as the landscape has been artificially modified for agriculture, lumbering, town and city development, and, most recently, urban sprawl. . . . There is precious little of what was here only 150 years ago. The future of the archaeological record for the Upper Mississippi River Valley depends upon preservation and recovery, and that will happen only through the mutual efforts of archaeologists, Native Americans, and the public.

From *Indian Nations of Wisconsin: Histories of Endurance and Renewal* (2001)

Patty Loew

The ancient people of the Driftless Area marked its hills, caves, and rock faces with works that expressed their imagination and spirit. Patty Loew has worked with members of the Ho-Chunk Nation in conveying their story as a Nation. Loew is an enrolled member of the Bad River Band of Lake Superior Ojibwe and professor in the Department of Life Sciences Communication at the University of Wisconsin–Madison. Before joining the UW faculty, Loew worked as a broadcast journalist and producer. She now teaches video production and analysis, with a special focus on working with tribal youth to connect science, culture, and storytelling through modern media.

A thousand years ago, after carefully preparing red, black, and blue-gray paints, an artist sanded the walls of a rock shelter hidden in a stand of mixed hardwoods in present-day Iowa County. Satisfied that the "canvas" was properly prepared, the artist—a historian, really—began to record a remarkable story. The walls filled with painted turtles, thunderbirds, and a mythic hero who wore human heads as earrings. Supernatural athletic contests and "giant" slayings unfolded in pictographic detail.

Members of the modern Ho-Chunk Nation recognize this composition as the story of Red Horn, an ancient Ho-Chunk hero. This origin epic, told by generations of tribal members and preserved in a cave known today as Gottschall, testifies to the enduring power of the spoken word and persistence of Native American oral tradition. Gottschall also provides other clues to the pre-Columbian Ho-Chunk past. Along with the Red Horn paintings, the cave contains pottery shards of the Effigy Mound Builders, whose earthen works first appeared about 3,000 years ago, and unusual soils associated with sacred rituals of the Mississippians, whose agriculture-based economy and impressive trade networks emerged about 1,000 years ago. The connection between Ho-Chunk oral history and the physical evidence at Gottschall suggests that rather than being separate peoples, later cultures evolved from and intersected with earlier ones.

The Gottschall site, a place of obvious cultural and religious significance, is just one of more than one hundred rock art sites identified in Wisconsin, most of them in the Driftless Area of the southwestern part of the state. From simple grooves and incised geometric designs to elaborate painted birds, animals, and human forms, these cave drawings may have been created for spiritual or sacred reasons, inspired by dreams, fasts, or rituals. Perhaps Native artists carved or painted these motifs to educate the young or commemorate the dead. It is likely that the ancestors of today's modern Indian nations used pictographs as mnemonic devices to help tribal members remember important events or complex ceremonies. . . .

Along with other intriguing fragments of the past, rock art, picture writing, and wampum are useful in reconstructing the experiences of Native cultures before they encountered Europeans. It is a history that encompasses a vast expanse of time. Although anthropologists believe that humans have occupied the Great Lakes region for at least 12,000 years, contemporary tribal historians resist such efforts to date human occupation of the area. According to the origin stories of most Indian nations in Wisconsin, the tribes have been here "from the beginning of time." . . .

From the stories and songs passed down to present generations of Native Americans, we can make inferences about the relationships early inhabitants had with the animals and plants that sustained them. The Ho-Chunk, for example, sing about their reverence for deer and a hill near present-day Black River Falls where their ancestors used to hunt. It was here that deer would beckon Ho-Chunk hunters by singing to them songs of love: "If he is there, let him come. If he is there, let him come," the deer would call. "An old man fasted there," the Ho-Chunk remember. "They took pity on them—that hill, the deer, and Earthmaker. Whatever that was sacred, they could bestow on him, they did." The hill remains a spiritual place where tribal members fast and pray. . . .

About 2,500 years ago, Native people began constructing earthen effigies, including turtles, bears, and humans. Some of the mounds were massive. The bird effigy near Muscoda in present-day Richland County, for example, had a wingspan of more than a quarter mile. Although many of the effigies contained human remains, some did not. It is likely that water held a special attraction for mound builders since many of the earthen effigies were located near lakes and rivers. Intriguingly, in Southern Wisconsin some of the mound groups correspond to Ho-Chunk clan divisions: eagles and thunderbirds from the sky world and bears representing the earth world. Some mound clusters include water panthers, which are symbolic of the underground spirits. There is some evidence that the tails of panther effigies often point to underground springs—entrances to the underworld, in the Ho-Chunk oral tradition.

Some researchers surmise that these mounds are the key to under-standing the cosmology of the culture that built them—the people the Ho-Chunk call "ancestors." There is speculation that mound groups may symbolize the clan structures of some contemporary tribes. Others suggest they may be gargantuan maps or, perhaps like the Mayan pyramids, calendrical or astronomical devices. There is no question that for the people who built them, these monumental cultural expressions were a form of communication. . . .

For Native Americans, research that combines oral history, mnemonics, and physical evidence represents a new approach to reconstructing the past. Had archaeologists not collaborated with Ho-Chunk elders, the priceless Red Horn composite at the Gottschall site might have remained an indecipherable mystery. The ancient songs, stories, and art of Native people are filled with symbolism and wisdom. In order to understand the cultural meaning of the people, places, and events that shaped their lives, we must not only *read* history, but also *listen* to it.

From "Notes Respecting Certain Indian Mounds and Earthworks, in the Form of Animal Effigies, Chiefly in the Wisconsin Territory, U.S." (1838)

RICHARD C. TAYLOR

Through the nineteenth century, observers came to appreciate the glob-ally unique concentration of ancient effigy mounds in the Upper Midwest, and especially along the river corridors in the Driftless Area. William Keating in his 1824 *Narrative* had noted the occurrence of "ancient tumuli or artificial mounds" along the route of the Long Expedition. Outside the Driftless, the Cahokia mound complex in Illinois was first recorded in the mid-1700s, and the Aztalan site in eastern Wisconsin in 1835. In 1838 geologist and archaeologist Richard C. Taylor (1789–1851) published the first full study of the region's effigy mounds.

During the past year, whilst traversing, in the society of some scientific friends, that portion of Wisconsin Territory which is bounded by Illinois to the south, and the beautiful Wisconsin River to the north, we frequently found our attention attracted by the singularly formed Indian mounds, of which the elevated prairies, as well as the rich valleys and the borders of the lakes and rivers of this region, afford such numerous specimens.

The existence of abundant traces, apparently monumental, of an ancient and now probably extinct nation, within the country under our present recognizance, was known long ago to its early explorers, of which the French were doubtless the first, in the seventeenth century, and has been mentioned by some of the travellers who have subsequently written concerning this country. But I was unprepared to discover in the forms of these remains, whose origin is so obscure, other than the usual simple tumuli. . . .

The earthworks which have been constructed in the shapes of animals, abound in the Iowa district of Wisconsin. . . . The site of [a] singular group of mounds . . . is about eighteen miles west of the Four Lakes, and seven miles east of the two remarkable natural hills called the Blue Mounds. . . . In this group there are seen the effigies of at least six quadrupeds; six mounds in parallelograms; one circular tumulus; one human figure, and one circle or ring which may have been formed by the Indians in their dances, whether peaceful or warlike, or may have been occupied for some such purpose, in by-gone times, as the torturing and destroying [of] their prisoners. The great Indian trail, or war-path, which leads from Lake Michigan, near Milwaukie, to the Mississippi above Prairie du Chien, passes along the edge of this chain of earthworks, and is now for many miles adopted as the route of the military road to the latter fort. We pursued this route for a great distance along the dividing ridge between the northern and southern waters; and we continually saw memorials of the character above described, along its borders.

What animals are represented by these rude monuments of earth, now covered with the rank prairie grass, is not made altogether apparent by their designers. . . . We were rather inclined, however imperfect the representation, to attribute the intention of the constructors to be that of exhibiting the figure of the Buffalo; an animal which had here the finest pasturage, and an almost boundless range, within one of the most ample hunting grounds, and were exceedingly numerous at the time of the first exploration of the country by the French. . . .

In the midst of this group, represented by our sketch, and forming a very important portion of it, we have now to notice the representation of a human figure, lying in an east and west direction; the head towards the west, and the arms and legs extended. Its length is one hundred and twenty five feet, and it is one hundred and forty feet from the extremity of one arm to that of the other. The body or trunk is thirty feet in breadth, the head twenty-five feet, and its elevation above the general surface of the prairie, is about six feet. Its configuration is so distinct, that there can be no possibility of a mistake in assigning it to the human figure. . . .

The site of this interesting series is an elevated open prairie, on the dividing ridge between the waters of the Wisconsin and Rock rivers. These monuments are covered with the same green carpet of prairie grass, intermixed with bright and brilliant flowers, as the prairie itself. There is an intervening space near the centre of the group, now overgrown with bushes, which probably conceal some unnoticed mounds. . . .

Beyond the Wisconsin Territory, on the north side of the river of that name, in the region still held by the Winnebagos, are innumerable mounds, both of the circular and most of the other forms we have figured. . . .

At the great savanna or prairie on the south bank of the Wisconsin river, called English prairie, are earthworks having the circular, the oblong, and the usual animal forms, and also some which bear resemblance to the Roman letter T. . . . Animal effigies occur fifteen miles to the southwest of the last mentioned locality, along the course of an ancient trail, and also of the present military road to Prairie du Chien from Fort Winnebago. Numerous others may be recognized between these and the Mississippi.

In the vicinity of the remarkable hills called the Blue Mounds, they occur abundantly. These hills were, until very lately, a great resort of the Indian inhabitants; as their existing paths, converging hither in singularly straight lines from every point of the compass, amply testify.

In the centre of the territory, at sites which it would be tedious to enumerate, we repeatedly passed by similar mounds, almost invariably contiguous to Indian paths, whose deeply-worn, but narrow tracks, attest their extreme antiquity and long use.

Between the interesting limestone hill, styled Sinsinnawa Mound, and the town of Galena, these animal representations are seldom out of sight, and are accompanied by earthworks of simpler forms. They prevail equally in the low meadow sites, as upon the higher prairie ridges.

Elevated circular tumuli rise from the flats on the margin of the Mississippi, at the old French village or trading station of Prairie du Chien.

All along the borders of the beautiful Wisconsin river, extending from its mouth to the Winnebago Portage, similar monuments are traceable on the high and dry lands. . . .

From the different structure and form of their monuments, it is not improbable that there always existed a variety of races upon this continent. And if in remote times those races were classified and designated in the mode which we have seen still exists, and long has existed,—that is to say, under the denomination of particular animals,—it is not altogether incompatible with probability, that the earthworks in which their dead were deposited, and which resemble certain animal figures, were in fact designed as representations of those national or family badges, and consequently pointed out the burial place of the members of those particular tribes.

From *Buried Indians: Digging Up the Past in a Midwestern Town* (2006)

Laurie Hovell McMillin

In her book *Buried Indians*, Laurie Hovell McMillin returned to her hometown of Trempealeau, Wisconsin, to explore the history, meaning, and cultural tensions surrounding the presence of effigy mounds in the local landscape. McMillin is a professor of rhetoric and composition at Oberlin College in Ohio, with a particular research interest in South Asian religion and culture.

Trempealeau Mountain is a bluff remnant of an island in the Mississippi; standing three hundred feet high and a third of a mile across, it was considered sacred ground by the Ho-Chunk and Dakota people who lived in the region. As the legend goes, the French explorer Nicolas Perrot landed near the mountain in 1685; Linctot's trading post, established in 1731, stood within a quarter mile of its banks. Later, when Dakota people moved into the area in the 1810s and 1830s, Chief Wabasha had a village near the mountain. In 1817, Lieutenant Zebulon M. Pike camped near it and "spoke glowingly of its scenery." The name of the bluff . . . comes from *la montagne qui trempe à l'eau,* French for the Winnebago name. In *Life on the Mississippi* Mark Twain describes Trempealeau Mountain in a speech by a long-winded tour guide of panoramas. The guide pontificates about "Trempeleau [*sic*] Island, which isn't like any other island in America, I believe, for it is a gigantic mountain, with precipitous sides, and is full of Indian traditions, and used to be full of rattlesnakes; if you catch the sun just right there, you will have a picture that will stay with you." When I was growing up there, local legend maintained that the Indians who used to live in the region considered "the mountain soaking in the water" to be the center of the world, the axis mundi, as Mircea Eliade would have it, around which people in the area oriented themselves.

These days Trempealeau Mountain is part of the Wisconsin State Park system, though it used to be private land, as my family will attest. My dad's boyhood friend Dale Chritzman used to own an arm of land off the mountain. My brother talks about being able to walk across the bay in the 1960s; my mother recalls being out on the mountain and nauseated with pregnancy; after a sip of cold coffee from a smelly thermos, she threw up. She was pregnant with me, she thinks. My family's boaters and water-skiers used to picnic and launch from the banks of the mountain, until the state condemned the land in order to seize it for the park.

Although the banks of the mountain were well trampled by my family, there is something foreboding about climbing its peak. Even now my uncle Clyde expresses surprise that I, a forty-year-old mother of two, would scale the mountain by myself in the dead of winter. Hiking just for pleasure is not really in his book. Other things conspire to keep people off the island and mountain too. For one, you have to walk on railroad tracks to get there. When I was a kid, I believed it was illegal to go there; perhaps because the railroad had put up forbidding signs; perhaps this was a story told by parents and other knowing adults. It added to the fun, in any case. To be sure, the number of trains on these tracks make going there a bit risky. In the old days part of the way was on a trestle over the river, and if a train came while you were crossing, the only place to go was in the water. Recently, however, the railroad has added a foot-path to this bridge; hikers and fishers use it, even if a sign proclaims it as the land of the Burlington Northern: keep off. Even now, though, if a train comes while you are on the tracks, you have to scramble down the bank while a hundred cargo boxes from China go barreling up the river. When I was a kid, other things kept you off as well: the rumor about rattlesnakes, which Twain cited. This rumor was repeated by my grandma Hovell, who, after one of my visits there, cried out in dismay: "You can't go there! There are rattlesnakes out there!" I doubt my grandmother knew she was echoing Twain; I assured her I'd never seen a snake, that I was careful. Certainly, she could not yet imagine that I would soon go to India, where cobras and vipers (and their owners) sometimes come knocking at the door, and snakes have their own special holiday. Anyway, she couldn't keep me away from the mountain— it was as exotic and romantic as I could get in those days, the center of someone else's world.

As a high-schooler, I probably went to Trempealeau Mountain three times a year, mostly alone. Romantic notions about Indians drew me, as did something about its forbiddenness. One time I was able to convince my cop brother and his fiancée to join me, and we scrambled up the rough trail to take a good look at the bluffs all around, the places where the land was reclaiming the bay in which we used to swim and water-ski, the trains, barges, and boats passing, the river running below us. At other times, when I climb nearby Brady's Bluff with a camera, I always took some shots of the mountain, which from that height rose out of the water like an isosceles triangle, or, in other terms, echoed in gigantic fashion the shape of the burial mounds constructed on it and that lined the opposite bank. The mount meant something to my dad too. His grandfather and dad helped build the road that limned the river (and thus the mountain) and extended into the state park. He had his memories of playing and boating in its shadow. Our shared attraction to the place gave my dad and me some connection. From his basement studio my dad turned out paintings of the mountain in many lights, at many times of year.

The centrality of the place to local self-conceptions is suggested by the decision to use the name of the mountain for the county when it was incorporated in 1854. Shortly after, in 1856, the name of the village also changed to Trempealeau. And Trempealeau Mountain continues to orient people there. The local café sports an enormous painting of the mountain. Pictures of it adorn park brochures. A county tourist pamphlet notes, erroneously, that "The French called the mountain, rising out of the Mississippi River, La Montagne qui [*sic*]. That is how the county got its name." In the 1960s a local band director wrote a "tone poem" about the site—"La Montagne qui trempe à l'eau"—that, in his words, explored something of what the place might have meant to native peoples here. Most recent is Harold Wilber's Trempealeau Mountain Golf Course. I am not immune to the mountain's pull, either. While staying in the area recently, I set out for a walk in the direction of the mountain and felt that old sense of excitement and reverence for the place.

That there are effigy mounds on Trempealeau Mountain is little known. Below a drawing of the mountain itself, brochures for Perrot State Park include images of the effigy mounds found on parkland: mounds in the shape of birds, deer, dogs, ovals, and wide straight lines, as well as conical burial mounds, but the park people don't tell you where to find them all. Archaeologists maintain that the effigy mounds were built sometime between 600 and 1200 CE, by the Late Woodland people, who have since become other peoples, changing their lifeways and taking on different names as time passed. Even though archaeologists cannot be certain who succeeded the mound builders in this region, members of the Ho-Chunk Nation, now the dominant native group in the region, believed that they were the mound builders. As the Ho-Chunk anthropologist Anna Funmaker told me, the mounds are clan totems.

Most local people know nothing of the effigy mounds on Trempealeau Mountain, and those who know where they are like it that way. And while most people these days have forgotten about them, there are also twenty-two burial mounds on the mountain, all of which were desecrated by amateur archaeologists and Sunday treasure seekers, by [early archeologist and author] George Squier himself. "Can you imagine digging in a cemetery? It's the same thing," John Ebersold said.

John learned of the effigy mounds on Trempealeau Mountain from copies of Theodore Lewis's extensive survey of mounds in the region from the 1880s. No one told John where to look; he had to scramble the steep banks until he found the right humps of dirt. John says that late spring is the best time to go looking, when the snow is gone but the brush has not yet grown tall enough to obscure them. Although it was high summer, John took T. S. and me out to see them in July 2001, surprising us by suggesting that we should go in the afternoon because the snakes would be sleeping then. (I had assumed that snakes were simply part of an old grandma's tale.) Because it was July, the brush was thick and had the potential to obscure the eroded figures. But John knew where to look. And, sure enough, after traveling through the brambles, he found the linear mound, a hump of dirt that sloped down the hill, and, below that, the shape of a bird mounded in dirt, facing the river. John held his arms out like wings to show us the shape of the bird, and then we could see it. Perhaps forty feet long and forty wide, the bird is poised at the edge of the slope, its wings spread wide. John reported that sometimes Ho-Chunk people come out here to pay their respects, leaving little packets of tobacco tied up in red-and-white thread strung up in the trees.

Effigy mounds, burial mounds, center of the world: the convergence of so many sacred structures in such a small area—Trempealeau Mountain—leads Rollie Rodell to posit that this part of the river area created a place of notoriety—others might say sacred power—among native peoples that continued into the seventeenth century. Rodell suggested to me in conversation that it may have been this fame that led Perrot to the area in the first place, directed by Ho-Chunk guides who left him at the Wisconsin River to find his own way. Certainly, a mountain and its effigies represent something of the sacred for a number of native groups. The Ho-Chunk claim them; the Dakota have their own stories about them.

And John told us one: Dakota people came into the area from Minnesota in the early nineteenth century. They too honored the mountain and maintained that, like themselves perhaps, it had floated down the Mississippi from upriver, from what is now Red Wing, Minnesota. When the mountain turned up missing, they sent scouts down to search for it; they made the seventy-mile journey by canoe. There, nestled among the other bluffs, they found the mountain and on it the thunderbird and linear effigies, still safe and sound, protected as they were by spirits—spirits in the form of rattlesnakes.

John put it together: there may well be snakes on the mountain, yet the story of rattlesnakes and the forbiddenness of the mountain was the tale—altered and rewritten—that Twain had passed along, the one my grandmother had told me, the one my dad had heard tell of—"There are rattlesnakes out there!"—a story transformed and translated but, as it was passed on, still intimating something of the holy out there.

Marching Bear effigy mound group (c. 1000). The Driftless Area and surrounding region is home to a concentration of effigy mounds unknown anywhere else in the world. Although the low relief of effigy mounds makes their shape and size difficult to perceive at ground level, their forms and position relative to other mounds and the landscape become apparent from above. In the 1970s Professor R. Clark Mallam of the Luther College Archaeological Center began to document mounds using aerial photography, outlining them using agricultural lime or painted stones. Mallam and colleagues used these mound images in research and efforts to promote their preservation.

From *Oneota Flow:*
The Upper Iowa River and Its People (2009)

David S. Faldet

In his book *Oneota Flow*, David Faldet surveyed the natural and cultural history of the Upper Iowa River and the Iowa portion of the Driftless Area. This selection is excerpted from his chapter "The Old Ones." Faldet lives in Decorah, Iowa, where he is Jones Professor of English at Luther College, teaching courses in rhetoric, creative writing, journalism, environmental writing, and English literature.

"The old ones" is a phrase Pete Fee uses for people of the past. "They're still with us," he maintains, "but in a different form. They're watching, and the women trill when you do something good." Fee points down at the round wooden surface of the table where we drink our cups of morning coffee. "You know, I'm sure, around this circle, if we could hear them right now, they'd be . . . ," and in a quiet, ghostly voice he gives a trill. "Those are the old ones." Fee has moved around a lot in his life, but today lives in a brown house that tucks into the bottom of the last bluff north of the Upper Iowa before its waters mix into the muddy flow of the Mississippi. Fee's house was the family home of his wife Alana, and across the road live his children and grandchildren. I sit at his kitchen table on a sodden October day because I've come to see if Pete and Alana can help me in a task as difficult as hearing the celebration trill of the dead: the task of understanding the old world of the river.

The people who were living on the Upper Iowa when prehistory became history were some of Pete Fee's ancestors. Until their story becomes part of the written record of European eyewitnesses, those old ones are called, by scholars, Oneota. When priests and traders showed up in the late 1600s, they gave these residents the name the Winnebago used for them: Ioway, the sleepy ones. The Ioway, however, call themselves *Baxoje*, the people whose noses are covered with ash.

Fee is an enrolled member of the Ioway tribe. The majority of his family still live on and around the reservation of the Northern Ioway in White Cloud, Kansas. He respects the old ones who lived here long before him and the stories his ancestors passed along. On the other hand, his children and grandchildren attend New Albin schools. He is a veteran of two tours of military duty, belongs to an electricians' union, and reads *Mother Earth News*. He respects the world he has experienced with his senses as well as the information learned from anthropologists, some of whom he calls friends.

The person who contributed most to understanding prehistory along the Upper Iowa had no formal training in anthropology or archaeology. Ellison Orr, who collected the last passenger pigeon egg in northeastern Iowa, kicked up arrowheads as a boy on a farm along the Yellow River. His passion for true archaeology was awakened in a campaign trip by buggy down the lower valley of the Upper Iowa in the fall of 1878. Only twenty-one, Orr had been convinced to run for county superintendent of schools on the Republican ticket. Roads were bare earth tracks. As he reached the river bottom where Bear Creek enters the Upper Iowa, Orr noticed pot fragments, grinding stones, and mortars in the dirt of the roadbed and its shoulder. Stopping to pick these up and gaining new additions as he canvassed from house to house, Orr had filled the back of his buggy by the time he reached New Albin. This abundance suggested to Orr the richness of the valley's prehistoric past. Fifteen years later, when an older man named Wilbur Dresser offered to dig artifacts for five dollars and a share of the finds, Orr agreed. Dresser dug in several of the hundreds of mounds in the valley that Orr had traveled. Dresser returned, Orr reported, with "a nice lot of pottery, pipes, knives, arrow-heads and bone and copper beads."

The pots and pot fragments Dresser dug up along the Upper Iowa River mark the separation of Woodland culture from its Archaic cultural past. With pottery, Woodland people could contain, carry, and heat water and mix and contain food far more easily than their ancestors. Woodland sites, like the Oneota sites that succeeded them, are scattered with pottery remains. Tempered by fire, a pot came from earth but did not become mud when it came in contact with water. Fired earthenware offered a new power. The fusion of fire, water, and earth in one circular vessel may have also fixed "the old ones" of the Woodland period more in place because, though they provided better storage, pots broke more easily in transit than skin bags or woven baskets.

Ellison Orr ran the Waukon office of the phone company from its earliest days, a job that included putting in the lines that eventually crisscrossed the countryside of Winneshiek and Allamakee counties. In his spare hours he dug, making notes and cataloging his finds. Orr distinguished himself from other amateur diggers in the Upper Iowa Valley by his meticulous method and by putting together a picture of the cultures whose artifacts he uncovered. Many of the landowners on whose property burial sites were situated had little sympathy with his passion. One farmer told him that when a pot, eighteen inches across, turned up in the soil of his barnyard, he smashed it because it was "haythen." Orr was careful with his finds. When he retired in 1930 from the phone company, he prepared his extensive collection to donate to the State Historical Society. At a 1933 academic conference, the culture of Oneota that had made its home in the Upper Iowa was given the name "Orr Focus."

The bulk of the materials in Orr's collection were Oneota, deposited between 1000 and 1670 C.E., but a number of finds didn't fit. Some smaller pots were tempered with sand rather than the pieces of shell that characterize an Oneota pot; many stone points had shapes far different than the triangle favored by Oneota craftsmen. Orr believed that another culture had also made its home along the river. He guessed that this culture was earlier, that it was Woodland, and that it was responsible for the creation of some of the mounds, but he had not produced hard evidence. When the Iowa State Planning Board began using Works Progress Administration (WPA) money to further cultural projects in the state, Orr served as field supervisor of an extensive archaeological study of the river valley to answer the question about this second culture. In the summer of 1934, at the age of seventy-seven, Orr began the full-time project that consumed the remaining fourteen years of his life.

There was urgency to the project's timing. When the antiquities of northeastern Iowa had been studied as part of two national surveys in the late nineteenth century, complete maps were created to mark the locations of Indian mounds, village sites, bank enclosures, rock shelters, and painted and carved rock. By the time Orr wrote up the reports of his own surveys, he recorded that 972 mounds along the Mississippi in Allamakee County had been totally obliterated by farming, construction, or erosion. Along the Upper Iowa, close to a hundred mounds had been totally erased. Of the eight recorded sites of banked enclosures, only three remained.

In the summer of 1934 the county relief officer assigned men to do the digging. One was in his seventies. Another had bad lungs from a gas attack during World War I. Due to a childhood illness, another required braces to keep his back straight. But all, Orr was relieved to find, were good with a shovel. On June 11 the group began its first excavation at the New Galena mound cluster on an oxbow up in the upper Iowa. Near the lead-mining region of the 1850s, called New Galena, the mounds were on a high flat terrace that looked east toward the most important juncture of streams in the lower Upper Iowa: where Bear Creek enters the river shortly after joining Waterloo Creek. Orr had entered the river valley near this spot in his electioneering buggy ride fifty-six years earlier. Twenty-five years earlier Orr had surveyed the site and found thirty-two mounds, some five feet in height. When Orr and his crew arrived to dig, they found only fifteen mounds, the highest rising two feet. The plowed site was growing young corn with bits of human bone evident among the rows. Selecting the center of what had been a large mound, the workers delineated a square. In the first day they uncovered bits of Oneota pottery, bone fragments, and an Oneota spear point.

The second day, however, Orr and his supervisor, Charles Keyes, found a burial that confirmed the theory they had set out to test. Having cleared away the black soil to the gravel of the terrace, they discovered a pile of gravel next to a similar-sized pit of black earth. After two and a half feet of slow digging, they uncovered in the pit of black earth the upper ridges of bone in five bundled skeletons. One skeleton was accompanied by copper button earrings. In the center of the group burial was a small, grit-tempered Woodland Indian bowl, exquisitely decorated with a design of incised lines and points. Woodland people had constructed the mound by first clearing away the earth to the gravel substratum. That done, they dug a pit in the gravel and heaped the displaced gravel next to the pit for the burial of the bone bundles. A mound of earth was raised over the entire excavation. The Oneota materials had been deposited higher and later in a mound of Woodland origins. The chief mound builders of the Upper Iowa Valley were the Woodland people, whose culture emerged fifteen hundred years before the Oneota. Though the WPA archeological project continued to map out the contents of sites for five summers, the accuracy of Orr's guess was clear at the end of that second day.

The uneasiness early people along the river felt about the powerful forces of water and soil may be signaled by the construction of the mound Orr and his WPA diggers excavated. Woodland mound builders chose ground that was safe from angry floods, and they cleared away the fertile and acidic topsoil, placing the bones in the buried subsoil. Bones were buried in a bundle after the body had been left to weather in a tree scaffold. Other mounds contain bones cremated by fire. The transforming powers of air and fire intervened with the substance of the flesh before the body and its spirit could be properly interred within the earth. Intrusive burials in some mounds suggest that in subsequent years, the Woodland people who made them or the people of later groups returned to enact ceremonies and place new bone bundles in the ground. Elaborate construction techniques suggest that the dead were respected, feared, or loved and that their proper passage from the world of the living into that of the dead required proper ritual. With hoes fashioned from the shoulder blades of elk or deer, Woodland people excavated a pit up to one hundred feet across. They shoveled sand and dirt with animal bone spades or clam shells into skins or baskets, carrying load after load to create a mound four or five feet deep. . . .

The clans of the Ioway tribe today are the Bear, the Buffalo, and the Eagle/Thunder. The clan unique to those Ioway who went south to Oklahoma is the Eagle/Thunder. Possibly those holy men who prayed to let the storm stop on the trip to Oklahoma were speaking to their Thunder ancestors. In the oral legends of the Ioway, the origin story of the Eagle/Thunder clan is also the origin story of the now defunct Pigeon clan. This story gives some sense of how people who lived on the Upper Iowa thought about the totem spirit that resided in the dark flocks of passenger pigeons. The story, related by an Ioway to J. Owen Dorsey in the 1880s, says the "Eagle and Pigeon people came to earth in the form of birds," warriors who came "to hunt men." The story continues: "They met the Bear and the Wolf people. After leaving them, they journeyed until they reached a certain place, where they made a village. They surrounded this with palisades, calling the settlement *MaⁿcúJoe*, Hill or Bank of Red Earth." Bear, Wolf, Eagle/Thunder, Pigeon, Elk, Owl, Beaver, Snake, and Buffalo are the nine traditional Ioway clans. In the old story, the people of the air, Pigeon and Eagle/Thunder, meet the people of the earth, Bear and Wolf. Together, their village makes a whole people. Some of the traditionalists who moved to Oklahoma have kept alive the bird half of that whole through their Eagle/Thunder clan. Spiritual relation with the animals and elements is the modern Ioway's most crucial piece of heritage from the world of the old ones.

In the last phase of Woodland culture, beginning fourteen hundred years ago and lasting until nine hundred years ago, a bird mound and bear mounds, honoring sky and earth, were constructed along the Upper Iowa. The single bird-shaped mound is cradled in a semicircular bend of the river. Ellison Orr measured the effigy: three feet high at its center and close to eighty feet across from wing tip to wing tip. It was, he wrote, "well proportioned, representing a flying nighthawk." Downstream from the bird mound, a bear effigy was constructed at a site called Voll farm. In the Sand Cove, behind the last set of bluffs along the Mississippi just south of New Albin, three bear mounds were created. In the Black Hawk Shelter, in the outcrop just above these mounds, Indian remains and a large number of bear bones were found.

Fee's clan affiliation is Bear. The ceremonial names of the people in his family connect back to the origin story of the Bear clan. "When that person being named makes his spirit journey, no matter how old he is, you want the people on the other side to say, 'There he comes, the one with that name. That's so-and-so's relative. Come on over, and we'll help you get through this spirit journey!' That's what it's for. So people will recognize you on the other side, in the spiritual world," Fee says. One of his granddaughters was given the name Comes With Them. This name "means that down through time she comes with them, comes with those bears." . . .

Pete Fee has a story about the demands that the dead place upon the living.

The Gottschall Head (c. 1000). This carved and painted head was
unearthed at the Gottschall Rockshelter, a site in the Wisconsin
River valley also known for its elaborate and well-preserved cave
paintings. The sculpture, made of local sandstone, is ten inches tall
with vertical stripes and a chin circle in blue pigment, and red
pigment at the mouth. Radiocarbon dating places it from AD 1000
to 1050. A team of archeologists led by Dr. Robert Salzer of Beloit
College has worked with members of the Ho-Chunk Nation to
interpret the paintings and other artifacts at Gottschall in light of
tribal history and mythology. Careful stratigraphy in the rockshelter
has suggested the site was host to a ritual that was practiced with
consistent core elements from 500 BC until AD 1100.

Winter time is coming up. That's the time we tell stories. I keep thinking about that, that we ought to do that more. You know, tell those stories: how we got here, clan stories. I can give you an example. My great aunt Pearl and a friend, an old lady named Irene Foster, would go into town for a bender. Now those people believed that when you went to the other side you would need things, and it was the job of the people here on this side to make offerings to give you what you wanted. Well, Pearl and her friend were walking down the street. It was Nemaha, which isn't a town more than a few blocks long, but it was dark. And it seems they would walk along and they'd hear footsteps coming along behind them. And so they'd stop, but when they'd stop, the footsteps would stop. Then they'd start walking again, and they'd hear those footsteps, and stop and they'd hear nothing. So finally they stopped, and my aunt Pearl said to her friend, "Give me that jug!" And she took it and she unscrewed the cap and she poured a little whiskey right there in the dirt and then put the cap back on. When they started walking again they listened, but those footsteps just stopped. And Pearl said, "You see, it was just somebody from the other side. They needed a little drink too."

Of this and the other old stories he's heard throughout his life, Fee says, "To me it's all about relationships. If you keep those old stories coming down, then you understand how we are related, not only to each other but to God, to the earth, to all that we know about. You know we *have* to be related. That's what's missing today, everywhere. We've forgotten how we're connected."

Wisconsin's Cave of Wonders (2003)

E. BARRIE KAVASCH

E. Barrie Kavasch is a poet, author, illustrator, and folklorist living in Connecticut. By background she is "Chicamagua Cherokee/Powhaton/ Muskogee Creek/English/German/Scotch-Irish." In her writing she explores her interests in family history, nature, spirituality, and Native foods. This poem appeared in her book *Ancestral Threads: Weaving Remembrance in Poetry and Essays and Family Folklore*.

Enter the Dream Lodge, access ancient wisdom,
journey into the Sacred Mystery much as
birch bark torches lit prehistoric
passage ways into three deep chambers.
Ritual ceremonial life unfolded here
beneath 1,300-year-old charcoal drawings
absorbed into native stone holding birds,
pregnant deer, bow-hunters dancing suspended
along cool rough walls of Earth's womb.
Vision quests tied closely to Nature add
Spirit prayers and offerings reflected in
this ancient rock art symbolizing origin myths,
ritual dances, feast times, family and clan lines.

Infants in cradleboards float across the
ceiling of the cave's entrance; evidence of
the ritual head flattening tied to the 1,500-year-old
Indian Mound nearby in western Wisconsin.
Charcoal line connects to Thunderbird,
perhaps an early "naming ceremony" commemorated
descendants of Ancient Effigy Mound Builders.
They recorded events in their lives with
pigments and carvings on pottery and stone.
Shamans danced journeying to the sources of
game, causes of illness, mysteries of healing.
Who can decipher these meanings in rock art
created like paper and ink in our society, yet

will our thoughts ever last this long?
This "Driftless Area" lay free of
glacial change ranging across
deep valleys in a rugged landscape;
Ho-Chunk homelands today embrace
ancient Earth wombs with stories to tell.

3

HISTORICAL ECOLOGIES

THE TERM "DRIFTLESS" SUGGESTS THAT the area's landscapes have resisted change—that having escaped the glaciers' effects, the Driftless terrain was (and has remained) a stable oasis. In fact, the region's plant and animal communities, like those everywhere, have always been dynamic, changing as climatic patterns shifted, fire regimes fluctuated, streams and their watersheds evolved, species arrived and flourished and declined and (in some cases) disappeared, and as human beings arrived and adopted different ways of living on the land. What was once tundra became boreal forest, which became mixed forest and woodland, which became oak savanna, which became prairie, which became more wooded again, all braided together by springs, streams, wetlands, and rivers. Over the millennia, the landscape mosaic comprising all these community types has continually varied in response to changing climatic, ecological, and cultural influences.

Today's Driftless Area is not the Driftless of ten thousand years ago, or one thousand years ago, or one hundred years ago, or ten years ago. Pieces of the Driftless past are gone forever. Many Pleistocene creatures disappeared. Topsoils have washed downhill and seaward. Waterways have been altered and plant communities frayed and fragmented. Other pieces persist, however, and even thrive, in specialized environments—on shady northern hillsides, on sun-baked goat prairies, in the hidden reaches of spring creeks, on nutrient-poor sand barrens, in chilly caves, along cool talus-slope vents, among gravestones in never-plowed cemeteries. We live in a permanent present that comprises all that has arrived and endured.

Some of these changes remain inscrutable or mythical to us, part of a distant prehistory. More recent changes we can trace through clues left in Native story and song and imagery, in the narratives of European

explorers and settlers and the notes of surveyors and naturalists, in newspapers and journal accounts, in soil deposits and tree rings, range maps
and genomes. Collectively these clues reveal that the Driftless Area,
because of its unique geology, topography, soils, waters, and history, has
provided time and space for biological oddities in the landscape: quirky
microhabitats, endemic and relict species of plants and animals, remnant ecological communities, specialized adaptations.

They also reveal a pattern of accelerated change over the last two centuries, and especially the last several generations. While recent transformations in land use have tended to simplify the landscapes and ecosystems of the Driftless (as they have across the continent and around the
world), the character of the area has to some degree buffered that trend.
Compared to the corn and soybean empire that dominates midwestern
landscapes to the south and west, and northern forests still recovering
from the wave of deforestation that peaked more than a century ago, the
life of the Driftless has followed a distinctive trajectory, its diverse mosaic
of life still adjusting to unique conditions on the land.

Meditations (1931)

LAURA SHERRY

In 1931 poet, actress, and theater advocate Laura Case Sherry (1876–
1947) published *Old Prairie du Chien*, a limited-edition collection of
poems portraying the "varied and interesting" lives of those inhabiting
her home town. After studying literature and drama at the University of
Wisconsin and Northwestern University, Sherry pursued her interest in
theater. In 1911 she founded the experimental Wisconsin Players in Milwaukee, dedicated to democratizing the theater experience and advancing amateur community theater across the state. Two other poems from
Old Prairie du Chien appear in other sections of this collection.

Red headed woodpeckers and yellow hammers[1] question in mystic
    councils.

---

1. A common name for the northern flicker.

Tall grasses in marsh gardens of wild rice, lotus, and cat tails
answer vaguely.
The Indian no longer summers at the mouth of the Wisconsin.
The echoing hoofs of the Buffaloe herds are ghosts on the Prairie.
Illusive themes flutter in the veins of the white birches and silver
poplars.
The chants in the ancient pines rise and swell deep-toned from
remembering.

From "Notes on the Journey West" (1861)

HENRY DAVID THOREAU

Following his doctor's advice to seek respite from his chronic tuberculo-
sis, Henry David Thoreau (1817–1862) traveled to Minnesota in the late
spring of 1861. Seventeen-year-old Horace Mann Jr., an aspiring naturalist and son of the eminent educator, accompanied Thoreau. Arriving by
train at East Dubuque, Illinois, on May 23, they then boarded the steamboat *Itasca* for the three-day trip up the Mississippi River to St. Paul. The
trip failed to improve Thoreau's health; he would die in Concord the following May. These notes from Thoreau's journal follow Walter Harding's
edited version in *Thoreau's Minnesota Journey* (1962). Thoreau remarks
not only on the plants and animals he observed, but on the continuing
Dakota presence, the emerging riverside towns, and a regional economy
dominated still by lead mining and wheat farming.

[May] 23
　　Chicago to Dunleith [now East Dubuque, Illinois]. Very level
1st 20 miles—then considerably more undulating. Greatest
rolling prairie without trees just beyond Winnebago [Illinois].
Last 40 miles in n[orth] w[est] of Ill[inois] quite hilly. Mississippi
backwater in Galena River 8 miles back. Water high now.
Flooded thin woods with more open water behind.
　　Much pink, flowered, apple-like tree (thorn-like) thru Illinois,
which may be the Pyrus coronaria [sweet-scented crabapple].

Distances on prairie deceptive. A stack of wheat straw looks like a hill in the horizon ¼ or ½ mile off. It stands out so bold and high.

Only one boat up daily from Dunleith by this line. In no case allowed to stop on the way.

Small houses without barns, surrounded & overshadowed by great stacks of wheat straw, it being thrashed on the ground. Some wood always visible, but generally not large. The inhabitants remind you of mice nesting in a wheatstack which [is] their wealth. Women working in fields quite commonly. Fences of narrow boards. Towns are, as it were, stations on a r[ail]-r[oad].

Staphylea trifolia [American bladder-nut] out at Dunleith.

[May] 24

Up river.

River, say 60 r[o]ds wide, or 3/4 to 1 mile between bluffs. Broad flooded low intervals covered with willow in bloom (20 feet high, rather slender) & prob[ably] other kinds & elm & white maple & cottonwood. Now boatable between the trees & prob[ably] many ducks there. Bluffs say 150 to 200 ft. high. Rarely room for a village at base of cliffs. Oaks on top (white?) ash, elm, aspen, Bass[wood] on slope & by shore. Kingfishers, small ducks, swallows, jays, & c.

[We] land on the shore often with a plank. Great rafts of boards & shingles 4 or 5 rods wide & 15 or 20 long. Very few small boats. Holes in sides of hill, at Cassville [Wisconsin] where lead [has been] dug. Occasionally a little lonely house on a flat or slope is often deserted. Banks in primitive condition bet[ween] the towns, which is almost everywhere. Load some 9 or 10 cords of wood at a landing. 20 men in 10 minutes. Disturb a bat which flies aboard. Willow shown floating horizontally across the river. Low islands occasionally. Macgregor [McGregor, Iowa] a new town op[posite] to Prairie du Chien [Wisconsin], the smartest town on the river. Exports the most wheat of any town bet[ween] St. Paul & St. Louis. Wheat in sacks. Great heaps at P[rairie] du Chien, covered at night & all over the ground & the only seed wheat.

At Prairie du Chien, Pulsatilla Nuttalliana [pasque-flower] out of flower. Very large. Viola pedata [bird-foot violet] also. Possibly a

white var[iety] of same without marks on the petal. Hoary
puccoon or alkanet (Lithospermum canescens) yel[low] flowered.
Root used to dye red by Ind[ians]. Common from Chicago &
before.

Red-wing b[lack]bird the prevailing [bird] to the Mississippi
R[iver].

On river—pigeons, king fishers, crows, jays, &c., &c., swallows
(white-bellied).

[May] 25th

Got to Prairie du Chien last even[ing]. At Brownsville
[Minnesota] about 6 this a.m. White pine began half a dozen
miles above La Crosse [Wisconsin], a few. Birches more [not?]
common. Cliffs high & interrupted or in promontories.

Fountain City [Wisconsin] about noon. Bluffs further apart &
channels more numerous than yesterday. 2 or 3 miles from bluff
to bluff. Take wood boat along with us. Oaks commonly open on
hills. Indians encamped below Wabashaw [Minnesota] with
Dacotah shaped wigwams. Loon on lake & fish leap. Every town
[has] a wharf with a *storage* building or several & as many hotels
as anything & commission merchants—"Storage, Forwarding, &
Commission"—one or all these words on the most prominent
new building close to the waterside. Perhaps a heap of sacks filled
with wheat on the natural quay or levee close by—or about
Dubuque [Iowa] & Dunleith a blue stack of pig lead which is in no
danger of being washed away. See where they have dug for lead in
the sides of the bluffs for many miles above Galena [Illinois].

The steamer whistles, then strikes its bell about 6 times
funereally & with a pause after the 3rd & You see the whole
village making haste to the landing—commonly the raw stony
or sandy shore. The postmaster with his bag, the passengers,
& almost every dog & pig in the town of commonly one
narrow street under the bluff & back yards at angles of about 45°
with the horizon. If there is more flat space bet[ween] the water
& the bluff, it is almost sure to be occupied by a flourishing &
larger town.

We deserted the outside at a few miles above Red Wing
[Minnesota] where there was a remarkable bluff (Red-Wing Bluff)

standing apart *before* the town as we *approached* it. Reached [St.] Pauls [*sic*] at 2 or 3 o'clock in the morning. The bluffs are here very much lower & even below Red Wing they had been far more interrupted by hollows. We wooded up again before making L[ake] Pepin, taking the boat along with us, now on this side, then on that. White maple, &c. See more & more white birch on bluffs.

"Monument Erected at Wyalusing State Park, Wisconsin, in Memory of the Passenger Pigeon," Hjalmar A. Skuldt (1947). On May 11, 1947, the Wisconsin Society for Ornithology dedicated at Wyalusing State Park a monument to the extinct passenger pigeon. The text of the monument's plaque reads: "Dedicated to the Last Wisconsin Passenger Pigeon Shot at Babcock, Sept. 1899. This Species Became Extinct through the Avarice and Thoughtlessness of Man." For the occasion the WSO issued a special publication, *Silent Wings: A Memorial to the Passenger Pigeon*. Its cover featured this scratchboard drawing of the scene by Hjalmar A. Skuldt (1905–1989), a Madison-area artist and teacher who was born and raised in the Town of Primrose, on the eastern edge of the Driftless Area.

From *Caddie Woodlawn* (1936)

CAROL RYRIE BRINK

Native peoples, explorers, and early settlers alike marveled at the immense flocks of passenger pigeons that periodically descended upon the Driftless Area's acorn-laden oak woodlands. In the chapter "Pigeons in the Sky" from the classic children's historical novel *Caddie Woodlawn*, Carol Ryrie Brink (1895–1981) described one episode in the "wholesale slaughter" that would drive the pigeon to extinction in just a few decades. Born in Idaho and orphaned as a girl, Brink was raised by her grandmother Caddie Woodhouse Watkins, who had grown up in Dunn County, Wisconsin, in the 1850s and 1860s. Watkins's stories of her childhood inspired Brink to write *Caddie Woodlawn*.

The next day was Sunday, and, of course, the school-house was opened and everyone went to church. Mrs. Woodlawn brought a bunch of her autumn flowers to decorate the desk. She had driven over early with her husband and Mr. Tanner to open and air the school-house which had been closed since summer. The children followed on foot. They had a mile to go, across a field and along a dusty road. They rubbed their feet through the tall grass by the schoolhouse gate to take the dust off their Sunday shoes. People from all the surrounding farms and homesteads had come to hear the circuit rider speak. Even Sam Hankinson was there, sitting in a back seat with his three little half-breed children about his knees. But his Indian wife stayed outside. Caddie peeped at them curiously through her fingers when Mr. Tanner's prayer grew very long. How would it be to have an Indian for a mother, she wondered? Then she looked at Mrs. Woodlawn, so fine in her full black silk with the cameo brooch and earrings and the small black hat, and she was glad that this was Mother. And yet, she thought, she would not be ashamed of an Indian mother, as Sam Hankinson seemed to be ashamed of his Indian wife.

The next day the circuit rider rode away on his horse. Father set his clock upon the shelf to be mended later, and life went on again as usual. But now the children began to talk about when Uncle Edmund would come, for Uncle Edmund always came with the pigeons in the fall. He made his annual visit when the shooting was at its best, for he was an eager if not a very skillful sportsman.

Mrs. Woodlawn sighed. "No one can say that I am not a devoted sister," she said, "but the prospect of a visit from Edmund always fills me with alarm. My house is turned upside down, my children behave like wild things, there is nothing but noise and confusion."

"But Ma—" cried Tom.

"Don't Ma me, my child," said Mrs. Woodlawn calmly.

"But, Mother," persisted Tom, defending his hero. "Uncle Edmund knows the most tricks—"

"And jokes!" cried Caddie.

"Remember when he put the hairbrush in Caddie's bed?" shouted Warren. "And the time he put a frog in a covered dish on the supper table, and when Mrs. Conroy lifted the cover—

"That is enough, Tom," said his mother. "We remember Uncle Edmund's tricks very well, and I've no doubt we'll soon see more of them."

But she looked forward to her younger brother's coming just the same, and when the pigeons came and there was no Uncle Edmund everyone felt surprised and concerned.

One night when they went to bed the sky was clear and the woods were still. But when they awoke in the crisp autumn morning the air was full of the noise of wings, and flocks of birds flew like clouds across the sun. The passenger pigeons were on their way south. They filled the trees in the woods. They came down in the fields and gardens, feeding on whatever seeds and grains they could find. The last birds kept flying over those which were feeding in front, in order to come at new ground so that the flock seemed to roll along like a great moving cloud.

"The pigeons have come!" shouted the little Woodlawns. "The pigeons have come!" Even baby Joe waved his arms and shouted.

Tom and Warren armed themselves with sticks and went out with the hired men. But for once Caddie stayed indoors. She liked hunting as well as the boys. But this was too easy. This was not hunting—it was a kind of wholesale slaughter. She knew that the Indians and the white men, too, caught the birds in nets and sent them by thousands to the markets. She knew that wherever the beautiful gray birds went, they were harassed and driven away or killed.

Something of sadness filled her young heart, as if she knew that they were a doomed race. The pigeons, like the Indians, were fighting a losing battle with the white man.

But John Woodlawn was not a glutton as some of his neighbors were. He said to Tom and the hired men: "There is not much grain left in the fields now. Drive the birds off and keep them from doing harm as well as you can, but don't kill more than we can eat. There is moderation in all things."

And so that night there was pigeon pie for supper. But on the Woodlawn farm no more birds were killed than could be eaten.

After supper Robert Ireton, strumming his banjo out by the barn, sang the song that everybody had on his lips at this time of the year:

> When I can shoot my rifle clear
> At pigeons in the sky,
> I'll bid farewell to pork and beans
> And live on pigeon pie.

The three children, huddled around him on the chilly ground, hummed or sang with him, and all about them in the darkness was the rustle and stir of wings.

A few days later the passenger pigeons had disappeared as suddenly as they had come. They had taken up their perilous journey toward the South. It was as if they had never passed by—except that the woods were stripped of seeds and acorns and dried berries, and some folks still had cold pigeon pie in their kitchens or dead birds on their truck heaps.

From "An Ecological Survey of the Driftless Area of Illinois and Wisconsin" (1909)

H. S. Pepoon

Appreciation of the Driftless Area's distinctive flora grew with the emergence of plant ecology in the American Midwest in the 1890s. H. S. (Herman Silas) Pepoon (1860–1941) was born in Warren, Illinois, studied botany at the University of Illinois, and then became a doctor. After practicing medicine in Nebraska and Illinois he returned to Chicago, where for thirty-eight years he taught botany and agriculture at Lake View High School. His important early ecological studies of the Driftless Area, first published in the journal *School Science and Mathematics*, have been republished in *H. S. Pepoon: Pioneer Conservationist of Northwest Illinois* (2011).

A plan long cherished by the writer, to make a botanical survey of that portion of Illinois and Wisconsin known to the geologist as the *driftless area*, was put into active operation during the summer of 1908, when continuous exploration was undertaken for sixty days during the months of July and August. Much work of a more or less desultory nature had been accomplished before this year, extending over a period of nearly thirty years, or from boyhood days, and resulting in many valuable observations and the accumulation of a large amount of data, much of which is now not obtainable at any cost.

Two main reasons may be given for the survey. The first is that this area was the birthplace of the writer, and from boyhood on he had traversed the hills and valleys and was familiar with every mile of its territory, and the familiarity was due to the zeal for botanical collection that actuated the miles and miles of tramping, spring, summer, fall and winter. The second and important reason from the standpoint of ecology is that, owing to the unique geological history of the area, hinted at in the term "driftless area" commonly applied to it, there might be found many interesting and peculiar features of plant life indicative of problems in distribution that would have solutions found in the exceptional geological history of the region. . . .

The Drift area of Stephenson County, on the east, and of Carroll County on the south, compared with the Driftless region in Jo Daviess County, leads me to conclude that fully ten per cent of the species present in the latter county are not present at all, or found but rarely in the Drift counties. This condition may arise, in part, from the development of forest on the Driftless soil, but the presence of many species point to an inherent difference, due to other influences. . . .

Speaking more in detail of a few forms, some of which are named above, it will be interesting to refer at the beginning to the [Bird's Eye] Primrose. This plant is so notoriously a boreal species that my statement of its abundance on the cliffs of Jo Daviess County was received by some botanical friends with some [in]credulity. Here on damp cliffs having a northern exposure, the plant is so common that the bare rock walls assume a lavender hue at the time of the blooming in late April. . . . The Canoe Birch, everywhere common on the bluffs, on north exposures, as before mentioned, is found so far as the writer has observed, at no other Illinois points except near Lake Michigan, and here it forms a zone around the south end, as if it were a relic of the great ice-mass that once filled the bed of the lake, encroaching everywhere on its border. The Pipsissewa and Rattlesnake Plantain reach their highest development in Canada, far to the northeast, and here are so excessively local that only one locality has been found for each, and each contains a score or so of plants. . . .

The area has from remote time been uncovered by the primeval waters, so that the surface has suffered merely the modifications due to erosive agencies of air and water; it might then with reason be expected that a commingling of southern and northern species would exist, and with all the more assurance because of the midway latitude of 42 degrees. During the long lapse of time some southern forms would gradually adapt themselves to a colder climate and some northern species would reverse the process. This is exactly what is found. For an astonishing example, the Pecan (Hicoria pecan) may be named. A notoriously warm temperate tree, it is yet found in the Mississippi bottom in the area, just on the 42 degree line, attaining a height of 90 feet, and a diameter of 3 feet, copiously fruiting also. The Coffee bean [Kentucky coffeetree, *Gymnocladus dioicus*] is locally common, particularly along the bluffs of the great river. The Mulberry (Morus rubra) is frequent along the Apple River, and was found in full fruit in 1908.

Not ten rods away from groups of the two latter species, Canoe Birch, Primrose, Moose-Wood (Dirca), Wild Snowball, and other cold temperature forms were common. It is true that the narrow gorge of Apple River is an exceedingly sheltered locality, both from heat and cold, and plants from either clime, by choosing the proper exposure, would easily find a genial temperature environment. Still it is no less interesting and noteworthy that they do grow in juxtaposition. . . .

Cases of peculiar habitat are abundant. Three or four very striking ones may be given, all contrary "to the books." The showy Lady-slippers (Cypripedium reginae) of "swamps and woods" grow here invariably on the bluffs, and some specimens sent to the Missouri Botanical Gardens were actually clinging to a crevice in a vertical limestone cliff. The only specimen of Limodorum (Grass Pink) found was on the bald crown of a high bluff, which place yielded Leptorchis loesellii or Twayblade; no Limodorum of "bogs and meadows" or Leptorchis of "wet thickets and springy banks" was found. The Fringed Gentian is a common cliff plant; this, however, must be noted, that abundant seepage of water constantly bathes the roots of all the above. . . . Shrubby Potentilla, a bog plant in Michigan, is a cliff plant here. White Pine grows nowhere but on the dry clefts of towering cliffs. Here, too, but lower down, the Wild Snowball grows, but only here; "low woods" say the books. Moose-wood (Dirca) is to be sought for on the bluffs; "woods and thickets" the books have it.

It appears to me that these peculiarities of habitat have a reasonable explanation in a gradual adaptation of the several species to life in far different topographic environments, but having a similar water content in the soil. This change in habitat may be a striking example of the effect of the removal of the fierce competition in the open bog or thicket, a few forms seemingly discovering the practical immunity from such struggle on the cliffs and adapting themselves to life there.

This has been done even at the expense of precarious foothold and lesser food supply. Here, then, we might expect to find the last stand of many ancient as well as modern forms of plant life. The only place where the three conifers, Pine, Red Cedar, and Yew, many ferns, several orchids, three liliaceous plants, the Primrose, and many more are to be found, is on these, to man often unattainable, cliff homes. . . .

While but little difference appears to exist in the plants of the upland varieties on the prairies, everywhere the topographic feature of the border between the two areas, one feature deserves particular mention, and that is the very sudden increase in number of pond and swamp forms, brought about by the imperfect drainage of the drift. The ponds, swamps, and wet prairies abound in sedges, juncus, potomogetons, polygonums, utricularias, naumbergias, and many more species entirely absent from the other side of that magic line, the drift margin. The prairies of drier nature are crowded with forms that reach their best development here, although many species are spread over the higher open lands within the Driftless area. The Meadow and the Turk's-Cap Lily abound, and astonishing to a degree, the White Fringed Orchis (Blephariglottis leucophoea) exists by thousands. The prairie Ranunculus, Violets, Phlox, Gentiana puberula, the cream-colored Wild Indigo, Asclepias sullivantia, Blazing Stars, and hordes of other original prairie plants greet the eye.

In this connection it is worth while noting the preservative influence of the Illinois Central [Railroad] on plant life. Built through this region in 1858, the right of way has never been cultivated, and the only unfavorable factor is the annual *burning off* in August. This comes too late to injure in the least spring and early summer forms, and even many Asters and late season types find havens of safety about telegraph posts and in the fence rows. It is here that genuine prairie plants are to be found, and a number of species are not to be obtained elsewhere. Of course migrant plants are much in evidence, and probably two-thirds of all introduced species can be found bordering the track bed. The purple Cone Flower, petioled Sunflower, False Dandelion (Nothocalais), Prairie Gentian (G. puberula), and Polygala incarnata are examples of species not seen in other localities. The weeds from the railroad initial vantage ground spread outward, and thus slowly take possession of waste places. . . .

In the sand area of the southwest portion of Jo Daviess county, bordering on the Mississippi River, a strip ten miles long by one to two miles wide, there exists a very peculiar and interesting community of plants, partaking in many of their features of the characteristics of desert plants. The land is a level plain, or with occasional minor elevations, having two well-marked zones of elevation, the low and the high prairie, a sand bluff bordering on the Mississippi, and a dune immediately inland from the bluff. A cross-section from river to valley bluff shows six zones of plant life, each markedly differing from the others. . . .

The whole prairie [near Savanna, Illinois] marks a former level of the great river, when it flowed four miles wide from the ice land at the north, and this was in comparatively modern times, geologically. The surface has since been eroded by the wind, numerous blowouts with their peculiar plant forms, notably, Cristatella, Talinum, and several grasses being common present features. Three hundred and fifty species were found upon this prairie during the year of 1908, of which 20 were peculiar to the bluff and dune, 10 to the oak belt, 25 to the high, and 15 to the low prairie, the balance being generally scattered, although many species are very rare, and only a few specimens found. As a whole this prairie reminds me of the elevated plains of northwestern Nebraska and South Dakota, having many plants identical or of related species. In fact, a number of species seem to have had their original home on these western lands and by some means have found their way far to the eastward. . . .

The proportion of plants found in different plant associations or societies has not been fully worked out, but approximately the results are shown in the following tabulated form:

Drift Area—

No. of Species	Prairie	Woodland	Bluff	Sand	Water.
850	250	445	40	15	100

Driftless Area—

No. of Species	Prairie	Woodland	Bluff	Sand	Water.
936	25	641	140	100	30

From *The Vegetation of Wisconsin* (1959)

JOHN T. CURTIS

Botanist and ecologist John T. Curtis (1913–1961) was born in Waukesha, Wisconsin, and received his PhD in botany at the University of Wisconsin in Madison. Years of intensive field work by Curtis and his students resulted in the book *The Vegetation of Wisconsin: An Ordination of Plant Communities*—a classic and globally influential work in the field of plant ecology. It includes this overview of the conditions shaping the distinctive vegetation of the Driftless Area.

In the southwestern part of Wisconsin lies an extensive area that has never been covered by glacial ice, although it is surrounded by lands that have been glaciated. Upon the usual glacial map it appears as an island, but in actual fact it never was surrounded completely by ice at any one time, because the glaciers to the east and to the west of it were present in different epochs. This area, the "Driftless Area," thus was open to direct colonization by plants at all times, but the fact that it was available is in itself no proof that plants actually did exist there during glacial times. The entire question of periglacial climates is involved. Without doubt the land surfaces immediately adjacent to the ice front were influenced by the temperatures of the ice, but considerable uncertainty exists as to the distance over which such an effect might persist. Some portions of the Driftless Area were at least 100 miles from the ice front, regardless of which sheet was present, and this distance is thought by many geologists to be far removed from direct effects of the ice. If recent theories on the climate necessary for glacier formation are correct, then the prevailing temperatures of the region may have been similar to those existing now or were slightly warmer. . . . Under such conditions of a warm, moist, growing season there is every reason to believe that a vegetational cover existed over most of the Driftless Area and furthermore, that the composition of the vegetation was very similar to that found today.

Unfortunately, no fossil record of any kind has been discovered which would prove or disprove this conclusion. [Botanist Norman] Fassett of the University of Wisconsin was deeply interested in the problem and from 1925 to 1950 devoted much effort to the study of the flora of the Driftless Area. He and his students succeeded in finding a number of species and varieties that were either endemic to the region, or were found there and in other places beyond the edge of the continental glaciation, but not in places which had been covered by ice. Among them were the species listed in Table 1. The rather remarkable distributions of *Aconitum noveboracense* [northern wild monk's-hood] and *Dodecathon amethystinum* [amethyst shooting star] are best explained by assuming that the plants have persisted within the Driftless Area from some past time when their range was continuous through the area now covered with drift. Both of these species and a number of others on the list have rather specialized habitat requirements, growing best on shaded, dripping cliffs. Some investigators have considered that the plants are confined to the Driftless Area because of the prevalence there of these cliffs. Such geological formations are naturally more common in the areas not subject to glaciation but they are also present in glaciated regions. In addition, other species on the list such as *Muhlenbergia cuspidata* [plains muhly or prairie satin grass] and *Psoralea esculenta* [prairie turnip] are prairie plants of open places and are in no way dependent upon special rock formations so the explanation would not hold for them. It would appear, therefore, that these species rightly may be called preglacial relics.

One of the peculiarities of the plants in Table 1 is that they have remained confined to the Driftless Area. Of course, this characteristic was instrumental in their original discovery but the point remains that they have shown an extraordinary tendency to a sedentary existence. Many other species may have persisted similarly within the Driftless Area during glaciation but had long since spread out and are no longer recognizable as to origin. A few species have rather small total ranges which center on the Area and are presumed to have spread in postglacial times. Included here is Hill's oak (*Quercus ellipsoidalis*). . . .

A variety of geological, climatological, and ecological evidence . . . strongly supports the hypothesis that the Driftless Area was at least partially covered with vegetation at all times and that it formed the source for the bulk of the plant cover which later spread out over the remaining parts of the state as these were deglaciated.

TABLE 1. Plants endemic in the Driftless Area or whose range in Wisconsin is restricted to that region

Aconitum noveboracense var. *quasiciliatum* [Columbian monk's-hood]
Adoxa moschatellina [moschatel muskroot]
Anemone caroliniana [Carolina anemone, prairie anemone]
Asplenium platyneuron [ebony spleenwort]
Azolla caroliniana [Carolina mosquito-fern, eastern mosquito-fern]
Callirhoe triangulata [clustered poppy mallow]
Cassia [Senna] marilandica [Maryland senna, southern wild senna]
Cheilanthes feei [slender lip fern]

Chrysopsis villosa [hairy golden aster, telegraph-plant]
Commelina erecta var. *greenei* [erect dayflower]
Dasistoma macrophylla [mullein-foxglove]
Dodecatheon amethystinum [amethyst (or jeweled) shooting star]
Elatine triandra [greater waterwort, long-stem waterwort, water-purslane]
Eliocharis wolfii [wolf's spike-rush]
Elymus riparius [riverbank wild-rye, streambank wild-rye]
Gerardia skinneriana [pale false foxglove, Skinner's false foxglove]
Gnaphalium saxicola [cliff cudweed]
Hibiscus militaria [halberd-leaf rosemallow]
Hypericum mutilum [small-flowered St. John's-wort]
Linaria canadensis [annual toadflax, blue toadflax, Canada toadflax]
Lycopodium selago var. *patens* [fir clubmoss, northern firmoss]
Muhlenbergia cuspidata [plains muhly, prairie muhly, prairie satin grass]
Myosotis laxa [bay forget-me-not, small forget-me-not]
Onosmodium occidentale [marble-seed, western false gromwell]
Pellaea atropurpurea [purple-stem cliff-brake]
Penstemon gracilis var. *wisconsinensis* [lilac penstemon, slender beard-tongue]
Psoralaea esculenta [prairie turnip]
Rhamnus lanceolatus [lanced-leaved buckthorn]
Rhododendron lapponicum [Lapland azalea]
Rhus trilobata [fragrant sumac, squaw-bush]
Solidago castrensis [showy goldenrod]
Solidago sciaphila [shadowy goldenrod]
Sullivantia reniformis [Sullivant's cool-wort]
Talinum rugospermum [prairie fame-flower]

From "Reconstructing Vegetation Past: Pre-Euro-American Vegetation for the Midwest Driftless Area, USA" (2014)

MONIKA E. SHEA, LISA A. SCHULTE, AND BRIAN J. PALIK

In a study published in the journal *Ecological Restoration*, the authors (ecologists with the University of Wisconsin–Madison, Iowa State University and the U.S. Forest Service) reconstructed the historic character of

Badger and Prairie Smoke, Dan Hazlett (2002). The American badger spends most of its life in burrows, hence the nickname for early miners who lived in their diggings in the Lead District of the Driftless Area. Today, much of this elusive carnivore's grassland and savanna habitat has been displaced by agriculture, but naturalist and artist Dan Hazlett of rural La Farge, Wisconsin, found one, depicted here in one of his distinctive colored pencil drawings of Driftless fauna and flora.

the Driftless Area's forests, savannas, and prairies. To do so, the authors analyzed detailed records and descriptions of soils, vegetation, and witness trees compiled by the U.S. public land surveyors in the mid-1800s.

Our reconstruction of pre-Euro-American vegetation for the Driftless Area depicts a landscape dominated by savanna and a variety of oak communities. [Our findings] are consistent with other work from this region, including qualitative reconstructions using [public land survey] witness tree records and surveyor notes to map vegetation in Minnesota, Wisconsin, Iowa, and Illinois. These early reconstructions also depict the Driftless Area as dominated by oak savannas, with several large patches of closed forest and prairie in roughly the same locations as we found. . . .

While dominated by oak species, our reconstructions [also] illustrate a complex landscape containing a variety of species assemblages, oak and non-oak. This diversity is likely due to a complex assortment of interacting factors (i.e., abiotic environment, disturbance history, disturbance regime, past community composition and structure, climate, etc.), which we cannot fully address given the scale of [land survey] data. Nevertheless, our study points to two elements that likely played a role in determining species composition and contributed to the Driftless Area's HRV[2]: disturbance and environmental conditions.

The preponderance of oak and, in particular, savanna supports previous assessments that suggest fire was widespread in the Driftless Area prior to Euro-American settlement. Savanna was likely maintained by low intensity fire with a frequent return interval of five to fifteen years, which created favorable conditions for the persistence of relatively fire-resistant, shade-intolerant oak species. Six of . . . eight oak-dominated cover classes[3] were highly associated with savanna and were dominated by species that display some degree of resistance to fire. Associations with environmental factors varied among these cover classes, suggesting that, while frequent low-intensity fire maintained oak savanna habitat

---

2. In ecology, the *historic range of variability*, or HRV, describes "the range of conditions possible within a given environmental context" over time. It provides insight into how humans have affected such ecological processes as fire and flooding.

3. A *cover class* is a distinct set of species comprising a plant community.

in general, environmental conditions played a role in separating oak species into different cover classes. Indeed, the Driftless Area's characteristically undulating topography generates a range of environmental conditions, predisposing the region to potentially support a diverse set of tree communities.

The biological requirements and limitations of tree species directed the compositional response to environmental conditions. Some oak species, such as black oak and northern pin oak, are limited to particular growing conditions: both are fairly intolerant of shade, drought tolerant and resistant to fire, and grow well in sandy, xeric[4] soils. In the Driftless Area, these two species dominated cover classes that generally occurred in areas that displayed xeric qualities: sandy soil, high topographic roughness, and far distance from waterways. White oak and bur oak are more versatile. These two species tolerate a wide range of soil and moisture conditions and white oak is also somewhat tolerant of shade. Versatility may be the reason these two species were a major part of multiple cover classes, each exhibiting an array of environmental associations. These two species' environmental associations sometimes overlapped: bur oak and white oak often occurred together, and they co-dominated the Bur Oak-White Oak cover class. Bur oak and white oak also dominated their own single-species cover classes, differing from one another in part by the Bur Oak cover class's strong association with low topographic roughness. This may be due to increased fire frequency in areas with more gentle topography; bur oak has extremely thick bark [and] is thought to be one of the most fire resistant oak species in North America.

While frequent low-intensity fires likely maintained savanna over much of the Driftless Area, variation in fire intensity and frequency would have contributed to the patterning of prairie, open woodland, and closed forest ecosystems. Variation in fire history can also affect tree species composition. For example, if fire is absent, an oak savanna is likely to develop into closed forest and may eventually become dominated by mesic[5] species, a process known as mesophication. In the Driftless Area,

---

4. *Xeric* refers to habitats or environments characterized by very dry conditions.

5. *Mesic* refers to habitats or environments characterized by moderate moisture conditions.

it is possible that the White Oak-Sugar Maple-Basswood-Elm and Sugar Maple cover classes originated from White Oak communities that were in various stages of mesophication, depending on time since fire disturbance. Similarly, less fire-tolerant northern red oak could have invaded white oak savannas in the absence of fire, forming the Red Oak-White Oak cover class. Red Oak-White Oak may have also arisen in places that experienced intense fire followed by a prolonged period without fire. In either case, fire may have occurred relatively recently prior to the time of the [public land] survey; this is because there were very few shade-tolerant mesic hardwoods recorded in the canopy of Red Oak-White Oak communities, despite the fact that mesic hardwoods readily establish in forests dominated by northern red oak. Small-diameter mesic hardwoods may have been present in these communities, but often were not recorded because surveyors favored medium-sized witness trees where they were available.

In addition to Sugar Maple, several non-oak cover classes were present in smaller portions of the Driftless Area. Elm and Birch-White Ash-Sugar Maple-Elm were both strongly associated with short distance from waterways and, given the species composition, probably comprised lowland forest communities. The Jack Pine-Red Pine and White Pine cover classes, which were mainly clustered in sections located on the northeastern edge of the Driftless Area, were strongly associated with sandy soils; these species are known to dominate Wisconsin forests in areas of sandy glacial outwash, which extends into the northeast margin of the Driftless Area. Elsewhere, isolated patches of the pine cover classes may be associated with relict pine communities, which occurred throughout the region on rocky cliffs. Both pine cover classes had greater than 70 percent of their sections occurring in savanna, suggesting that frequent fires maintained pine barrens in an open landscape. Aspen occurred throughout the Driftless Area, but was only dominant in the northern part of the region. Clonal reproduction allows aspen to rapidly establish in recently disturbed or open spaces like prairies, particularly in areas with flat to moderate topography. The dominance of aspen in the north may be due to lower topographic roughness combined with proximity to prairies. . . .

The dominance of savannas and oak communities, and the presence of other fire-dependent communities, such as those dominated by aspen or pine species, indicates that fire played a key role . . . in the Driftless

Area prior to Euro-American settlement. In the absence of fire, the region's annual rainfall is more than adequate for supporting closed forests composed of mesic species, as is the case today. While browsing by elk and deer, and potentially bison, may have also had an impact on vegetation dynamics, fire with a frequent return interval (one to fifteen years) would have been required to maintain open vegetation types over such large extents. Fire likely was a major determinant of the Driftless Area's HRV for several thousand years; indeed, paleoecological investigations at locations within or near the Driftless Area revealed that oak ecosystems were . . . dominant during the late Holocene leading up to Euro-American settlement.

Today, about 47 percent of the Driftless Area is used for agriculture, 13 percent is developed, and 34 percent is forested, mainly in fragmented closed forest patches. Very little savanna remains, having been converted into pasture and crop fields or developed into closed forest with fire exclusion. While oak species sometimes dominate these forests, they are being replaced by more shade-tolerant and mesic species, such as maple, ash, and elm. This mesophication of the forests is due in part to a sustained lack of fire disturbance since Euro-American settlement, a phenomenon that is occurring throughout much of the eastern U.S. As oak savannas gave way to oak forests, which are now giving way to mesic hardwood forests, it is likely that much of the compositional diversity found in the pre-Euro-American vegetation . . . is being lost. These declines may be further compounded with climate change: current projections for tree species habitat response to climate change predict substantial reductions in importance values for currently prominent oak species, white oak and northern red oak, in the Driftless Area ecoregion. These potential declines may be compensated by increasing importance of other oak species, black oak, post oak (*Quercus stellata*), and chinkapin oak (*Q. muehlenbergii*). Additionally, several non-oak species, including hackberry, box elder, and honey locust (*Gleditsia triacanthos*), are also projected to increase in dominance.

Given the prevalence and diversity of oak communities prior to Euro-American settlement, we consider restoring oak ecosystems an urgent restoration goal for the Driftless Area. Oaks are often foundational species where they occur, supporting a diverse array of plant and animal species. We expect declines in oak dominance and loss of oak communities to be indicative of substantial changes in ecosystem structure and function across the Driftless Area. To ameliorate oak declines due to mesophication, and to inhibit the potential negative impacts of climate change on oak ecosystems in the Driftless Area, it is important to restore a diverse array of oak communities and for them to be present in their appropriate structural condition (i.e., savanna, closed forest) to provide a broad template on which climate change will act.

Changes in Wildlife Over Time (2012)

WISCONSIN DEPARTMENT OF NATURAL RESOURCES

In a 2012 report, *Ecological Landscapes of Wisconsin*, researchers in the Wisconsin Department of Natural Resources summarized the historical changes in populations of many of the most prominent wildlife species of the Driftless Area.

The Western Coulees and Ridges [region of Wisconsin] was important historically for a number of wildlife species, especially those using oak savanna and oak openings, oak and floodplain forests, prairies, bluffs, caves and rock outcroppings, and large river systems. This ecological landscape was particularly important for elk (*Cervus canadensis*), American bison (*Bos bison*), wild turkey (*Meleagris gallopavo*), passenger pigeon (*Ectopistes migratorius*), sharp-tailed grouse (*Tympanuchus phasianellus*), greater prairie chicken (*Tympanuchus cupido*), northern bobwhite (*Colinus virginianus*), timber rattlesnake (*Crotalus horridus*), and eastern massasauga (*Sistrurus catenatus catenatus*). In the mid-nineteenth century, the ecological landscape was settled by EuroAmericans, wild fires were prevented and controlled, and wildlife populations changed.

Although the distribution of the passenger pigeon has been described as covering the eastern half of North America, its nesting habitat was limited by the presence and abundance of mast (primarily beechnuts and acorns). [A. W.] Schorger reported from newspaper accounts and interviews that passenger pigeons nested by the millions in Wisconsin. With a large presence of oak, this ecological landscape was undoubtedly an important nesting area for passenger pigeons during years of high mast production.

Passenger pigeons were clubbed, shot, and trapped during the nesting season and squabs taken from nests and shipped to markets in
Milwaukee, Chicago, and cities on the east coast by the trainload. Since
the passenger pigeon was thought to lay only one egg each year, nested
only in communal roosts, and was dependent on abundant mast for the
production of young, the heavy kill of passenger pigeon led to its extinction. The last known passenger pigeon died in 1914 at the Cincinnati
Zoo. . . .

Elk were found throughout Wisconsin but flourished in open woodlands, oak openings, and at the border of grasslands and forests. Elk
were most numerous and abundant in the southern and western parts
of the state and were especially abundant in this ecological landscape.
The Chippewa, Kickapoo, Trempealeau, and Mississippi River valleys
were often mentioned as having abundant elk populations, and there
was a report that elk were "astonishingly abundant" around the Platte-
ville area. Elk were still abundant in this ecological landscape during the
1850s but declined rapidly after that. The last reliable report of elk in
Wisconsin is from west of Menomonie in 1866. Beginning in [the] 1930s,
attempts have been made to restore free-ranging elk in Wisconsin. . . .

American bison historically occupied the prairie areas of the state
and were abundant in this ecological landscape. A map of southwestern
Wisconsin published in 1829 by R. W. Chandler, a pioneer settler of
Galena, Illinois, stated that "not more than a tenth is covered by timber
in detached groves, the remainder being prairies." [Edward] Daniels
estimated that only one-third of southwestern Wisconsin was prairie in
1854. He attributed this rapid change from prairie to timber to the cessation of fires and rapid growth of young trees on the open prairie.
American bison occurred from Racine along Lake Michigan, north to
Lake Winnebago, and over to Burnett County in the northwestern part
of the state. Both the Wisconsin and Chippewa River valleys are mentioned as having abundant American bison populations. The last Wisconsin American bison was killed near the Trempealeau River in 1832.

White-tailed deer (*Odocoileus virginianus*) were found throughout
the state and were likely more abundant in southern Wisconsin than
in the northern part of the state at the time of Euro-American settlement. Deer were reported as plentiful in southwestern Wisconsin in the
1830s, and [Charles] Hoffman reported that he saw "large herds" on the
prairies in February 1834. However, as settlers arrived in southwestern

Wisconsin in subsequent years, they depended on venison for food, and professional market hunters sent tons of venison to the large eastern cities. The severe winter of 1856–1857 caused many deer to starve or be easily killed by settlers in southwestern Wisconsin. Snow six feet deep was reported in some places with a thick half-inch crust making movement of deer very difficult. Within a decade, the deer population seemed to recover somewhat, and they were reported to be numerous again in southwestern Wisconsin in the mid-1860s. Subsistence harvest, together with market hunting, likely reduced the deer population to its lowest level late in the nineteenth century. Deer were considered uncommon throughout southwestern Wisconsin from 1900 through the 1960s. However, since the early 1980s, deer populations have increased dramatically in this ecological landscape, and deer are now very abundant. Today the white-tailed deer is an important game species but causes crop damage, vehicle accidents, damage to forest regeneration, and negative impacts to many forest herbs. Chronic Wasting Disease (CWD) was discovered in the eastern part of this ecological landscape (Dane and Iowa counties) in 2002. Since then, special hunting seasons and regulations have been implemented to reduce the deer herd and thereby contain the disease. Ongoing testing for this disease is occurring to monitor its incidence and spread and to inform hunters of sick deer they may have shot.

The gray wolf (*Canis lupus*) occurred statewide prior to Euro-American settlement. Wisconsin wolf numbers then declined gradually due to loss of food sources, shooting, trapping, and poisoning. By the early 1960s, they were thought to have been extirpated from the state. The gray wolf population has since reestablished itself and expanded from northwest to northeast and into central Wisconsin. No gray wolves are known to be resident in this ecological landscape at this time but are sporadically observed here.

American black bears (*Ursus americanus*) were historically found throughout the ecological landscape but were probably more abundant in the heavily wooded areas to the north. The last historical appearance of black bears here was from the early to mid-1900s. Today the American black bear range is expanding south and southwest in the state. The northeastern edge of the ecological landscape, in Dunn, Chippewa, and Eau Claire counties, is considered secondary range for the American black bear, and northwestern Jackson County is considered primary range. Recent sightings of American black bears have occurred in other parts of the Western Coulees and Ridges.

The historical range of the wild turkey was in southern Wisconsin below a line from Green Bay to Prairie du Chien. However, since the wild turkey was at the northernmost part of its range, the number of turkeys close to this line fluctuated in response to severe winters. Wild turkeys were most abundant in southwestern Wisconsin and in the southern part of this ecological landscape. In 1816, James Lockwood stated, "It was not an uncommon thing to see a Fox Indian arrive at Prairie du Chien with a hand sled, loaded with twenty to thirty wild turkeys for sale, as they were very plentiful about Cassville, and occasionally killed opposite Prairie du Chien." Due to persistent hunting by settlers for food, changes to habitat, and the severe winter of 1842–1843, wild turkeys were rare by 1860. The last historical documented wild turkey was seen in Lafayette County in 1881. . . .

It wasn't until 1976 that the wild turkey became reestablished in Wisconsin, when forty-five wild turkeys trapped in Missouri were released in Vernon County. These wild turkeys were obtained in a trade for 135 ruffed grouse trapped in this ecological landscape. Other reintroductions followed, and a total of 334 Missouri wild turkeys were released in Buffalo, Iowa, Sauk, Trempealeau, Jackson, La Crosse, Vernon, Dane, and Lafayette counties. Once established in these areas, the Wisconsin DNR trapped and relocated wild turkeys throughout the state. Although the wild turkey is now established in all sixteen ecological landscapes, the Western Coulees and Ridges Ecological Landscape has the highest densities for this bird in Wisconsin, providing excellent hunting and wildlife viewing opportunities.

The sharp-tailed grouse was considered widely distributed in the state in open and brushy habitats before Euro-American settlement and was likely common in this ecological landscape, primarily occupying the extensive oak openings and barrens. Sharp-tailed grouse probably expanded into additional areas as dense growths of shrubs and saplings created brushy habitat with the cessation of fire. Sharp-tailed grouse later declined, as the oak openings grew into dense forests, and agriculture became increasingly intensive. No sharp-tailed grouse occur in this ecological landscape today.

The greater prairie chicken was found throughout southern Wisconsin prior to EuroAmerican settlement, although the sharp-tailed grouse may have been more abundant. Through the 1850s, the greater prairie chicken was considered abundant in southern Wisconsin, but it later declined. The spread of agriculture initially seemed to lead to an increase in the greater prairie chicken population, but populations declined as farming became more intensive and the prairies disappeared. The greater prairie chicken was forced north as prairies were plowed for agriculture in the south while forests were cleared in central and northern Wisconsin. As forests regrew in the north, the range of the prairie chicken contracted to its present location, primarily in the Central Sand Plains. . . . The greater prairie chicken is not found in this ecological landscape today.

The northern bobwhite must have been distributed throughout the open areas of southern Wisconsin, though populations fluctuated widely depending on winter severity. Northern bobwhite . . . reached peak numbers in 1854, [then] declined quickly thereafter due to unregulated trapping and shooting and adverse weather. . . . At the close of the nineteenth century, the northern bobwhite population increased temporarily in the Mississippi valley. Schorger noted that "they were abundant in 1896 at Prairie du Chien and more numerous than usual at Trempealeau. . . ." The increase continued through 1900, and they "were to be found everywhere in the country districts at Prairie du Chien for the first time in many years." Northern bobwhite populations have decreased dramatically since 1900 due to changes in land use and other causes, but this ecological landscape has the best populations remaining in the state. The Wisconsin DNR made an effort to increase northern bobwhite habitat and populations here during the 1970s and 1980s by planting hedgerows and winter food plots on private land. These efforts met with little success because habitat was not maintained by private landowners. Up to 60 percent of annual variability in northern bobwhite numbers could be explained by winter severity, but long-term declines are due to habitat loss.

Both the timber rattlesnake and eastern massasauga were historically abundant in this ecological landscape. The timber rattlesnake was found in the uplands, especially where there were rock outcroppings and rock crevices where they could hibernate. Historically, they have been restricted to southwestern Wisconsin and have never been found east of Madison. The eastern massasauga was found in marshy areas, low prairies, and along streams throughout southern and central Wisconsin.

Populations of both rattlesnake species have been dramatically reduced by land use changes and continued persecution. The Cooke family killed 150 rattlesnakes during their first year near Gilmanton in 1856. [E.] Messeling stated that he killed a thousand rattlesnakes for their bounty each year. As late as the mid-1960s, Crawford County paid a bounty for 10,000–11,000 rattlesnakes a year. Early settlers also used pigs, which kill and eat snakes, to control rattlesnakes on their farms.

The eastern massasauga is more sensitive to habitat changes, is now listed as Wisconsin Endangered, and is a candidate for federal listing. In the Western Coulees and Ridges, it is still occasionally found locally along the Chippewa and Black rivers. Timber rattlesnake populations have also been reduced; it is a Wisconsin Special Concern species and is protected from harvest by state law. As this is the only Wisconsin ecological landscape that has both the timber rattlesnake and eastern massasauga and suitable habitat for them, this is the only place where management for this species can feasibly occur.

Desoto Hills (1951)

Cecile Houghton Stury

Cecile Houghton Stury (1881–1971) was born and raised on a farm in Walworth County, Wisconsin, attended Northwestern University, and became a teacher and writer. She published prolifically—articles, plays, children's books, poems, stories. "Desoto Hills" appeared in *Sun Across Wisconsin*, a collection of poems depicting the Wisconsin landscape from Lake Michigan to the Mississippi River. "Desoto Hills" was the closing poem of the collection.

The stone-faced hills along the Mississippi
Know so much but stand in silence there
Scorning to betray a fox or wildcat—
A deer within their bosom's secret lair.

Quite undisturbed by lonely whip-poor-will
Or flash of cardinal or thrush

They ever dwell on memories of the days
When out of darkness and eternal hush

They shook the waters from their hoary heads
To clothe themselves in robes of motley green—
While on and on, dividing east and west,
The river flowed serene and safe between.

Mount Winnishiek and all the other mountains
know so much of struggles fierce and long
Yet take no sides with children red or white—
Rejoice in not one victory of the strong.

These hills hide depths of joy and sorrow under
Thin blue veils before the snow
While peering down from phantom castles over
Barges slipping through the locks below.

Untitled wood engraving, Frank Utpatel (1966). Woodcut artist Frank Utpatel (1905–1980) was a lifelong resident of Wisconsin who studied under John Steuart Curry and lived in his later years in Mazomanie. Through his friendships with Sauk Prairie writers August Derleth and Mark Schorer, Utpatel became a prolific illustrator of popular science fiction, horror, and fantasy books. He also provided illustrations for nonfiction literature, including this engraving from Derleth's 1966 poetry collection *The Only Place We Live*.

4

NATIVE VOICES

EOPLE HAVE INHABITED THE DRIFTLESS AREA since the first Paleoindians arrived in the aftermath of the Wisconsin glaciation. In
historic times the region has witnessed dramatic and disruptive
changes in the lifeways of Native peoples. By the mid-1600s Euro-
Americans had displaced Native tribes over much of what is now the
northeastern United States. Disease, war, land alienation, and forced
removal frayed the fabric of Native communities and drove eastern tribes
into the western Great Lakes and Mississippi River basins. The Menominee, Ho-Chunk,[1] Dakota, and Ioway (Báxoĵe), present in the land since
time immemorial, were now joined by Ojibwe clans in the north; and
by Potawatomi, Odawa, Sauk and Fox (Mesquakie), Mescouten, Miami,
and Kickapoo in the south.

Over the next two centuries, the Driftless landscape became the stage
for complex, evolving, and often tragic relationships among the tribes,
and between the tribes and the European empires. With the spread of
the French fur trade across the old Northwest, the forces of intercultural
contact and an expanding global economy gathered momentum, inten-
sifying pressures on the region's natural and social systems. At the mid-
continent's cultural crossroads, the Driftless Area saw the unfolding of
critical episodes in the history of Native America: key trading posts aris-
ing at Prairie du Chien and La Crosse; incursions of non-Native miners
from the south and east into the lead district; consequential meetings

---

1. The portion of the tribe that in the 1800s remained in or returned to
Wisconsin is known as the Ho-Chunk Nation of Wisconsin. The portion that
was removed and relocated to Nebraska is known as the Winnebago Tribe of
Nebraska.

between the tribes and the new United States government in the early
1800s; fraught negotiations that yielded land divisions, treaties, and cessions in 1825, 1829, 1832, and 1837; the tragedy of the Black Hawk War in
1832; the removal, return, and determined persistence of the Ho-Chunk
people in their home lands.

That history did not end with the momentous events of the nineteenth
century. The Native voice does not speak just from the past; it is a voice
of continuing presence in the Driftless landscape—in Ho-Chunk communities across the region and the Mdewakanton Dakota community
at Prairie Island (Tinta Winta); in stories and place names, cultural features and controversies; in mediation over the contemporary meaning
of effigy mounds, revered landmarks, and new archeological findings; in
conversations about land and water, economies and education, recognition and reconciliation. It is a voice that contains both echoes from the
past and deepening resonance for the future.

Native Names on the Land

The indigenous experience in the Driftless Area is recorded in the many
place names derived from individual and tribal names, translated descriptions, landmarks, and events. This sample is drawn from several published compilations of places names in the region.

It is most probable that whites manufactured *Allamakee* from An-a-
mak-ee, a Sauk-Fox word for "thunder," and the name of one of their
clans, to which Black Hawk belonged.

Waukon Decorah . . . is perhaps the most notable of the [Decorah] family. He signed five treaties between 1828 and 1846, in which he is listed
under his Winnebago name Wau-kon-haw-kaw (variously spelled), translated in the treaties as "Snakeskin." . . . [H]e lived to see his given name,
shortened to *Waukon*, attached to the seat of Allamakee County, Iowa,
and his family name, *Decorah*, to the seat of Winneshiek County in that
state.

Illinois is derived from *ininiwek* or *ininiok*, altered to *illiniwek* and finally to *Illinois* by the French. The term, signifying "men," was the collective name of the confederacy of six tribes, once a mighty host, which formerly occupied this state and surrounding regions.

The name of the state comes from that of the *Iowa* (or Ioway) Indian tribe, by way of the Iowa River.

As place names suggest, the Kickapoo people once lived in Vernon and Crawford counties in southwestern Wisconsin. Reportedly they were on the Kickapoo River before 1700. . . . James Mooney traced the tribal name *Kiwigapawa*, meaning "he stands about" or "he moves about, standing now here, now there." This could perhaps be freely translated as "wanderers," a term which correctly describes the tribe's mobile ways.

Mazomanie, the name of a Dane County [Wisconsin] village near Madison, is a corruption of Mau-ze-mon-e-ka, "Iron Walker," the name of a Winnebago Indian, son of Whirling Thunder. . . . There is, however, a more direct and more likely source of the name. *Mazomanie* was the name of at least two generations of leaders of the Sioux on the Minnesota River in the second quarter of the nineteenth century.

Manomini, the "wild rice people," was the name given by the Ojibwa to the Menominee, for whom wild rice was a major food source. . . . The city and town of *Menomonie*, in Dunn County [Wisconsin], are located far from the area of Menominee occupation and are doubtless named for the grain.

Minneiska township . . . and its village [in Minnesota] . . . are named from the White Water river, which is a translation of its Dakota or Sioux name (Minne or Mini, water, ska, white).

The Dakota or Sioux name *Minnesota* means sky-tinted water (*Minne*, water, and *sota*, somewhat clouded). . . .

In January 1699 the Jesuit priest Julien Binneteau wrote from Illinois, "I have recently been with the Tamarois, to visit a band of them on the bank of one of the largest rivers of the world which, for this reason, we call the *Missisipi* or 'the great river.'" Concurring, Father Hennepin, a chaplain with La Salle, declared that the river of the Illinois "falls into that of Meschasipi; that is, in the language of the *Illinois*, the Great River."

Muscoda . . . clearly approximates the word for "prairie" (or "meadow") in several Algonquian languages.

According to [William] Keating's account, the meaning of the stream name [*Pecatonica*] "in the Sauk language is *muddy*, and it is remarkable that the same name has been applied to the Missouri by the Sauks."

Since the middle of the eighteenth century, this place in Sauk County [Wisconsin] has been called *Sauk Prairie* in English, and for it are named the twin village of *Prairie du Sac* and *Sauk City*. . . . *Sac* is the usual French spelling of this tribal name.

Doane Robinson, historian of the Sioux, writes in the "Handbook of American Indians" (1910): "red wing [is] the name of a succession of chiefs of the former Khemnichan band of Mdewakanton Sioux, residing on the west shore of Lake Pepin, Minn., where the city of *Red Wing* now stands."

Sinnipee Creek in Grant County [Wisconsin] has a name composed of Sauk *assini*, "rock," plus *nipi* or *nipee*, "water."

The first part of [*Sinsinawa*] could be corrupted from *aseniki*, Sauk-Fox for "stony," or from *assini*, "stone"; the last part could represent *nawi*, Sauk-Fox for "middle."

Tomah [refers to] Thomas Carron, a Menominee leader in the Green Bay area in the late eighteenth and early nineteenth century. There is a local tradition (unfounded) that Tomah called a conference on Council Creek to encourage cooperation between Menominees and Winnebagos.

Viroqua . . . probably recognizes a popular novel of the day, *Viroqua; or, The Flower of the Ottawas, a Tale of the West,* by Emma Carra, published in 1848. (The actual author is unknown, since Emma Carra was a collective pseudonym used by a number of writers.) The novel, based loosely on historical events, tells of the romance between an English officer and Viroqua, the beautiful daughter of an Ottawa chief, set in the time of Pontiac's siege of Detroit in the early 1760s.

Wabasha . . . commemorates a line of Dakota or Sioux chiefs . . . Wapa-shaw (variously spelled) was the name, in three successive generations, of the hereditary chiefs having greatest influence among the Mississippi bands of the Sioux.

Wahcoutah Island in the Mississippi, Pepin County [Wisconsin], is named for a notable Sioux warrior whose name is usually spelled Wacouta, "The Shooter." . . . He was a nephew of the notable Red Wing, of Minnesota, and a member of Wabashaw's band.

The probability is that *Waumandee*, Wisconsin, is named for the Santee Sioux Indian [Wa-man-de-tun-ka] . . . among the signers of [the] treaty at Prairie du Chien on August 19, 1825 . . . [and] another treaty at Washington on June 19, 1858.

Waupeton is a spelling variation of *Wahpeton*, "people of the leaves," the name of one of the seven major divisions of the Sioux or Dakota nation.

Wauzeka is from Ho-Chunk "pine tree," perhaps named from a particular Winnebago leader or local figure.

Winnebago [township in Minnesota] is drained by Winnebago creek, which, with the township, received its name from the Winnebago Indians, many of whom, after the cession of their Wisconsin lands, in 1832, were removed to northeastern Iowa. Their hunting grounds then extended into this adjoining edge of Minnesota, until they were again removed in 1848 to Long Prairie, in central Minnesota.

Winneshiek . . . was the name borne by several generations of prominent Winnebago chiefs during the last two hundred years. . . . John Black-hawk, a grandson of Winneshiek II, maintained that the name was composed of *Winne* (short for "Winnebago") and *shiek*, "leader."

[*Winona*] was named for a Dakota woman, Winona, cousin of the last chief named Wabasha, both of whom were prominent in the events attending the removal in 1848, of the Winnebago Indians from Iowa to Wabasha's prairie (the site of the city of Winona) and thence to Long Prairie in Todd County [Minnesota].

Of all the states of the American union, none has a name that has been spelled in more ways, or interpreted more variously, as *Wisconsin*. Among the spellings are Mesconsin, Meskousing, Mishkonsing, Ouisconsens, Ouisconsin, Ousiconsing, Oiscousing, Ouiskonsin, Owisconsing, Quisconsing, Weeskonsan, Wisconsan, Wisconsin, Wishkonsing, and Wiskonsin. The name has been attributed to the French, Menominee, Ojibwa, Potawatomi, Sauk-Fox, and Winnebago languages. The definitions of Wisconsin include "stream of a Thousand Isles," "Gathering of the Waters," "small lodge of a beaver or muskrat," and "Gathering River."

Devil's Lake Sunrise, John Miller (2012). Devil's Lake (in Ho-Chunk, *Day-wa-kun-chunk* or "Sacred Lake") in the Baraboo Hills sits at the eastern edge of the Driftless Area. One of the few natural lakes within the Driftless, it was formed when the terminal moraine of the Wisconsin glacier plugged at both ends the quartzite gorge in which it lay. In this inkjet print, Madison artist John Miller depicts the sun rising over the east bluff above the lake.

Witoka [Minnesota] . . . was named for "the daughter of the war chief of Wabasha's band. Witoka was captured by the Sacs (Sauks) near the present site of Witoka, and was rescued by her father's daring dash."

The name of the village and town of *Wonewoc*, in Juneau County [Wisconsin], is . . . a derivation from Ojibwa *wonowag*, pronounced *wo-no-waug*, signifying "they howl, e.g., wolves."

Wyalusing is from Munsee Delaware *machiwihilusing*, "place of the old man," often translated figuratively as "home of the old warrior."

The Story of Devils Lake (1930)

ULYSSES S. WHITE

Day-wa-kun-chunk (Devils Lake), on the eastern edge of the Driftless Area in Wisconsin, is an anomaly within an anomaly: the only upland natural lake in the region. Ulysses White (1877–1949) recorded this story of the origin of Day-wa-kun-chunk in 1930. White, a member of the Ho-Chunk Nation, lived in Wisconsin Rapids and Milwaukee. As a member of the Wisconsin Winnebago Business Committee, formed in the late 1940s, White was a leader in the tribe's efforts to seek payment on millions of acres of ceded land and to strengthen tribal governance under the 1934 Indian Reorganization Act.

The Winnebago formerly had their winter quarters on the north shore of Devils Lake, three miles south of Baraboo. In those days a young Winnebago went on a fast. Then fasting was the only thing they depended on. In fasting, the Indians put up a wigwam out where no one could bother the person who was fasting. As a general rule no one was allowed to visit it, excepting the old men, warriors and medicine men, or those who had experience in fasting and had been blessed by some spirit. These can advise him. He fasts in order that he may be blessed by certain spirits and become a warrior or medicine man among his people. Fasting months are December, January, February and March. In the summer time the Indians fast just as the corn is ripe.

This particular young man and his people put up a wigwam on the south shore of the Lake, where the [Chicago and Northwestern Railroad] tracks now are. He was blessed by a water spirit. This spirit told the young Winnebago to come to the Lake, that the water spirit would there show himself to him on a certain day. He would tell him what medicine to use to heal general sickness, what war paint to use, etc.

When the day came the young Winnebago came to the lake near the place [for] fasting, on the southeast shore of the lake. The day was clear, nothing but blue sky above. At noon the water of the lake began to move and become wavy. Then the water spirit appeared and the waters became quiet.

There was a small cloud moving towards them from the west. Just as soon as this cloud came above them a streak of lightning from the sky struck the water spirit and he was raised from the water; all of the water coming up with him like gum or syrup. From this the water spirit could not separate himself. A thunder bird did the striking, the thunder bird and the water spirit being enemies; they struggled for some time, pulling each other four times into and above the lake.

The thunder bird said to the young man, "My Brother, shoot this water spirit for me. He is getting me exhausted. He may take my life. I will bless you with everything I have control of above and on the earth." (These Winnebago were a thunder clan.)

The young Indian had a bow and arrows but he was confused because each of them wanted him to kill the other. The water spirit said, "Don't shoot me. If you shoot me don't ever come near any water on this earth. This thunder bird should have blessed you long ago. He knows that you were fasting all winter." The thunder bird said, "Don't mind him. He is not the only one who has water. I have water too." But finally the young Winnebago shot the thunder bird who was drawn down until he could be heard under the water. Then a great thunder storm came from the west and lightning struck all around the lake bluffs. The cliffs were all struck, and the rocks rolled down as we now see them. The young man received many blessings from the water spirit. This is the reason why the Winnebago call this lake by a name meaning holy lake or sacred lake. But the white people call it Devils Lake.

Statement to U.S. Indian Commissioners at Prairie du Chien (1829)

HOOWANEKA/HⱵWĄNⱵKA (LITTLE ELK)

The United States government acquired Native lands in the Driftless Area through treaties involving the Sauk and Fox (1804, 1830, and 1832), Ojibwe (1816), Potawatomi and Ottawa (1829), Ho-Chunk (1829 and 1837), and Dakota (1837 and 1851). In 1829 Andrew Jackson appointed Caleb Atwater (1778–1867), a politician, lawyer, and archaeologist from Ohio, as Indian commissioner, charged with negotiating a land cession treaty with the Ho-Chunk Nation. Atwater, struck by the bearing and eloquence of the Ho-Chunk chief Hoowaneka (1774–1831), recorded this statement, delivered in July 1829. Hoowaneka recounts Ho-Chunk interactions with Europeans and recalls his visit to Washington, D.C., the year before to meet President John Quincy Adams.

The first white man we knew, was a Frenchman—he lived among us, as we did, he painted himself, he smoked his pipe with us, sang and danced with us, and married one of our squaws, but he wanted to buy no land of us! The "Redcoat" came next, he gave us fine coats, knives, and guns and traps, blankets and jewels; he seated our chiefs and warriors at his table with himself; fixed epaulets on their shoulders, put commissions in their pockets, and suspended medals on their breasts, but never asked us to sell our country to him! Next came the "Bluecoat," and no sooner had he seen a small portion of our country than he wished to see a map of the whole of it, and having seen it, he wished us to sell it all to him. Gov[ernor] Cass, last year, at Green Bay, urged us to sell all our country to him, and now, you fathers, repeat the request. Why do you wish to add our small country to yours, already so large? When I went to Washington, to see our great father, I saw great houses all along the road, and Washington and Baltimore. Philadelphia and New York are great and splendid cities. So large and beautiful was the

President's house, the carpets, the tables, the mirrors, the chairs, and every article in it, were so beautiful, that when I entered it, I thought I was in heaven, and the old man there, I thought was the Great Spirit; until he had shaken us by the hand, and kissed our squaws, I found him to be like yourselves, nothing but a man! You ask us to sell all our country, and wander off into the boundless regions of the West. We do

Battle of Bad Axe, Ernest Heinemann and William de la Montagne Cary (c. 1876). Men, women, and children following the Sauk leader Black Hawk were pursued through the Driftless along a trail that can be retraced today via Wisconsin historical markers and places with names such as Black Hawk, Militia Ridge, Soldiers Grove, Retreat, Battle Bluff, and, lastly, Victory, which lies near present day Blackhawk Park on the Mississippi River. It was reportedly at this site that Black Hawk's band was fired upon when trying to surrender. This engraving depicts the Battle of Bad Axe, in which at least 150 Sauk and Fox were killed by militiamen, their Native American allies, and the gunship *Warrior*; many also drowned in trying to escape across the Mississippi.

not own that country, and the deer, the elk, the beaver, the buffalo, and the otter, now there, belong not to us, and we have no right to kill them. Our wives and our children now seated behind us, are dear to us, and so is our country where rest in peace the bones of our ancestors. Fathers! pity a people, few in number, who are poor and helpless. Do you want our country? yours is larger than ours! Do you want our wigwams? you live in palaces! Do you want our horses? yours are larger and better than ours! Do you want our women? yours now sitting behind you . . . are handsomer and dressed better than ours! Look at them, yonder! Why, Fathers, what can be your motive?

From *Life of Black Hawk or Mà-Ka-Tai-Me-She-Kià-Kiàk* (1833)

BLACK HAWK

The Black Hawk War of 1832 was a turning point in the history not only of the Driftless Area but of relations between Native tribes and the United States government throughout the midcontinent. In the 1820s the Sauk-Fox were divided internally over the terms of the 1804 treaty they had signed with the United States. One faction, under Black Sparrow Hawk (1767–1838), refused to be removed west of the Mississippi River from their main village at Saukenuk, Illinois. In a complicated series of events, tensions escalated until the spring of 1832, when the U.S. Army began its pursuit of Black Hawk and his "British Band" up the Rock River, west through southern Wisconsin, then across the Wisconsin River and the Driftless landscape. The war culminated in the tragic Battle of Bad Axe on August 2, when more than 250 Sauk were killed fighting and fleeing across the Mississippi River. Black Hawk's autobiography, written while he was in captivity, was the first Native American autobiography to be published in the United States. In it Black Hawk recounted the final stages of the conflict.

During our encampment at the Four Lakes [present-day Madison] . . . there was but little game of any sort to be found—and fish were equally scarce. The great distance to any settlement, and the impossibility of bringing supplies therefrom, if any could have been obtained, deterred our young men from making further attempts. We were forced to dig *roots* and *bark trees*, to obtain something to satisfy hunger and keep us alive! Several of our people became so much reduced, as actually *to die with hunger!* And, finding that the army had commenced moving, and fearing that they might come upon and surround our encampment, I concluded to remove my women and children across the Mississippi, that they might return to the Sac nation again. Accordingly, on the next day, we commenced moving, with five Winnebagoes acting as our guides, intending to descend the Ouisconsin.

Ne-a-pope, with a party of twenty, remained in our rear, to watch our enemy, whilst we were proceeding to the Ouisconsin, with our women and children. We arrived and had commenced crossing them to an island, when we discovered a large body of the enemy coming towards us. We were now compelled to fight, or sacrifice our wives and children to the fury of the whites! I met them with fifty warriors (having left the balance to assist our women and children in crossing) about a mile from the river, when an attack immediately commenced. I was mounted on a fine horse, and was pleased to see my warriors so brave. I addressed them in a loud voice, telling them to stand their ground, and never yield it to the enemy. At this time I was on the rise of a hill, where I wished to form my warriors, that we might have some advantage over the whites. But the enemy succeeded in gaining this point, which compelled us to fall back into a deep ravine, from which we continued firing at them and they at us, until it began to grow dark. My horse having been wounded twice during this engagement, and fearing from his loss of blood, that he would soon give out—and finding that the enemy would not come near enough to receive our fire, in the dusk of the evening—and knowing that our women and children had had sufficient time to reach the island in the Ouisconsin, I ordered my warriors to return, in different routes, and meet me at the Ouisconsin—and were astonished to find that the enemy were not disposed to pursue us.

In this skirmish, with fifty braves, I defended and accomplished my passage over the Ouisconsin, with a loss of only six men; though opposed by a host of mounted militia. I would not have fought there, but to gain time for my women and children to cross to an island. A warrior will duly appreciate the embarrassments I labored under—and whatever may be the sentiments of the *white people*, in relation to this battle, my nation, though fallen, will award to me the reputation of a great brave in conducting it.

The loss of the enemy could not be ascertained by our party; but I am of opinion, that it was much greater, in proportion, than mine. We returned to the Ouisconsin, and crossed over to our people. . . .

Myself and band having no means to descend the Ouisconsin, I started, over a rugged country, to go to the Mississippi, intending to cross it, and return to my nation. Many of our people were compelled to go on foot, for want of horses, which, in consequence of their having had nothing to eat for a long time, caused our march to be very slow. At length we arrived at the Mississippi, having lost some of our old men and little children, who perished on the way with hunger.

We had been here but a little while, before we saw a steam boat (the *Warrior*) coming. I told my braves not to shoot, as I intended going on board, so that we might save our women and children. I knew the captain [Throckmorton] and was determined to give myself up to him. I then sent for my *white flag*. While the messenger was gone, I took a small piece of white cotton, and put it on a pole, and called to the captain of the boat, and told him to send his little canoe ashore, and let me come on board. The people on board asked whether we were Sacs or Winnebagoes. I told a Winnebago to tell them that we were Sacs, and wanted to give ourselves up! A Winnebago on the boat called to us *"to run and hide, that the whites were going to shoot!"* About this time one of my braves had jumped into the river, bearing a white flag to the boat— when another sprang in after him and brought him to shore. The firing then commenced from the boat, which was returned by my braves, and continued for some time. Very few of my people were hurt after the first fire, having succeeded in getting behind old logs and trees, which shielded them from the enemy's fire.

The Winnebago, on the steam boat, must either have misunderstood what was told, or did not tell it to the captain correctly; because I am confident that he would not have fired upon us, if he had known my wishes. I have always considered him a good man, and too great a brave to fire upon an enemy when sueing for quarters.

After the boat left us, I told my people to cross, if they could, and wished: that I intended going into the Chippewa country. Some commenced crossing, and such as had determined to follow them, remained—only three lodges going with me. Next morning, at day break, a young man overtook me, and said that all my party had determined to cross the Mississippi—that a number had already got over safe, and that he had heard the white army last night within a few miles of them. I now began to fear that the whites would come up with my people, and kill them, before they could get across. I had determined to go and join the Chippewas; but reflecting that by this I could only save myself, I concluded to return, and die with my people, if the Great Spirit would not give us another victory! During our stay in the thicket, a party of whites came close by us, but passed on without discovering us!

Early in the morning a party of whites, being in advance of the army, came upon our people, who were attempting to cross the Mississippi. They tried to give themselves up—the whites paid no attention to their entreaties—but commenced *slaughtering* them! In a little while the whole army arrived. Our braves, but few in number, finding that the enemy paid no regard to age or sex, and seeing that they were murdering helpless women and little children, determined to *fight until they were killed!* As many women as could, commenced swimming the Mississippi, with their children on their backs. A number of them were drowned, and some shot, before they could reach the opposite shore.

One of my braves, who gave me this information, piled up some saddles before him, (when the fight commenced,) to shield himself from the enemy's fire, and killed three white men! But seeing that the whites were coming too close to him, he crawled to the bank of the river, without being perceived, and hid himself under it, until the enemy retired. He then came to me and told me what had been done. After hearing this sorrowful news, I started, with my little party, to the Winnebago village at Prairie La Cross. On my arrival there, I entered the lodge of one of the chiefs, and told him that I wished him to go with me to his father—that I intended to give myself up to the American war chief, and *die*, if the Great Spirit saw proper! He said he would go with me. I then took my *medicine bag,* and addressed the chief. I told him that it was "the soul of the Sac nation—that it never had been dishonored in any battle—take it, it is my life—dearer than life—and give it to the American chief!" He said he would keep it, and take care of it, and if I was suffered to live, he would send it to me.

During my stay at the village, the squaws made me a white dress of deer skin. I then started, with several Winnebagoes, and went to their agent, at Prairie du Chien, and gave myself up.

On my arrival there, I found to my sorrow, that a large body of Sioux had pursued, and killed, a number of our women and children, who had got safely across the Mississippi. The whites ought not to have permitted such conduct and none but *cowards* would ever have been guilty of such cruelty which has always been practiced on our nation by the Sioux.

The massacre, which terminated the war, lasted about two hours. Our loss in killed, was about sixty, besides a number that were drowned. The loss of the enemy could not be ascertained by my braves, exactly; but they think that they killed about *sixteen*, during the action.

I was now given up by the agent to the commanding officer at Fort Crawford (the White Beaver [General Henry Atkinson] having gone down the river.) We remained here a short time, and then started to Jefferson Barracks [near St. Louis], in a steam boat, under the charge of a young war chief, [Lieut. Jefferson Davis] who treated us all with much kindness. . . .

On our way down [to Jefferson Barracks], I surveyed the country that had cost us so much trouble, anxiety, and blood, and that now caused me to be a prisoner of war. I reflected upon the ingratitude of the whites, when I saw their fine houses, rich harvests, and every thing desirable around them; and recollected that all this land had been ours, for which me and my people had never received a dollar, and that the whites were not satisfied until they took our village and our grave-yards from us, and removed us across the Mississippi.

From *A Canoe Voyage Up the Minnay Sotor* (1847)

GEORGE WILLIAM FEATHERSTONHAUGH

The British-born George Featherstonhaugh (1780–1866) (pronounced *fan-shaw*) came to the United States in 1806, settling in upstate New York and gaining success as an investor in the development of railroads and canals. An interest in geology led to his appointment, in 1834, as the first U.S. government geologist. In 1835 he embarked on a survey of the Upper

Mississippi River. In his account of that journey, Featherstonhaugh describes his encounter at present-day Trempealeau with Ompaytoo Wakee and other members of the Dakota. Two years later, a treaty removed the Dakota from Wisconsin to lands west of the Mississippi River.

September 6.— . . . Having ascended to the crest of this Trempe à l'eau, I found it to be a non-fossiliferous limestone, only three or four yards wide, running from north to south about 200 yards, and falling off in a steep precipice to the west, with compact sandstone at its base. Whilst I was contemplating the magnificent view around me, I saw three Sioux Indians in a canoe approach our fire, and descending, I found the serjeant talking with them, and getting such information from them about the state of the upper country as the few words he possessed enabled him to do. Taking out my list of Sioux words, and pointing to the water, the fire, the trees, &c., they gave me the true pronunciation of the Indian names of these natural objects. I then asked them the name of the mountain at the base of which we were, and they answered "Minnay Chon ka hah,"—literally, as I afterwards found, "Bluff in the Water,"— than which nothing could be more descriptive.

We left this place about 4 p.m., and landed for the night at six, at a blacksmith's shop built by the United States Government, for the use of a band of Indians in this neighbourhood, but now abandoned. There was, however, a log hut, a blacksmith's shop, an anvil, some iron and steel, but nobody to take care of them. As soon as the tent was pitched, and our fires lighted, a very respectable old-looking Sioux Indian, who had espied us from an island in the river, crossed over to our camp in his canoe with two children, a boy and a girl about nine and ten years old. He walked up to me as I was entering some memoranda in my note-book, and extending his hand, said "Capitaine! Capitaine!"—the only word he knew out of his own language. I now took out my vocabulary, and sending for the serjeant, we soon got into a way of understanding each other. About the names of things we had little or no difficulty, for he soon saw that I wanted him to give me the pronunciation, and when I pointed to anything, he would name it two or three times, and when I had caught the sound, and pronounced it to him from my book, he would give an approving grunt and smile. But when I wanted to ask him questions about their enemies, the Ojibways, whether any marauding bands of either nation were out, and whether I was likely to meet with any of them before I reached Fort Snelling, we got into a perfect colloquial bog. I knew nothing but the names of substantial things. . . .

The old man remained very contentedly about two hours; I gave him a part of my supper, and biscuits and sugar for his children, which they were quite delighted with, the word "washtay" escaping them several times when they licked the fair white loaf sugar, which they put by after tasting it. When my supper was over, he rose, took his children to the canoe, and I saw him by the moonlight paddling over to the island. I now entered the tent and began my evening's work of bringing up my notes, at the close of which, hearing some unknown voices at my fire, I looked out, and lo! my Indian acquaintance, his two children, and two of his wives, each of them carrying a male papoose. I now understood why he had taken his departure so abruptly, without bidding me "Good bye"; the truth being, that, pleased with my kind treatment of him, he had determined to bring his ladies to my camp, and introduce them to the *Capitaine*. I received them of course very kindly. . . .

Beau Pré now came up and said that L'Amirant had passed several winters amongst the upper Sioux, and spoke the Yankton dialect pretty well. I was delighted to hear this, and sending for him, asked him if he really could converse with these people. Upon which he immediately addressed the man, and in a few minutes I found, to my perfect satisfaction, that he could interpret betwixt us.

The Indian now informed me that his name was *Ompaytoo Wakee*, or Daylight; that he was brother to Wabeshāw, a celebrated chief, who with his band resided at their village built on a prairie on the right bank of the Mississippi, which we should see as we passed up the river. *Minnay Chon ka hah*, the outlier we had visited in the afternoon, was in fact, he said, a sort of island, as there was an obscure passage round it. Finding I could now keep up a conversation with him, I asked him "where the moon went to when it set?" and he answered that "it went travelling on until it came up on the east again." I then asked him "who was the father of the two little papooses?" when he answered that he was. We now came back to the old question which the serjeant had so bungled, and I asked him "who was the maker of the moon?" when he immediately replied "*Wakōn*." I asked him "who Wakōn was?" and he said that every Indian knew that the moon (*wee*), the sun (*wee ompaytoo*, "sun day"), the lakes (*minday*), the river (*wāhpadah*), the trees (*chagn*), the sky (*māhpayah*), the stars (*weechāhpee*), were all made by Wakōn; and here he pointed to the heaven, and said that the Indians after death went to the hunting-ground where the sun rises, and afterwards to *Wakōn*. I asked him if they ever offered anything to *Wakōn*, and he replied that good Indians never forgot to offer to him; and said that it was the custom of his band to go to the top of *Minnay Chon ka hah* at the season for hunting wild geese, and that they made offerings to Mangwah Wakōn ("wild goose god"), that he might be favourable to them in their hunting.

Ompáytoo seemed pleased to be talked to about such matters; he expressed himself like a sensible and rational man, and convinced me that the Indians entertained juster opinions of natural theology than they had credit for. When we parted I gave the women pork and biscuit, and they presented me with some teal in return. At the last moment I desired L'Amirant to tell *Ompáytoo* that all good white men believed Wakōn made everything as well as he did, and that they prayed to him to be good to them. That there was only one *Wakōn*; and, as he made both the Indians and the white men, they were brothers, and *Wakōn* was their father. That, therefore, we ought all to love one another, and that I hoped he would tell the Indians a white man had said so. He shook hands very kindly with me, and it was late in the night when they left my camp to go to their *weetah*, or island.

From "Narrative of Spoon Decorah" (1887)

SPOON DECORAH

The Ho-Chunk chief Spoon Decorah (c. 1805–1889) lived through the many turbulent changes in the lives of his people in the nineteenth century. Born in his father's village near the mouth of the Baraboo River, he was among the Ho-Chunk who were removed to northeast Iowa in 1840. He was also among those who resisted further removal to reservation lands and steadfastly returned to Wisconsin. In March 1887, historian Reuben Gold Thwaites interviewed Decorah at his home in Adams County, Wisconsin.

I have heard my father say that his father often told him about certain white medicine-men in black gowns being among our people; but I never heard the names of any of them. In my day, we have not been much troubled by white medicine-men, but have been allowed to keep to the religion of our fathers. Very few of my friends are Christians. Our spirits are the same spirits our fathers believed in.

Our people once owned the lead mines in Southwestern Wisconsin. I have seen Winnebagoes working in them, long before the Black Hawk War. There were a good many at work in this way, nearly all the time in summer. Some dug lead for their own use, but most of them got it out to trade off to other Indians for supplies of all sorts. They made lead-mining their regular work. Every fall and spring hunters would go down to the mines and get a stock of lead for bullets, sometimes giving goods for it and sometimes furs. When the whites began to come among the mines, the Big Father said to his Winnebago children: "I want this land and will have my own people to work it, and whenever you go out hunting come by this way, and you will be supplied with lead." But this agreement was never carried out by the Big Father or his agents. Never was a bar of lead or a bag of shot presented to us. This was a very great sorrow to our people. For many years there was much sorrowful talk among the Winnebagoes, at the manner in which the Big Father had treated them, with regard to the mines. No, we never saw any of our lead again, except what we paid dearly for; and we never will have any given to us, unless it be fired at us out of white men's guns, to kill us off. . . .

I am getting very old. My memory is poor. But what I have told you I know to be true. I wish you had come when I was younger. I could have told you much about my tribe. I could have told you more about the old chiefs and our traditions. When I was a boy we were proud of them. My father gave me good talk about our tribe. He liked to speak of those things. Now the Winnebagoes are poor. They have not so much pride. Very few of them care about the old times. Most of them care only for firewater. We get a very poor living, now. Our farms have not good soil. The game is not as plenty as it was. The white traders cheat and rob us. They make our young men drunk. It would be better if we had an agent. We think the Big Father does not care for us any longer, now that he has all our best land. Perhaps it will not be long before he will want the poor land we now live on. Then we must go to the reservation. Life on the reservation is hard. The Winnebagoes in Wisconsin do not want to go there. They want to die on their own land. They like best the

streams and woods where their fathers and uncles have always hunted
and trapped. . . .

From *Mountain Wolf Woman,*
Sister of Crashing Thunder (1961)

XEHAĆIWIŊGA (MOUNTAIN WOLF WOMAN)

Mountain Wolf Woman, or Xehaćiwiŋga (1884–1960), was born into the
Thunder Clan of the Ho-Chunk Nation near Black River Falls. Her life
story was recorded in early 1958 by her adopted niece, Nancy Oesterich
Lurie, who had earned a PhD in anthropology at Northwestern University.
Their collaboration resulted in one of the first published autobiographies
of a Native American woman. Lurie later served as professor of anthropology at the University of Wisconsin–Milwaukee, head curator of anthropology at the Milwaukee Public Museum, and president of the American
Anthropological Association. In this passage, Xehaćiwiŋga recounts her
family's removal and quest to reclaim a home in the Driftless Area.

Mother said she had me at our grandfather's home,—at East Fork [of
the Black] River. We lived there in the spring, April, at the time they
were making maple sugar. She said that after a while the weather became pleasant, everything was nice and green, and we moved from this
place back to where we usually lived,—at Levis Creek, near Black River
Falls. There father built a log house. I suppose it took a long time to
build it because mother said the log house was newly finished when I
walked there for the first time. There, where we regularly lived, mother
and father planted their garden. . . .

It was about the time that my older sister Bald Eagle was born that
they went to Nebraska. Mother used to say they were taken to Nebraska
that winter; they were moved from one land to another. Many Winnebago were moved to Nebraska and there mother took her three children.
Grandmother had relatives in Nebraska. Grandmother was the oldest
daughter in her family. In Nebraska she saw her sisters, the second and
third daughters. They were very eager to see their relatives. But, mother

said, some of the Wisconsin Winnebago did not like the removal. Some even cried because they were taken there. However, mother used to say, "The fact that we would see my relatives made me happy that we were going. And when we reached the Missouri River, our uncles came to meet us. When they heard we were coming, Squeaking Wing and Captures The Lodge and a third uncle Hágaga came to meet us."

Emma Big Bear, Florence Bird (2008). At the Mississippi River Sculpture Park in Prairie du Chien, the plaque next to this figure reads:

(Wa' ka' ja' ze Winga. b. 1869, near Tomah, Wisconsin: d. 1968, Waukon, Iowa), a Ho-Chunk (Winnebago) woman of the Bear tribal family, who walked in silence, kindness and humbleness, was the daughter of Chief Big Bear and Mary Blue Wing. She was the wife of Henry Holt (Floating in Air), and mother of Emmaline. As a direct descendant of Winnebago Chief Waukon Decorah, she instilled in her bloodline the fortitude to be honest, strong in beliefs and to march ahead, never complaining of the hardships she encountered and endured.

Outliving her husband and daughter, Emma Big Bear made a living by selling her black ash baskets, beaded jewelry and ginseng, and by accepting food and assistance offered by the caring, local people of McGregor and Marquette, Iowa. She didn't wander far from the graves of her ancestors. She lived out her days as the last in the tradition of ancestors who inhabited the prehistoric site near the Effigy Mounds sacred space along the Mississippi River in northeast Iowa.

As their uncle Squeaking Wing came through the train he called out "Bends The Boughs, where is she? Bends The Boughs, where is she?" At last he found them and there was much rejoicing when they saw one another. Brother Crashing Thunder was dressed in a fringed buckskin outfit, and when my uncles saw him they lifted him up in the air and they said, "Oh, how cute our nephew is!" Eventually they arrived at the reservation.

It was winter. Everyone had his own camping outfit, and they all made their homes here and there. They built wigwams. Then spring came and mother said that the Winnebago died in great numbers. Deaths occurred almost every day. When someone died, the Winnebago carried away their dead, crying as they walked. All those who had a death in the family cried as they walked along. They were going to the graveyard, and there was much weeping.

Mother was frightened. "Why do we stay here?" she said. "I am afraid because the people are all dying. Why do we not go back home?" They were with some uncles at the time. The first was called Good Village, the next was called Big Náqiga and the third was called Little Náqiga. In the spring they moved to the Missouri River where they cut down some big willow trees and made dugout canoes big enough for two, mother said. She must have been talking about fairly big boats that they made. There in the spring when the weather is very pleasant, mother used to say, a large group went down the Missouri River. Thus she returned home with some of her relatives. They went down the Missouri to River's Mouth Place as they used to call St. Louis. From there they travelled back on the Mississippi River, they travelled upstream on the Mississippi.

Eventually they stopped at a certain place where they saw some white people. Nobody knew how to speak English, so they said, "Where is Hénaga? Where is Hénaga? He is the only one who knows the name of that place." They meant Captures The Lodge, who was just a little boy. When they brought him they said to him, "Say it! Say it!" He was the only one who knew that one word, and he said, "Prarsheen? Prarsheen?" I guess he was saying "Prairie Du Chien." Then the white people understood him,—he said it was Prairie Du Chien. They stopped there for a while and eventually they left and arrived at La Crosse. They lived there for a time and then they moved out towards Black River Falls.

It seems that many Winnebago came back to Wisconsin. My family were evidently not the only ones who returned. Also, some of the Winnebago in Wisconsin lived way out in the country a great distance from any town. These people said that they had not been found so they did not go to Nebraska, mother said. Thus, not all of the Winnebago left in the removal.

It must have been at this time that my parents took up land, that is, a homestead. Some of them acquired homesteads there at Black River Falls. However, father was not interested in such things. Even when they were in Nebraska his brother said, "Register, older brother, claim some land for yourself and claim some for your children." But father did not do it, so they did not have any land in Nebraska. Mother and her uncles did not take any land, but some of the Winnebago took land in Nebraska so they had property, but eventually they sold it. However, my parents did not realize what they were doing and that is why they acted as they did. Some of the Indians took homesteads but father did not understand so he did not take a homestead. That was when my mother took a homestead. There was an old man who was a grandfather to us who took land. His name was Many Trails. I used to seek him; he was a little old man. He said to my mother, "Granddaughter, why do you not claim some land? I claimed some and if you take a homestead right next to me, then we can live beside each other." So mother took forty acres.

Indians did not look ahead to affairs of this sort. They never looked to the future. They only looked to the present insofar as they had enough to sustain themselves. This is the way the Indians used to live. The fact that my father did not care to obtain any land was because he was a member of the Thunder Clan. "I do not belong to the Earth," he said, "I do not belong to the Earth and I have no concern with land." This is why he was not interested in having any land. But mother was also one,— one of the bird clan people; she belonged to the Eagle Clan. She said, "By this means we will have some place to live," and so she took forty acres. Here my father built the log house where we usually lived. . . .

We probably went back to our home again that spring as it must have been at that time that I was sick. I was very sick and my mother wanted me to live. She hoped that I would not die, but she did not know what to do. At that place there was an old lady whose name was Wolf Woman and mother had them bring her. Mother took me and let the old lady hold me. "I want my little girl to live," mother said, "I give her to you. Whatever way you can make her live, she will be yours." That is where they gave me away. That old lady wept. "You have made me think of myself. Let it be thus. My life, let her use it. My grandchild, let her use my existence. I will give my name to my own child. The name that I am going to give her is a holy name. She will reach an old age." There they named me with a Wolf Clan name; Xehaćiwiŋga they called me.—It means to make a home in a bluff or a mountain, as the wolf does, but in English I just say my name is Mountain Wolf Woman.

Bird Effigy, Truman Lowe (1997). Many native voices have explored their storied relationships with Driftless Area mounds. Artist Truman Lowe, originally of Black River Falls, created the sculpture *Bird Effigy* in a form that links the mounds with his family's membership in the Thunderbird clan of the Ho-Chunk Nation. *Bird Effigy* was first installed in the Jacqueline Kennedy Garden at the White House and is now in the collection of Western Michigan University. The sculpture is a lattice of solid aluminum, with 20 feet, 6 inches in wingspan, and 11 feet, 8 inches from head to tail.

5

EXPLORATIONS

THE FIRST NON-NATIVE AMERICAN EXPLORERS of the Driftless Area
followed the callings of wealth, faith, curiosity, dominion, military
competition, and diplomacy. Along the rivers and overland routes
came representatives of the European powers, private interests, the Christian faith, and, later, the United States government. The landscape long
known to its ancient and Native inhabitants would now become increasingly connected to a wider world.

Initially the remoteness of the region delayed inroads. In 1541 the
Spanish explorer Hernando de Soto became the first European to reach
the Mississippi, but came upriver only as far as present-day Tennessee.
The first French to reach the western Great Lakes—the interpreter-guides
Étienne Brûlé (1622–23) and Jean Nicolet (1634), and the fur-traders
Pierre-Esprit Radisson and Médard des Groseilliers (1654–1660)—followed the shores of Lakes Michigan and Superior. Nicolet, Radisson,
and Groseilliers penetrated inland and upstream at least as far as the
Wisconsin and Chippewa Rivers, but crossed only briefly, it seems, into
the Driftless. Only with the 1673 expedition of the twenty-seven-year-old
fur trader Louis Joliet and the thirty-five-year-old Jesuit Father Jacques
Marquette did Europeans first come into and traverse the Driftless Area,
traveling by canoe up the Fox River from Lake Michigan, crossing over
the "carrying place" at Portage, and paddling down the Wisconsin River
to the Mississippi.

Over the next century the fur trade remained the main economic driver
of European exploration and empire. As early as the late seventeenth century, however, French fur traders and explorers—Henri Joutel, Louis Hennepin, Nicolas Perrot, Pierre-Charles Le Sueur—recognized the potential
for exploitation of the minerals of the lead district. With Julien Dubuque's

arrival in the region in 1785 mining began its rise to dominance in the local economy. The Spanish, French, and British spheres of influence overlapped in the Driftless, and would do so until eventually the Treaty of Paris (1783) and the Louisiana Purchase (1803) brought the territory under the control of the United States.

The allure of unknown geographies, especially the quest to find the source of the Mississippi River and the elusive Northwest Passage, spurred several of the subsequent expeditions in the old Northwest Territory. Aligned with this was the aim of the young United States to establish economic and military control at the edge of its expanding political sphere, and to establish claims upon lands held by the Native tribes. In the first half of the nineteenth century, the Driftless Area became the crucible of this profound cultural conflict. The explorers' knowledge of the landscape came to serve the interests of those intent on using that knowledge in pursuit of wealth and power. Yet, for at least some of those at this far edge of empire, exploration provided an opportunity to appreciate for their own sake the natural and cultural features of the Driftless. And latter-day explorers continue to locate mystery and revelation within the Driftless Area.

La Crosse at Ninety Miles an Hour (1953)

RICHARD EBERHART

Poet and teacher Richard Eberhart (1904–2005) was born in Austin, Minnesota. He taught for thirty years at Dartmouth College and published more than a dozen collections of poetry. Eberhart served as U.S. Poet Laureate (1959–1961) and received, among other honors, the Pulitzer Prize (1966), the National Book Award (1977), and the Frost Medal of the Poetry Society of America (1986).

Better to be the rock above the river,
The bluff, brown and age-old sandstone,
Than the broad river winding to the Gulf.

The river looks like world reality
And has the serenity of wide and open things.
It is a river of even ice today.

Winter men in square cold huts have cut
Round holes to fish through: I saw it as a boy.
They have a will to tamper with the river.

Up on the high bluffs nothing but spirit!
It is there I would be, where an Indian scout was
Long ago, now purely imaginary.

It is a useless and heaven-depended place,
Commodious rock to lock the spirit in,
Where it gazes on the river and the land.

Better to be rock-like than river-like;
Water is a symbol will wear us all away.
Rock comes to the same end, more slowly so.

Rock is the wish of the spirit, heavy symbol,
Something to hold to beyond worldly use.
I feel it in my bones, kinship with vision,

And on the brown bluffs above the Mississippi
In the land of my deepest, earliest memories,
Rushing along at ninety miles an hour,

I feel the old elation of the imagination.
Strong talk of the river and the rock.
Small division between the world and spirit.

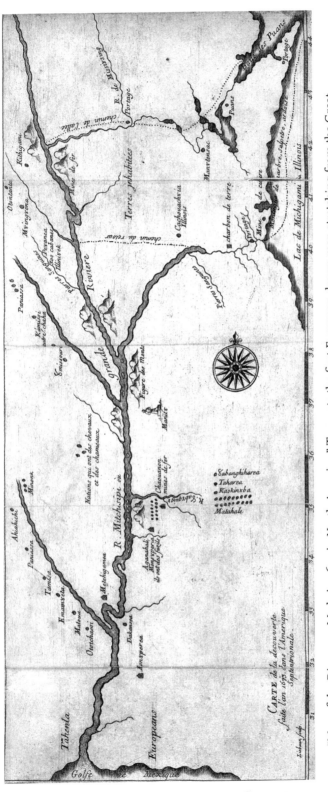

"Map of the Discovery Made in 1673 in North America." To create the first European-drawn map stretching from the Great Lakes to the Gulf of Mexico, cartographer Melchisédech Thévenot and engraver Henri Liebaux used original maps and descriptions from Jacques Marquette and Louis Joliet's 1673 expedition down the Mississippi River. Note the location of their *portage* from the Fox to the Wisconsin near where the city of Portage stands today; the erroneously designated *Mines de fer* [iron mines] would become the lead district; and the hills depicted at the confluence of the *Mississing* [Wisconsin] and *Mitchisipi* [Mississippi] rivers.

From *Le Premier Voÿage qu'a Fait Le P. Marquette . . . [Of the First Voyage Made by Father Marquette . . .]* (1674)

Jacques Marquette

Father Jacques Marquette (1637–1675) was a French Jesuit missionary who in 1668 established Michigan's first European settlement, Sault Ste. Marie. In the spring of 1673 Father Marquette joined the expedition of French-Canadian fur trapper and explorer Louis Jolliet (1645–c. 1700), seeking passage into the Mississippi River basin. Accompanied by five Métis voyageurs, they became the first Europeans to cross from the Great Lakes watershed and into the Mississippi basin. Marquette described the journey down the Wisconsin River to its confluence with the Mississippi.

We left the Waters flowing to Quebeq, 4 or 500 Leagues from here, to float on Those that would thenceforward Take us through strange lands. Before embarking thereon, we Began all together a new devotion to the blessed Virgin Immaculate, which we practiced daily, addressing to her special prayers to place under her protection both our persons and the success of our voyage; and, after mutually encouraging one another, we entered our Canoes.

The River on which we embarked is called Meskousing [Wisconsin]. It is very wide; it has a sandy bottom, which forms various shoals that render its navigation very difficult. It is full of Islands Covered with Vines. On the banks one sees fertile land, diversified with woods, prairies, and Hills. There are oak, Walnut, and basswood trees; and another kind, whose branches are armed with long thorns. We saw there neither feathered game nor fish, but many deer, and a large number of cattle. Our Route lay to the southwest, and, after navigating about 30 leagues, we saw a spot presenting all the appearances of an iron mine; and, in fact, one of our party who had formerly seen such mines, assures us that The One which We found is very good and very rich. It is Covered with three feet of good soil, and is quite near a chain of rocks, the base of which is covered by very fine trees. After proceeding 40 leagues on This same route, we arrived at the mouth of our River; and, at 42 and a half degrees Of latitude, We safely entered Missisipi on The 17th of June, with a Joy that I cannot Express.

Here we are, then, on this so renowned river, all of whose peculiar features I have endeavored to note carefully. The Missisipi River takes its rise in various lakes in the country of the northern nations. It is narrow at the place where Miskous empties; its current, which flows southward, is slow and gentle. To the right is a large chain of very high mountains, and to the left are beautiful lands; in various places, the stream is divided by islands. On sounding, we found ten brasses of water. Its width is very unequal; sometimes it is three quarters of a league, and sometimes it narrows to three arpents. We gently followed its course, which runs toward the south and southeast, as far as the 42nd degree of latitude. Here we plainly saw that its aspect was completely changed. There are hardly any woods or mountains; the islands are more beautiful, and are covered with finer trees.

From *The Expeditions of Zebulon Montgomery Pike to Headwaters of the Mississippi River* (1810)

ZEBULON MONTGOMERY PIKE

French exploration of the Upper Mississippi and Driftless Area continued in the century following the expedition of Marquette and Joliet. In 1766 Jonathan Carver became the first English-speaking explorer to venture into the region and west of the upper Mississippi River. (Historians would later call into question the veracity of his influential account, published in 1778.) In 1805 Zebulon Pike (1779–1813), then a lieutenant in the U.S. Army, led an expedition into the upper reaches of the newly organized Louisiana Territory, with the aim of determining the source of the

Mississippi River. Pike and his twenty-man crew departed from St. Louis on August 9, traveling upriver by keelboat. The expedition failed to find the "true source" of the Mississippi at Lake Itasca, but gathered valuable information on the territory and its Native inhabitants before returning to St. Louis at the end of April 1806.

Sunday, Sept. 1st. Embarked early; wind fair; arrived at the lead mines [at Dubuque] at twelve o'clock. A dysentery, with which I had been afflicted several days, was suddenly checked this morning, which I believe to have been the occasion of a very violent attack of fever about eleven o'clock. Notwithstanding it was very severe, I dressed myself, with an intention to execute the orders of the general relative to this place. We were saluted with a field-piece, and received with every mark of attention by Monsieur [Julien] Dubuque, the proprietor. There were no horses at the house, and it was six miles to where the mines were worked; it was therefore impossible to make a report by actual inspection. . . .

Dined with Mr. D., who informed me that the Sioux and Sauteurs [Ojibwe] were as warmly engaged in opposition as ever; that not long since the former killed fifteen Sauteurs, who on the tenth of August in return killed ten Sioux, at the entrance of the St. Peters [Minnesota river]; and that a war-party, composed of Sacs, Reynards [Fox], and Puants [Ho-Chunk], of 200 warriors, had embarked on an expedition against the Sauteurs; but that they had heard that the chief, having had an unfavorable dream, persuaded the party to return, and that I would meet them on my voyage. . . .

Sept. 2d. After making two short reaches, we commenced one which is thirty miles in length; the wind serving, we just made it, and encamped on the E. side [near Cassville, Wis.], opposite the mouth of Turkey river. In the course of the day we landed to shoot pigeons. The moment a gun was fired, some Indians, who were on the shore above us, ran down and put off in their perogues with great precipitation; upon which Mr. Blondeau informed me that all the women and children were frightened at the very name of an American boat, and that the men held us in great respect, conceiving us very quarrelsome, much for war, and also very brave. This information I used as prudence suggested. We stopped at an encampment about three miles below the town, where they gave us some excellent plums. They dispatched a perogue to the village, to give notice, as I supposed, of our arrival. It commenced raining about dusk, and rained all night. Distance forty miles. . . .

Sept. 3d. . . . It is surprising what a dread the Indians in this quarter have of the Americans. I have often seen them go round islands to avoid meeting my boat. It appears to me evident that the traders have taken great pains to impress upon the minds of the savages the idea of our being a very vindictive, ferocious, and warlike people. This impression was perhaps made with no good intention; but when they find that our conduct toward them is guided by magnanimity and justice, instead of operating in an injurious manner, it will have the effect to make them reverence at the same time they fear us. Distance twenty-five miles.

Sept. 4th. Breakfasted just below the Ouiscousing [Wisconsin river]. Arrived at the Prairie des Cheins about eleven o'clock; took quarters at Captain Fisher's, and were politely received by him and Mr. Frazer. . . .

Sept. 7th. My men beat all the villagers jumping and hopping. Began to load my new boats. . . .

Sept. 10th. Rain still continuing, we remained at our camp. Having shot at some pigeons, the report was heard at the Sioux lodges, the same to whom I spoke on the sixth at the Prairie [du Chien] . . . Mr. Frazer and the interpreter went home with the Indians. We embarked about one o'clock. Frazer, returning, informed me that the chief [Wabasha] acquiesced in my reasons for pressing forward, but that he had prepared a pipe (by way of letter) to present me, to show to all the Sioux above, with a message to inform them that I was a chief of their new fathers, and that he wished me to be treated with friendship and respect. . . .

Some of my men who were going up with me I caused to leave their arms behind, as a mark of confidence. At the chief's lodge I found a clean mat and pillow for me to sit on, and the before-mentioned pipe on a pair of small crutches before me. The chief sat on my right hand, my interpreter and Mr. Frazer on my left. After smoking, the chief spoke to the following purport:

"That, notwithstanding he had seen me at the Prairie [du Chien], he was happy to take me by the hand among his own people, and there show his young men the respect due to their new father [President

Jefferson]. That, when at St. Louis in the spring, his father [General Wilkinson] had told him that if he looked down the river he would see one of his young warriors [Pike] coming up. He now found it true, and he was happy to see me, who knew the Great Spirit was the father of all, both the white and the red people; and if one died, the other could not live long. That he had never been at war with their new father, and hoped always to preserve the same understanding that now existed. That he now presented me with a pipe, to show to the upper bands as a token of our good understanding, and that they might see his work and imitate his conduct. That he had gone to St. Louis on a shameful visit, to carry a murderer; but that we had given the man his life, and he thanked us for it. That he had provided something to eat, but he supposed I could not eat it; and if not, to give it to my young men."

I replied: "That, although I had told him at the Prairie my business up the Mississippi, I would again relate it to him." I then mentioned the different objects I had in view with regard to the savages who had fallen under our protection by our late purchase from the Spaniards; the different posts to be established; the objects of these posts as related to them; supplying them with necessaries; having officers and agents of government near them to attend to their business; and above all to endeavor to make peace between the Sioux and Sauteurs. "That it was possible on my return I should bring some of the Sauteurs down with me, and take with me some of the Sioux chiefs to St. Louis, there to settle the long and bloody war which had existed between the two nations. That I accepted his pipe with pleasure, as the gift of a great man, the chief of four bands, and a brother; that it should be used as he desired." I then eat of the dinner he had provided, which was very grateful. It was wild rye [rice?] and venison, of which I sent four bowls to my men. . . .

We embarked about half-past three o'clock; came three miles, and encamped on the W. side. Mr. Frazer we left behind, but he came up with his two perogues about dusk. It commenced raining very hard. In the night a perogue arrived from the lodges at his camp. During our stay at their camp, there were soldiers appointed to keep the crowd from my boats, who executed their duty with vigilance and rigor, driving men, women, and children back, whenever they came near my boats. At my departure, their soldiers said, "As I had shaken hands with their chief, they must shake hands with my soldiers." In which request I willingly indulged them.

Sept. 11th. . . . Supposed to have come sixteen miles this day. Rain and cold winds, all day ahead. The river has never been clear of islands since I left Prairie Des Chein. I absolutely believe it to be here two miles wide. Hills, or rather prairie knobs, on both sides.

Sept. 12th. It raining very hard in the morning, we did not embark until ten o'clock, Mr. Frazer's perogues then coming up. It was still raining, and was very cold; passed the Racine [Root] river; also a prairie called Le Cross [La Crosse], from a game of ball played frequently on it by the Sioux Indians. This prairie is very handsome; it has a small square hill, similar to some mentioned by Carver. It is bounded in the rear by hills similar to [those of] the Prairie Des Chein.

On this prairie Mr. Frazer showed me some holes dug by the Sioux, when in expectation of an attack, into which they first put their women and children, and then crawl themselves. They were generally round and about ten feet in diameter; but some were half-moons and quite a breastwork. This I understood was the chief work, which was the principal redoubt. Their modes of constructing them are: the moment they apprehend or discover an enemy on the prairie, they commence digging with their knives, tomahawks, and a wooden ladle; and in an incredibly short space of time they have a hole sufficiently deep to cover themselves and their families from the balls or arrows of the enemy. They [enemies] have no idea of taking those subterraneous redoubts by storm, as they would probably lose a great number of men in the attack; and although they might be successful in the event, it would be considered a very imprudent action. . . .

Sept. 14th. . . . Mr. Frazer, Bradley, Sparks, and myself, went out to hunt. We crossed first a dry flat prairie; when we arrived at the hills we ascended them, from which we had a most sublime and beautiful prospect. On the right, we saw the mountains which we passed in the morning and the prairie in their rear; like distant clouds, the mountains at the Prairie Le Cross; on our left and under our feet, the valley between the two barren hills through which the Mississippi wound itself by numerous channels, forming many beautiful islands, as far as the eye could embrace the scene; and our four boats under full sail, their flags streaming before the wind. It was altogether a prospect so variegated and romantic that a man may scarcely expect to enjoy such a one but twice or thrice in the course of his life. . . .

Sunday, Sept. 15th. Embarked early. Passed the riviere Embarrass [Zumbro river], and Lean Clare [i.e., l'Eau Claire; Clear, White Water, or Minneiska river], on the W., which is navigable 135 miles. Encamped opposite the river Le Bœuf [Beef or Buffalo river], on the W. shore. At the head of this river the Chipeways inhabit, and it is navigable for perogues forty or fifty leagues. Rained in the afternoon. Mr. Frazer broke one of his canoes. Came about three miles further than him. Distance twenty-five miles.

Sept. 16th. . . . We made the sandy peninsula on the east at the entrance of Lake Pepin, by dusk; passed the Sauteaux [Chippewa] river on the east, at the entrance of the lake. After supper, the wind being fair, we put off with the intention to sail across; my interpreter, Rosseau, telling me that he had passed the lake twenty times, but never once in the day; giving as a reason that the wind frequently rose and detained them by day in the lake. But I believe the traders' true reason generally is their fears of the Sauteurs, as these have made several strokes of war at the mouth of this river, never distinguishing between the Sioux and their traders. However, the wind serving, I was induced to go on; and accordingly we sailed, my boat bringing up the rear, for I had put the sail of my big boat on my batteau, and a mast of twenty-two feet. Mr. Frazer embarked on my boat. At first the breeze was very gentle, and we sailed with our violins and other music playing; but the sky afterward became cloudy and quite a gale arose. My boat plowed the swells, sometimes almost bow under. When we came to the Traverse [crossing-place], which is opposite Point De Sable [Sandy Point], we thought it most advisable, the lake being very much disturbed and the gale increasing, to take harbor in a bay on the east. One of the canoes and my boat came in very well together; but having made a fire on the point to give notice to our boats in the rear, they both ran on the bar before they doubled it, and were near foundering; but by jumping into the lake we brought them into a safe harbor. Distance forty miles.

Sept. 17th. Although there was every appearance of a very severe storm, we embarked at half-past six o'clock, the wind fair; but before we had hoisted all sail, those in front had struck theirs. The wind came on hard ahead. The sky became inflamed, and the lightning seemed to roll down the sides of the hills which bordered the shore of the lake. The storm in all its grandeur, majesty, and horror burst upon us in the Traverse, while making for Point De Sable; and it required no moderate exertion to weather the point and get to the windward side of it. Distance three miles. . . .

Sept. 18th. Embarked after breakfast. Mr. Cameron, with his boats, came on with me. Crossed the lake, sounded it, and took an observation at the upper end. I embarked in one of his canoes, and we came up to Canoe [Cannon] river, where there was a small band of Sioux under the command of Red Wing, the second war chief in the nation. He made me a speech and presented a pipe, pouch, and buffalo skin. He appeared to be a man of sense, and promised to accompany me to St. Peters [the Minnesota river]; he saluted me, and had it returned. I made him a small present.

We encamped on the end of the island, and although it was not more than eleven o'clock, were obliged to stay all night. Distance eighteen miles. . . .

Sept. 20th. Embarked after sunrise. Cloudy, with hard head winds; a small shower of rain; cleared up in the afternoon, and became pleasant. Encamped on a prairie on the east side, on which is a large painted stone, about eight miles below the Sioux village. The traders had not yet overtaken me. Distance twenty-six and a half miles.

From *Narrative Journal of Travels through the Northwestern Regions of the United States* (1821)

HENRY R. SCHOOLCRAFT

In the spring of 1820 explorer, geologist, and ethnologist Henry Rowe Schoolcraft (1793–1864) joined an expedition led by Michigan Territorial

Governor Lewis Cass to explore Lake Superior and the upper Mississippi River. Their route took them from Detroit, across the upper Great Lakes, down the Mississippi River, up the Wisconsin River, and then on to Lake Michigan. This selection is drawn from Schoolcraft's 1821 account of that journey. Later, in 1832, he led the expedition that would identify the source of the Mississippi at Lake Itasca (which he named). Schoolcraft, who married a half-Ojibwe woman, Obabaamwewe-giizhigokwe, served as Indian agent to the Ojibwe and continued to write influential studies of Native American cultures for the remainder of his life.

LXXII. Day.—(*August 3d.*) . . .

At twelve o'clock we arrived at the Sioux village of Talangamane, or the Red wing, which is handsomely situated on the west banks of the river, six miles above Lake Pepin. It consists of four large, and several small lodges, built of logs in the manner of the little Raven's village. Talangamane is now considered the first chief of his nation, which honour it is said he enjoys both on account of his superior age and sagacity. He appears to be about sixty, and bears all the marks of that age. Very few of his people were at home, being engaged in hunting or fishing. We observed several fine corn fields near the village, but they subsist chiefly by taking sturgeon in the neighbouring lake, and by hunting the deer. The buffalo is also occasionally killed, but they are obliged to go two days journey west of the Mississippi, before this animal is found in plenty. . . .

Half a mile east of Red wing's village there is an isolated mountain, standing upon the brink of the river, called the Grange, from the summit of which you enjoy the most charming prospect. The immense valley of the Mississippi, with the numerous channels and islands of the river—the prairies and forests—with the windings of a number of small rivers which flow into the Mississippi, spread like a map below the eye. The calcareous bluffs which bound this valley, and terminate the prospect towards the west, in a line of lofty grey cliffs, throw an air of grandeur upon the scene, which affords a pleasing contrast with the deep green of the level prairies, and the silvery brightness of the winding river. Turning the eye towards the east, Lake Pepin spreads its ample sheet across the entire valley of the river, from bluff to bluff, and the indentures of its shores recede one behind another, until they become too faint to be distinguished, and are terminated on the line of the horizon.

The second Fort Crawford (c. 1840). The first Fort Crawford was built after
the U.S. Army recaptured Prairie du Chien from the British in the War of
1812. In 1825 more than five thousand Native Americans from a dozen tribes
gathered at the fort to sign the treaty of Prairie du Chien, which set the
boundaries used in later land cessions. The fort was abandoned shortly
thereafter, but in response to conflicts known as the "Winnebago War"
between Ho-Chunks and settlers, future U.S. president Col. Zachary Taylor
directed construction of the second Fort Crawford between 1829 and 1835, on
a bank above the Mississippi about two miles north of the mouth of the
Wisconsin River.

The altitude of this mountain cannot fall short of eight hundred feet
above the bed of river. It presents an abrupt mural precipice towards the
Mississippi, but slopes off gradually towards the south, and is covered
with grass, and a few scattering oaks. Its sides are strewed with beautiful
crystals of violet coloured, and radiated quartz, and with masses of iron
ore crystallized in cubes and octagon hedrons. A specimen of lead ore
(*galena*) was also shewn to us by one of Talangamane's people, and a
mine is reported to exist in the vicinity, but we could procure no information which is to be relied upon, concerning is situation and extent. . . .

At one o'clock in the afternoon we entered Lake Pepin. This beautiful
sheet of water is an expansion of the Mississippi river, six miles below
the Sioux village of Talangamane, and one hundred below the falls of
St. Anthony. It is twenty-four miles in length, with a width of from two
to four miles, and is indented with several bays, and prominent points,

which serve to enhance the beauty of the prospect. On the east shore, there is a lofty range of limestone bluffs, which are much broken and crumbled—sometimes run into pyramidal peaks—and often present a character of the utmost sublimity. On the west, there is a high level prairie, covered with the most luxuriant growth of grass, and nearly destitute of forest trees. From this plain several conical hills ascend, which, at a distance, present the appearance of vast artificial mounds or pyramids, and it is difficult to reconcile their appearance with the general order of nature, by any other hypothesis. This lake is beautifully circumscribed by a broad beach of clean washed gravel, which often extends from the foot of the surrounding highlands, three or four hundred yards into the lake, forming gravelly points upon which there is a delightful walk, and scalloping out the margin of the lake, with the most pleasing irregularity. . . . There is no perceptible current in the lake, during calm weather, and the water partakes so little of the turbid character of the lower Mississippi, that objects can be distinctly seen through it, at the depth of eight or ten feet.—It is plentifully stored with a variety of fish, the most remarkable of which is the *shovel-nosed sturgeon*, which is so called from a protuberance which extends from the end of the nose about fourteen inches—is four in width, and quite thin, in which respect, as well as in the shape of this process, it bears a striking resemblance to a physician's *spatula*. In other respects its size and general appearance corresponds with the small sturgeon of lakes Huron and Superior. This extension of the nose, appears designed to enable the animal to agitate the mud along the shores, and on the bottom of the Mississippi, in quest of certain animalcula, which are supposed to be its favourite food. The shores of this lake, also, appear favourable to the growth of crustaceous fish, and an examination of the different varieties which are presented, would probably result in the discovery of one or two new species. In no place have I ever noticed the fresh water muscle, attain so large a size. One of these, which I procured, measures seven inches in length, by five and half in width, and the thickness, taken at right angles with the most convex part of the shell, is a little than four inches. . . .

LXXIII. Day.—(*August 4th.*)—We proceeded on our descent at five o'clock. The rain had ceased before day light, but the morning remained cloudy. The lake is two miles and a half wide, opposite the spot of our encampment, but narrows gradually towards its outlet, which is ten miles below. The scenery during this distance is highly picturesque and beautiful. The precipices on the east are high, and shoot up into spiral points, yet are covered partially with grass and shrubbery. On the west we observe nothing but an elevated level prairie. The contrast produces the finest effect. At the precise point of exit of the Mississippi river, from Lake Pepin, the Chippeway, or Sauteaux river, comes in from the east. It is half a mile wide at its mouth, and its sources are connected with the Montreal river of Lake Superior. Below the junction of this stream, the Mississippi has an increased width, and contains a great number of small willow and cotton-wood islands, and the navigation is rendered more difficult, on account of the innumerable sand bars which here first make their appearance. They are attributable, in a great measure, to the immense quantity of sand brought down by the Chippeway river. . . .

LXXIV. Day.—(*August 5th.*)—It is ninety miles from the spot of our encampment to Prairie du Chien. We embarked a few moments after three in the morning, and reached the Prairie, at six in the afternoon. As we descend, the Mississippi has a gradual increase of size, and its valley a corresponding width.—The calcareous bluffs continue on either shore. In the course of this day, the river has been swelled by the rivers Embarras [Zumbro], La Claire [White], and Badaxe, the two former uniting at the point of their entrance into the Mississippi.

The village of Prairie du Chien is pleasantly situated on the east bank of the river, on the verge of one of those beautiful and extensive natural meadows, which characterize the valley of the Mississippi. It consists of about eighty buildings, including the garrison, the principal part of which are of logs, arranged in two streets parallel with the river, and is estimated to have an aggregate population of five hundred. This, is exclusive of the garrison, now consisting of a company of infantry, ninety-six strong, under the command of Capt. Fowle.

The village of Prairie du Chien takes its name from a family of Fox Indians who formerly resided there, and were distinguished by the appellation of *Dogs.* The present settlement was first begun in 1783, by Mr. Giard, Mr. Antaya, and Mr. Dubuque. There had formerly been an old settlement about a mile below the site of the present village, which existed during the time that the French held possession of the Canadas, but it was abandoned, chiefly on account of its unhealthy situation, being near the borders of an extensive tract of overflowed grounds. The early settlers, according to the principles adopted by the French colonists in the Canadas, intermarried with Indian women, and the present population is the result of this connexion. . . .

LXXVIII. Day.—(*August 9th.*) . . . We left Prairie du Chien at half past ten in the morning, and entering the Ousconsing three miles below, ascended that river eighteen miles. It is a wide, and shallow stream, running over a bed of sand—with transparent waters—and chequered with numerous small islands, and sand bars. It has an alluvial valley, of a mile in width, bounded on each side by calcareous hills—which frequently, present naked precipices towards the river.—The predominating trees, are oak, elm and maple.

LXXXIX. Day.—(*August 10th.*)—Quitting our encampment at five o'clock, A.M. we ascended the river thirty-six miles. During this distance, it is joined by a small tributary from the right bank, called Blue river. It is a stream of small size—with clear water—and originates in highlands, near the banks of Rock river. No change is observed in the appearance of the Ousconsing—there is no perceptible diminution, either in the width of the river, or its valley. The bluffs, continue to bound the river on both sides. The weather was fair and warm during the fore part of the day, but suddenly clouded up, in the afternoon, when we had a shower of rain, attended with thunder and lightning.

LXXX. Day.—(*August 11th.*)—On ascending the river sixteen miles, we passed the mouth of Pine river, a stream of thirty yards wide, entering on the left, at the junction of which, there is a village of Winnebagoes, of four lodges. Here we stopped a few moments. The Indians appeared friendly, and presented us some dried venison:—we engaged two of them to pilot us up the river, to the portage, and make some mineral discoveries. The navigation of the river above, is considerably impeded by sand bars, and small islands, and some time is lost, in searching for the proper channel. The water is shallow—clear—and very warm.— The current is strong, although without any falls or rapids. Numerous muscle, and other shells, are strewed along the sandy shores, some of which are very large, others, exceedingly small, with transparent shells, and colours beautifully variegated.—The plover, wild goose, king-fisher, and small yellow bird, are seen along this part of the river. The river bluffs continue, sometimes receding a mile or two from the river, and giving place to bottom lands, and patches of prairie, then shutting in close upon the water's edge. In the course of the day, we overtook a barge and Indian canoe, which had been dispatched in advance, from the Prairie, on the eighth, under the charge of Mr. Chase. We encamped at twilight, at the head of the *Spruce Channel*, having ascended the river thirty-four miles.

LXXXI. Day.—(*August 12th.*)—Proceeded up the river at twenty minutes before five—weather fair.—Ascended forty miles, and encamped on a sand bar, on the left shore. Highlands continue.—Trees, oak, elm, and maple. Alluvial bottom lands: and prairies, occasionally, on either shore. Rock strata, compact lime stone, reposing upon white sandstone. A shower of rain, at six in the evening.

LXXXII. Day.—(*August 13th.*)—Ascended thirty-eight miles.

LXXXIII. Day.—(*August 14th.*)—A rain storm after twelve o'clock at night—cleared off at seven in the morning, when we embarked, and reached the portage between the Ousconsing and Fox rivers, at one o'clock P.M.—distance sixteen miles. Crossed over the portage, and encamped on the head of Fox river.

Recess in the Bluffs near MacGregor (1863)

JOHN MUIR

In the summer of 1863 naturalist and writer John Muir (1838–1914) was a twenty-five-year-old student at the University of Wisconsin, having emigrated in 1849 with his family from Dunbar, Scotland, and settled on land near Portage. Newly excited by the study of botany, considering a career in medicine, and burdened by the prospect of entering the Civil War, he had come to a turning point in his early life. He and two companions

embarked upon an excursion down the Wisconsin River to Iowa, studying the valley's plants and geologic features along the way. From their
"recess in the bluffs," Muir reported his experiences in several letters to
his friend Emily Pelton, with whose family he had boarded in Prairie du
Chien two years before.

July 7th 1863

   Dear Friend Emily

   This evening finds us encamped near M'cGregor. We have spent a
toilsome day, but it has not been without interest. In the morning we
were directed to a romantic glen down which a little stream sought a
path, turning the mosses to stone as it went, and watering many interesting flowers. "The road that leads to it," said the man, "lies close along
the river bank—it is not very far and a loghouse marks the Glen's narrow entrance." We remarked, that in following our directions, when
we had inquired more particularly about the exact position of the loghouse after we had proceeded some distance on our way, the person
we inquired of gave us some very curious glances which we could not
understand. As we proceeded on our way we could not withstand the
temptation to climb the bluffs that butted so majestically overhead, and
after many vain attempts we at last found a place where the ascent
was practicable. We had to make many a halt for rest, and made as
much use of our hands as of our feet, but the splendid view well repaid
the toil.

   After enjoying the delightful scenery and analyzing some specimens
which we gathered on our way, we began to wish ourselves down again,
as the afternoon was wearing away and we wished to visit the glen before night, but descending was still more difficult and we several times
reached an almost unstoppable velocity. We found the first specimen of
Desmodium in this vicinity and several beautiful *Labiatus*.

   After travelling a good way down the river we began to fear that we
had already passed the object of our search but when the sun's rays
were nearly level and we had just emerged from a mass of low leafy
trees we were suddenly struck with the most genuine astonishment at
the unique and unexpected sight so full before us. We expected that
a loghouse in such a place would be a faultless specimen of those pioneer establishments with outside Chimney, the single window, and
door over run with hopvine or wild honeysuckle, the dooryard alive with

The Mississippi River along Highway 35, Paul Vanderbilt (1962). All Driftless
waterways run to the Mississippi, so the river has been a regional travel
corridor from the days of Oneota canoes to contemporary barge traffic.
Railways from Milwaukee reached the river at Prairie du Chien and La Crosse
in the 1850s and connected the two cities in the 1870s. Throughout the
twentieth century, expanding roadways, electrical lines, and telecommuni-
cation networks increasingly connected the Driftless and opened it to the
wider world. Photograph by iconographer Paul Vanderbilt.

poultry and pigs and the barn yard at hand with its old strawstack and
street of dilapidated stables and sheds, with cows, dirty children, and
broken plows, sprinkled over all.

But judge, Emily, of our surprise when upon a piece of ground where
the bluffs had curved backward a little from the river we at once saw the
curious old house with four gaudily dressed females in an even row in
front with two idle men seated a little to one side looking complacently
upon them like a successful merchant upon a stock of newly arrived
goods. Not a broken fence, dirty hog, or squealing pig was to be seen
but there on such a background, the old decaying logs and the dark
majestic hills on which the soft shades of evening were beginning to
fall, there in clothes which had been dipped many times in most glaring
dyes sat the strange four. It was long before I could judge of the character of the establishment but I saw at once there was something very
strange about it, and instinctively fell behind my companion. He was

equally ignorant but boldly marched forward and asked for the glen where fossils were found. This was a subject of which they knew but little. They told us that the path was no farther—that the hills were unclimbable, etc. We then took the alarm—gained the summit of the bluffs after an hours hard labor—built our camp fire, congratulated each other on our escape and spoke much from the first chap. of Proverbs.

You will perhaps soon hear from us again.

Truly your friend, JM

2nd Day July 8th, 1863

Dear Friend Emily,

When morning had dawned after our evening log house adventure, we found ourselves upon the brink of one of the highest points overhanging the river. It seemed as though we might almost leap across it. The sun was unclouded, and shone with fine effect upon the fleecy sea of fog contained by its ample banks of bluffs—later it flowed smoothly away as we gazed and gave us the noble Mississippi in full view.

Breaking the spell which bound us here so long we leisurely proceeded to explore the pretty glen which we passed before in the dark, here we spent some hours of great interest and added some fine plants and fossils to our growing wealth, and soon found ourselves upon the shore of the great river. The genuine calm of a July morning was now master of all—the river flowed on, smooth as a woodland lake, reflecting the full beams of the dreamy light while not on all the dark foliage which feathered its mountain wall, moved a single breeze. We stood harnessed and half asleep with the settled calm, looking wistfully upon the cool waters, when suddenly the thought struck us "How fine it would be to purchase a boat and sail merrily up the Wisconsin to Portage." We would read and work the oars by turns as our heavy packs would be packed snugly away beneath the seats and every few miles we would land at an inviting place and gather new spoils—and so in a few minutes we had our effects packed snugly as I have described in a pretty boat, and were joyfully floating on the bosom of the Father of Waters.

But alas, how vain our large hopes of promised bliss. We reached the mouth of the river, Wis. and soon our bright faces grew less and less bright till gloomy as a winters day as we paddle with all our might shooting bravely on against the current at the fearful velocity of *ten rods per*

two hours. At last completely exhausted we give up for the present in dispair and are instantly returned to the Mississippi by the boiling current but we were not yet beaten for holding a counsel of war against the bustling stream we determined to *"Try Try Again."* So landing we procured a pair of boards by a necessitous act of self appropriation and proceeded to make two pair of oars—they were nearly made before dark—we found a new camping ground and sought repose with hearts again trimmed with fresh hope. But now goodbye for the present. I shall write you again this evening and give you the result of today's labor. I wish you would write immediately on receiving this. Address to Wauzeka, Wisconsin. I shall pass near that place in a few days.
Truly your friend,
J Muir.

From "Landscape and Home: Environmental Traditions in Wisconsin" (1990)

WILLIAM CRONON

Environmental historian William Cronon grew up in Madison and studied at the University of Wisconsin–Madison and Yale University. Shortly after publishing the essay from which this reading is excerpted, Cronon returned to UW–Madison, where he has since served as Frederick Jackson Turner and Vilas Research Professor of History, Geography, and Environmental Studies.

When I was eleven years old, I fell in with a group of University of Wisconsin students and became a cave explorer. As I look back on that event from the distance of nearly a quarter century, I suddenly realize that spelunking—caving—was among the formative experiences of my life, and has informed my sense of place in Wisconsin ever since.

My first visit to a wild Wisconsin cave was to Pop's Cave, in Richland County. I still remember the trip quite vividly. After a drive along the Wisconsin River and through the hills of the Driftless Area, we parked our cars by an old church and headed out across the waist-high weeds of a farmer's meadow. To reach the cave, we clambered through several barbed-wire fences and climbed to the top of what then seemed to me a very steep hill. There, we found a deep sinkhole filled with refuse. At the bottom was a narrow slit sending clouds of steam into the cold December air, and leading down into darkness. We lit our carbide lamps—modern remnants of Wisconsin's lead-mining days—and edged gingerly down into the world below.

Entering such a place is always magical. You're suddenly engulfed in darkness, and it takes a minute or two before your eyes adjust to the dim yellow glow of the lamps. If you've arrived as we did in the winter, the air at 47 degrees Fahrenheit is suddenly warm and very humid, with an indescribable odor of clay and damp stone that is like an ancient farm cellar but older and less human. Behind you, the blue light of day becomes ever fainter as you move away from the entrance. When the last glimmer vanishes and you realize that your lamp is now your only lifeline back to the outside world, you suddenly understand that you have entered a wild place, which people can visit but cannot call home. The contrast with the day-lit countryside above could hardly be more stark.

As caves go, Wisconsin's are a humble and unpretentious lot. The glacier did away with most that might have existed outside the Driftless Area, so there are only a few hundred left. Our thinly bedded dolomites just can't compete with the great limestones of Kentucky or New Mexico, so our caves have none of the mileage or grandeur one finds elsewhere. More than a century of human vandalism has removed most of the calcite formations they once contained. Pop's Cave is fairly typical. The steeply sloping entrance room leads down to a series of chambers and tight crawlways for a total of about eight hundred feet. Thick wet mud covers nearly every surface, and soon covers you as well. Soda straw stalactites hang next to a few dew-covered bats from various places on the ceilings, and water drips everywhere. At the far back of the cave are some wonderfully delicate rimstone pools, where calcite has built up in a series of steps to produce a frozen cascade of water, like nothing so much as a Yellowstone hot spring. Elsewhere, the floor is covered with broken slabs of stone, grim reminders that the ceiling is gradually collapsing as the cave migrates upward. Eventually, it will produce new sinkholes and then cease to exist altogether.

The attractions of such a place are completely lost on some people. You either feel them or you don't. Indeed, I should confess to some ambivalence about them myself. I never, for instance, got over a lingering fear of the dark. The thought of my lamp going out was akin to the dread of being caught without a night-light to hold back the terrors that lurk behind the closet doors of every child's bedroom. I never lost a mild claustrophobia, the fear that I might be "buried deeper cheaper," as we cavers said with our gallows wit. I worried that I might catch rabies from a bat. And I was openly terrified of heights, the places where we had to use ropes and ladders to drop into dark pits in order to continue our explorations.

All of these, of course, were actually about a much more basic fear—the fear of dying. Caves, I think, remind us all too easily of the grave, and there are many people who have no eagerness to look into that place any sooner than they have to. But the places that most remind us of death are often the places where we also confront our own fears and discover the strength we need to live in their presence. The wilderness—for that is what these caves were to me—is always a place of adventure, where young people especially learn to push the limits of their own courage in a struggle with nature and the self which is finally about growing up. The thought that I walked across a perfectly ordinary cornfield and suddenly dropped down into an extraordinary secret world below had all the wonder of Alice's unexpected trip down the rabbit's hole, Bilbo Baggins' near-fatal encounter with Gollum, or Lucy's discovery of Narnia at the back of the wardrobe. At the outermost edge of my daylight world, caves were a wonderful passage into the realm where childhood fantasy met grownup adventure. Even their terrors were compelling.

I was soon spending an inordinate amount of time driving around southwestern Wisconsin with my new spelunker friends looking for caves. In between our weekend excursions, I spent endless hours reading about caves, making lists and maps cataloging where they might be found, and planning new expeditions. My parents were wise enough not to interfere with this peculiar new hobby, and in fact even encouraged me in it without revealing too many of their own fears about it. And so I moved on from plain spelunking to speleology, the more serious study of caves, becoming involved with the Wisconsin Cave Survey in a collective effort to locate and describe all the caves of the state. . . .

Looking back on my eight or so years as a spelunker, I now realize that the caves themselves were actually less important than the sense of place that went with them. Caving taught me a much more general passion for land and history that has come to define my adult life. It showed me the fascination of trying to read the landscape as a place of many stories: of the achingly slow sedimentation that produced the rocks around us; of the dissolution of that rock by acidic groundwater to create a cave; of the plants and animals whose habitats were affected by that cave's existence; of the human lives that eventually became entangled in its history. Despite their different time scales, all these stories seem equally fascinating to me, and come to define in my own mind the field called environmental history. I no longer care so much about caves, but the questions they taught me to ask—about reading landscapes and telling their stories—have stayed with me ever since.

I take another lesson from my caving experience as well. I think we acquire our most vivid sense of place when we discover a special passion—often when we are still quite young—for some small part of the land around us. The original focus of that passion probably doesn't matter very much. For me, it began with caves, but for someone else it might just as easily start with hunting or birdwatching or farming or even just owning a piece of land. The simple act of declaring an *interest* carries us across the threshold that leads outward from ourselves to the world around us. It gives us an ever more detailed knowledge about the object of our desire, and an ever greater intimacy with its special qualities. Because nothing in nature stands alone—caves lead to the world above just as a hunter's quarry leads to the larger habitat in which that animal lives—our original fascination more often than not becomes a much broader affection for the land itself. Our passion teaches us to care, so that the land becomes not an abstraction called "environment," but a familiar place filled with limestones and sinkholes, cat-tails and geese, oak groves and white-tailed deer. The details matter in an entirely new way; we have experienced them at first hand, as members of a landscape we have learned to call home. Their stories mingle with our own, and we come to share a common history.

From *Gathering Moss: A Natural and Cultural History of Mosses* (2003)

ROBIN WALL KIMMERER

Botanist, ecologist, and writer Robin Wall Kimmerer explored the sandstone cliff faces of the Kickapoo River valley early in her career, while studying at the University of Wisconsin–Madison. Kimmerer teaches at the State University of New York, where she also founded and directs the Center for Native Peoples and the Environment. *Gathering Moss* was her first book and included this chapter, "Kickapoo."

I finally got around to refinishing the bottom of my canoe. After the duct tape wore off. Ahh, duct tape, the great enabler of the procrastinator. I peel it off, layer after layer, where I'd slapped it on after a collision with a rock on the Oswegatchie, and where the stern bumped down hard on a ledge of the New River. Inspecting the various cracks and chips is like taking inventory of great canoe trips. Here's a souvenir of the rapids on the Flambeau and here the gravel beds of the Raquette. Along the gunnel there is a smudge of red paint, running for six inches or so along the sky blue fiberglass. I puzzle over that one for a moment and then I remember the Kickapoo and the summer I spent immersed.

The Kickapoo River runs through southwestern Wisconsin in a region known as the Driftless Area. The glaciers which covered the upper Midwest skipped this one little corner of Wisconsin, leaving a landscape of steep cliffs and sandstone canyons. I discovered the stream with a fellow graduate student as she surveyed the area for rare lichens. We paddled down the river, stopping at cliffs and outcrops to scan the species. All along the river I was struck by the distinctive pattern on the cliffs. The upper reaches of the cliff were spattered with lichens, but at the foot of the sheer wall were horizontal bands of moss in different shades of green, rising from the water. I was looking to find a thesis question and this one found me. What was the source of the vertical stratification that striped the cliff?

I had some ideas, of course. I'd climbed too many mountains not to notice the changes in vegetation with elevation. Elevational zonation usually results from temperature gradients and it gets cooler the higher you go. I imagined that there would be some kind of environmental gradient that changed as the cliff rose from the water, and the moss pattern would follow.

The next week I went back to the Kickapoo by myself, ready to look more closely at the banded cliffs. I put my canoe in at the bridge and paddled upstream. The current was swifter than it looked and I had to paddle hard. I maneuvered alongside the rock face, but there was nowhere to moor the canoe. Every time I stopped paddling to look at the mosses I'd be pulled downstream. I could hang on with my fingers wedged in a crack, just long enough to snatch a clump of moss, and then I'd drift away again. Any kind of systematic study was clearly going to require a different approach.

I beached the canoe on the opposite bank and decided to see if I could wade over to the cliff. The bottom was sandy and the river only knee deep. The cool water, swirling around my legs, felt wonderful on a hot day. This was starting to feel like the perfect research site. I waded over within arm's reach of the cliff. Suddenly, the bottom dropped away. The current had undercut the cliff and I found myself chest deep and clinging to the rock. But what a great face-to-face view of the mosses.

Right next to the water, extending upward for a foot or so, was a dark band of *Fissidens osmundoides*. *Fissidens* is a small moss. Each shoot is only 8 mm high, but it is tough and wiry. *Fissidens'* form is very distinctive. The whole plant is flat, like an upright feather. Each leaf has a smooth thin blade, atop which sits a second flap of leaf, like a flat pocket on a shirtfront. This envelope of leaf seems to function in holding water. All crowded together, the shoots make a rough-textured turf. *Fissidens* has well-developed rhizoids, root-like filaments that attach firmly to the grainy sandstone. At the waterline *Fissidens* formed a virtual monoculture. I saw hardly any other species, save a snail or two hanging on for dear life.

About a foot above water, the *Fissidens* disappeared and was replaced by assorted clumps of other mosses. Silky tufts of *Gymnostomum aeruginosum*, mounds of *Bryum* and glistening mats of *Mnium*, all are arrayed in a patchwork of different greens amidst empty patches of tawny sandstone.

Higher still, just at the limit of what I could reach from my underwater perch, began a dense mat of *Conocephalum*, a thallose liverwort. . . . This plant has no distinct leaves, just a sinuous flattened thallus ending in three round lobes like the triangular head of a viper. Its surface is divided into tiny diamond-shaped polygons, contributing to its reptilian appearance. Closely appressed to the surface, it snakes its way over rock or soil, held loosely in place by a line of scraggly rhizoids on its underside. Brilliant green, exotic, *Conocephalum* completely covers the cliff at this height, making a striking contrast to the darker mosses below.

I was captivated by these plants and their layered distribution on the cliff. The fact that I could paddle to my research site cinched my choice of thesis topic. The only problem was logistics. How could I make all the detailed measurements I needed while chest deep in the river? Over the next few weeks I tried lots of things. I tried anchoring the canoe and leaning out toward the cliff. The number of dropped pencils and rulers was disheartening, as was the constant threat of capsizing. I tied little Styrofoam floats to all my equipment, but the current just carried them away, bobbing merrily downstream before I could grab them. So I tethered all my gear to the thwarts of the canoe and you can imagine the resulting tangle of camera straps, data books, and light meters. Eventually, I abandoned ship and simply planted my feet on the river bottom. I devised a kind of floating laboratory with the canoe anchored beside the cliff and me standing in the river where I could reach both rocks and canoe. Data books were impossible to manage. I kept dropping them in. So I collected my measurements using a tape recorder. The machine sat securely duct-taped to the seat of the canoe and the microphone was looped around my neck. I could then have both hands free to position my sampling grids and collect specimens, and still have a free leg to snare the canoe rope when it began to drift. I felt like the one-man band of the Kickapoo. It must have made quite a picture as I was talking to myself, immersed in the river, and singing out the locations and abundance of mosses: *Conocephalum* 35, *Fissidens* 24, *Gymnostomum* 6. I marked all the plots with dabs of red paint, which still decorates my canoe.

In the evenings I'd transcribe the tapes, converting my recorded litany to real data. I wish I'd kept some of those tapes, just for entertainment value. In between the hours of droned numbers were bursts of inspired cursing as the canoe started to drift away, tightening the microphone around my neck. I recorded any number of squeals and frantic splashes when something nibbled at my legs. I even had tape of an entire conversation with passing canoeists who handed me a cold Leinenkugels Ale as they floated by.

The vertical stratification of species was very clear with *Fissidens* at the bottom, *Conocephalum* at the top, and a variety of others sandwiched in between. But my hypothesis about the cause of the pattern was not supported. There were no significant differences in light, temperature, humidity, or rock type along the face of the cliff. The pattern had to be caused by something else. Standing in the river day after day I was becoming vertically stratified myself—shriveled toes at the bottom, sunburned nose at the top, and muddy in between.

Oftentimes, an abrupt pattern in nature is caused by an interaction between species, such as territorial defense or one tree species shading out another. The pattern I was observing might well be the result of some competitive "line in the sand" between *Conocephalum* and *Fissidens*. I gave the two species a chance to tell me about their relationship, by growing them side by side in the greenhouse. Alone, *Fissidens* did fine. *Conocephalum* likewise. But when they were grown together there was clear evidence of a power struggle, which was consistently lost by *Fissidens*. Time after time *Conocephalum* extended its snaky thallus over the top of diminutive *Fissidens*, completely engulfing it. Their separation on the cliff became clearer. *Fissidens* had to keep away from the liverwort in order to survive. But, if competition was so important, why didn't *Conocephalum* grow all the way to the waterline and simply obliterate the other species?

One day in late summer I noticed a wad of grass snagged on a branch high above my head—a high-water mark. Clearly the river was not always at wading depth. Perhaps the vertical stratification was due to differences in how the species tolerated flooding. I collected clumps of each species and submerged them in pans of water for various times: 12, 24, 48 hours. The *Fissidens* remained perfectly healthy even after three days, as did *Gymnostomum*. But after only twenty-four hours the *Conocephalum* was black and slimy. So here was a piece of the pattern. *Conocephalum* must be confined to the higher levels of the cliff by its inability to withstand flooding.

I wondered how often floods like the one I'd simulated actually happened. Could it be often enough to create a barrier for *Conocephalum* expansionist tendencies? As luck would have it, the Army Corps of Engineers was wondering the same thing, albeit for a different reason. They were considering constructing a flood-control dam on the river and had installed a gaging station at the bridge below my cliffs. They had amassed five years of daily measurements of water levels on the Kickapoo. I could use their data to calculate the frequency with which any point on the cliff had been underwater. I could also call in to the automated phone number to learn the current water level at the ridge. I've not been much of a cheerleader for the Corps, given their propensity for spoiling rivers, but these data were invaluable.

All winter long I analyzed the data to match time to the distribution of mosses on the cliff. Not surprising, the gaging station data matched the elevational zonation of the bryophytes very well. The water level was most frequently lapping at the base of the cliff where *Fissidens* dominated the vegetation. It was tolerant of flooding and its wiry streamlined stems allowed it to withstand the frequent company of the current. Flood frequency declined with rising elevation on the cliff. The zone dominated by loosely attached *Conocephalum* was inundated very rarely. High above the water, *Conocephalum* could safely spread its snaking thallus over the rock in an uninterrupted blanket of green. One species dominated where flood frequency was high. Another species dominated where disturbance was low. But what about the middle? Here was a tremendous variety of species, as well as patches of open rock as bare as a billboard advertising "space available." In the zone of intermediate flood frequency no one species dominated and diversity was high. As many as ten other species were sandwiched here between the two superpowers. . . .

The Kickapoo cliffs helped to generate what has become known as the Intermediate Disturbance Hypothesis, that diversity of species is highest when disturbance occurs at an interval between the extremes. Ecologists have shown that in the complete absence of disturbance, superior competitors like *Conocephalum* can slowly encroach upon other species and eliminate them by competitive dominance. Where disturbance is very frequent, only the very hardiest species can survive the tumult. But in between, at an intermediate frequency, there seems to be a balance that permits a great variety of species to flourish. Disturbance is just frequent enough to prevent competitive dominance and yet stable periods are long enough for successional species to become established. Diversity is maximized when there are many kinds of patches of all different ages. . . .

When the ice went out on the Kickapoo the next spring I called the gaging station and an electronic voice informed me that the river was in flood. So I jumped in my car and drove down to see what the mosses looked like now. The river was chocolate brown with dissolved farmland. Logs and old fenceposts were pushed along in the torrent, bumping against the cliff. My red paint marks were nowhere to be seen. By the next morning the waters had receded as quickly as they had come and the aftermath was revealed. The *Fissidens* had emerged unscathed. The mid-level mosses were sodden with mud and battered by the logs and the pull of the water. A few more bare patches had been made. The *Conocephalum* had not been submerged long enough to die, but it was torn away in great swaths, hanging from the cliff like ripped wallpaper. Its flat loose form had made it particularly vulnerable to the pull of water, while *Fissidens* was unaffected. The open patches created by the removal of *Conocephalum* made temporary habitats for a new generation of mosses which would persist there until *Conocephalum* gathered its strength and returned. These are the species which are not able to compete with *Conocephalum*, nor to withstand the frequent flooding. They are fugitives between two forces, living in the crossfire between competition and the force of the river.

I like to think of the satisfying coherence in that pattern. Mosses, mussels, forests, and prairies all seem to be governed by the same principle. The apparent destruction of a disturbance is in fact an act of renewal, provided the balance is right. The Kickapoo mosses had a piece in telling that story. Sandpaper in hand, I looked at the splotch of red paint on this old blue canoe and decide to let it be.

Old Man Fishing (1960)

AUGUST DERLETH

August Derleth (1909–1971) of Sauk City, Wisconsin, was a prolific writer in varied genres—historical and detective novels, short stories, science fiction, memoir, nature essays, poetry. Much of his writing, including his multivolume *Sac Prairie Saga*, focused on the local landscape of the lower Wisconsin River valley in and around Sauk Prairie, where the river crosses into the Driftless Area. "Old Man Fishing" appeared in Derleth's poetry collection *West of Morning.*

One old man, as all old men before him,
sitting at the river's edge, eyes to the west,
with the glacier at his back (centuries on the rim),
an old cane pole held up against his breast—
all Midwest America unfolding here
before his rheumy eyes, going past anew
down river—
Jonathan Carver in 1766:

> *"There are Indians here,*
> *Saukies they call themselves . . ."*

LaHontan, Marquette, Joliet, Red Bird—
each leaving here his mark, each his word,
fur-traders, voyageurs, pioneers,
Captain Maryatt, Chief Black Hawk with his braves' own blood
    and tears—
> *"I loved my cornfields.*
> *I fought for them . . ."*
One old man fishing. He could see the Rockies,
he could see the far Pacific, he could see past Sauk
and Winnebago, the far Sioux: Lakotah, Arapaho,
the Minneconjou, the Oglala—Crazy Horse, Sitting Bull,
Jim Bridger, Kit Carson, the U. P. Trail, a land full
of wildness and bright with endless tomorrows.

One old man fishing in water and in time.
Crow cry and wind's rune are something starting over,
and one old man alone divides all time
between the here and now and what was yesterday forever,
the glacier at his back, Los Alamos on the distant rim,
all America going by in two boys paddling a canoe—

> *"Catching any fish, Grandpa?"*

Fish out of water—one bullhead, one pike, four
bright sunfish: and out of time a hundred years or more—
what must a century measure in a sunbeam?
An old man fishing to while away a dream
which began—how many years ago?
He must be seventy, eighty perhaps—he could be
as old as all America; he could see
years past since it began, with the glacier at his back
and the wilderness before,
the wild Wisconsin and the Indian country on the far side.
A dream's as long and wide
as any gauge of time or any similar measure.
Who's to fix its boundaries? The wind's talk,
the field sparrow's sweet lament, the wheeling hawk—
all are older here than 1953:
below them one old man is young as a sapling tree.

He sits musing with the wind in his beard
and his eyes half-closed, with his hat pushed low
to shut out sun so he can see
what's going on—a bobbing cork, or a rippling wave,
a Winnebago passing by, or an engagé,
a fragment of a day or year gone by, or just today,
canoe, keelboat, steamboat, launch: a raft of logs,
an otter flashing past: fur-traders, pioneers—
time beginning once again,
time that was starting over
when the least pebble turned under a red man's heel,
when the sand washed back from General Dodge's step,
when the stage-coach rode by in ruts gone with the next rain,
when the wilderness fell back and the leaves turned
where Bob LaFollette passed, and time burned
on the iron rails . . .

One old man fishing under the sun,
hearing the wind and the sound time makes. . . .

6

EARLY ECONOMIES

THE DRIFTLESS AREA'S STRATEGIC LOCATION and abundant natural assets have long attracted and supported an array of economic activities. Lead, copper, and zinc lay embedded in the Driftless bedrock. Historically the region's network of waterways invited travel, trade, fishing, agriculture, and manufacturing. Its soils and sufficient annual rainfall allowed agriculture to thrive. Forests, savannas, prairies, and riparian wetlands offered plants for food, medicines, forage, fuels, and construction, and other materials for tools, clothing, wares, and artworks. The resident game animals and furbearers and the annual passage of migratory waterfowl made it a rich region for hunting and trapping.

People have known and made use of all of these assets for millennia. Native peoples fished, hunted, and trapped, extracted minerals, built shelters and villages, cultivated garden beds, foraged for foods and medicines, and fashioned household goods. The Native economies of the region were linked by trade routes that carried minerals and furs out of the Driftless and brought in copper from Lake Superior, pipestone from southwestern Minnesota, obsidian from the Rocky Mountains, chert from southern Iowa, flint and jasper from Ohio, shell beads from the Gulf of Mexico. These Native economies and trade networks evolved through the Paleoindian, Archaic, Woodland, and Mississippian periods, and into the historic time of modern Native Americans.

With the contact of Native and European cultures, the character and pace of economic activity in the Driftless Area changed profoundly. Europeans not only brought new tools and techniques but new systems of organized capital, transportation, and trade. Markets that had previously developed along waterways and across portages now stretched overland and across oceans. In the century after the arrival of the first voyageurs, a mixed French-Indian culture and economy emerged and grew—with important effects on the mid-continent's native wildlife and ecosystems and with the potential at least for continuing cultural accommodation. Those possibilities were soon overwhelmed by the relentless reality of American economic expansion. The Indian treaties of the 1820s and 1830s prepared the way. As historian William Cronon observed in *Nature's Metropolis: Chicago and the Great West*, "The hybrid cultural universe of Indians and Euromericans that had existed . . . for decades was finally to be shattered by different conceptions of property and real estate." ·

Over the next century those conceptions of property manifested themselves in the official documents of government, in the ledger books of private enterprise, and in the working of the land. In the long run, farming would come to dominate the economic landscape of the Driftless. As agriculture developed, however, three other major economic forces would hold sway across the region: the continuing fur trade, a boom in lead mining, and an epic wave of pine logging that forever changed the forests to the north while shaping the Driftless Area's river towns, rail networks, and farm communities.

Diggings (2011)

ALICE D'ALESSIO

Alice D'Alessio is a poet and writer from Middleton, Wisconsin. She has published three books of poetry, taught writing for Elderhostel, and led workshops at The Clearing in Door County, Wisconsin.

Land rolling and first rate. thinly timbered with oak
until I enter the prairie. Sylvester Sibley, Deputy Surveyor

The 13th day of February, 1832.
Cold. He walks the land
that will be one day ours,
wading through snow, leaning
against a crotch of oak.
to write with frozen fingers,

At 50 chains, Morrison's house and double-eye furnace
he wrote; *about 18 chains east of line*
the Horine house and Bowman's house.

A little to left of line, diggings
almost whole length.
"Delving for Galena," they called it
gouging the earth
in hopes of instant wealth.

Only 180 years ago, but as gone as snow,
as smoke that hung over the valley
from wood-fired smelters.
At night, the coals glowed, like dragon eyes.

Two dollars a section
they paid him for his work. I'd give him that
and more to tell me where the diggings were,
the houses, the furnaces. Only the words are left,
their thin black lines.
Time's merciful silting thickens over.

Life in the Diggings (1898)

HENRY E. LEGLER

The lead district's early mining boom had passed into history when librarian and scholar Henry Eduard Legler (1861–1917) recalled the period in this excerpt from his 1898 book *Leading Events of Wisconsin History: The Story of the State.* Legler served as a Wisconsin state assemblyman; as secretary of the Milwaukee School Board and the Wisconsin Library Commission; as director of the Chicago Public Library; and as president of the American Library Association.

With the keen scent of birds of prey, gamblers and other adventurers flocked to the lead diggings of southwestern Wisconsin during the great mining excitement that occurred in the early '20s. As was the case later

Pl. IX

Cross-section of a Lead Mine, David Dale Owen (1844). In 1839 the United
States General Land Office commissioned physician and geologist David Dale
Owen (1807–1860) to undertake a survey of the mineral resources of the
Mineral Point, Galena, and Dubuque Land Districts in eastern Iowa and
southern Wisconsin. Under this commission, Owen and a corps of more than
one hundred assistants surveyed eleven thousand square miles in the lead
region in just two months. Owen's *Report of a Geological Exploration of Part of
Iowa, Wisconsin, and Illinois* was published in 1844. A gifted illustrator, Owen
prepared the maps, diagrams, sketches, and plates for the report, including
this vertical cross-section of a typical lead mine.

in California, gambling dens and grog shops were constructed in the midst of the cabins of the miners, and the fruit of the prospector's thrift often went into the coffers of the card shark. During the years when the lead mines were being developed, the aggregation of cabins that dotted the region were the typical frontier camps of a mineral country, with their swagger and utter disregard of any law but their own—prototypes of the later gulch towns of the far West. Their names were characteristic, too, and some of them yet retain a place on the map of Wisconsin. Among them were Hardscrabble Diggings, Buncome, Snake Hollow, Shake-the-Rag-Under-the-Hill, Rattle Snake Diggings, Big Patch, and other places with more euphonious, if less descriptive, names.

It was about 1822 that the so-called discovery of the lead diggings in southwestern Wisconsin occurred. For nearly two centuries the existence of the ore in that region had been known to white men, but the Indians were unwilling to let them penetrate to the mines. This was especially the case when the pushing Americans began to travel from the southern states to the upper Mississippi in quest of fortune. Before this, Frenchmen had been given permission to work the mines to some extent, for the Indian was ever wont to fraternize with the representatives of this volatile race, but Americans were rigidly excluded. The introduction of firearms among the Indians had taught them the value of the lead as an article of barter. It was stated in a letter written to the secretary of war in 1810 by Nicholas Boilvin, agent at Prairie du Chien, that the quantity of lead exchanged by Indians for goods during the season was about 400,000 pounds.

Doubtless none but Frenchmen had been at the mines previous to the war of 1812, but in 1816 a St. Louis trader named John Shaw succeeded in penetrating to the mines of the Fever river district by passing himself as a Frenchman. He was one of the traders who made periodical trips to Prairie du Chien, propelling the boats by means of poles and sails. It required from two weeks to a month to make the trip up the river, while the return journey occupied from a week to ten days. The boats carried miscellaneous supplies to Prairie du Chien, and their return cargo consisted principally of lead.

Shaw saw about twenty smelting places, the mineral being smelted in the crudest way imaginable. This was Shaw's description of the process: "A hole or cavity was dug in the face of a piece of sloping ground, about two feet in depth and as much in width at the top; this hole was made in the shape of a mill-hopper, which was about eight or nine inches square; other narrow stones were laid across grate-wise; a channel or eye was dug from the sloping side of the ground inwards to the bottom of the hopper. This channel was about a foot in width and in height, and was filled with dry wood and brush. The hopper being filled with the mineral, and the wood ignited, the molten lead fell through the stones at the bottom of the hopper; and this was discharged through the eye, over the earth, in bowl-shaped masses called plats, each of which weighed about seventy pounds."

Glowing notices of the richness of the lead mines of the upper Mississippi appeared in St. Louis newspapers in 1822, and started a migration thitherward. In order to overawe the Indians, who would not let white men enter the district, the government dispatched detachments of troops from Prairie du Chien and the Rock Island forts. Finding that resistance would be futile, the Indians quietly submitted to the invasion of their mineral territory. Thus began, a few miles south of the present border of the state, what at one time was the leading industry of Wisconsin, as the fur trade had been up to that period. The newcomers were mainly from the southern states and territories, and thus the first seeds of American origin in Wisconsin were the planting of men from Kentucky, Tennessee, and Missouri. They came by boat and in caravans on horseback. Soon the prospector's shovel was upturning the sod on the hillsides of southwestern Wisconsin, the Indian occupants in sullen resentment biding their time for mischief. Galena became the center of the mining region.

Some of the adventurers who came in the expectation of acquiring sudden wealth were doomed to disappointment. There were some who sought to avoid the rigors of a Northern winter by coming in the spring and returning to their genial Southern climate when snow began to fly. These tenderfeet were denominated "suckers" by the hardier miners, an appellation that was later transferred to the state of Illinois. Their superficial workings were called "sucker holes."

Despite muttered threats from the Indians, and other disheartening circumstances, population rapidly increased. Red Bird's disturbance [in 1827] caused a temporary exodus, but the frightened miners soon returned. How busily pick and shovel were plied may be gathered from the reports of lead manufactured. It was soon seen that negro labor could be well utilized, and some of the Southerners brought slaves to do the work. The population rapidly increased. In 1825 it was estimated that there were 200 persons; three years later fully 10,000, one-twentieth being women and about 100 free blacks. The lead product had increased in the same period from 439,473 pounds to 12,957,100 pounds.

Most of the miners followed the Indian plan of smelting in a log furnace. It was a crude device, and there was much wastage. They likewise imitated the Indian mode of blasting—heating the rock and then splitting it by throwing water on it. "I saw one place where they (the Indians) dug forty-five feet deep," says the account of Dr. Moses Meeker, a pioneer of the period. "Their manner of doing it was by drawing the mineral dirt and rock in what they called a mocock, a kind of basket made of birch bark, or dry hide of buckskin, to which they attached a rope made of rawhide. Their tools were a hoe made for the Indian trade, an axe, and a crowbar made of an old gun barrel flattened at the breech, which they used for removing the rock. Their mode of blasting was rather tedious, to be sure; they got dry wood and kindled a fire along the rock as far as they wished to break it. After getting the rock hot they poured cold water upon it, which so cracked it that they could pry it up. At the old Buck Lead they removed many hundred tons of rock in that manner, and had raised many thousand pounds of mineral or lead ore."

During this period there came to Wisconsin some of the men who became most notable in its territorial history. Among them were Henry Dodge, afterwards governor, who brought with him from Missouri a number of negro slaves; Ebenezer Brigham, pioneer of Blue Mounds; Henry Gratiot and Col. William S. Hamilton. The latter was a son of Alexander Hamilton, who was killed by Aaron Burr, in a duel.

Some of the miners realized what in those days were considered great fortunes. One man sank a shaft near Hazel Green on the site of an old Indian digging. "At four and a half feet he found block mineral extending over all the bottom of his hole," in the language of Dr. Meeker's narrative. "He went to work and cut out steps on the side of the hole, to be ready for the next day's operation. Accordingly, the next day he commenced operations. The result of his day's work was seventeen thousand pounds of mineral upon the bank at night."

After raising about a hundred thousand pounds, the diggings was abandoned. Another prospector took possession and secured more than a hundred and fifty thousand pounds.

Most of the lead that was smelted went to Galena, to be transported thence to St. Louis and New Orleans. Long caravans of ore wagons, some of them drawn by as many as eight yoke of oxen, wore deep ruts into the primitive road that went by way of Mineral Point and Belmont to this metropolis of the mines. About $80 a ton was obtained for the ore. . . .

Doubtless the typical mining camp in Wisconsin when the lead excitement was in its heyday was Mineral Point. Its straggling lines of huts were ranged along a deep gorge, and at all hours the sound of revelry could be heard emanating from the saloons and gambling houses. Dancing and singing, with the accompaniment of rude music, and drinking and gambling furnished the entertainment for the wilder spirits. The town bore the appellation of the Little Shake-Rag, or Shake-Rag-Under-the-Hill. The origin of the peculiar name is explained by an early-day traveler in this wise:

"Females," says this account of sixty years ago, "in consequence of the dangers and privations of the primitive times, were as rare in the diggings as snakes upon the Emerald Isle. Consequently the bachelor miner from necessity performed the domestic duties of cook and washerwoman, and the preparation of meals was indicated by appending a rag to an upright pole, which, fluttering in the breeze, telegraphically conveyed the glad tidings to his hungered brethren upon the hill. Hence this circumstance at a very early date gave this provincial sobriquet of Shake-Rag, or Shake-Rag-Under-the-Hill."

Public Land Sale (1847)

JAMES M. GOODHUE

In the 1830s and 1840s, as the mining boom in the lead district subsided, farming grew in significance. Agriculture expanded dramatically as lands were sold out of the United States land office in Mineral Point: 74,000 acres in 1846, 117,500 acres in 1847, and 53,500 in 1848. On June 5, 1847, James Goodhue, the editor of the *Wisconsin Herald* in Lancaster dutifully described how the miners and others from across the region were now coming into farmland, then committed the story to verse.

The sale of mineral lands has gone off beautifully. Col. Parris, the Register of the Land Office, has been obliging to us all and has done all in his power and all that was consistent with his duties to facilitate the sales, and no more. Nearly all the reserved lands have been sold at $1.25 per acre—all the lands at Platteville and everywhere else, I believe, except a few plots at Beetown. In fact, the weather is so dry and has been for a long time, that nearly all the diggings have petered. It was in evidence that they had petered—the best of diggings will peter. Every thing went off quietly; nearly all claims have been adjusted. There was, however, some show for a row amongst the claimants at New Diggings. Mineral Point has been thronged with people of all sorts and descriptions. There seemed to be an abundance of money for all who had lands to enter. Mr. Phillips of Boston, had cash to loan—cords of it. We have here during the sales, the fullest representation from the diggings that has ever assembled in the mines.

> New Diggings, Shake Rag, Benton, Snake
> Are all on hand and wide awake;
> Black Jack, Black Leg, Swindler's Ridge
> Claim with the rest their privilege.
> Franklin is there and Centerville
> Crawls from its elevated hill.
> Dodgeville, Schullsburg, Hamilton
> Are there to see to number one.
> Burlesqueburgh, Platteville, White Oak, Whig,
> Scrabble, the Little Patch, the Big.
> Red Dog, Pin Hook, Nip and Tuck
> Are on hand to try their luck.
> Beetown and Pigeon thither fly
> With money in their hands to buy.

> And last, and least inclined to nab
> Her share of mineral lands, is Grab.

From "Recollections of Antoine Grignon" (1914)

ANTOINE GRIGNON

Fur trader, storekeeper, mediator, and student of Indian customs, Antoine Grignon (1828–1913) embodied the complex intercultural relationships that characterized the changing communities and economy of the Upper Mississippi in the mid-nineteenth century. Born at Fort Crawford to a French/Ho-Chunk father and a French/Dakota mother, he was among the last survivors of the fur-trading era in Wisconsin when he was interviewed in the last year of his life.

In looking back over the departed years, I can see Prairie du Chien as it was when I played along its streets as a boy. The strange, wild life of the hunters, traders, and trappers thrilled me, and I was often on hand to see the fleets of canoes from the northland with their throng of painted Indians or, to see the voyageurs arrive with their bateaux of furs. Indians came from far and near to trade at Prairie du Chien, which was in reality a big post with stores and warehouses belonging principally to the American Fur Company. From the north, the region along Minnesota and Chippewa Rivers, and the upper Mississippi, came the Sioux, Winnebago, Chippewa, and Menominee. Down the Wisconsin came bands of Indians belonging to different tribes. The Iowa, Sauk, and Foxes came from the river below Prairie du Chien. The Indians traveled mostly by river in canoes, but a few came on ponies, afoot, and horseback from the interior.

When the Indians came down or up the river, they were painted in their most gaudy colors, the bucks using red, yellow, and green to decorate their faces, while the squaws used vermilion, and painted a round spot of this color on each cheek and a streak down the middle of their hair where it was parted. The canoes used in these journeys were both the dugout and the birch bark, and a fleet usually consisted of a dozen or fifteen boats, but I have seen as many as forty in one flotilla. The Indians brought with them furs, wild game, and pemmican made out of clean, fat venison pounded to a pulp, or of buffalo meat treated in the same manner. They also brought venison and buffalo meat that had been jerked, scorched, and smoked. They likewise brought baskets, mats, wild honey, maple sugar, berries in season, and dried lotus-root, which when cooked tasted like a potato. The Indians also made brooms out of birch, hickory, or ash wood. With these commodities they bought or secured in barter flour, pork, coffee, tobacco, blankets, hatchets, knives, dress-goods, ribbons, ammunition, and trinkets of many kinds. I must not forget to mention bows and arrows which the Indians made and sold to the whites, especially to the young boys; they also sold buckskin and moccasins. These bands of Indians would remain a week or two to trade at Prairie du Chien and the surrounding neighborhood. While there they would feast and dance and enjoy life that had a tinge of civilization in it. You could hear the tum-tum beating all night when a dance was in progress, and mingled with the crude song and the yell of the dancers, it made night hideous; silence was a luxury on nights of the Indian dance.

It was customary for the fur-trader to leave for the Indian country sometime during September. Some, who had shorter distances to travel left later, along in October. They took their supplies in large canoes, in barges, and in "a-la-cordelle." The barges were poled with long poles, while the cordelles were drawn with ropes from shore, although oars were also employed. The canoes were paddled by the French voyageurs, who sometimes used oars in the swift cross currents. The traders took along as supplies hatchets, knives, ammunition (powder and lead), blankets, and woolen dress-goods, calico, and trinkets, such as beads, ribbons, and silver ornaments of large plates and round and square silver pieces. The squaws used the latter on their dresses, while the bucks were fond of silver for decorating their hair.

Among Indian goods must be included traps for catching animals, and, last but not least, rum. A few kegs or barrels of rum would often get the trader more furs than any of his other goods. As a general thing the Indian would give more for rum or whisky than for anything else; he would even sell his squaw for fire-water. However, the trader was usually shrewd in dealing out liquor, and would give the Indian but a

small amount. A reckless trader often did a great deal of damage by selling quantities of liquor to the Indians. When a crowd of them got drunk,
fighting followed and shooting affrays. Trouble with the whites could
usually be traced to over-indulgence in fire-water.

The trader penetrated to the remote parts of the country in quest of
furs, and dispersed his trappers into the interior; then at his trading
quarters he would deal with the Indians and collect furs during the

Rafting pine on the Upper Mississippi River (c. 1900). The Upper Mississippi
River and its network of tributaries from the north and passing through the
Driftless Area saw a logging and milling boom that lasted for three-quarters of
a century. Beginning in the 1830s, white pine (and to a lesser extent Norway,
or red, pine) from the northern "pineries" was cut and floated downriver for
use in building the burgeoning cities, towns, and farms of the Midwest. At
the peak of the boom in the 1890s, Winona and Dubuque were major lumber
towns. Red Wing, Alma, Lansing, Prairie du Chien, Guttenberg, and Cassville
were also milling centers (as were many cities further downstream). Log and
lumber rafts disappeared as the northern pine was depleted. In August 1915
the steamboat *Ottumwa Belle* guided a symbolic last pine raft downstream
from Hudson, Wisconsin, to Fort Madison, Iowa. This photograph shows the
Mississippi's first floating railway bridge, between Prairie du Chien and
Marquette, which opened via steam-powered pontoons, allowing for passage
of lumber rafts, boat traffic, and ice floes.

fall, winter, and spring. Then when the spring trapping was over, with his boats loaded with fur, he would depart for the fur company's headquarters. Voyageurs were paid by the year and furnished provisions for the season; these consisted of hulled corn, peas (for soup), and hardtack, with plenty of salt and pepper, but no tea or coffee. They also had salt pork in small quantities. The foreman or boss of the trading expedition always had a drinking cabinet and carried the best of rum and whisky. He kept this under lock and key and each day would give his men a few drinks, and on rare occasions after a hard day's work would allow them an extra drink to keep up their spirits or to show them their work was rewarded.

After the spring trapping was over the trader would pack his furs and set out for the trading post. On these return journeys, the voyageurs were a merry set. They would sing their French songs by the hour, keeping time with their paddles, thus making the journey homeward a pleasant one. How often have I heard the music of these boatmen's songs float out over the valley of the Mississippi, and then watched the canoes, bateaux, and barges round a bend and appear in sight with the head canoe flying the American flag at its bow.

The traders and voyageurs remained all summer at Prairie du Chien, and then in the fall took their way into the wilderness again. The voyageurs were as a rule illiterate, and knew nothing but their work. After completing their time for the fur companies, many of them returned to Canada, though a few settled in this country. They were an honest people and many of them married among the Indians. When they went to work for the fur company they were required to sign a contract, and this bound them for a term of years. It was about the same as enlisting in the army.

From *A Raft Pilot's Log* (1930)
WALTER A. BLAIR

The logging of northwoods pine was intimately tied to the development of the Upper Mississippi River. The rafting of raw logs and sawn lumber to downstream mill sites and railroad towns provided the connection between forest and farm country. Late in his life, veteran riverboat pilot and boat-owner Walter Blair (1856–1939) recounted his experience floating the immense rafts down the Mississippi in *A Raft Pilot's Log: A History of the Great Rafting Industry on the Upper Mississippi, 1840–1915*. Blair was born in Galena and was said to have "lived his entire life on or within sight of the river."

Rafts of both logs and lumber were made up of long strings each sixteen feet wide and about four hundred feet long. The string was composed of logs placed in rows, close together, side by side and butt to butt, and the rows held together by sixteen-foot poles laid across the string and fastened to each log by hickory or elm lockdowns and wooden plugs. The lockdown was bent over the pole, the ends stuck down into one and one-quarter inch holes in the log, and then the plugs driven in to hold them.

Lumber was built in strongly framed cribs at the mill where it was sawed, and slid off into the river by a tilting cradle on which it rested.

Rafts were not made up to size until they were safely out on the Mississippi. About seven cribs long and four strings wide was the usual size run on the tributaries.

The crew lived on the raft on its voyage down to the mill, where it was to be sawed, or to the market to be sold.

There was so much objection to any structure that would catch wind and cause more work at the oars, that they were contented with very small tents made of rough boards. If any ambitious members of the crew built higher shanties they were usually told to knock them down, the first windy day. Failure to comply with this suggestion frequently resulted in a fight that was sure to end in defeat for the owner, because the pilot or the rest of the crew would knock it down anyway.

They generally had a low wide "cook-shanty" in which they sat down to eat; but often the cooking was done with only a cover to keep the rain off the stove, and the grub was served out in the open, the men standing to eat. The success of the cook depended more on his ability to lick any man in the crew than on his skill in the culinary art. Even the pilot had to give in to the cook, at least until the end of the trip. Most of the cooks were only known by their nick-names, such as Sailor Jack, Spike Ike, Calfskin Ben, Steubenville Jim, Kelly the Cutter, Hayden the Brute, Slufoot Murphey, Double Headed Bob, and many more just as musically named; all good cooks and most of them agreeable when sober, but real bad actors when liquored up.

One day two of them especially noted for their skill as cooks and also for their bibulous habits, met in the Lansing boat store and strange to tell both of them sober.

After friendly greeting Hayden said to Luker, "I thought you were on the 'Caffrey.'"

"I was."

"Why leave her; she furnishes well?"

"I couldn't give satisfaction, I was paid off."

"Where did the Icicle come from, the cabin or the messroom?"

"Why the messroom, of course. The officers were delighted with me work. The captain had tears in his eyes when I left the boat; but I couldn't please the men."

"Well Jimmie Luker! I'm really surprised that a 'cuke' of your experience should fail to handle a common situation like that. Why didn't you fill them up on sweet stuff—pie and cake and candy?"

"That's just what I did. I sat up nights making candy and gave them pie and cake three times a day and for midnight lunch and then the reprobates set up the howl for 'puddin' and I quit her right there." . . .

The first lumber was rafted down the Chippewa river in 1831, and from a small beginning the industry developed rapidly. . . . There was lively work bringing this [lumber] down the Chippewa to Read's landing, where small rafts or pieces were made up into a large Mississippi raft for downriver. . . .

The first trace of rafting on the Black river was in 1844, when Myrick and Miller sent some logs to Saint Louis, but about two years before this, the Mormons had got out some timber for their buildings at Nauvoo. . . .

The lumber handled by the Galena yards nearly all came from sawmills on the Wisconsin river. It was floated down the Wisconsin and Mississippi and towed up the Fevre river by some of the small boats, or pulled and poled up by hand, when the conditions were favorable.

Logs to supply the local sawmill came from the northern pineries in the same way. Considerable Galena capital was invested in lumbering in the Wisconsin pineries. Many of the men who worked on the boats as deckhands in summer went up to the pineries in winter and helped cut and bank the logs and in early spring, to get the logs down to the sawmills. . . .

The earliest lumbering was probably done on the Wisconsin river. Pierre Grignon had a sawmill operating in 1822, and possibly earlier, on Dutchman's creek. Some of the product was floated out and down the Mississippi, but records are very meager. By treaty with the Indians in 1836, Governor Henry Dodge secured the rights for lumbering, and by 1840 many mills were located, and some in operation.

The first raft taken through to Saint Louis of which we have reliable record, was run by Honorable Henry Merrill, who took charge of it at Portage, Wisconsin, rebuilt and refitted it at the mouth of the Wisconsin river, and delivered it in Saint Louis in 1839. The early sawmills in Galena and Dubuque were supplied with logs prior to this long trip to Saint Louis.

By 1857, three thousand men were engaged in lumbering on the Wisconsin, and the value of the log crop was estimated at $4,000,000.00. As all the lumber had to be floated out of the Wisconsin and down the Mississippi, rafting grew into a great business, and was handled quite systematically, by a hardy, rough, but industrious and reliable lot of men, working under such floating-raft pilots as Dave Philomalee, Bill Skinner, Bill Simmons, Wild Penny Joe Blow, and Sandy McPhail.

Some went through direct to Saint Louis, others peddled by string or crib to dealers in the towns along the way, and the trips would often end at Davenport, Muscatine, or Quincy. Then the crew would take passage on a steamboat going north to start another trip down. They had no work to do going up river, and usually made it one long carousal, so that by the time they reached the mouth of the "Wisconse" or Black river they were broke and glad to go to work again.

From *History of the White Pine Industry in Minnesota* (1949)

AGNES M. LARSON

In her authoritative history of the white pine industry in Minnesota, Agnes Mathilde Larson (1892–1967) described the market system that connected the white pine forests of the north, Winona and the other mill towns of the Upper Mississippi, and the timber consumers of the prairie hinterlands. Larson was born in Preston, Minnesota, and pursued her studies in history at St. Olaf College, Columbia University, and Radcliffe College. Larson returned to St. Olaf, teaching there from 1926 to 1960.

In the southern part of Minnesota Territory was located the county of Wabashaw, so named for the great Sioux chief who was active in the negotiation of the Indian Treaty of 1851. Wabashaw County was not the size of an ordinary county in Minnesota today; it was bounded on the south by Iowa, on the east by the Mississippi, on the west by the Missouri, and on the north by a line drawn westward from the junction of the St. Croix and the Mississippi. This section had no extensive forest of white pine as did much of Minnesota Territory, but it did have the finest farming land in the region. A substantial market for white pine would develop in the process of settlement in the region.

In the southeastern portion of Wabashaw County the first installment of lands surveyed by the United States in this newly acquired "Suland" was offered for sale in 1855. Then began settlement, which as usual followed the river valleys branching off from the Mississippi. The rich farmlands of the Whitewater, the Rollingstone, and the Zumbro valleys, all reaching westward from the Mississippi, were settled first. A point on the Mississippi where a number of these small valleys converged became the center of trade for that region. The place was first called Wabasha Prairie, but shortly people of a romantic mind gave it the name of Winona in memory of the comely Indian maid whose loyalty had become a legend in Minnesota.

Winona, on flat land on the west bank of the Mississippi, was snugly protected by hills at her back, and beyond those hills lay some of Minnesota's richest farm land. The pioneers on that farm land had to have shelter, which meant lumber. Winona became the point of lumber manufacture. There was no commercial white pine in the vicinity of Winona, but logs came from the St. Croix or the Chippewa in the form of rafts, and at Winona those logs were changed into lumber with which to build farm homes. . . .

From 1858 to 1868 Winona produced 160,000,000 feet of lumber. A small portion of this was marketed downriver, but the larger share was sold to the incoming settlers of the uplands above. Winona in the sixties could hardly keep pace with the demand for lumber. . . .

Untitled drawing by Lawrence E. Blair (c. 1948). Overland transport of goods
was difficult for early Europeans in the Driftless Area. Exports such as fur,
lead, timber, and wheat were generally gathered near trade centers located on
riverways, where they were exchanged for provisions. This drawing, which
suggests the challenge of travel from the Driftless uplands into the river
valleys, was commissioned by the Wisconsin Highway Commission as part of
a series of works depicting the development of transportation in the state.

Farmers came to Winona all the way from Owatonna, Clinton Falls,
and Blooming Prairie to buy their lumber; all these towns were located
in Steele County, in the fourth tier of counties west of the Mississippi.
The length of the smoothly paved state highway from Owatonna to Winona at the present time is ninety miles, a distance comfortably covered
in two hours by automobile. But in the late 1850s and early 1860s it was
a long and hard trip.

Farmers would travel in groups with four, six, or eight teams of oxen.
These grizzled men of the new West were accustomed to the cold, so
they could sleep out in the open under the winter sky. They carried their
food because inns were few and far between. A round trip from Blooming Prairie to Winona required at least six days. Stockton, located on the
western edge of the Winona hills, marked the gateway from the plateau
to the valley below. To reach the river town from the uplands was a
rough, winding drive of eleven miles. Before beginning the descent into

the valley the farmers from the back country spent the night at Stockton's well-known inn. After a long day's trip from Stockton to Winona
and back, they again spent the night at the inn before they started on
their tedious journey homeward. They usually carried wheat to Winona
and brought back lumber and groceries.

Winona lumbermen considered the region westward, including Owatonna and its environs, their market in the days of oxen. They sensed
early the need for better roads, and on August 13, 1857, a meeting was
called in Winona to plan the building of a road up the Stockton Hill.
These men of business in Winona were always mindful of the market
in the interior. In 1857 Laird, Norton and Company urged their "interior
friends" to note that they could "supply all our inland towns" with lumber "of qualities to satisfy the most particular." Lumber advertisements
stating that "grain will be taken in part pay at cash prices" were not
unusual. Steele County, Olmsted, and Fillmore were all a part of the back
country whose market belonged to Winona, although farmers in southern Fillmore County sometimes hauled their lumber from McGregor,
farther south on the Mississippi in Iowa. But that lumber, too, was white
pine from the Upper Mississippi which had been rafted downriver.

The long haul to the river town was fraught with difficulty and danger.
The roads were little better than prairie trails and forest paths. The present generation speeding up Stockton Hill on a beautifully constructed
piece of road, which cost the state of Minnesota about $700,000, can
hardly imagine the unfordable streams of the spring and the heavy,
almost impassable roads where the pioneer made his way when the winter thaw was passing. Much hauling was done in the winter, but the snow
drifts, the pitch holes, and the sharp, cold wind made the trip to market
one the farmers dreaded. There were the Indians, too, and at times there
were robbers. The trip to market was no small incident in pioneer life.

From *Order Upon the Land* (1976)

HILDEGARD BINDER JOHNSON

The rolling topography of the Driftless Area resisted the imposition of
the land surveyors' rigid grid of township and range lines, so evident in

the checkerboard pattern of other midwestern landscapes. Intrigued by this contrast, geographer Hildegard Binder Johnson (1908–1993) explored the origins and history of the U.S. public land survey system and its impact on the American landscape in *Order Upon the Land: The U.S. Rectangular Land Survey and the Upper Mississippi Country*. Johnson was born in Berlin, fled Germany in 1934, and after World War II came to Minnesota, where she founded the geography department at Macalester College. In this excerpt Johnson reviews the evolution of overland travel routes through the Driftless Area.

During the Black Hawk War, a secure route from the lead-mining region to Lake Michigan was needed, and in 1832 Congress appropriated $50,000 for the survey of the road that connected Fort Howard on Lake Michigan to Fort Crawford at Prairie du Chien. The 234-mile route ran southwest from Green Bay to Portage and Fort Winnebago, turned south to Poynette and the northern shore of Lake Mendota, and then bent west to follow the divide between the Wisconsin and Rock rivers (the "Military Ridge"), passing through Dodgeville and Monfort (both lead-mining towns dating from the 1820s) to Fennimore and Patch Grove, where it bent back across the Wisconsin to Prairie du Chien. The commandants of the three forts were responsible for construction of the road, which was begun in 1835 and completed in 1837. Described in the 1840s as "very high and commanding a fine view," on road maps today it is designated as a "scenic route."

The Military Road had many more ascents, inclines, and curves than modern Highway 18, which follows it closely. But it was important for the shipping of lead until railroads began to reach the lead-mining region in the mid-1850s. Before the road was built, lead from southwestern Wisconsin was shipped to Milwaukee via New Orleans, New York, the Erie Canal (where shipments of Wisconsin lead were granted special rates), and the Great Lakes back to Wisconsin's shore on Lake Michigan.

For an example of the persistence of roads marked by the surveyors on their maps let us follow the journey of a man from Braintree, Vermont, who according to his diary was determined to reach River Falls on the Kinnickinnic River at the northernmost edge of the Hill Country. Leaving Vermont in late fall 1855, he traveled by railroad to Chicago and continued by wagon to Galena. In February 1856 he and a party of

THEORETICAL MAP OF WISCONSIN
DURING THE SECOND GLACIAL EPOCH.

EXPLANATION.

Glaciers, Glacial Lakes and Rivers in blue.
Outlines and Non-glacial Streams in black.

THE EXTENT OF THESE MARGINAL LAKES IS UNDETERMINED

Plate 1. "Theoretical Map of Wisconsin during the Second Glacial Epoch,"
T. C. Chamberlin (1883). This map of the Driftless Area, hemmed in by lobes
of glacial ice during the Pleistocene, was prepared by T. C. Chamberlin for the
1883 volume *Geology of Wisconsin: Survey of 1873–1879, Volume 1,* which
Chamberlin edited. The map distilled information from advances in
glaciology and field studies within and beyond the Driftless Area over the
prior sixty years.

Plate 2. Main bison panel, photograph by Geri Schrab (2016). Exposed stone faces on steep hillsides are characteristic of the Driftless Area, as are caves within the hills. Throughout the millennia humans have found these faces a natural canvas. Many marks of ancient inhabitants have been sufficiently durable to withstand natural wear and secluded enough to escape inadvertent or willful destruction. The site photographed here is in a part of Wisconsin's Driftless where remains of bison are rare, but shoulder blade bones used as hoes have been found near prehistoric settlements. The detail of these forms further suggests that the artists had intimate experience with bison, which in general were more common on the plains to the west of the Driftless. Unlike most petroglyphs, which are outlined by grooves carved into the stone, several of these figures were created by sanding down a depression, creating a three-dimensional form.

Plate 3. *Third Buffalo Hiding*, Geri Schrab (2016). Ancient voices endure in the unique rock art throughout the Driftless Area. Many compositions represent striking expressions of universal forms, and many are also subtle and enigmatic. As shown in this painting of the adjacent panel, Geri Schrab renders rock art in reverent watercolors, translating the works of the early artists of the Driftless Area onto the modern page. In *Hidden Thunder: Rock Art of the Upper Midwest*, Schrab writes, "I do not grasp all the science, and I do not know the full story of this site, but the spirit of the land . . . connects my heart to these ancient, sacred places. It is my love of the land and its spirit that I paint."

Plate 4. *Black Hawk, Prominent Sac Chief,* George Catlin (1832). Perhaps the most famous and tragic of Native Americans associated with the Driftless Area, Chief Black Sparrow Hawk, or *Mà-ka-tai-me-she-kià-kiàk,* led more than one thousand Sauk, Fox, Potawatomi, and Kickapoo on an ill-fated attempt to return to their homeland in 1832. After pursuit across the Driftless and the massacre of his band at the Battle of Bad Axe, Black Hawk surrendered. He was painted several months later while imprisoned near St. Louis by the renowned portraitist George Catlin.

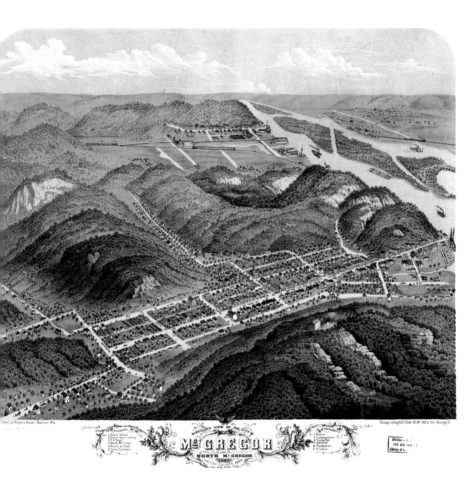

Plate 5. "Bird's Eye View of the City of McGregor and North McGregor, Clayton County, Iowa 1869." While serving with the Ohio Volunteers in the Civil War, Prussian immigrant Albert Ruger sketched images of the Union camps from an overhead perspective. Ruger settled in Michigan after the war and began to adapt his technique to depict the burgeoning towns and cities of mid-America. He soon teamed up with Joseph J. Stoner of Madison to produce panoramic, or "bird's eye view," maps. Over the next three decades the industry thrived across the Unites States. Southern Wisconsin became an incubator of panoramic map artists, with Ruger among the most prominent. This view of McGregor, Iowa (with Prairie du Chien in the background) was among the earliest products of the Ruger and Stoner partnership.

Plate 6. *Boyhood Home of Hamlin Garland,* Hans John Stoltenberg (1937).
Wisconsin artist Hans Stoltenberg (1879–1963), a German immigrant who
had studied at the Milwaukee Art Institute, often portrayed rural landscapes
in his work and favored several sites within the Driftless Area. In the summer
of 1937 Stoltenberg painted this scene near Onalaska and was later informed
by a neighbor that it was the childhood home of Hamlin Garland. Stoltenberg
sent a photo of the painting to Garland, who was then living in Hollywood,
California, asking him to confirm the connection, which Garland did.

Plate 7. *Wisconsin Farm Scene*, John Steuart Curry (1941). John Steuart Curry (1897–1946) was already a highly regarded regionalist, closely identified with his native Kansas, when in 1936 he became the first artist-in-residence at any American university, at the University of Wisconsin in Madison. Curry studied at the Art Institute of Chicago and in Paris and was living in Connecticut at the time of his appointment. Significantly, the residency was based within the university's College of Agriculture, and Curry would devote himself to teaching and promoting the visual arts in rural communities. *Wisconsin Farm Scene*, an adapted perspective of the lower Wisconsin River valley, was one of Curry's last works.

Plate 8. *Residence of Mr. Martin Lutscher. Town Honey Creek. Wis.*, Paul Siefert (c. 1880). The farmyards and houses of rural Iowa, Richland, and Sauk counties in Wisconsin were the focus for the watercolor works of folk artist Paul Adolph Siefert (1846–1921). Siefert was born in Dresden, Germany, and studied forestry and horticulture before immigrating to Gotham, Wisconsin, in 1867. Siefert began painting his farm portraits in the late 1870s, selling them to his farmer clients for $2.50. His exacting style captured the configuration of the diversified farms of the time, embedded amid the natural setting of Driftless bluffs. Siefert's work gained posthumous recognition beginning in the 1950s, and in recent years his works have become treasured by museums and private collectors.

Plate 9. *Milking Time*, Lavern Kammerude (1981). Lavern Kammerude of Blanchardville left school in eighth grade for a career of farm work. He began painting later in life and was largely self-taught. Kammerude's paintings, and the vanishing aspects of country life they carefully depict, evoke nostalgia for many Driftless residents.

Plate 10. *Contour Farming*, Jim Klousia (2013). Plowing and planting crops along the land's contours—rather than in straight rows up and down sloping fields—was a major advance in limiting the rampant soil erosion on farms in the Driftless Area. Beginning in the 1930s, Coon Valley was home to the nation's first watershed conservation project, in which farmers, university scientists, CCC workers, engineers, and government officials cooperated in adapting conservation practices suited to the landscape. Along with the contoured rows, this photograph from the Coon Creek watershed shows other soil conservation measures still in practice throughout the Driftless: wooded hillsides, check dams and terraces, and strips of different annual crops interspersed with perennial forages and pastures. Photographer Jim Klousia captured this scene while airborne for *Edible Madison* magazine, where he is creative director.

Plate 11. *Cow Crossing in Grant County*, Kerry G. Hill (2012). Kerry Hill, a photographer from Madison, took this image of an Amish boy herding cows along a roadside in Grant County, Wisconsin, between Fennimore and Lancaster.

Plate 12. Hmong Pa Dau (c. 1990). Many Hmong were allies of United States military in Southeast Asia during the Vietnam conflict and fled the persecution that followed. Many of these refugees came to Wisconsin and Minnesota. As they did elsewhere, the Hmong who settled in Decorah, Iowa, produced textile art both to maintain tradition and to generate income. Called Pa Dau (an American adaptation of *paj ntaub*, meaning "flowery cloth"), the intricate craft helps communicate stories and symbols in a culture that originally lacked a written language. This Pa Dau features a cucumber seed motif, one of many Hmong designs that reflect natural forms in their hilly ancestral lands. Now in the collection of Luther College's Anthropology Department, it was a gift to a Decorah resident who had helped Hmong people adapt to their new life in the Driftless.

Plate 13. *Syttende Mai 2015*, Lauren Louise Anderson (2015). Decorah, Iowa, is one of several Driftless communities where descendants of Norwegian settlers celebrate the National Day of Norway, Syttende Mai. Lauren Louise Anderson, professor of African American History at Luther College in Decorah, describes her composition *Syttende Mai 2015* this way: "This woman dressed in a traditional Norwegian bunad who sips coffee from a paper cup, where in time does she belong? Must she choose a time or can she belong to both?"

Plate 14. Steamboat *J. S.* on the Mississippi River (c. 1900). The first steamboat to come to the Upper Mississippi River was the *Virginia*, arriving in the lead region in 1823. Over the next century, steamboats remained the dominant form of transportation on the river. In this color postcard from the early twentieth century, the sternwheel excursion steamboat *J. S.* prepares to leave La Crosse for Winona, Minnesota. The crane on the front of the steamer is attached to a passenger boarding bridge.

Plate 15. *Traffic Serenade*, Paul Bergquist (2012). This familiar view down 4th Street in downtown La Crosse was painted by plein air artist and physician Paul Bergquist of Viroqua.

Plate 16. *The Remarkable Cow*, John Craig (2016). From his collection *Lost Treasures from the Heart of the Driftless*, illustrator John Craig of rural Rolling Ground, Wisconsin, penned the following to accompany this print:

There once was a lovely Holstein, and on her hide
was a perfect silhouette of the now-famous Driftless Area.
When lost travelers passed by and asked,
"Where are we, son?"
The young lad would put a finger on her spot and say,
"Why . . . you're right here."

other travelers arrived at Prairie du Chien and proceeded to Viroqua, a small village in the "timber" on a ridge, where they were delayed for a few days by a snowstorm. Continuing on the height that divides the Kickapoo River from Raccoon Creek and the La Crosse River, they descended to the flats of the La Crosse and the settlement of Sparta, where they transferred to sleds for the journey to Black River Falls. The route continued around the ravines of the headwaters of the Trempealeau River to "Beef River Station" on the Buffalo River, to Eau Claire, and to Wilson's Mills on the Red Cedar River. The Vermonter reached River Falls on the Kinnickinnic in March. His route may be followed on the surveyors' plats, which are marked with notations such as "Road from Prairie du Chien to Lake Superior" or "Wagon Road to Black River Falls." The course of this route, which is followed for roundly 220 miles between Prairie du Chien and River Falls by modern roads and in part by an interstate highway, was dictated most of all by topography. Complaints that a stage traveler in the 1850s expressed about the "perilous succession of ups and downs" did not refer to steep ascents and inclines, which are a feature of straight roads in the Hill Country today, but to the jolts caused by wagon wheels hitting the not-infrequent stumps in the road.

Some stagecoach routes could be followed by the railroads. Railroads require a nearly "water-level route" as the Burlington Railroad calls its line from Chicago to St. Paul, which follows the Mississippi floodplain from Savanna, Illinois, to the Twin Cities. Laying tracks on alluvial plains and broad ridges was not difficult, and the major lines used these easy thoroughfares. The Milwaukee & Mississippi Railroad from Madison to Prairie du Chien, completed in 1854, followed the Wisconsin River Valley. The Northwestern Railroad out of Madison followed the Military Ridge west of Mount Horeb. The Milwaukee and St. Paul Railroad, completed in 1867, skirted the northern edge of the Hill Country, connecting towns which originated near the sites of early sawmills, such as Eau Claire and Menomonie. But pulling trains from the river bottoms to the upland involved rock cuts, sharp turns around hills, and bridges over swales and ravines. Many roadbeds were laid on narrow, band-like terraces cut from the hillsides and on embankments across valleys, and wooden trestle bridges were frequent. Few of these bridges remain today, most of them having been dismantled after branch lines were discontinued. Cast-iron bridges, patented in 1876, were rare, although one stands on the Upper Iowa River near Bluffton, Iowa.

Crossing the Mississippi presented another problem during the westward movement of settlers and the eastward movement of wheat, the
first major cash crop west of the Mississippi. Ferries worked around
the clock between Prairie du Chien and McGregor on the Iowa side of
the river transporting railroad cars—one at a time—across the water, a
time-consuming and risky procedure. In 1874, however, the ingenious
construction of the wooden pontoon bridge, the largest of its kind, eliminated the awkward loading and unloading of cars and permitted trains
to cross the river without impeding navigation.

Motor transport increasingly replaced railroads in the twentieth century. The Great River Road follows the earliest transportation route in
the Upper Mississippi Country, and in several stretches runs parallel to
or directly over earlier roads. Interstate Highway 94 follows the Vermonter's route of 1856 between Black River Falls and Menomonie, and
Interstate 90 runs through the alluvial flats of the La Crosse River between Sparta and La Crosse. On the opposite side of the Mississippi out
of La Crescent the interstate highway is projected to continue over the
ridge separating the Root River and the Whitewater River watersheds.
These examples must suffice to illustrate the enduring relationship
between roads and topography. It makes the study of their antecedents,
the trails and roads in the surveyors' notes, meaningful in historical
geography.

Dreamers (1931)

LAURA SHERRY

In 1931 poet, actress, and theater advocate Laura Case Sherry (1876–1947)
published *Old Prairie du Chien*, a limited-edition collection of poems portraying the "varied and interesting" lives of those inhabiting her home
town. After studying literature and drama at the University of Wisconsin
and Northwestern University, Sherry pursued her interest in theater. In
1911 she founded the experimental Wisconsin Players in Milwaukee, dedicated to democratizing the theater experience and advancing amateur
community theater across the state. Two other poems from *Old Prairie
du Chien* appear in other sections of this collection.

Prairie du Chien
Quick with the blood of French adventurers
Preserves the stone walls of an old fur trading post
By the changing sands of the Mississippi.
John Jacob Astor
Bartered with the Indians at the mouth of the Wisconsin.
John Jacob Astor
Cornered the pelts of the Northwest.

Fifth Avenue
Builds and wrecks and builds again.
Fifth Avenue
Caught in the quick of its changing sands
Does not preserve stone walls
Of old fur trading posts.

Brisbois Fur Trading Post (c. 1920). This stone warehouse was built in 1828
by Québécois Jean Joseph Rollette, a prominent Prairie du Chien fur trader
who was among those residents who fought for the British when they
overtook Fort Shelby there during the War of 1812. Rollette became an agent
of John Jacob Astor's American Fur Company and this building, also known
as the Astor Fur Warehouse, served as a principal outpost of that global
empire. A museum of the fur trade now occupies the building.

7

SETTLER STORIES

F OR SEVERAL CENTURIES, the Driftless Area provided raw materials
for the hungry Spanish, French, and British empires. The earliest
European settlements arose along major rivers and overland trails
to feed the fur trade, lead mines, and, later, the lumber market. Prairie du
Chien, Dubuque, and Mineral Point swelled to populations larger than
the young cities of Milwaukee and Chicago to the east.

As migration brought more people into the region, the appetite for
the fruits of the land grew. Farmsteads sprouted across the Driftless
hills and valleys, and camps that once comprised mostly frontiers*men*
grew into frontier communities with families. Outposts and crossroads
became villages and towns. Churches, commerce, and municipalities
took root. The new settlers constructed bridges, dug wells, dammed
rivers, and built granaries and sawmills. The face of the Driftless was
changing.

As the young United States expanded and elbowed its way into the
interior, it pushed aside Native peoples and European powers alike. The
new nation converted the land itself into a commodity. Federal land surveyors superimposed the grid of town and section lines over the region's
natural boundaries of winding ridgelines and sinuous rivers. Now subject to uniform measure and standard legal description, land could be
bought, sold, "improved," and taxed as private property.

Americans from the east and European immigrants acquired land
and settled the Driftless. They arrived in waves and persisted in many
places as distinct ethnic enclaves: Welsh in Mineral Point, Norwegians
in Westby, Italians in Genoa, Germans in Guttenberg, African Americans in Cheyenne Valley. Places such as Czechville, Irish Coulee, French
Island, and Yankeetown bear their history in their names. The process of

settlement has never stopped, even as the motives of subsequent generations changed. The back-to-the-land movement saw disaffected flower
children channeling the idealism of the 1960s into latter-day homestead-
ing. At the same time, the Driftless became home to Hmong, Hispanic,
and Amish peoples.

The story of the settlement of the Driftless is also one of disposses-
sion. Most fundamentally, Native peoples were removed to make way
for the new immigrants. The historic military outpost at Fort Crawford
reminds us of this violent history. Others, too, have lost their Driftless
homes. In 1941 the U.S. government claimed ten thousand acres at the
eastern edge of the Driftless, in Sauk Prairie, uprooting more than eighty
farm families to build the Badger Army Ammunition Plant. At La Farge,
the government took possession of some 140 farms for a planned dam
on the Kickapoo River that was never built. In a twist of history, the Ho-
Chunk Nation acquired portions of both these public properties, adding
these common lands to other parcels that tribal members have purchased in the effort to reclaim their place in the Driftless.

To whom any land ultimately belongs is a question that may never be
settled. But for many who have settled here, there has never been a question that they belong to the Driftless.

Sesquicentennial Song:
For Wisconsin Statehood, 1848 (2008)

Thomas R. Smith

Thomas R. Smith lives in River Falls, Wisconsin, and teaches poetry at
the Loft Literary Center in Minneapolis. Smith's poetry has appeared in
many journals and in seven published volumes. "Sesquicentennial Song"
was included in Smith's chapbook *Kinnickinnic*.

In Ouisconsin the Blackrobes wanted souls, but the traders wanted
furs and squaws, and the settlers who followed them wanted
land, lumber, and wheat.

At Portage a mile-and-a-half-long trail fifteen thousand years old
tied the knot of Empire, marrying the North Atlantic to the Gulf
of Mexico.
Immigrants wrote to relatives in Germany and Sweden of the sails
on Milwaukee Harbor, struck out following maps that repeated
the same speculators' errors for decades.
At night on raw farmsteads still moist with native blood, enraged
spirits hissed in the trees while candle-light caught the gilt-edged
Bible.
We who were born in the shadow of the shot towers took lead in
through the soles of our shoes, grew heavy-footed with a drunken
shuffling.
We never looked askance at our assumed innocence, nor at the
crowded docks on Lake Michigan, convinced that our bad luck,
depression, and illness were only our own.

From *Wau-Bun: The Early Day in the Northwest* (1856)

JULIETTE KINZIE

Juliette Augusta Magill Kinzie (1806–1870) was born in Connecticut and
came to Wisconsin in 1830 when her husband, John Kinzie, was appointed
Indian sub-agent to the Ho-Chunk Nation, stationed at Fort Winnebago
(the portage point between the Fox and Wisconsin Rivers). The Ho-
Chunk had recently signed treaties ceding lands to the east and south,
and the Black Hawk War would commence in 1832. In *Wau-Bun*, her narrative of her experiences at Fort Winnebago, Kinzie recounts an overland
trip to Chicago that she and her husband took in March of 1831. Instead
of the more direct southeast route—passage over the Rock River being
"impossible at this season of the year"—they traveled via the "Four
Lakes" (Madison), the "Blue Mound," and Ridgeway; Hamilton's Diggings (present-day Wiota), a lead mine established by William Hamilton,
a son of Alexander Hamilton; and Kellogg's Grove in Illinois.

Sketch of Mineral Point, Aaron Bohrod (1973). This Mineral Point street
scene, sketched by Aaron Bohrod (1907–1992), appeared in the book
Wisconsin Sketches (1973). Bohrod was a native of Chicago, where he studied at
the School of the Art Institute. In 1948 he succeeded John Steuart Curry as
artist-in-residence at the University of Wisconsin–Madison, a position he held
for the next twenty-five years.

The next morning, after a cheerful breakfast, at which we were joined
by the Rev. Mr. Kent, of Galena, we prepared for our journey. I had re-
conciled my husband to continuing our route [from "Blue Mound"]
towards Chicago, by assuring him that I felt as fresh and bright as when
I first set out from home.

There seemed some apprehension, however, that we might have
difficulty in "striking the trail" to Hamilton's *diggings*, our next point of
destination.

The directions we received were certainly obscure. We were to pursue a given trail for a certain number of miles, when we should come
to a crossing into which we were to turn, taking an easterly direction;
after a time, this would bring us to a deep trail leading straight to Hamilton's. In this open country there are no landmarks. One elevation is so

exactly like another, that if you lose your trail there is almost as little hope of regaining it as of finding a pathway in the midst of the ocean.

The trail, it must be remembered, is not a broad highway, but a narrow path, deeply indented by the hoofs of the horses on which the Indians travel in single file. So deeply is it sunk in the sod which covers the prairies, that it is difficult, sometimes, to distinguish it at a distance of a few rods.

It was new ground to Mr. Kinzie, whose journeys from the Portage to Chicago had hitherto been made in the direct route by Kosh-ko-nong. He therefore obliged Mr. Morrison to repeat the directions again and again, though Plante, our guide, swaggered and talked big, averring that "he knew every hill and stream and point of woods from that spot to Chicago."

We had not proceeded many miles on our journey, however, before we discovered that Monsieur Plante was profoundly ignorant of the country, so that Mr. Kinzie was obliged to take the lead himself, and make his way as he was best able, according to the directions he had received. Nothing, however, like the "cross trails" we had been promised met our view, and the path on which we had set out diverged so much from what we knew to be the right direction, that we were at length compelled to abandon it altogether.

We travelled the livelong day, barely making a halt at noon to bait our horses and refresh ourselves with a luncheon. The ride was as gloomy and desolate as could well be imagined. A rolling prairie, unvaried by forest or stream—hillock rising after hillock, at every ascent of which we vainly hoped to see a distant fringe of "*timber*." But the same cheerless, unbounded prospect everywhere met the eye, diversified only here and there by the oblong openings, like gigantic graves, which marked an unsuccessful search for indications of a lead-mine.

So great was our anxiety to recover our trail, for the weather was growing more cold, and the wind more sharp and piercing, that we were not tempted to turn from our course even by the appearance, more than once, of a gaunt prairie-wolf, peering over the nearest rising-ground and seeming to dare us to an encounter. The Frenchmen, it is true, would instinctively give a shout and spur on their horses, while the hounds, Kelda and Cora, would rush to the chase; but the bourgeois soon called them back, with a warning that we must attend strictly to the prosecution of our journey. Just before sunset we crossed, with some difficulty, a muddy stream, which was bordered by a scanty belt of trees, making a tolerable encamping-ground; and of this we gladly availed ourselves, although we knew not whether it was near or remote from the place we were in search of.

We had ridden at least fifty miles since leaving Morrison's, yet I was sensible of very little fatigue; there was, however, a vague feeling of discomfort at the idea of being lost in this wild, cold region, altogether different from anything I had ever before experienced. The encouraging tones of my husband's voice, however, "Cheer up, wifie—we will find the trail to-morrow," served to dissipate all uneasiness.

The exertions of the men soon made our "camp" comfortable, notwithstanding the difficulty of driving the tent-pins into the frozen ground, and the want of trees sufficiently large to make a *rousing* fire. The place was a *stony side-hill*, as it would be called in New England, where such things abound; but we were not disposed to be fastidious, so we ate our salt ham and toasted our bread, and lent a pleased ear to the chatter of our Frenchmen, who could not sufficiently admire the heroism of "Madame John" amid the vicissitudes that befell her.

The wind, which at bed-time was sufficiently high to be uncomfortable, increased during the night. It snowed heavily, and we were every moment in dread that the tent would be carried away; but the matter was settled differently by the snapping of the poles, and the falling of the whole, with its superincumbent weight of snow, in a mass upon us.

Mr. Kinzie roused up his men, and at their head he sallied into the neighboring wood to cut a new set of poles, leaving me to bear the burden of the whole upon my shoulders, my only safety from the storm being to keep snugly housed beneath the canvas.

With some difficulty a sort of support was at length adjusted for the tent-covering, which answered our purpose tolerably well until the break of day, when our damp and miserable condition made us very glad to rise and hang round the fire until breakfast was dispatched, and the horses once more saddled for our journey.

The prospect was not an encouraging one. Around us was an unbroken sheet of snow. We had no compass, and the air was so obscured by the driving sleet, that it was often impossible to tell in which direction the sun was. I tied my husband's silk pocket-handkerchief over my veil, to protect my face from the wind and icy particles with which the air was filled, and which cut like a razor; but, although shielded in every way that circumstances rendered possible, I suffered intensely from the cold.

We pursued our way, mile after mile, entering every point of woods, in hopes of meeting with, at least, some Indian wigwam at which we could gain intelligence. Every spot was solitary and deserted; not even the trace of a recent fire, to cheer us with the hope of human beings within miles of us.

Suddenly, a shout from the foremost of the party made each heart bound with joy.

"*Une clôture! une clôture!*" (A fence! a fence!)

It was almost like life to the dead.

We spurred on, and indeed perceived a few straggling rails crowning a rising ground at no great distance.

Never did music sound so sweet as the crowing of a cock which at this moment saluted our ears.

Following the course of the inclosure down the opposite slope, we came upon a group of log cabins, low, shabby, and unpromising in their appearance, but a most welcome shelter from the pelting storm.

"Whose cabins are these?" asked Mr. Kinzie, of a man who was cutting wood at the door of one.

"Hamilton's," was his reply; and he stepped forward at once to assist us to alight, hospitality being a matter of course in these wild regions.

We were shown into the most comfortable-looking of the buildings. A large fire was burning in the clay chimney, and the room was of a genial warmth, notwithstanding the apertures, many inches in width, beside the doors and windows. A woman in a tidy calico dress, and shabby black silk cap trimmed with still shabbier lace, rose from her seat beside a sort of bread-trough, which fulfilled the office of cradle to a fine, fat baby. She made room for us at the fire, but was either too timid or too ignorant to relieve me of wrappings and defences, now heavy with the snow.

I soon contrived, with my husband's aid, to disembarrass myself of them; and, having seen me comfortably disposed of, and in a fair way to be thawed after my freezing ride, he left me, to see after his men and horses.

He was a long time absent, and I expected he would return accompanied by our host; but when he reappeared it was to tell me, laughing, that Mr. Hamilton hesitated to present himself before me, being unwilling that one who had been acquainted with his family at the East should see him in his present mode of life. However, this feeling apparently wore off, for before dinner he came in and was introduced to me, and was as agreeable and polite as the son of Alexander Hamilton would naturally be.

The housekeeper, who was the wife of one of the miners, prepared us a plain, comfortable dinner, and a table as long as the dimensions of the cabin would admit was set out, the end nearest the fire being covered with somewhat nicer furniture and more delicate fare than the remaining portion.

The blowing of a horn was the signal for the entrance of ten or twelve miners, who took their places below us at the table. They were the roughest-looking set of men I ever beheld, and their language was as uncouth as their persons. They wore hunting-shirts, trowsers, and moccasins of deer-skin, the former being ornamented at the seams with a fringe of the same, while a colored belt around the waist, in which was stuck a large hunting-knife, gave each the appearance of a brigand. . . .

Mr. Hamilton passed most of the afternoon with us; for the storm raged so without, that to proceed on our journey was out of the question. He gave us many pleasant anecdotes and reminiscences of his early life in New York, and of his adventures since he had come to the Western wilderness. When obliged to leave us for awhile, he furnished us with some books to entertain us, the most interesting of which was the biography of his father.

Could this illustrious man have foreseen in what a scene—the dwelling of his son—this book was to be one day perused, what would have been his sensations?

The most amusing part of our experience was yet to come. I had been speculating, as evening approached, on our prospects for the night's accommodation. As our pale, melancholy-looking landlady and her fat baby were evidently the only specimens of the feminine gender about the establishment, it was hardly reasonable to suppose that any of the other cabins contained wherewithal to furnish us a comfortable lodging, and the one in which we were offered nothing of the sort to view, but two beds, uncurtained, extended against the farther wall. My doubts were after a time resolved, by observing the hostess stretch a cord between the two, on which she hung some petticoats and extra garments, by way of a partition, after which she invited us to occupy one of them.

My only preparation was, to wrap my cloak around me and lie down with my face to the wall; but the good people were less ceremonious, for at the distance of scarcely two feet, we could not be mistaken in the sound of their garments being, not "laid aside," but whipped over the partition-wall between us.

Our waking thoughts, however, were only those of thankfulness for so comfortable a lodging after the trials and fatigues we had undergone; and even these were of short duration, for our eyes were soon closed in slumber.

The next day's sun rose clear and bright. Refreshed and invigorated, we looked forward with pleasure to a recommencement of our journey, confident of meeting no more mishaps by the way. Mr. Hamilton kindly offered to accompany us to his next neighbor's, the trifling distance of twenty-five miles. . . .

The miner who owned the wife and baby, and who, consequently, was somewhat more humanized than his comrades, in taking leave of us "wished us well out of the country, and that we might never have occasion to return to it!"

"I pity a body," said he, "when I see them making such an awful mistake as to come out this way; for comfort never touched this Western country."

We found Mr. Hamilton as agreeable a companion as on the preceding day, but a most desperate rider. He galloped on at such a rate that, had I not exchanged my pony for the fine, noble Jerry, I should have been in danger of being left behind.

Well mounted as we all were, he sometimes nearly distanced us. We were now among the branches of the Pickatonick, and the country had lost its prairie character and become rough and broken. We went dashing on, sometimes down ravines, sometimes through narrow passes, where, as I followed, I left fragments of my veil upon the projecting and interwoven branches. Once my hat became entangled, and, had not my husband sprung to my rescue, I must have shared the fate of Absalom, Jerry's ambition to keep his place in the race making it probable he would do as did the mule who was under the unfortunate prince.

There was no halting upon the route, and, as we kept the same pace until three o'clock in the afternoon, it was beyond a question that when we reached "Kellogg's," we had travelled at least thirty miles. . . .

Macaja Revels Camped at a
Stream of Water (2013)

Fabu

In the mid-nineteenth century former slaves and free black settlers established several African American communities in the Driftless Area. The
best known and documented of these communities were in Wisconsin's
Cheyenne Valley in Vernon County and Pleasant Ridge in Grant County.
Around 1854 Macaja Revels came to Cheyenne Valley to settle and farm.
Poet Fabu's reflection on his migration appeared in the collection *Echolocations: Poets Map Madison*. Fabu lives in Madison, where she studied
African languages and literature at the University of Wisconsin and where
she has served as poet laureate.

In *Black Settlers in Rural Wisconsin*
there is a notation that a Black man
Macaja Revels, born in 1800 on the Cherokee reservation
migrated to Dane county and camped at a stream of water
eighteen miles north of the village of Madison.
Macaja traveled on to buy land elsewhere.
There is no record of physical description; light, dark or
    medium
what he accomplished or who his parents were.
In 1800, a Black man was both an oddity and invisible
but the land welcomed him.
The land was cheap, fertile with plenty
there was schooling for children and protection for escaped
    slaves
so Macaja could rest briefly.
Who remembers Macaja Revels, Black settler in the 1800's
Who camped at a refreshing stream

Eighteen miles north of the village of Madison
but moved on, maybe knowing there would be no welcome in
    Madison.
Who remembers that Black people came to Wisconsin
to be free?

Cemetery at Pleasant Ridge (c. 1958). In 1848 freed slaves who had moved
from Virginia with their former owner settled in the community of Pleasant
Ridge (now Beetown), five miles west of Lancaster in Grant County,
Wisconsin. Other former slaves would come to Pleasant Ridge from Missouri,
Arkansas, and Tennessee. Along with the settlement at Cheyenne Valley in
Vernon County, it was one of several rural African American communities in
Wisconsin's portion of the Driftless Area. The black population eventually
declined as younger members moved away. In this photo from the late 1950s,
Charles Green, the last surviving member of the African American
community at Pleasant Ridge, stands beside the community graveyard.

From *A Badger Boy in Blue* (1862)

CHAUNCEY COOKE

Chauncey Cooke (1846–1919) and his family came to Wisconsin in 1855 and were the first white settlers in Buffalo County's Dover Township. In the fall of 1862, when Cooke was sixteen years old, he lied about his age, traveled to La Crosse, and joined the Twenty-fifth Wisconsin Volunteer Infantry. Expecting to be sent immediately to the South, he was instead detailed to Fort Snelling in St. Paul to await possible assignment in suppressing the Sioux Uprising in western Minnesota. In early 1863 Cooke's unit left for Kentucky, taking part that spring in the Vicksburg Campaign. After the war Cooke returned to Buffalo County and became a teacher and farmer. Late in his life Cooke edited and published his Civil War letters, including this selection that first appeared posthumously in the *Wisconsin Magazine of History* in 1920. His collected letters were published in 2007 as *A Badger Boy in Blue: The Civil War Letters of Chauncey H. Cooke.*

New Richmond, Minn.
Co. G. 25th Regt.
Nov. 4th, 1862.

Dear sister Doe: Your favor of Oct. 25th rec'd yesterday. It seemed so good to me that I read it over twice before stopping. I am just like other soldiers I suppose, crazy to get letters from dear ones at home. I wrote mother only a day or two ago but that makes no difference, I am glad for an excuse to write home. . . .

I am real glad you are making such headway in your books. You are father's girl alright. Do you know, sister, I used to think father was a curious kind of person because he differed with so many people, and I didn't know what to think about it, but I know now our father is a sensible man. He opened my eyes about this Indian question which I am finding every day to be true, and I believe his opinion about the slaveholders to be just as true. I cannot forget his words in the grove at Rufus

Fuller's when we started for Alma after that big dinner. He said, "Be true to your country my boy, and be true to the flag, but before your country or the flag be true to the slave." I never saw tears in father's eyes before. . . .

Give the old dog a hug for me. There is lots of game here and I wish I had old Prince with me.

Obed Hilliard and I have bought a lot of traps and as soon as I get strong I am going to set them. The boys have shot a lot of rats and minks with their muskets.

The news came just now that McClellan had captured 30,000 rebs and had cornered the rest of Lee's army, and the war was at an end. We hear things like this nearly every day. Nobody believes it.

Your brother,

Chauncey.

Richmond, Minn.,
Nov. 20, 1862.

Dear Parents:—

I had no letters the past week but look for one this afternoon. Things go on rather quiet most of the time. Our log shanties are all finished and I am now with the boys. I'll tell you, I am keeping a diary and I will give you a copy of it for a week in this letter:— . . .

Nov. 11—A nice Indian summer day, a smoky, hazy, dreamy day. Took my gun and went rat hunting. Shot five but got only four. Came back to camp hungry as a dog. Had a glorious supper of beef, bread, potatoes, cranberry sauce, and pie. A big supply train bound for Fort Abercrombie pulled in for the night. Gen. Pope has ordered all infantry south. We may get to see Dixie yet. Hurrah! Snow all gone and big prairie fires to the east tonight.

Nov. 12— . . . I found some papers at the hotel called *The Dacota Friend*, that I have been reading. They were left by a woman who had been stopping. This paper was a missionary paper for the Indians and had letters in it from Bishop Whipple. He is certainly a good man. I read some of his letters about the honesty of the Indians when the white man was honest with them. It made me think of good old One Eye and his band that came so many times to our place. I spoke of Bishop Whipple to the trappers and what he said of their honesty, but they said Whipple was an old woman in breeches.

Nov. 13— ... In this miserable Indian war I often wonder what has become of Lightfoot (father gave him that name because he could beat me in a race) and of his brothers and of Owena. They promised to come back in the fall of 1860 when they broke camp the spring before two miles below us but they never came. I haven't lived long, but long enough to think this is a strange world. When I think of the Indians and remember how good they were to me and my father and mother, and reading in this *Dacota Friend* paper how the traders have made them drunk in order to cheat them, and how the government bought 35,000,000 acres of them and has been owing them for it against their promise for thirty years, and because they were starving and broke into a warehouse for food, and this brought on a war. I am for the Indians as much as the whites. ...

Your boy,
Chauncey.

Nov. 22— ... I have been studying the *Dacota Friend* the woman left here in the hotel, and I believe there is something terribly wrong in this war. I know the Indians have been wronged and mistreated. But what can a fellow like me do? I could not eat any supper tonight and I dared not tell the boys what I was thinking about. I knew they would joke me and make fun of me. I feel that Obed Hilliard is nearer to me than any of the boys and yet he says the Indians ought to be shot. I seem to think different from any of them. I may not be right but I can't help it. ...

Nov. 25— ... Final orders to begin our return march to Fort Snelling near St. Paul came late last night. We were up bright and early. Some of the boys said they were fixing all night to get ready. I was hard to wake, because I had gone to bed so late after my night's jaunt gathering in my traps. I had paid a dollar and a quarter a piece for the traps, and the merchant said I had had such bad luck, he would take them back at cost and charge me $2 for the use of them. I thanked him from the bottom of my heart as I had expected a much harder deal. Some of the fellows, one or two from Mondovi had spent a good part of the night at one of the saloons just across the Sioux River and they were singing "Dixie" and "Johnny comes marching home" long before the morning drum beat. ...

All the forenoon its been Dixie, Dixie. A lot of the nearby settlers came in to see the boys go away. Some of them said its all right for us to go south, they weren't afraid any more the Indians had been scared away, others wished we would stay. I think there were four or five pretty girls from the Sioux River that felt sorry for reasons of their own to see the boys go away. It was near noon when we started out in hit or miss order for St. Cloud. We straggled into St. Cloud late in the evening. . . .

Nov. 26—I am tired tonight; marched all day with heavy overcoat, haversack, gun, and two big blankets. I made but eighteen miles and when it began to get dark I dropped out of the squad I was with and went to a private house where I saw a light shining among the trees. A young woman and child were the only persons there. She told me her husband had gone to the war and she was carrying on the farm alone with a little help her brother gave her who came once in a while. She told me she had but one bed in the house but I was welcome if I could sleep on the lounge in the kitchen. I asked to sleep on the floor, but she said, "No." I told her where I slept the night before and she just looked at me without saying a word. She asked me why my mother let me go into the army when I was so young. When I told her I tried to get my mother's consent a year before, she said, "O, you must be a crazy fellow." . . .

Nov. 28th—Fort Snelling, Minn. Arrived this noon. A few of the company still here, most of them come and gone. The right wing of our Reg't came down the Minnesota some days ago bringing with them 1,700 captured Sioux, wives, children, and old men and women of the hostiles. They are camped on the bottoms just below the Fort at the junction of the Minnesota and Mississippi rivers. They are a broken-hearted, ragged, dejected looking lot. They have a million dogs almost, and you can hear them barking for miles. There are 156 tepees. A Minnesota Reg't is in charge of them and no soldier is allowed inside the tepees. Papooses are running about in the snow barefoot and the old Indians wear thin buckskin moccasins and no stockings. Their ponies are poor and their dogs are starved. They are going to be shipped West into the Black Hills country. Like the children of Israel in the Bible story they are forced to go forever from the homes of their childhood and the graves of their fathers to dwell in the mountains and on the barren plains of a strange land. I lifted up the flaps of a number of their tepees and looked in. Every time I looked in I met the gaze of angry eyes. Nearly all of them were alike. Mothers with babies at their breasts, grandmothers and grandsires sat about smouldering fires in the center of the tepee, smoking their long stemmed pipes, and muttering their plaints in the soft guttural tones of the Sioux. The white man's face was their hate and their horror and they showed it by hate in their eyes and their black lowering brows. Why shouldn't they? What had they done? What was their crime? The white man had driven them from one reservation to another. They were weary and broken hearted and desperate at the broken promises of the government. And when they took up arms in desperation for their homes and the graves of their sires they are called savages and red devils. When we white people do the same things we are written down in history as heroes and patriots. Why this difference? I can't see into it. I often think of what father said of justice in the world. That is, that it is the winning party, the lions of the earth, that write its history. . . . My fingers are numb. The cold west wind hits me here and I must quit. I must look for a warm place to sleep tonight and start for home in the morning by the way of Hudson and Eau Claire.

Camp Randall, Madison, Wis.
Co. G. 25th Wis. Vol. Inft.
Dec. 16, 1862.

Dear Parents: After just one week of varying incident from the time of leaving my old dear home I am seated to write to you. We did not find our regiment at Winona as we expected, they had gone to La Crosse. There were twenty-seven of us in the crowd so we hired three liveries and drove all night and reached La Crosse at 6 o'clock in the morning. We nearly swamped in the Black river crossing McGilvery's ferry the ice was running so, but we got over all right. We stayed in La Crosse one night and came on to Madison the next night. The people of La Crosse were good to us, they gave us a fine dinner in the biggest hall in town but mother it did not taste half as good as the last one you gave me of bear meat and venison and hot biscuit and honey. It may be I did not do right when I sneaked out of the house and got Billy and rode away without saying good bye, but I couldn't help it. I knew it hurt you to say good-bye and that's why I did it.

Well, we are in Madison, the Capital of the state. How long we are to stay nobody knows. They say we need drilling and must get more disciplined before we go to the front. Well I hope we won't stay here long. These barracks are awful cold, and my bunk is on the top tier, next to the shingles—too hot in the evening—cold in the morning. I am wearing father's moccasins yet. I didn't get time to buy me boots in La Crosse or Winona.

Tell father to use my money and buy him some more. We are to be paid soon and I will send you some money. You need not lay it up as you did before but use it, and don't think of me, I am all right. I never want to see father wear patches again. I don't believe this war is for long. I expect to be home next year to help with the work. Maybe not, but we'll see.

I forgot to tell you that we came in the cars to Madison from La Crosse. It was a new experience to me, I was wide awake the whole way. I was afraid we were off the track every time we crossed a switch or came to a river. At the towns, girls swarmed on the platforms to ask the boys for their pictures and to kiss the best looking ones. A young Frenchman, we called him the pony of the regiment because he was so small and quick, got the most kisses. He was so short the boys held him by the legs so he could reach down out the windows to kiss the girls. Many times some old fellow held the girls up so she could be reached. It was fun anyway.

I never think but I am all right, except when I try to double quick for a half hour or so. My wind gives out. Lieutenant Parr says, "Your measles stay with you yet." "Warm weather," he says, "will fix you all right." Love to all.

Your son,
Chauncey

From *The Kickapoo Valley:* *The Gem of Wisconsin* (1896)

GERTRUDE FRAZIER AND ROSE B. POFF

Parts of the Driftless became infamous for harboring scoundrels and miscreants. Not content to have their valley besmirched, and eager to attract more reputable settlers, Gertrude Frazier and Rose B. Poff in 1896 wrote "[a] brief history of the Kickapoo Valley, its early settlement, progress and development, illustrated with half-tone engravings of buildings, scenery, representative men, etc." This locally beloved volume of boosterism was reprinted in 2007 by the Friends of the Kickapoo Valley Reserve.

In presenting this handsome little volume to the public, we are prompted to do so by hearing and reading many fictitious reports about the Kickapoo Valley and its inhabitants. Out of loyalty to the country, love for our homes and local institutions, our high esteem for the citizens of the Kickapoo Valley, and the great admiration we have for the beauties of Nature which we behold in any direction we may turn, we undertake this publication. . . .

The Kickapoo Valley and its inhabitants have an established unsavory reputation, extending throughout the state of Wisconsin and even beyond that it is a territory some fifty miles long, wild and undeveloped, inhabited by illiterate people who are designated timber thieves, horse thieves and desperadoes. That such statements are wholly false, we will prove by the indisputable evidence herein. The engravings we present to the reader will give some idea of the development, enterprise, industry and progression of the inhabitants of this far famed and much abused Kickapoo region. . . .

This fairest and most gorgeous of Wisconsin gems of scenery lies in the western part of the state, north of the Wisconsin River into which the Kickapoo empties. Surrounded by tall waving grass and sheltered by a clump of trees, the Kickapoo River wells up to the surface a few miles to the northward of Wilton, in Monroe County. At first it is only a brook across which a child might jump, but it is soon augmented by many other brooks and becomes a river.

It waters a region about eighty miles in length but is itself much longer, for it is as its name in the Indian tongue indicates, a "crooked river." Its general course is to the southwest. On its way to the Wisconsin it crosses the counties of Vernon and Crawford and the northwest corner of Richland. In some places, especially near the mouth, the valley is narrow and the cliffs on either side stand like sentinels guarding some sacred treasure. At other points the valley suddenly widens out and smilingly invites the husbandman to garner in the riches so profusely spread out.

Not only in the valley is the scenery very beautiful, but a view from the top of one of the bluffs presents a new world. As far as the eye can reach is shown a succession of hilltops, each crowned with cultivated fields and substantial residences. . . .

The Kickapoogians as a whole are not a moneyed class, but they believe with the apostle that "If any provide not for his own, and specially for those of his own house, he hath denied the faith, and is worse than an infidel." There are many individuals among their number who are possessed of much houses and lands and flocks and herds and bank stock, but the vast majority are in moderate circumstances only. Nineteen-twentieths of the farmers own the land they till. Very nearly as large a proportion of the villagers own the house and lot on which they live.

There is practically no pauper class here. Out of a population of 14,779, throughout the eighty miles of the Kickapoo Valley there were about one hundred and fifty persons who received some aid from the public treasury last year. The amount paid was $679.55, an average of about $4.50 to each. One township, that of Forest in which Viola is situated, received none.

The homes on the Kickapoo are characterized by comfort rather than by display. While many of them are elegant in their appointments, a few are of a primitive style. But to the rich and to the poor alike, the stately bluffs add dignity, and the smiling valleys, murmuring streams and diversified woodlands give beauty.

Just here let it be noted that no more charming spots for camping in tents or in cottages can be found in Wisconsin than are *hundreds* of locations on the Kickapoo River and its tributaries. The cost of living is not great, and with the hunting, fishing, boating and delightful excursions by team or bicycle a most enjoyable season may be passed.

Among a people so nearly on a par with each other financially, and each one a free American citizen residing in his own house and tilling his own land, one does not expect to find marked class distinctions. Social divisions are made in accordance with a high, if sometimes narrow standard of moral living. Mutual tastes and ambitions, intellectual power and environment produce "sets" in society just as it universally does. No one is ashamed to work. Some may be too lazy to do so but such are few. The children of both the well-to-do and of the poorer parents are taught that it is no disgrace to be a worker, but that the shirker is to be despised.

Like true Americans everywhere, the people residing in this Valley take an active interest in both national and international affairs. The great dailies of Chicago and Milwaukee, usually the former, have hundreds of subscribers in this region, and their readers are well qualified to argue each his own political creed, or to discuss matters of general interest. Poor indeed is the home in the Kickapoo Valley into which some one of the local weekly papers do not go. Magazines and religious papers are found on every hand, and scarcely a family but has at least a few books. The religious belief of the professed followers of Christ is not of that superstitious variety that "troubles one like a gadfly" as Mrs. Humphrey Ward says, but has a healthful tone manifesting itself in upright living and a firm belief in the ultimate triumph of right. As a whole the people may be classed as conservative but not stubbornly so. They are open to conviction. Many aggressive workers against sin and unrighteousness are to be found in every community. They receive the cordial support of the general public. The temperance cause has always had a large following and warm advocates. The villages of Star, La Farge, Readstown and Barnum are habitually no-license towns. Viola for twenty years or more was free from the saloon curse; but three years ago license carried in the town of Liberty, Vernon County, in which a portion of the village is located. In the town of Forest there is yet an overwhelming majority for no license.

Churches and schools and all public institutions are well supported. Not every one takes advantage of the opportunities open to him. But many persons who are far from being scholarly, like Whittier's "Barefoot Boy" are rich in "knowledge never learned of schools," and possessed of a refinement which springs from an inborn sense of justice and a love for truth and for humanity.

Hospitality is considered one of the prime virtues. It is bestowed with a disinterestedness and homely charm that warms the heart of any but the most cynical.

A letter from Rev. William Haughton, pastor of Congregational Church at Retreat, Wisconsin . . . expresses so well some facts concerning the Kickapoo Valley and its inhabitants, that with his permission extracts are here made from it: . . . "I am surprised that any should advertise the Kickapoo Valley in adverse terms. I traveled up and down that Valley twice a year for five years or more, and never have I met more generous or hospitable people. I have preached frequently in Readstown, Bloomingdale, Rockton, Seeleyburg, Gays Mills, Ontario and on up the Kickapoo and always found a quiet, orderly and appreciative audience. And some of the kindest and most Christian homes I have ever lodged in were on the Kickapoo and the plains about it. I am surprised that any one should defame the dear old Kickapoo. To be sure there were some "roughs" there as there are in all other places, but this is the exception not the rule.—Well I always love to look upon the bright side of everything and every place, and indeed the Kickapoo has many bright spots for me and lingers very tenderly in my recollection. Good Christian men and women there, able men and women intellectually, and many generous hearts. Some of our best Vernon County teachers came from the Kickapoo. I remember them well. It is unfair and unkind to speak evil of the Kickapoo.—I am glad to be able to give my honest testimony as regards the good people of that part of Vernon County watered by the dear old Kickapoo."

"Every Time I Travel the Great River Road . . ." (1990)

PEARL SWIGGUM

Pearl Swiggum (1914–2015) was among the Driftless Area's most prolific local journalists, writing her weekly "Stump Ridge Farm" stories from 1958 until retiring in 2004 at the age of ninety. Her column characteristically mixed reminiscence, witty vignettes of farm life, and tireless response to readers. Originally published in the *Crawford County Independent*, Swiggum's column was syndicated in newspapers throughout the region, including the *Wisconsin State Journal*.

Every time I travel the Great River Road I come down with a case of nostalgia. How sad I am not to see the passenger trains that used to travel up and down the valley and years ago stopped at every station along the way. Every village had a depot, even Charm, which has itself disappeared, too.

In those days the river itself wasn't so great appearing. Oh, it was there, but hard to see. Streams, every one with a name, spread out from creeks that came from every coulee. They meandered all over the vast valley floor, forming islands where we picnicked, sand bars for wading before they reached the main channel which, near Ferryville, was way over on the Iowa side.

Train from Coon Valley to Viroqua (c. 1919). The La Crosse and Southeastern Railroad ran from La Crosse through Stoddard, Chaseburg, Coon Valley, and Westby to Viroqua. It ceased service in 1933, but the line from Chaseburg to Westby was used through 1972. Railroads such as the Galena and Southern, the Ettrick and Northern, the Chicago and Tomah, the Dubuque and Minnesota, the Mineral Point, the Cazenovia Southern, and the Kickapoo Valley "Stump Dodger" once transported passengers and freight throughout the hills and valleys of the Driftless.

In those days the sight of the river was so different from passenger trains and from the dinky I rode upriver Monday morning, downriver Friday nights. It was early Mondays—had to be—when Dad made my breakfast, always oatmeal, and walked me up to the depot in the dark.

I can't remember train time but I reached La Crosse in time to get to the home where I and five other girls did light housekeeping, then to Central High School before 8:30. I must have done a lot of running in those days.

If you haven't consulted your dictionaries yet, a dinky was homely (as in simple, domestic, familiar) and I think had a crew of only two. Take a train engine, a small one, a caboose, and squash them together.

Just an engine and a small compartment attached to it for a very few passengers. It traveled from Prairie du Chien to La Crosse—I think that was the extent of its route.

There was a lot of excitement in the country back in the late '20s, I think it must have been. King Haakon of Norway was making a train trip across the United States. At every whistle stop the king appeared on the open platform at the end of the train, waved and possibly he spoke but I didn't hear him.

The day he went through Ferryville Dad and I were climbing the bank along the right-of-way as the train neared. I had spent the day helping him with the clamming. We stood alongside the tracks as the train passed, slowing for the station in the village. A distinguished look-ing gentleman, the king, stood on the rear platform.

At the supper table there was much discussion about how, at every train stop, people had doffed their hats and even bowed for the king. Someone asked if Dad had done so. He hadn't removed his dark old felt and after a lot of jabbering about whether he should or shouldn't have paid some homage to the king, the table was about evenly divided.

Since Dad could do no wrong in my eyes, I was his champion. And finally someone asked him why he didn't, since it sounded like every-one else in the country had. This Norwegian-born, naturalized citizen of America settled it quietly and shut everyone up with four words: "He's not my king."

Yanys (2010)

JACQUELINE WEST

Jacqueline West lives amid the bluffs of Red Wing, Minnesota, where she is a poet and writer of short fiction for children and young adults. "Yanys" is among the poems in the chapbook *Cherma*, in which West explores the lives and experiences of Bohemian immigrants who came to western Wisconsin's Pierce County in the late nineteenth century.

She did not know how to begin
that first letter for sending home

knowing how her mother's hands would tremble
veins raised like small mountains over the bones
as she tore through the American seal.

She did not know if she should tell
how, of the seventy-four who sailed
only thirty-eight remained alive,
how the rest had slid from a wet deck
in makeshift shrouds, their landings divots in the waves.

Most of the Dvořák cousins were gone,
three of the Jansas, five of the Mareks,
and all of the children who could not subsist
on biscuits soaked in salty leakage,
on crates of flour curled with worms.

In that first letter she could not write
of the loneliness that ate this land,
the spreads of dense and hungry woods
that swallowed cries from neighbor to neighbor,
the places where there was no road at all,
of the jewelers and teachers and newspapermen
now splitting their skin against an axe handle.

So instead she wrote of the land that they had found
which looked like home, of the hillsides
that folded just like the Orlické
into low troughs that ran with rain,
the robins that chirped in the berry trees,
the soil dark as karakul.

She would say that at last they had plenty to eat,
that the land was cheap
and the china unbroken
and outside the tent where they slept on the dirt
clumps of violets grew wild in the ruts.

8

FARMING LIVES

ODAY MUCH OF THE DRIFTLESS AREA is farm country. Traffic jams happen in single file, tractors and combines leading cars on roads too narrow or winding for them to pass. These roads trace a topography that is more varied and less friendly to extensive, large-scale agriculture than much of the rural Midwest. Still, the land—if it is not too steep or marshy, and sometimes even if it is—is largely devoted to farming.

Indigenous people cultivated squash, beans, corn, and tobacco, and residents of the early trading outposts grew sustenance crops. Not until the mid-nineteenth century, however, did farmers begin in earnest to carve fields out of native prairies, oak savannas, and woodlands. Driftless soil—built of weathered sandstone and limestone, loess deposits, decomposed roots, leaf mold, sod, and fungi, and the work of animals and microbes—was bared and made to bear sheaves for the first time. Wet meadows, grasslands, and savannas, once the province of mammoth and bison, now accommodated sheep and cows. Diverse branches of old-world agriculture, grafted onto the stock of new land, yielded bountifully.

Wheat was the Driftless Area's first significant cash crop, and was often planted after clearing the land—and then season after season until the soils were exhausted and the crops diseased. As the wheat frontier pushed west across (and then beyond) the region, other crops came to prominence. Hogs, tobacco, and hops all had their heyday, but dairying became the iconic face of farming in the Driftless. Due in part to writers who have memorialized the era, many Driftless residents recall—even mythologize—a time when every coulee held a dairy barn and a herd of thirty Jerseys. Cheese factories graced the crossroads, large farm families filled one-room schoolhouses, and small towns achieved peaks in population and enjoyed relative prosperity.

This fondly remembered golden age was short-lived. When the Great Depression hit, many farm families fared better than those who could not provide for themselves, but other farms throughout the Driftless were lost. On many "two-story farms" of ridgetop and valley-bottom fields, settlers had cleared the flatter areas first. But other early farmers worked fields in rows running up and down the steep slopes, to avoid tipping their teams over sideways. By the 1930s, these and other old-world practices had proven ruinous. Soil erosion reached crisis proportions. In response, farmers—at first in the Coon Creek watershed in Wisconsin and then across the Driftless—pioneered the adoption of contour plowing and other techniques to conserve soils and restore damaged watersheds.

As farming became industrialized after World War II, smaller farms continued to fold under the economic imperative to "get big or get out." With the farm crisis of the 1980s, some farmers began to consider alternatives and adopted organic agriculture. The region's unique mix of multigenerational dairy farms, back-to-the-land homesteads, strong cooperatives and organizational ties, and a legacy of land conservation allowed the Driftless Area to become home to an expanding network of organic farms and associated businesses unmatched elsewhere in the country.

More than any other human activity, agriculture has profoundly changed the Driftless landscape. At the same time, the Driftless land imposes certain limits and requirements upon those who seek to cultivate it. Soil conservation, organic farming, perennial agriculture, and local food movements all have roots among farms and communities here. The Driftless will continue to be farmed as long as the rain continues to fall and the soil stays in place. *How* it will be farmed remains at issue.

Me and My Man (1931)

LAURA SHERRY

In 1931 poet, actress, and theater advocate Laura Case Sherry (1876–1947) published *Old Prairie du Chien*, a limited-edition collection of poems portraying the "varied and interesting" lives of those inhabiting her home town. After studying literature and drama at the University of Wisconsin and Northwestern University, Sherry pursued her interest in theater. In

1911 she founded the experimental Wisconsin Players in Milwaukee, dedicated to democratizing the theater experience and advancing amateur community theater across the state. Two other poems from *Old Prairie du Chien* appear in other sections of this collection.

Bes' thing of all, I like to be
Me and my man, live in coulee
On nice farm we work so long
While men all 'round sing ol' French song.
Same ol' song we used to sing
When young blood tell us it was Spring
And we paddle skiff 'till we come through
To big Mississip' from little bayou.

Sometime I think of the big worl'
I used try think when I was girl—
What was out there, and it seem to me
That I go mad if I can't see.
Well I don't get a chance to go
And my mind get sick with bother me so.
Nice French boy come along and say—
You marry me, we go some day.
Well, I marry him and I forget
Big worl' out there. I aint goin' fret
If lot children mak' the money spen',
My man, he is the bes' of men.

My worl' is live in the old coulee.
Ba gosh! it big enough for me.
I aint got time to think nor fret.
Ten boy and girl mak' me, you bet,
Keep fill the day with cook and sew
'Till I aint even got time to go
With load of wood to Prairie du Chien,
That biggest place I ever seen.
But I aint complain and I tell you
I prefer coulee and little bayou
With my old man and my boy and girl.
Maybe that mak' for me big worl'!

From *Incidents of a Journey from Pennsylvania to Wisconsin Territory* (1837)

WILLIAM RUDOLPH SMITH

Lawyer and legislator William Rudolph Smith (1787–1868) was born in Pennsylvania, served in the War of 1812, and in 1837 became U.S. Commissioner to the Chippewa Indians of Upper Mississippi. He migrated to Mineral Point the following year, and later served as a delegate to the first Wisconsin Constitutional Convention in 1846. In his journal from 1837, he provided this evocative description of the southwestern Wisconsin landscape from the Military Ridge, capturing the wonder of the native tallgrass prairie in full flower, even as it was being replaced by the "incipient farms" of newly arrived emigrants.

August 29th. Gov. Dodge sent in his carriage, and we accompanied Augustus, his son, to Belmont. This place is situated on the prairie at the foot of the Platte mounds. These mounds are three in number, the distance between the east and west being about two miles, a small mound lying between the two. The east and west mounds are well covered with timber. The center mound is bare, excepting a few large straggling rocks. The lands between the Pekeetolica after leaving Mineral Point and Belmont, are well cultivated. Several fine farms and most beautiful and rich situations. The town of Belmont contains about half a dozen well-built frame houses, built at Pittsburg and sent round in steamboats to Galena, painted white, with red roofs; fronts built up with battlements. This place, since it has lost the chance of being selected as the seat of government, is going down. The Legislature sat here at its first session, last winter. It cannot at present be supported as a town or place of business, as the country is not sufficiently farmed. . . . The east and west mounds are about twenty feet high. The center mound is elevated from the general level of the surrounding prairie about 100 feet.

It rises from the plain with a gentle ascent about half a mile from its base, until it assumes abruptly its conical form, and rises about fifty feet until its apex is completely a point. . . . The view from this mound, as well as from the flat near the summit of the eastern mound, beggars all description. An ocean of prairie surrounds the spectator, whose vision is not limited to less than thirty or forty miles. This great sea of verdure is interspersed with delightfully varying undulations, like the vast waves of the ocean, and every here and there, sinking in the hollows or creating the swell, appear spots of wood, large groves, extensive ranges of timber, small groups of trees, as if planted by the hand of art for the purpose of ornamenting this naturally splendid scene. Over the extended view, in all directions, are scattered the incipient farms of the settlers, with their luxuriant crops of wheat and oats, whose yellow sheaves, already cut, form a beautiful contrast with the waving green of the Indian corn and the smooth, dark surface of the potato crop. Throughout the prairie the most splendid variety of flowers are seen rising above the thickly set grass, which has here and there in large and small patches been mowed for hay, presenting a curious checkered appearance of the table beneath us. The prairie flowers are various in hue, the dark purple masonic or mineral flower, the tall bright purple and red feather, the prairie sunflower, the golden rod, the several small and beautifully variegated flowers interspersed amongst the grass, all render the scene indescribably beautiful. To the north, the Wisconsin hills are seen, bounding the view; to the east, prairie and wood are limited by the horizon, and the blue mounds form a background and a landmark. To the south the view over the rolling country extends far into the State of Illinois, and to the west the view is only bounded by the Dubuque mound and the hills west of the Mississippi, distant about thirty miles, and to the northwest high grounds through which the river breaks its sweeping way close the view. Below us, on the prairie, is the little village of Belmont, with its bright painted dwellings. The brown lines in the general green carpet indicate the roads public and private over the prairie. The grazing cattle are scattered over the broad surface, looking like sheep or dogs, whilst in the distance are seen traveling wagons of emigrants, ox-teams hauling lumber, pleasure and traveling carriages whirling rapidly over the sward, as if the country had been improved for a century past, instead of having been only five years reclaimed from the savages. The picture is not exaggerated. It fails of the original beauty in the attempt to describe that which is worth a journey of a thousand miles to contemplate in a summer day's calm sunset as I have viewed it.

From *A Son of the Middle Border* (1917)

HAMLIN GARLAND

Hamlin Garland (1860–1940) was born on a farm near West Salem, Wisconsin, and became a celebrated novelist, poet, essayist, and short story writer. After a youth spent on several midwestern farms he moved east to Boston in 1884 to pursue a writing career. In his writing he often returned to his midwestern life and landscapes, and to themes of rural life and progressive economic reform. His autobiography, *A Son of the Middle Border*, was published to wide acclaim in 1917. Its sequel, *A Daughter of the Middle Border*, garnered a Pulitzer Prize for biography.

All of this universe known to me in the year 1864 was bounded by the wooded hills of a little Wisconsin coulee, and its center was the cottage in which my mother was living alone—my father was in the war. As I project myself back into that mystical age, half lights cover most of the valley. The road before our doorstone begins and ends in vague obscurity—and Granma Green's house at the fork of the trail stands on the very edge of the world in a sinister region peopled with bears and other menacing creatures. Beyond this point all is darkness and terror.

It is Sunday afternoon and my mother and her three children, Frank, Harriet and I (all in our best dresses) are visiting the Widow Green, our nearest neighbor, a plump, jolly woman whom we greatly love. The house swarms with stalwart men and buxom women and we are all sitting around the table heaped with the remains of a harvest feast. The women are "telling fortunes" by means of tea-grounds. Mrs. Green is the seeress. After shaking the cup with the grounds at the bottom, she turns it bottom side up in a saucer. Then whirling it three times to the right and three times to the left, she lifts it and silently studies the position of the leaves which cling to the sides of the cup, what time we all wait in breathless suspense for her first word.

Threshing scene, Frank Feiker (c. 1905). A native of Milwaukee, Frank Feiker
(1876–1950) moved around 1905 to Cassville, where he purchased a
photography studio. Over the next fifty years Feiker documented daily life in
and around the Mississippi River town in his landscapes, studio portraits,
postcard views, and town, river, and farming scenes. Here he captured the
annual ritual of threshing, carried out at that point through a combination of
human-, horse-, and steam-power.

"A soldier is coming to you!" she says to my mother. "See," and she
points into the cup. We all crowd near, and I perceive a leaf with a stem
sticking up from its body like a bayonet over a man's shoulder. "He
is almost home," the widow goes on. Then with sudden dramatic turn
she waves her hand toward the road, "Heavens and earth!" she cries.
"There's Richard now!"

We all turn and look toward the road, and there, indeed, is a soldier
with a musket on his back, wearily plodding his way up the low hill just
north of the gate. He is too far away for mother to call, and besides I
think she must have been a little uncertain, for he did not so much as
turn his head toward the house. Trembling with excitement she hurries
little Frank into his wagon and telling Hattie to bring me, sets off up the

road as fast as she can draw the baby's cart. It all seems a dream to me and I move dumbly, almost stupidly like one in a mist. . . .

We did not overtake the soldier, that is evident, for my next vision is that of a blue-coated figure leaning upon the fence, studying with intent gaze our empty cottage. I cannot, even now, precisely divine why he stood thus, sadly contemplating his silent home,—but so it was. His knapsack lay at his feet, his musket was propped against a post on whose top a cat was dreaming, unmindful of the warrior and his folded hands.

He did not hear us until we were close upon him, and even after he turned, my mother hesitated, so thin, so hollow-eyed, so changed was he. "Richard, is that you?" she quaveringly asked.

His worn face lighted up. His arms rose. "Yes, Belle! Here I am," he answered.

Nevertheless though he took my mother in his arms, I could not relate him to the father I had heard so much about. To me he was only a strange man with big eyes and care-worn face. I did not recognize in him anything I had ever known, but my sister, who was two years older than I, went to his bosom of her own motion. She knew him, whilst I submitted to his caresses rather for the reason that my mother urged me forward than because of any affection I felt for him. Frank, however, would not even permit a kiss. The gaunt and grizzled stranger terrified him.

"Come here, my little man," my father said.—"*My little man!*" Across the space of half-a-century I can still hear the sad reproach in his voice. "Won't you come and see your poor old father when he comes home from the war?"

"My little man!" How significant that phrase seems to me now! The war had in very truth come between this patriot and his sons. I had forgotten him—the baby had never known him.

Frank crept beneath the rail fence and stood there, well out of reach, like a cautious kitten warily surveying an alien dog. At last the soldier stooped and drawing from his knapsack a big red apple, held it toward the staring babe, confidently calling, "Now, I guess he'll come to his poor old pap home from the war."

The mother apologized. "He doesn't know you, Dick. How could he? He was only nine months old when you went away. He'll go to you by and by."

The babe crept slowly toward the shining lure. My father caught him despite his kicking, and hugged him close. "Now I've got you," he exulted.

Then we all went into the little front room and the soldier laid off his heavy army shoes. My mother brought a pillow to put under his head, and so at last he stretched out on the floor the better to rest his tired, aching bones, and there I joined him.

"Oh, Belle!" he said, in tones of utter content. "This is what I've dreamed about a million times." . . .

Our farm lay well up in what is called Green's Coulee, in a little valley just over the road which runs along the La Crosse river in western Wisconsin. It contained one hundred and sixty acres of land which crumpled against the wooded hills on the east and lay well upon a ridge to the west. Only two families lived above us, and over the height to the north was the land of the red people, and small bands of their hunters used occasionally to come trailing down across our meadow on their way to and from La Crosse, which was their immemorial trading point.

Sometimes they walked into our house, always without knocking— but then we understood their ways. No one knocks at the wigwam of a red neighbor, and we were not afraid of them, for they were friendly, and our mother often gave them bread and meat which they took (always without thanks) and ate with much relish while sitting beside our fire. All this seemed very curious to us, but as they were accustomed to share their food and lodging with one another so they accepted my mother's bounty in the same matter-of-fact fashion. . . .

Our postoffice was in the village of Onalaska, situated at the mouth of the Black River, which came down out of the wide forest lands of the north. It was called a "boom town" for the reason that "booms" or yards for holding pine logs laced the quiet bayou and supplied several large mills with timber. Busy saws clamored from the islands and great rafts of planks and lath and shingles were made up and floated down into the Mississippi and on to southern markets.

It was a rude, rough little camp filled with raftsmen, loggers, mill-hands and boomsmen. Saloons abounded and deeds of violence were common, but to me it was a poem. From its position on a high plateau it commanded a lovely southern expanse of shimmering water bounded by purple bluffs. The spires of La Crosse rose from the smoky distance, and steamships hoarsely giving voice suggested illimitable reaches of travel. Some day I hoped my father would take me to that shining market-place whereto he carried all our grain. . . .

Month by month the universe in which I lived lightened and widened. In my visits to Onalaska, I discovered the great Mississippi River, and the Minnesota Bluffs. The light of knowledge grew stronger. I began to perceive forms and faces which had been hidden in the dusk of babyhood. I heard more and more of La Crosse, and out of the mist-filled lower valley the booming roar of steamboats suggested to me distant countries and the sea. . . .

The road which led from our farm to the village school crossed a sandy ridge and often in June our path became so hot that it burned the soles of our feet. If we went out of the road there were sand-burrs and we lost a great deal of time picking needles from our toes. How we hated those sand-burrs!—However, on these sand barrens many luscious strawberries grew. They were not large, but they gave off a delicious odor, and it sometimes took us a long time to reach home.

There was a recognized element of danger in this road. Wildcats were plentiful around the limestone cliffs, and bears had been seen under the oak trees. In fact a place on the hillside was often pointed out with awe as "the place where Al Randal killed the bear." Our way led past the village cemetery also, and there was to me something vaguely awesome in that silent bivouac of the dead. . . .

Green's Coulee was a delightful place for boys. It offered hunting and coasting and many other engrossing sports, but my father, as the seasons went by, became thoroughly dissatisfied with its disadvantages. More and more he resented the stumps and ridges which interrupted his plow. Much of his quarter-section remained unbroken. There were ditches to be dug in the marsh and young oaks to be uprooted from the forest, and he was obliged to toil with unremitting severity. There were times, of course, when field duties did not press, but never a day came when the necessity for twelve hours' labor did not exist.

Furthermore, as he grubbed or reaped he remembered the glorious prairies he had crossed on his exploring trip into Minnesota before the war, and the oftener he thought of them the more bitterly he resented his up-tilted, horse-killing fields, and his complaining words sank so deep into the minds of his sons that for years thereafter they were unable to look upon any rise of ground as an object to be admired.

It irked him beyond measure to force his reaper along a steep slope, and he loathed the irregular little patches running up the ravines behind the timbered knolls, and so at last like many another of his neighbors he began to look away to the west as a fairer field for conquest. He no more thought of going east than a liberated eagle dreams of returning to its narrow cage. He loved to talk of Boston, to boast of its splendor, but to live there, to earn his bread there, was unthinkable. Beneath the sunset lay the enchanted land of opportunity and his liberation came unexpectedly.

Sometime in the spring of 1868, a merchant from La Crosse, a plump man who brought us candy and was very cordial and condescending, began negotiations for our farm, and in the discussion of plans which followed, my conception of the universe expanded. I began to understand that "Minnesota" was not a bluff but a wide land of romance, a prairie, peopled with red men, which lay far beyond the big river. And then, one day, I heard my father read to my mother a paragraph from the county paper which ran like this, "It is reported that Richard Garland has sold his farm in Green's Coulee to our popular grocer, Mr. Speer. Mr. Speer intends to make of it a model dairy farm."

This intention seemed somehow to reflect a ray of glory upon us, though I fear it did not solace my mother, as she contemplated the loss of home and kindred. She was not by nature an emigrant,—few women are. She was content with the pleasant slopes, the kindly neighbors of Green's Coulee. Furthermore, most of her brothers and sisters still lived just across the ridge in the valley of the Neshonoc, and the thought of leaving them for a wild and unknown region was not pleasant.

To my father, on the contrary, change was alluring. Iowa was now the place of the rainbow, and the pot of gold.

From *Little House in the Big Woods* (1932)

Laura Ingalls Wilder

The Little House books of Laura Ingalls Wilder (1867–1957) are among the most beloved and enduring classics in American children's literature. Wilder was born near the village of Pepin, Wisconsin, but her family

removed to Kansas before she was two years old. The family returned
to Wisconsin in 1871 and remained there for the next four years. These
years provided the background for *Little House in the Big Woods*, the
first in Wilder's series of eight autobiographical novels. In Chapter 11,
"Harvest," Wilder notes that "the stumps were so thick"; set in the Big
Woods, her story in fact evokes a landscape that was quickly being converted to agriculture.

Pa and Uncle Henry traded work. When the grain got ripe in the fields,
Uncle Henry came to work with Pa, and Aunt Polly and all the cousins came to spend the day. Then Pa went to help Uncle Henry cut his
grain, and Ma took Laura and Mary and Carrie to spend the day with
Aunt Polly.

Ma and Aunt Polly worked in the house and all the cousins played
together in the yard till dinner time. Aunt Polly's yard was a fine place
to play, because the stumps were so thick. The cousins played jumping
from stump to stump without ever touching the ground.

Even Laura, who was littlest, could do this easily in the places where
the smallest trees had grown close together. Cousin Charley was a big
boy, going on eleven years old, and he could jump from stump to stump
all over the yard. The smaller stumps he could jump two at a time, and
he could walk on the top rail of the fence without being afraid.

Pa and Uncle Henry were out in the field, cutting the oats with
cradles. A cradle was a sharp steel blade fastened to a framework of
wooden slats that caught and held the stalks of grain when the blade
cut them. Pa and Uncle Henry carried the cradles by their long, curved
handles, and swung the blades into the standing oats. When they had
cut enough to make a pile, they slid the cut stalks off the slats, into neat
heaps on the ground.

It was hard work, walking around and around the field in the hot sun,
and with both hands swinging the heavy cradles into the grain and cutting it, then sliding it into the piles.

After all the grain was cut, they must go over the field again. This
time they would stoop over each pile, and taking up a handful of the
stalks in each hand they would knot them together to make a longer
strand. Then gathering up the pile of grain in their arms they would
bind it tightly around with the band they had made, and tie the band,
and tuck in its ends.

After they made seven such bundles, then the bundles must be shocked. To make a shock, they stood five bundles upright, snugly together with the oat-heads up. Then over these they put two more bundles, spreading out the stalks to make a little roof and shelter the five bundles from dew and rain.

Every stalk of the cut grain must always be safely in the shock before dark, for lying on the dewy ground all night would spoil it.

Pa and Uncle Henry were working very hard, because the air was so heavy and hot and still that they expected rain. The oats were ripe, and if they were not cut and in the shock before rain came, the crop would be lost. Then Uncle Henry's horses would be hungry all winter.

At noon Pa and Uncle Henry came to the house in a great hurry, and swallowed their dinner as quickly as they could. Uncle Henry said that Charley must help them that afternoon.

Laura looked at Pa, when Uncle Henry said that. At home, Pa had said to Ma that Uncle Henry and Aunt Polly spoiled Charley. When Pa was eleven years old, he had done a good day's work every day in the fields, driving a team. But Charley did hardly any work at all.

Now Uncle Henry said that Charley must come to the field. He could save them a great deal of time. He could go to the spring for water, and he could fetch them the water-jug when they needed a drink. He could fetch the whetstone when the blades needed sharpening.

All the children looked at Charley. Charley did not want to go to the field. He wanted to stay in the yard and play. But, of course, he did not say so.

Pa and Uncle Henry did not rest at all. They ate in a hurry and went right back to work, and Charley went with them.

Now Mary was oldest, and she wanted to play a quiet, ladylike play. So in the afternoon the cousins made a playhouse in the yard. The stumps were chairs and tables and stoves, and leaves were dishes, and sticks were the children.

On the way home that night, Laura and Mary heard Pa tell Ma what happened in the field.

Instead of helping Pa and Uncle Henry, Charley was making all the trouble he could. He got in their way so they couldn't swing the cradles. He hid the whetstone, so they had to hunt for it when the blades needed sharpening. He didn't bring the water-jug till Uncle Henry shouted at him three or four times, and then he was sullen.

After that he followed them around, talking and asking questions. They were working too hard to pay any attention to him, so they told him to go away and not bother them.

But they dropped their cradles and ran to him across the field when they heard him scream. The woods were all around the field, and there were snakes in the oats.

When they got to Charley, there was nothing wrong, and he laughed at them. He said:

"I fooled you that time!"

Pa said if he had been Uncle Henry, he would have tanned that boy's hide for him, right then and there. But Uncle Henry did not do it.

So they took a drink of water and went back to work.

Three times Charley screamed, and they ran to him as fast as they could, and he laughed at them. He thought it was a good joke. And still, Uncle Henry did not tan his hide.

Then a fourth time he screamed, louder than ever. Pa and Uncle Henry looked at him, and he was jumping up and down, screaming. They saw nothing wrong with him and they had been fooled so many times that they went on with their work.

Charley kept on screaming, louder and shriller. Pa did not say anything, but Uncle Henry said, "Let him scream." So they went on working and let him scream.

He kept on jumping up and down, screaming. He did not stop. At last Uncle Henry said:

"Maybe something really is wrong." They laid down their cradles and went across the field to him.

And all that time Charley had been jumping up and down on a yellow jackets' nest! The yellow jackets lived in a nest in the ground and Charley stepped on it by mistake. Then all the little bees in their bright yellow jackets came swarming out with their red-hot stings, and they hurt Charley so that he couldn't get away.

He was jumping up and down and hundreds of bees were stinging him all over. They were stinging his face and his hands and his neck and his nose, they were crawling up his pants' legs and stinging and crawling down the back of his neck and stinging. The more he jumped and screamed the harder they stung.

Pa and Uncle Henry took him by the arms and ran him away from the yellow jackets' nest. They undressed him, and his clothes were full of yellow jackets and their stings were swelling up all over him. They killed the bees that were stinging him and they shook the bees out of his clothes and then they dressed him again and sent him to the house.

Laura and Mary and the cousins were playing quietly in the yard, when they heard a loud, blubbering cry. Charley came bawling into the yard and his face was so swollen that the tears could hardly squeeze out of his eyes.

His hands were puffed up, and his neck was puffed out, and his cheeks were big, hard puffs. His fingers stood out stiff and swollen. There were little, hard, white dents all over his puffed-out face and neck.

Laura and Mary and the cousins stood and looked at him.

Ma and Aunt Polly came running out of the house and asked him what was the matter. Charley blubbered and bawled. Ma said it was yellow jackets. She ran to the garden and got a big pan of earth, while Aunt Polly took Charley into the house and undressed him.

They made a big panful of mud, and plastered him all over with it. They rolled him up in an old sheet and put him to bed. His eyes were swollen shut and his nose was a funny shape. Ma and Aunt Polly covered his whole face with mud and tied the mud on with cloths. Only the end of his nose and his mouth showed.

Aunt Polly steeped some herbs, to give him for his fever. Laura and Mary and the cousins stood around for some time, looking at him.

It was dark that night when Pa and Uncle Henry came from the field. All the oats were in the shock, and now the rain could come and it would not do any harm.

Pa could not stay to supper; he had to get home and do the milking. The cows were already waiting, at home, and when cows are not milked on time they do not give so much milk. He hitched up quickly and they all got into the wagon.

Pa was very tired and his hands ached so that he could not drive very well, but the horses knew the way home. Ma sat beside him with Baby Carrie, and Laura and Mary sat on the board behind them. Then they heard Pa tell about what Charley had done.

Laura and Mary were horrified. They were often naughty, themselves, but they had never imagined that anyone could be as naughty as Charley had been. He hadn't worked to help save the oats. He hadn't minded his father quickly when his father spoke to him. He had bothered Pa and Uncle Henry when they were hard at work.

Then Pa told about the yellow jackets' nest, and he said, "It served the little liar right."

After she was in the trundle bed that night, Laura lay and listened to the rain drumming on the roof and strewing from the eaves, and she thought about what Pa had said.

She thought about what the yellow jackets had done to Charley. She thought it served Charley right, too. It served him right because he had been so monstrously naughty. And the bees had a right to sting him, when he jumped on their home.

But she didn't understand why Pa had called him a little liar. She didn't understand how Charley could be a liar, when he had not said a word.

From *The Land Remembers:*
The Story of a Farm and Its People (1975)

BEN LOGAN

Ben Logan (1920–2014) grew up on a ridge farm near Gays Mills, Wisconsin. After graduating from the University of Wisconsin in Madison (where he studied with Aldo Leopold), Logan joined the U.S. Navy and entered World War II. He returned to the university for further studies after the war, and went on to a successful career in journalism and public relations in New York. In 1975 he published his memoir *The Land Remembers.* In 1986 Logan purchased his boyhood farm, Seldom Seen Farm, and returned there with his wife, Jacqueline, upon his retirement. *The Land Remembers* has been published in multiple editions, becoming one of the most widely admired portraits of early twentieth century American farm life. This excerpt is from the second chapter, "Hilltop World."

There is no neat and easy way to tell the story of a farm. A farm is a process, where everything is related, everything happening at once. It is a circle of life; and there is no logical place to begin a perfect circle. This is an unsolved paradox for me. Part of the folly of our time is the idea that we can see the whole of something by looking at the pieces, one at a time.

Tobacco weeding, Andrew John Mueller (1968). Tobacco was an important
cash crop for many farms in the Driftless Area. Even as other field crops were
mechanized, care of tobacco required significant manual labor, and work
parties represented an important social activity for rural communities. This
photograph by Andrew Mueller features a farmer hoeing his field in rural
La Farge, Wisconsin.

Yet how else tell the story of the farm?

There were two hundred sixty acres of cultivated fields, woods, and pasture land sprawled out along the narrow branching ridgetop. There was the cluster of buildings, dominated by the main barn with its stanchions for dairy cows, stalls for work horses. Attached to the barn was a tall silo, which oozed the strong smell of fermented silage when it was filled and made a marvelous, echoing place to yell into when it was empty. A second barn, mostly for hay and young cattle, had a machine-shed lean-to. An eight-foot-tall wood windbreak connected the two barns. Across the barnyard, like the other side of the compound in the fort, was the great tobacco shed. It stood on poles rather than foundations and it creaked and groaned in the wind.

There were the bulging granary, with bins for oats; a slatted corncrib with white and yellow ears showing; a hog house with roof ventilators turning restlessly in the wind; a milkhouse next to the tall steel-towered windmill; and a woodshed with sticks of oak for the kitchen range and heating stoves.

There was the house. It had two wings, the walls of the old one very thick because the siding hid what it had once been—a log house. "You can say you grew up in a log cabin, even if it doesn't show," Mother used to tell us.

In the yard around the house were lilacs, elms, box elders, junipers, white pines, and one immense soft maple tree that looked as if it had been there forever. On the east side of the yard was the orchard with its overgrown apple, cherry, and plum trees. On the west was the rich black soil of the garden.

The farmstead stood on a hilltop, like a castle, like the center of the world. A dusty road went straight into the woods to the west and wound over knolls and swales to the east until it disappeared down the big hill that led to Halls Branch Valley. Look in any direction and there were other ridges, with dots of houses and barns, and the blue shadows of other ridges still beyond them, each a whole world away from the next narrow ridge. Down below, in the valley, was yet another world. The valleys had different trees and animals. Even the seasons were different— watercress stayed green all winter in the valley springs.

Below our orchard, a ravine led down to a timbered hollow which broadened and joined the crooked valley of the Kickapoo River. That ravine and hollow brought to us the whistle of the "Stump Dodgers," the steam locomotives of the Kickapoo Valley and Northern Railroad, so loud on foggy nights the engine seemed to be coming right through the house. That whistle was joined sometimes, when the wind was in the west and the air just right, by the sound of trains along the Mississippi, nine miles to the west.

The nearest neighbors were a half mile away and seemed farther because the buildings were half hidden by a hill and because each farm was its own busy place.

In our own hilltop world there were Father, Mother, and four boys: Laurence, the oldest; then Sam, Junior; then Lee, and me, the youngest. There were two years between each of us. We were as alike as peas in a pod, as different from one another as the four seasons.

There was someone else to make seven of us. Lyle Jackson came as a hired man the year I was born. He stayed on and became such a part of us that even the neighbors sometimes called him the oldest Logan boy.

If the farm had a name before Lyle came, it was soon lost. Lyle, who had grown up near the village of Gays Mills, was used to more people. He took one look out along that isolated ridge, shook his head, and said, "Hell and tooter. We better call it Seldom Seen."

From then on Seldom Seen was the only name ever used for that farm. The seven of us, and the land with all its living things, were like a hive of bees. No matter how fiercely independent any one of us might be, we were each a dependent part of the whole, and we knew that.

Father was the organizer of our partnership with the land. Because he had come from out beyond the hill country, I was always searching for his past, but I could not easily ask him questions, nor could he easily answer. It was as though his earlier years did not belong to us. That part of his life had happened in a foreign language and did not translate into a new place and time.

He came from the Old Country, as he put it. That meant southern Norway and the community of Loga, which was once a little kingdom. "You are descendants of royalty," our Uncle Lou used to tell us.

Born fourth of eight sons and daughters, Father was named Sigvald Hanson Loga. The year was 1880. . . .

Father ran away from home and went to sea when he was fifteen, on an old schooner sailing with timbers for the coal mines of England. "Windjammers," he called the ships, with a mixture of ridicule and pride. For three years he lived with the windjammers. Then there was a voyage when a great storm took his ship. For eleven days it was carried far out into the open Atlantic. Finally the storm ended. Half starved, the crew rerigged enough sail to get the battered schooner headed back toward Norway. Almost every crewman was from that one little community. They came home to families who thought they were dead.

Father was eighteen then.

Here glimpses of his mother appear, the grandmother I never knew, though she lived to be ninety: a stern-faced woman in a metal picture with mountains in the background, a brass candlestick, a tin box for matches, a letter in a foreign language each Christmas, and a silver spoon inscribed with the words *Sigvald, fra Mudder.*

She gathered her sons after that stormy voyage and told them, "I would rather never see you again than to have you lost, one by one, to the sea."

She brought out the box. To each son went passage money to the New World. To the village silversmith she took a pair of old candlesticks. He melted them down and made for each son a silver serving spoon.

Father and three brothers landed in New York in 1898. At Ellis Island an immigration official suggested they had an "n" to the name Loga to make it "more American." They didn't know if they had a choice were not, so they left Ellis Island with the name Logan.

Father also left that island with "not a word of English, ten dollars in my pocket, and the whole country before me." The ten dollars took him to south-central Wisconsin, where his first job was grubbing stumps from newly cleared land. His pay—fifty cents a day. "Young Norwegians were cheaper than blasting powder in those days," he told us.

Father had worked as a hired man on many different farms. He and Lyle talked about their experiences sometimes on summer evenings under the big maple tree. It was endless, adult talk. I could run a mile into the dark woods and come back to find the talk still going on.

They had seen what happens on farms given mostly to tobacco, with the other fields going to ruin. They learned about different combinations of beef, dairy cattle, and hogs. They had worked for men who loved the land, treating it with respect, working with it. Other farmers seemed to hate the land, taking a living from it, giving nothing back.

They found people were different on ridge and valley farms. Some were happier down below where the days were shorter, the wind gentle, storms hidden by steep hillsides. Others were happier on the hilltop, where you could prove yourself by standing against the summer storms and winter blizzards, enduring the stony fields and loneliness, with other ridges beyond yours, like great rollers on the sea.

When he was ready to buy land, Father chose the ridge.

People who came to visit us on our hilltop talked as if they were on an expedition to the end of the world. A cousin of Mother's always drove miles out of the way to avoid the steep hill coming up from Halls Branch Valley. Outsiders just weren't used to the ups and downs of southwestern Wisconsin. It was a small area, missed by the glaciers that had flattened out the country all around it.

Lyle nodded when he first heard about the glaciers. "That figures. Even the ice had sense enough to stay out of these hills. Now wouldn't you think people would be as smart as ice?"

Some of our visitors were from towns. They climbed carefully out of their cars, looking down at the ground with every step, expecting a bear or timber wolf or rattlesnake to get them any minute. They recoiled up from every leaf because it might be poison ivy, and they asked questions we couldn't answer. It would have meant educating them about a world they didn't even know existed.

One of the summer-night voices I remember is that of a bachelor neighbor who shaved once a month, whether he needed it or not. He didn't care much for town people. "I got relatives," he said, "that come when the strawberries are ripe and leave before milkingtime. I guess it must be different in town. Don't know. Never lived there. I guess in town a man can be a banker, barber, storekeeper, just be good at one job. A farm needs a man who's some kind of revolving son of a bitch. You got to help calves get born, nursemaid a dozen different crops, be your own blacksmith, cut the testicles out of male pigs, fix machinery, keep the windmill going . . ."

"Of course, that's just before breakfast," Lyle interrupted with his cat-that-ate-the-canary grin.

The hill country was filled with voices that I remember. Some of them, the older ones mostly, were forever trying to put the past in proper order. I heard them at ice-cream socials, at school picnics, at stores in town, and under our own big maple tree.

"Was it eighteen ninety-five that we didn't get but fourteen inches of rain?"

"I thought it was twelve inches."

"When was it frost came in the middle of August? Never saw so much soft corn in my life."

A small group might come over to Father. "Say, Sam, we been talking about your farm. Wasn't it Banty McPherson who broke the first land?"

"That's what we been told."

"Well, when was that?"

"The deed says eighteen sixty-four."

"There, I told you! I said the Civil War was still going on."

"Well, I thought Pat Mullaney lived there then. He used to tell about Indians crossing his land just below where the buildings are now. They was carrying lead from some little mines down in Hall's Branch. Carried it down to the Kickapoo and took it by canoe clean down to Illinois someplace. Was lead still that scarce after the war was over?"

The voices went on and on, putting events and past years together.

Years were hard to separate on the farm. A year is an arbitrary, calendar thing. Our lives revolved around the seasons. Spring was each year's genesis, the beginning of new life, the awakening of the sleeping land. Summer was heat, sun, harvest, and always work, with muscles aching, shirts covered with dust and sweat and the white rings of salt from earlier sweat.

Fall was the end of harvest, end of the growing season, a glorious burst of color and sun-warmth before killing frost turned the land gray and cold. Fall was a moody time, full of both life and death, a time when we were reminded of the power outside us, reminded that the seasons happen to us. We do not invite the change to come.

Winter was in-between time, the frozen land resting under blowing snow. The farm seemed to shrink in winter, with the farmstead bigger and more important. The animals were inside the barns, the fields were empty. Even the winter birds gathered near the buildings. We were in the house more, and it was a time when we reached out past the frozen fields to explore a bigger world in our books and conversation.

Then, magically, spring again, and rebirth of the rolling seasons, the unfailing promise of the awakening land.

It Is Natural (2006)

Lynne Burgess

Lynne Burgess is a poet, short story writer, and illustrator who lives with her husband on a farm in La Crosse County, Wisconsin.

It is natural
that the ridges would rise in my work,
ancient rims of rock that sustain
always unfolding color, sometimes blue
sometimes green, white, lines of trees
sculpting the sky. This morning,
this morning of the lamb's death
the sun shot yellow across the top
of Catback Ridge and the grasses
kept rising to meet it, the first cut
rolled and baled, stored for winter.
I snip my hair and let the ends fall
curling, over the deck rail to the soil below.
A vulture whirls and stirs the air,
crying above the chicken coop
where the rooster hurries the hens.
It marks the lamb's carcass
and prepares to feed. It is natural
that lamb, raptor, and the woman
who lives with them both, with them all
would emerge, wordless, moving
into the coulee's encircling ridges,
the coulee suffused with mourning light.

Before the Heat of the Day, Kathie Wheeler (2010). Farming in the Driftless Area has had many faces over the centuries: diverse Native horticultures, the wheat boom, the rise of dairy, the advent of soil conservation, and the recent surge of interest in local and organic foods. In recent decades, the Driftless has become home to a growing number of Hmong farmers. Following the Vietnam War, in which the Hmong of Laos were American allies, tens of thousands of Hmong people resettled in the Upper Midwest. The Driftless Area holds the first certified organic Hmong-owned farms in Wisconsin. Painter Kathie Wheeler, who lives on a farm in the Driftless, portrays here a crew of Hmong workers weeding their way down a valley field.

9

WATERWAYS

WATER DEFINES LIFE AND LAND in the Driftless Area. Sands and sediments deposited under Paleozoic seas built its layered sandstones, limestones, and dolomites. Over the eons, surface waters carved its dendritic network of ridges, valleys, and streams. Groundwater seeped into and through its soils and fractured rock, opened its caves, filled its aquifers, and replenished its cold springs and creeks. Water in its solid form—glaciers—spared the Driftless. Water in its liquid form has shaped it since. At the end of the Wisconsin ice age, melted glacial water formed large lakes along the edges of the Driftless, rising until they overtopped and broke through their ice dams and inundated the valleys of the Wisconsin, Black, Mississippi, and other rivers. Over the millennia since, thirty-four inches of annual rain (more or less) have watered the Driftless, sustaining its aquifers, springs, wetlands, creeks, and rivers and all the life that depends upon them.

Water defines the Driftless Area culturally as well. River names speak the region's history and ecology: Mississippi, Saint Croix, Red Cedar, Cannon, Chippewa, Zumbro, Whitewater, Trempealeau, Black, La Crosse, Root, Pine, Bad Axe, Upper Iowa, Baraboo, Kickapoo, Wisconsin, Yellow, Turkey, Grant, Platte, Pecatonica, Sinsinawa, Galena, Maquoketa, Apple. Since people first came into the Driftless, water routes have borne them in, and borne them away. Along waterways, Native mound builders constructed their effigies and buried their dead. Explorers, voyageurs, and Métis traders traveled by canoe and keelboat. On riverbanks, wars were waged, boundaries set, treaties drawn. The Sauk and Fox, Ho-Chunk, and Dakota were removed across the Mississippi. Dissatisfied, Black Hawk and Yellow Thunder and the Decorahs brought their people back across and up the Great River. In 1832, where the Mississippi met the Bad Axe, the waters ran red with the blood of the Sauk. Trade and commerce followed, flowing along by log raft, paddleboat, steamboat, and barge.

What was the Driftless's blessing could also become its curse. For any river, floods are a given, part of its character and behavior. In the corrugated landscape of the Driftless, creeks and rivers are prone to flash floods—especially where land has been made vulnerable by excessive development or intensive agriculture—and the main stem of the Mississippi is given to the periodic epic overflow. Learning to live not just along the waterways but *with the waters* has long been a theme of Driftless existence. In *The Driftless Land*, Kevin Koch writes of the Mississippi: "We all share this river. It hosts our picnics, and we boat on it and float barges on it. Sometimes it drowns our children, and sometimes it floods our towns. It is what it is, and communicates nothing and feels nothing. This is not out of insolence. The river was here first and is not required to be on our terms."

The Pinery Boy (1926)

Collected by Franz Rickaby

The era of white pine logging and rafting in Wisconsin and Minnesota peaked in the 1880s and 1890s, and faded as the old pine was depleted. In August 1915 a final ceremonial pine raft was assembled and floated down the Upper Mississippi River. In addition to billions of board feet, the era yielded a trove of songs and stories, legends and place names. Folklorist, poet, and musician Franz Rickaby (1889–1925) was teaching at the University of North Dakota when he compiled the collection *Ballads and Songs of the Shanty-Boy* (1926). According to his field notes, his source for "The Pinery Boy" was Martha Olin of Eau Claire, Wisconsin, who in turn had learned it around 1867 from a local boy named Thomas Ward.

> Oh, a raftsman's life is a wearisome one.
> It causes many fair maids to weep and mourn.
> It causes them to weep and mourn
> For the loss of a true love that never can return.

Maiden's Rock, Lake Pepin, Alfred Waud (1874). This bluff over Lake Pepin, Maiden Rock, takes its name from the widely known legend that a Dakota woman named Winona leapt to her death here rather than wed one she did not love. Engraved in wood by J. Kilmer after a drawing by Alfred Waud.

"O father, O father, build me a boat,
That down the Wisconsin I may float,
And every raft that I pass by
There I will inquire for my sweet Pinery Boy."

As she was rowing down the stream,
She saw three rafts all in a string.
She hailed the pilot as they drew nigh,
And there she did inquire for her sweet Pinery Boy.

"O pilot, O pilot, tell me true,
Is my sweet Willie among your crew?
Oh, tell me quick and give me joy,
For none other will I have but my sweet Pinery Boy."

"Oh, auburn was the color of his hair,
His eyes were blue and his cheeks were fair.

His lips were of a ruby fine;
Ten thousand times they've met with mine."

"O honored lady, he is not here.
He's drownded in the dells, I fear.
'T was at Lone Rock as we passed by,
Oh, there is where we left your sweet Pinery Boy."

She wrung her hands and tore her hair,
Just like a lady in great despair,
She rowed her boat against Lone Rock
You'd a-thought this fair lady's heart was broke.

"Dig me a grave both long and deep,
Place a marble slab at my head and feet;
And on my breast a turtle dove
To let the world know that I died for love;
And at my feet a spreading oak
To let the world know that my heart was broke."

From *Life on the Mississippi* (1883)

MARK TWAIN

Mark Twain, born Samuel Langhorne Clemens (1835–1901), is forever associated with the Mississippi River, but primarily the middle and lower river where he spent his early life and career as a printer's apprentice and steamboat pilot. Following publication of *The Adventures of Tom Sawyer* (1876), and while working on *Adventures of Huckleberry Finn* (1885), Twain published *Life on the Mississippi*, a hybrid memoir and contemporary travelogue. In the spring of 1882, as Twain was at work on the book, he returned to the river on an exploratory trip. Accompanied by his publisher and a stenographer, Twain boarded the steamboat *Minneapolis* at Hannibal, Missouri, on May 17 for a four-day tour of the Upper Mississippi to St. Paul.

We move up the river—always through enchanting scenery, there being no other kind on the Upper Mississippi—and pass Moline, a center of vast manufacturing industries; and Clinton and Lyons, great lumber centers; and presently reach Dubuque, which is situated in a rich mineral region. The lead mines are very productive, and of wide extent. Dubuque has a great number of manufacturing establishments; among them a plough factory which has for customers all Christendom in general. At least so I was told by an agent of the concern who was on the boat. He said—

"You show me any country under the sun where they really know *how* to plough, and if I don't show you our mark on the plough they use, I'll eat that plough; and I won't ask for any Woostershyre sauce to flavor it up with, either." . . .

The majestic bluffs that overlook the river, along through this region, charm one with the grace and variety of their forms, and the soft beauty of their adornment. The steep verdant slope, whose base is at the water's edge, is topped by a lofty rampart of broken, turreted rocks, which are exquisitely rich and mellow in color—mainly dark browns and dull greens, but splashed with other tints. And then you have the shining river, winding here and there and yonder, its sweep interrupted at intervals by clusters of wooded islands threaded by silver channels; and you have glimpses of distant villages, asleep upon capes; and of stealthy rafts slipping along in the shade of the forest walls; and of white steamers vanishing around remote points. And it is all as tranquil and reposeful as dreamland, and has nothing this-worldly about it—nothing to hang a fret or a worry upon.

Until the unholy train comes tearing along—which it presently does, ripping the sacred solitude to rags and tatters with its devil's warwhoop and the roar and thunder of its rushing wheels—and straightway you are back in this world, and with one of its frets ready to hand for your entertainment: for you remember that this is the very road whose stock always goes down after you buy it, and always goes up again as soon as you sell it. It makes me shudder to this day, to remember that I once came near not getting rid of my stock at all. It must be an awful thing to have a railroad left on your hands. . . .

We added several passengers to our list, at La Crosse; among others an old gentleman who had come to this northwestern region with the early settlers, and was familiar with every part of it. Pardonably proud of it, too. He said—

"You'll find scenery between here and St. Paul that can give the Hudson points. You'll have the Queen's Bluff—seven hundred feet high, and just as imposing a spectacle as you can find anywheres; and Trempeleau Island, which isn't like any other island in America, I believe, for it is a gigantic mountain, with precipitous sides, and is full of Indian traditions, and used to be full of rattlesnakes; if you catch the sun just right there, you will have a picture that will stay with you. And above Winona you'll have lovely prairies; and then come the Thousand Islands, too beautiful for anything; green? why you never saw foliage so green, nor packed so thick; it's like a thousand plush cushions afloat on a looking-glass—when the water's still; and then the monstrous bluffs on both sides of the river—ragged, rugged, dark-complected—just the frame that's wanted; you always want a strong frame, you know, to throw up the nice points of a delicate picture and make them stand out."

The old gentleman also told us a touching Indian legend or two—but not very powerful ones.

After this excursion into history, he came back to the scenery, and described it, detail by detail, from the Thousand Islands to St. Paul; naming its names with such facility, tripping along his theme with such nimble and confident ease, slamming in a three-ton word, here and there, with such a complacent air of 't isn't-anything,-I-can-do-it-any-time-I-want-to, and letting off fine surprises of lurid eloquence at such judicious intervals, that I presently began to suspect—

But no matter what I began to suspect. Hear him—

"Ten miles above Winona we come to Fountain City, nestling sweetly at the feet of cliffs that lift their awful fronts, Jovelike, toward the blue depths of heaven, bathing them in virgin atmospheres that have known no other contact save that of angels' wings.

"And next we glide through silver waters, amid lovely and stupendous aspects of nature that attune our hearts to adoring admiration, about twelve miles, and strike Mount Vernon, six hundred feet high, with romantic ruins of a once first-class hotel perched far among the cloud shadows that mottle its dizzy heights—sole remnant of once-flourishing Mount Vernon, town of early days, now desolate and utterly deserted.

"And so we move on. Past Chimney Rock we fly—noble shaft of six hundred feet; then just before landing at Minnieska our attention is

attracted by a most striking promontory rising over five hundred feet—
the ideal mountain pyramid. Its conic shape—thickly-wooded surface
girding its sides, and its apex like that of a cone, cause the spectator to
wonder at nature's workings. From its dizzy heights superb views of the
forests, streams, bluffs, hills and dales below and beyond for miles are
brought within its focus. What grander river scenery can be conceived,
as we gaze upon this enchanting landscape, from the uppermost point
of these bluffs upon the valleys below? The primeval wildness and awful
loneliness of these sublime creations of nature and nature's God, excite
feelings of unbounded admiration, and the recollection of which can
never be effaced from the memory, as we view them in any direction.

"Next we have the Lion's Head and the Lioness's Head, carved by
nature's hand, to adorn and dominate the beauteous stream; and then
anon the river widens, and a most charming and magnificent view of the
valley before us suddenly bursts upon our vision; rugged hills, clad with
verdant forests from summit to base, level prairie lands, holding in their
lap the beautiful Wabasha, City of the Healing Waters, puissant foe of
Bright's disease, and that grandest conception of nature's works, incom-
parable Lake Pepin—these constitute a picture whereon the tourist's eye
may gaze uncounted hours, with rapture unappeased and unappeasable.

"And so we glide along; in due time encountering those majestic
domes, the mighty Sugar Loaf, and the sublime Maiden's Rock—which
latter, romantic superstition has invested with a voice; and oft-times as
the birch canoe glides near, at twilight, the dusky paddler fancies he
hears the soft sweet music of the long-departed Winona, darling of
Indian song and story.

"Then Frontenac looms upon our vision, delightful resort of jaded
summer tourists; then progressive Red Wing; and Diamond Bluff, impressive and preponderous in its lone sublimity; then Prescott and the
St. Croix; and anon we see bursting upon us the domes and steeples
of St. Paul, giant young chief of the North, marching with seven-league
stride in the van of progress, banner-bearer of the highest and newest
civilization, carving his beneficent way with the tomahawk of commercial enterprise, sounding the warwhoop of Christian culture, tearing off
the reeking scalp of sloth and superstition to plant there the steam-plow
and the school-house—ever in his front stretch arid lawlessness, igno-
rance, crime, despair; ever in his wake bloom the jail, the gallows, and
the pulpit; and ever—"

"Have you ever traveled with a panorama?"

"I have formerly served in that capacity."

My suspicion was confirmed.

"Do you still travel with it?"

"No, she is laid up till the fall season opens. I am helping now to work up the materials for a Tourist's Guide which the St. Louis and St. Paul Packet Company are going to issue this summer for the benefit of travelers who go by that line."

"When you were talking of Maiden's Rock, you spoke of the long-departed Winona, darling of Indian song and story. Is she the maiden of the rock?—and are the two connected by legend?"

"Yes, and a very tragic and painful one. Perhaps the most celebrated, as well as the most pathetic, of all the legends of the Mississippi."

We asked him to tell it. He dropped out of his conversational vein and back into his lecture-gait without an effort, and rolled on as follows—

"A little distance above Lake City is a famous point known as Maiden's Rock, which is not only a picturesque spot, but is full of romantic interest from the event which gave it its name. Not many years ago this locality was a favorite resort for the Sioux Indians on account of the fine fishing and hunting to be had there, and large numbers of them were always to be found in this locality. Among the families which used to resort here, was one belonging to the tribe of Wabasha. We-no-na (first-born) was the name of a maiden who had plighted her troth to a lover belonging to the same band. But her stern parents had promised her hand to another, a famous warrior, and insisted on her wedding him. The day was fixed by her parents, to her great grief. She appeared to accede to the proposal and accompany them to the rock, for the purpose of gathering flowers for the feast. On reaching the rock, We-no-na ran to its summit and standing on its edge upbraided her parents who were below, for their cruelty, and then singing a death-dirge, threw herself from the precipice and dashed them in pieces on the rock below."

"Dashed who in pieces—her parents?"

"Yes."

"Well, it certainly was a tragic business, as you say. And moreover, there is a startling kind of dramatic surprise about it which I was not looking for. It is a distinct improvement upon the threadbare form of Indian legend. There are fifty Lover's Leaps along the Mississippi from whose summit disappointed Indian girls have jumped, but this is the only jump in the lot that turned out in the right and satisfactory way. What became of Winona?"

"She was a good deal jarred up and jolted: but she got herself together and disappeared before the coroner reached the fatal spot; and 'tis said she sought and married her true love, and wandered with him to some distant clime, where she lived happy ever after, her gentle spirit mellowed and chastened by the romantic incident which had so early deprived her of the sweet guidance of a mother's love and a father's protecting arm, and thrown her, all unfriended, upon the cold charity of a censorious world."

I was glad to hear the lecturer's description of the scenery, for it assisted my appreciation of what I saw of it, and enabled me to imagine such of it as we lost by the intrusion of night.

Swimming in the Mississippi River, Gerhard Gesell (c. 1890). Gerhard Gesell (1845–1906) emigrated from Germany in the 1860s and began his career in photography in 1873 in Reads Landing, Minnesota. In 1876 Gesell moved across the Mississippi River to Alma, Wisconsin, where he would operate a photography studio for the next thirty years. While developing a business around portraits of Alma's townspeople, he was also devoted to recording images of everyday life along the Mississippi.

From *American Places* (1981)

WALLACE STEGNER

Almost a century after Twain's riverboat excursion on the Mississippi, Wallace Stegner (1909–1993) plied the same waters. Stegner was widely known as a novelist, short story writer, biographer, essayist, and historian; as an influential writing teacher at Stanford University; and as a staunch advocate of the nation's public lands and wilderness preservation. Although Stegner is generally associated with the American West, he had midwestern roots. He was born in Lake Mills, in north-central Iowa, while his wife Mary hailed from Dubuque. Stegner's subdued account of his trip, "The River," reflected on the Upper Mississippi at a time when, for him, its "wonder ha[d] worn off."

When my wife tells people that she is from Dubuque, she says the name a little challengingly, knowing that the only thing most people know about Dubuque is that *The New Yorker* is not written for an old lady from there. And she takes pains to mention that Dubuque is on the Mississippi, another fact they are unlikely to know. It was a good town to be born in and grow up in, and she lived there without noticeable cultural undernourishment until I induced her to move. She learned to swim in the Mississippi when the undammed current was strong enough to carry a swimmer halfway to Quincy before he could struggle back ashore. Some of the romantic nights of her youth—and mind— were spent on the excursion boats that in the early 1930s still operated out of Dubuque, Davenport, and other towns. Old sternwheelers converted into floating dance floors, they were equipped with bands and drew big crowds of young people.

On such night-time excursions it was customary for the captain to get his blazing palace up into some dark reach, away from the lights of any town, and abruptly shut off both lights and engines. A band stopped, the wheel rolled over and died, all noise and conversation came to a halt.

You could hear the watery stillness. You were afloat on the dark river in the middle of the dark continent, in touch for a brief theatrical moment with the force and mystery of that mighty flood.

A minute, perhaps, of flowing dark. Then the searchlight awoke on the pilothouse and probed a smoking hole in the night and picked out, far downstream, a jungled point. From the point it swept up the black wooded face of the bluff, then down to the living surface of the water, then restlessly wide to find an island, then clear across to the bluffs of the opposite shore. Following that probing light was like standing and breathing shallowly while a doctor holds a stethoscope to your chest. Young men found it a good time to put their arms around their girls.

The searchlight went out. A moment of total black, a feeling like breakdown, like panic. Then the boat's lights blazed on, the band burst out, the held breath was released, the wheel resumed its lazy roll, the minute of mystery was over. But not forgotten. Those captains knew what they were doing. . . .

Seen from the river, with their splendid bluffs behind them, the little towns on the Iowa shore—Marquette, McGregor, Guttenberg—are as picturesque as anything between St. Paul and St. Louis. Even with the sun low above the rim and the towns in shadow, they excite Mary with recollections, for these were the towns of Sunday excursions in her childhood. In the morning, front-lighted, their steeples like tall candles, they would show even better.

But they are not lively towns. Marquette and McGregor have a good deal going through them on the highway, which here runs along the shore, and across the Marquette bridge, the only crossing between Lansing and Dubuque. But the streets are somnolent in the late afternoon. As for Guttenberg, it went quietly to sleep a long time ago, and is not likely to awaken, or realize any of the high aspiration that went into its founding.

Even more than other American regions, the rich farmland of the Middle West attracted idealists and perfectionists—Owenites, Icarians, Hutterites, Amanites, socialists and Christian communists of many varieties, pentecostal sects pursuing New Jerusalem with the same hope of sectarian isolation and social asepsis that brought the Pilgrims to Plymouth Rock. New soil, new social compacts. New frontiers, new moralities and religions and political systems.

The whole Turkey River valley, which joins the Mississippi a few miles below Guttenberg, was a province of the perfected society. Up the Turkey a few miles, French and German Christian communists founded in 1847 a colony called Communia. In 1850 a dozen Scottish families established a cooperative colony at Clydesdale. At Spillville, up near Decorah, there flourished for a good while a colony of Bohemians, including the Bily brothers, notable carvers of wooden clocks; and among the Bohemians, for a short period in the 1890s, lived Anton Dvořák. It is Iowa's boast, in the best American tradition of going well dressed in borrowed clothes, that Dvořák's *String Quartet in F Major* and the final movement of his *New World Symphony* were both written in Spillville.

Earlier than any of these Turkey River communities was Guttenberg. It was founded in 1845 by a group of German intellectuals who in a glow of aspiration named their town after the inventor of movable type. But what happened to the town's name—first mispronounced, then misspelled, then added to the map in its corrupted form—is not unlike what happened in general to imported culture and millennial dreams in America. Their surety was tainted by contact with unwashed neighbors, internal discords multiplied, young people were lured away, enthusiasm waned, and after a generation or two or three what was to be a rural Athens was only another sleepy village from which the liveliest intelligences and the most ambitious talents yearned to escape.

The country westward from Guttenberg, seen from any high point, is a vision of rural opulence out of "America the Beautiful"—white houses, red barns, silver silos, hayfields with great rolls of hay, fields full of grazing dairy herds. But the best Guttenberg can show is a certain threadbare tidiness. The church is big and solid, with double spires, but the streets are nearly empty, the riverfront warehouses of local limestone are closed, nobody is stirring around the commercial fishing dock, the lock and dam don't seem to have brought any business. Like the river, the Milwaukee Railroad seems to run *through* the town, not in any real sense *to* it. Without any significant industry, Guttenberg has only the limited future of a farming center, and perhaps as a bedroom community for industrial towns such as Dubuque.

Our anachronistic steamboat swims through the lock, navigating between nostalgia and faded idealism, past the mouth of the Turkey, where in 1780 the British captured an American fur barge during the only Revolutionary War battle fought in Iowa. In the dusk, before going down to dinner, we search the darkening water in vain for the thing that Marquette reported seeing along here: "a monster with the head of a tiger, a sharp nose like that of a wildcat, with whiskers and straight, Erect ears; the head was gray and the Neck quite black."

Explorers always have the best of it. They get to see things before the wonder has worn off. Nevertheless we look forward to Dubuque in the morning; a reunion with . . . old friends, a look at familiar tree-heavy streets, a ride on the Fourth Street elevator, a treat of smoked sturgeon, which has it over smoked salmon as far as salmon has it over carp. We are not hunting the future or an ideal society, only the present and the real one.

Water Song (2013)

CATHERINE YOUNG

A poet and essayist, Catherine Young has worked as a naturalist, geographer, and national park ranger. She lives and writes on her family's farm near Blue River, Wisconsin.

I wake and listen for it—often in the middle of the night: the sound of the spring creek below our house. I hear it gushing from the springbox, and as it leaves the culvert, it tumbles over the weeping willow's roots, talking loudly in spring and fall when detritus is gone; softer in summer beneath swallows, beside grasses. In winter, the spring creek purls a clear, clear ringing until deep cold freezes fairy bridges across it in places. The creek is an ever-present, resonant spiral of sound.

More than voice of our Wisconsin Driftless Area farm, the spring creek is an artery in a water heart—alive and pulsing. It is a twig on a water tree, and its course shapes the branch of a trout stream called Dieter Hollow Creek, which in turn, is part of the great water tree called the Mississippi River. In spring, the winged ones in the sky follow the trail of water from trunk to twig and then in fall, back again from twig to trunk.

The coursing of the waters shapes the course of our lives—just as it surely has for all the people who have lived here over millennia. A century ago, people who spoke Norwegian filled the hollow along this creek. The family who lived here kept butter and milk in the spring house beneath our weeping willow. Stories handed down from them tell how the spring was the center of the sugarbush for indigenous people who gathered and distilled the sweet waters of this place.

Like all of the people who lived here before us, we are here because of the water.

The waters which flow from these hills begin as artesian springs pushing out of layers of sandstone and limestone.

The phrase *artesian spring* is alluring. A lure. I walk upstream to one of the many springs on our farm in Dieter Hollow to follow a thread of water. In the woods, I find cool trickles seeping and trace the trails through moist brown leaves to their source. I pull away the leaves, wait, and watch for the muddy swirling to settle. It reveals a roiling porridge of water bubbling through fine sand, creating patterns that beg to be deciphered. Stories swirl in those patterns—and sustain the voices of the ancients. . . .

I plunge into the stream. Silt fills around the ankles of my waders, and I remind myself that I can get stuck in stream silt. Under one arm, I hold the stadia rod used for surveying a cross-section of this south-western Wisconsin stream. Under the other, I hold the steel soil probe, used for coring the soil in the cornfield on the streambank ahead of me. I work as a fluvial geomorphologist in Wisconsin—*the place of the gathering of waters*. I have sought these water-shaped lands of the Driftless Area, where no glacial ice has ever smoothed hills or filled valleys; a land of springs and streams all running to the Mississippi River. My job is to measure the flood history along all the tributaries to the Galena and Kickapoo rivers. The sound of the word, *fluvial*, laps against my heart.

I wade into the cornfield, set up the surveying rod, and wave a signal to my work partner across the stream. All around me, corn waves its glossy green leaves. The reflection from sunlight on corn plants blinds me. At my feet, I see the red tubular roots of each stalk anchored in coffee-and-cream colored soil as smooth as paste.

When the surveying equipment is properly set up, we will plunge the probe into the surface, deeper and deeper, until we find an almost black layer: the original prairie soil surface from the 1830s. We will plunge the core in again and again. We will use the samples to look at what the stream has laid over these past 150 years, and how often and with what force it has flooded. Sometimes we will reach the original surface at three feet. At other times we will reach the prairie soil at fifteen feet. All of the deposits on the stream banks are the result of large-scale farming. The yellowish soils here on top of the very dark original surface have been deposited from years of accelerated erosion.

Along stream banks, we can see the exposed bones of the Driftless landscape: the layers of golden limestone or verdigris-covered white sandstones. Sometimes we can see the buried prairie soil, the soil developed under the care of indigenous people over many, many centuries.

I learn the unglaciated Driftless land through layers of sediment: deposits of gravels and silts laid down, flood after flood. I read its history. Sometimes I wade into a stream and stand, becoming a part of the living trail of water. I feel its gentle push. The water of the Driftless landscape calls to me, and I want to answer, calling it *home*.

The weeping willow at our farm's spring creek fills the sky. Its roots are the sounding board for water's music, allowing the cold, clear water to drop and speak. The willow watches over the creek and us.

In April, my young daughter and I wake before dawn and take a thermos of tea down to the water. We plunk our boots into the creek facing our willow. Lazily, we pull out browned stems of last year's weeds and forbs. My daughter and I pluck yellow willow wands, and weave them into bracelets. Soon, fragrant catkins will appear, and the tree will hum with our honeybees. Willow nectar is their first spring food.

In June, my feet land in the spring creek, bare-naked, crushing mint and stepping into woven strands of sunlight. In I plunge—and out! Such ache, I cannot believe my feet are a part of me. The spring waters that course so seemingly frigid in summer actually flow from the ground at the same temperature year round. And though my skin aches from the cold, other creatures stay in the spring water all year. Tiny gravelly tubes rise from stones in the stream, like an underwater garden: caddis fly larvae. Snails in black spiraled shells smaller than a letter on this page cling to golden gravel. Side swimming scuds (a name I adore) float along the creek's edges among spearmint, purple-stemmed peppermint, watercress, and jewelweed. My daughter and I pluck the jewelweed leaves. We drape them over our hands like the softest cloth, and then hold them underwater to see them shine silver. . . . All along the streams where we live, the jewelweed blooms orange and thick, telling us where there is running water; telling us wildlife and humans have played at the waters.

In January, snow makes visible the trails of deer, turkeys, skunks, and opossum who visit the waters while we sleep. The creek becomes the central pathway through a crystal garden and the voice which sets the crystals ringing. In this monochrome landscape of snow and wintry skies, crystallized water seeds the air and coats the trees and bushes. We wake to watch the sunrise set millions of frozen droplets on fire in every color of the rainbow. We call to one another to come to the window and see! Come see, before the sun melts the hoarfrost and allows water to flow once again. We have even seen a crystallized rainbow shimmer in our barnyard: a snowbow in the metallic colors of a soap bubble: of rust red, gold, blue, and silver. The snowbow showed no green; it magnified only what was present on the landscape.

When rain falls, we listen. Each drop of water that falls on our headwaters farm connects us to the Mississippi River water tree. When waters rise on the Mississippi, we watch, helpless to stop the floodwaters and damage farther down in Iowa and Missouri.

And when the Mississippi River is low as it was last year, with patches of duckweed instead of open water, it is because, in part, our branch of water has thinned.

Living on this headwaters farm, we've tried our best to be stewards of the soil and guardians of the waters. To protect the integrity of our branch of the water tree, we farm organically, and we fence our herd of dairy goats away from the trout stream and springs. We know that whatever we do affects the waters upstream as well as downstream—a subtle shift in water flow goes both directions. And though we work hard to protect the waters, we have learned that so much is beyond our control.

In a quarter century of living beside these waters, we have seen the extremes of drought and flood. And we wonder: How does a stream that is normally as deep as a shoe and as wide as a shovel rise to a height twice as tall as any of us in our family and swell as wide as a county highway?

My husband and I are driving with our children to a celebration a few miles from our home. Rain has fallen all week; rain has fallen all day, but all at once the daylight darkens. Halfway in the journey, the *sound* of the rain changes.

We are blinded by rain as we head downhill. Through the windshield, we see a blurry line of headlights come toward us—away from the gathering. At the spillway we see why everyone is leaving: water shoots up into the air higher than the cars trying to cross over and get out. A flash flood. All the creeks are going to rise. All I can think is: *We've got to get home. We've got to get home and see if we can get back to our house.*

The same highway we just drove on minutes before becomes a moving glass surface. Alarm surges up from my core—I know what is coming. "Watch," I say, pointing my finger. Streams beside the road rise as if I have said an incantation, as if the energy of my pointing finger pulls the waters up, turns them round and wild, and sends them roaring through every streambed along every mile back to our hollow. We race through the rains, and none of us says a word as the water pounds against the car.

We top the last ridge to our own hollow and speed downward. Next to the road, a stream that has never ever been there before churns over a pasture and into the ravine we follow.

We turn onto our driveway to face the culvert at the main channel. Can we cross? In the deepening dark, brown waters fill the stream banks. We speed to the house to get the children inside, and then my husband races our vehicles back across the waters and onto the road.

We fill jugs of clean water and wait, on edge. In the darkness, all we can hear is the sound of rain as it beats against the house. Though lightning flashes, there is nothing to see but water. Then a new sound rises—louder than the storm—the *roar* of flood. "Listen," I say to my children. "*Listen.* Dieter Hollow Creek—that's what a really bad flood sounds like."

When a flood comes, you don't see all the damage at once. You can't see anything, because everything is covered and hidden by water, mud, and disbelief. Everything you see confuses you. Your world has changed, and at first you have no words for it.

I didn't want to admit that we lost our farm road. I didn't want to admit that the lower garden was gone and with it, all of the food we raise to survive through a year.

Twenty inches of rain fall that night.

Afterwards, we hear how a road mudslide trapped families in for a few days near where we had driven, and how two horses above Readstown were washed a mile downstream, unharmed. No one saw them go—the waters were too high—and no one knows what kind of ride they had. Hundreds of creeks carve the hollows of the Driftless Area. Every single one has flooded. Sewage and dead and decaying livestock were everywhere. The scent of antibiotics hangs in the air.

We find this:

Our poultry and livestock are alive, but have nowhere to stand out of the wetness. All of the golden gravel that had composed the surface of our long driveway is gone; it lines the spring creek. Trenches in the driveway go down six feet. Boulders appear that we never knew were there—from the farmers long ago who built this road up to the house. Midden piles emerge everywhere—on the road, in the back yard, in the fields—popping out porcelain lids for ancient-style canning jars and decayed saddle shoes. Though we are a headwaters farm, pieces of fencing and stock tank (which are not ours) are strewn atop the mud-covered garden. Huge logs, long-dead trees, lie against the upstream side of the culvert. Our spring-house spring beneath the willow is buried, and so many rivulets are flowing, it's hard to tell where exactly the spring was.

Ten days after the first flood, rains pound and the waters gather a second deluge. We watch in confusion as both creeks rise, coffee-and-cream color; as the driveway beside our house—now without gravel—becomes a river rushing into the spring creek at the willow tree. We see it all happen in morning light.

The spring creek is washed clean of golden gravel. Gray clay and coarse sand line the gouged banks. Beneath the weeping willow, all of the jewelweeds and mints are gone. Strewn here and there, broken branches of the willow lie partially buried in clay. We have fences to fix; logs to cut. We must clean barn and coop, re-roof, re-batten, and re-gravel the farm road.

We are dazed. On edge. Each drop of rain gets our attention. We listen, as if dreading the approach of a beast that has been terrorizing the neighborhood.

Nearby, the Kickapoo River town of Gays Mills succumbs, and the residents decide to relocate the village. Some leave the area.

In the hills and hollows of the Driftless Area, water has always determined the shape of the land; it makes it possible for us to live. We learn to make peace with rain and ask as we make our homes here: *What does the water bring to us, and what does it carry away?*

New waterfalls sing as the spring creek plunges into a sequence of pools. My daughter and I walk down to the weeping willow. We drop our feet into the water. On the banks around us, sapling willow trees sprout from buried branches. They root; take hold; begin a new generation.

From *Crossing the Driftless: A Canoe Trip through a Midwestern Landscape* (2015)

LYNNE DIEBEL

In *Crossing the Driftless* author and long-time paddler Lynne Diebel recounts a 359-mile trip by canoe and portage that she and her husband made in 2009 from Faribault, Minnesota, to Stoughton, Wisconsin. Diebel grew up in southern Minnesota and lives in Stoughton.

June the thirtieth. At dawn, the cold heavy fog and its accompanying sense of mystery drench the river. Alive with the possibilities of the day, we slide our canoe into the current downstream of Lock & Dam 6. We know that by afternoon boredom will have set in and all the trees will look alike, but for now the river runs through our veins. Once again, we're the only boat on the river, yet we are not alone. Herons and egrets fish the shallows and eagles soar above. The eyes of a big snapping turtle watch us, disappearing swiftly and silently as we get too close.

We follow the channel and the channel follows the Minnesota shore, where a stately line of half-dome bluffs rises over five hundred feet above the river, a precipitously steep wooded array of cliffs, faced in places with rocky outcrops of St. Peter sandstone or of the Prairie du Chien Formation, the rocky layers of ancient seabed that built these bluffs. Across the Mississippi in Wisconsin, the top of a ghostly pointed bluff, twin brother to Trempealeau Mountain, appears to float on the surface of the low-lying mist. We're in the embrace of the bluffs now and I feel the visual power of this familiar landscape in a way that only happens for me on the river. Viewing the river valley from acreage or an overlook is a snapshot, a static moment. Floating the river is a movie. It's a subtle but telling difference. As we travel down this wide, deep valley, the ebb and flow of shape and form, the ever-evolving view, slide past my eyes in a visual narrative, and the grandeur of the Upper Mississippi builds.

I find a kindred sense in the accounts of early explorers, who at first believed the lines of bluffs were mountain ranges, and in the many accounts of writers who followed. In *Letters and Notes*, George Catlin wrote, "From day to day, the eye is riveted in listless, tireless admiration, upon the thousand bluffs which tower in majesty above the river on either side, and alternate as the river bends, into countless fascinating forms."

The paddler finds that the morning fog shapes a different image than does the late afternoon sun. On every passage down the river, the angle of the light, the hues and textures of water and land change. When Catlin painted the familiar forms of the Mississippi bluffs, many were treeless; today, after centuries of wildfire suppression, most are thickly forested. I recall historic accounts and art as we float, and the images blur into one. We're traveling down a river valley peopled by the ghosts of paddlers past.

But the river is quite real, and very soon, it seems, Pool 7 comes to an end. As we pass Dresbach Island, both the speedboat traffic and our ever-present tailwind begin to rise. A fight ensues between the wakes and the waves and we're caught in the middle of the muddle. We paddle cautiously into Lock & Dam 7 through water that our paddling friend Warren would call "squirrely," a chaos of current, cross-chopped waves, and boat wakes bouncing off the concrete walls that guide the river craft into the lock's inner sanctum.

From within, I look downstream, over top of the lock gates, all the way to the bridge that carries Interstate 90, the bridge I have crossed so many times in my life. I'm about to see it from underneath for the first time. Already I sensed how disconnected the bridge is from the river, how foreign its linear shape and concrete materials are in this curvaceous riverine world. When we crossed the same bridge in our car, concrete sidewalls prevent us from looking down to the river that flows directly below us; only distant water is visible.

My perfect bridge is one built of wood or stone, with see-through railings that afford a clear view of the river, a tacit acknowledgment that the river should be seen, has beauty and importance. A bridge with solid sidewalls one cannot see through is a statement that what lies below is not worth looking at, that all that matters is crossing the river. In the same way, locking through forces us to encounter the river as a human construct rather than a natural flow of water over land.

Beyond the bridge, a glimpse of a distant cluster of moored house-boats—a house on the water has definite allure—alongside scattered sandbar encampments—even better—returns me to an intimate relationship with the river. We're at the upstream end of the long river town of La Crosse and also at the upstream end of an elaborate riverine highway interchange. The Black and the La Crosse both flow into the Mississippi from Wisconsin at this sprawling confluence, and the Root River joins the Mississippi from Minnesota at the downstream end of town. . . .

When the Corps impounded the Mississippi in the 1930s, the final reach of the Black's main channel, which runs parallel to the Mississippi for about ten miles, disappeared under the waves of Lake Onalaska, the wide shallow expanse of open water behind Lock & Dam 7, separated from the main channel of the Mississippi by a string of low wooded islands. Within the lake, the Black's now amorphous main channel hugs the shoreline, forming again when it slides between the shore and French Island. Downstream of an earthen dam and concrete spillway between the island and Onalaska, and downstream of Lock & Dam 7 and the interstate bridge, the Black reaches its historic and true confluence with the Mississippi, slyly subverting the lock.

Here on the river I feel as though I'm starting to understand this complex confluence, at least a little. These recent chapters in the story of the Black River's relationship with the Mississippi are on record, but I wonder too what permutations the Black went through before written history. Some clues lie upstream. When Bob and I first canoed the Black, it was between the towns of Irving and North Bend, a particularly lovely and remote stretch of river that rambles through the steep hills of the Driftless. The wide gorge, sandy bottom, and frequent sandbars along this reach reflect the lower Black's ancient past as an early outlet for Glacial Lake Wisconsin, and the dark water for which the river was named comes from organic compounds at its headwaters in northeastern Taylor County, a little way south of Timm's Hill, outside the Driftless. After the river crosses into the Driftless at the city of Black River Falls, it traverses the unglaciated area from northeast to southwest. The river valley, carved into the ancient bedrock, grows deeper as it nears the Mississippi River valley, and the underlying geology of the Driftless is visible along this reach. We walked into the mouth of one of its tributaries, Roaring Creek, a small stream with a steep gradient, and up the narrow sandstone canyon that flanks its final drop into the Black, to see a series of small waterfalls drop over sharp-edged hard bedrock ledges. On one tall bluff we paddled next to, the moist Cambrian sandstone bedrock of the sheer cliff face was covered with the small leathery leaves of liverwort plants, anchored by their rhizoids in rock fractures, doing their part to disintegrate this rock face: a very long-term project, and one tiny piece of the Driftless Area's master plan to erode the Paleozoic bedrock.

White pine tops the bluffs and the lower banks are densely wooded with hardwood trees and river birch. Because little of the Black's watershed is agricultural and much is forested, phosphorus and other nutrient

Along the Kickapoo River, Adam Haydock (2014). The Kickapoo River is the longest river that winds its way entirely within the Driftless. Historically, the Kickapoo halted the fires that created oak savanna and prairie to its west, allowing forests to develop east of the river in the heart of the Driftless. Logging occurred here on a smaller scale than in the northwoods, but timber was abundant enough for sawmills to sprout along the banks of the Kickapoo in the nineteenth century, with the river providing power and an avenue to markets downstream. This photograph highlights the river's contemporary draw as a popular stretch for paddlers.

levels are low compared to the nearby Trempealeau and the water is clear. In the shallows, we spotted live mussels and their tracks in the sand. In deeper water were northern pike, bass, redhorse, and huge schools of minnows. And the many bald eagles that flew over us are further testament to the river's abundant fishery. That day the river was low, only about a third of its usual flow, and we had to follow quite a meandering downriver course, occasionally grounding in the shallows and wading for a bit. The channel split at one point; searching for higher water, we wandered off into an alternate Black River, a channel with more flow and fewer deadfalls.

To the paddler, Driftless rivers seem to be all about change. Water levels rise and fall, sometimes dramatically. When the river floods, whole trees are scoured from the banks and carried downstream to be dumped carelessly on sandbars or in sandy shallows, where their presence helps shape the ever-shifting sandy outlines of the channel. The Black shares its past with the Wisconsin River—both drained Glacial Lake Wisconsin and both were log transport routes from lumber camps to the Mississippi during the logging of the north woods. Though the Black is a smaller river, in the eyes of the paddler they look very similar, as do their sandbars, ever moving and shifting.

War (1956)

Joseph Langland

Joseph Thomas Langland (1917–2007) was born and raised in Spring Grove, Minnesota. He studied at the University of Iowa, then served as an infantryman in Europe in World War II. After the war he taught at the Universities of Iowa, Wyoming, and Massachusetts–Amherst. In his poetry Langland often returned to the experiences of his rural childhood, growing up on the Driftless Area farm that his Norwegian grandfather had homesteaded in 1877. "War" recounts Langland's experience of learning, while serving in Europe, that his brother had been lost in combat in the Philippines.

When my young brother was killed
By a mute and dusty shell in the thorny brush
Crowning the boulders of the Villa Verde Trail
On the island of Luzon,

I laid my whole dry body down,
Dropping my face like a stone in a green park
On the east banks of the Rhine;

On an airstrip skirting the Seine
His sergeant brother sat like a stick in his barracks
While cracks of fading sunlight
Caged the dusty air;

In the rocky rolling hills west of the Mississippi
His father and mother sat in a simple Norwegian parlor
With a photograph smiling between them on the table
And their hands fallen into their laps
Like sticks and dust;

And still other brothers and sisters,
Linking their arms together,
Walked down the dusty road where once he ran
And into the deep green valley
To sit on the stony banks of the stream he loved
And let the murmuring waters
Wash over their blood-hot feet with a springing crown
of tears.

10

CONSERVING LANDS

THE TRANSFORMATION OF THE DRIFTLESS landscape quickened through the nineteenth century as land was surveyed and sold, settlers migrated, markets grew, and railroad lines expanded. New technologies came on: the telegraph, steamboats, band saws, steel plows, punt guns, dredges, steam shovels. The settlers carried methods of farming developed in the eastern United States or in the Old World—and not necessarily well suited to the hilly topography, loess soils, and hard rains of the Driftless. Before the dairy revolution took hold in the late nineteenth century, farmers in the Driftless Area grew primarily wheat, oats, corn, and other grains, leading to the depletion of soil nutrients.

By the early twentieth century these trends were destabilizing what Aldo Leopold called the "land community" of the Driftless Area. The northern pineries that fed the downstream sawmills were all but vanquished. Agricultural expansion brought about the near-total conversion of the native oak savannas, prairies, and wetlands. Plowing and hard grazing rendered the soils on the steep Driftless slopes highly vulnerable to erosion. Rains fell onto open ground, washing sediments downhill into increasingly flood-prone streams. Populations of fur-bearing mammals had yet to recover from the fur industry's decades of exploitation, while overhunting depleted even once-common game species. The advent of the internal combustion engine and the mechanization of farm life, beginning in the 1910s and 1920s, further intensified these trends.

In these same decades, however, a counterforce emerged: the conservation movement. The Driftless Area would became a landscape of both controversy and innovation in conservation. In the early 1920s sportsmen promoted establishment of the Upper Mississippi National Wildlife and Fish Refuge. In the mid-1930s farmers in the Coon Creek watershed came together in a radical experiment in watershed restoration and land stewardship. Early state parks, forests, and preserves—Wyalusing (1917), Apple River Canyon (1932), Yellow River (1933), Pike's Peak (1935), Beaver Creek Valley (1937), Wildcat Mountain (1948)—protected special places within the Driftless landscape. In 1949 Effigy Mounds National Monument was created to safeguard its nationally significant concentration of intact mounds.

But conservation in the Driftless was not only about protecting the special, rare, and threatened. It was, and is, about readjusting the social, economic, and ecological relationships between people and land more generally. In recent years conservation has embraced the adoption of new agricultural practices that protect and regenerate soils, waters, plant communities, and wildlife. In the Kickapoo Valley, at Sauk Prairie, and elsewhere, conservation has entailed new ways of resolving historic disputes and building upon shared conservation values. It has involved reimagining how the built environment can fit within the contours of the land—inspired in part by the works of a visionary child of the Driftless, Frank Lloyd Wright. Now conservation faces sobering new realities. How can the cities, towns, farms, and economies of the Driftless Area—how can we—respond to climate change, biodiversity loss, compromised food and food systems, intensified demands on our soils and freshwaters, energy infrastructure and development pressures, the sand mining boom, and other environmental challenges? Will we regard them as inexorable trends or as conservation challenges and opportunities?

From *Wisconsin Sketches* (1973)

ROBERT E. GARD

The fostering of the arts in rural communities was a passion for Robert Gard (1910–1992). Gard was a Kansas native who joined the faculty of the University of Wisconsin in Madison in 1945. For the next four decades he was a leading organizer and advocate of the arts in Wisconsin and nationally. He helped to establish a number of arts organizations, including the Wisconsin Regional Writers Association, the Wisconsin Arts

Foundation and Council, the School of the Arts at Rhinelander, and the National Community Theatre Center.

I awoke one clear morning and said
I will certainly do something great today
I will move a mountain
Or at least cause a bell to chime
Celebrating some minor victory.
Instead, near Spring Green,
I crossed a star-flowered prairie,
Sat down in the middle of tall grass
And simply stared upward
At white clouds in a spring sky.

A Wisconsin meadow
In spring
With shooting stars
And sweet star grasses
Can make a fulfilled astronomer
Of any earthbound, astral
Day seeker.

Coon Valley: An Adventure in Cooperative Conservation (1935)

ALDO LEOPOLD

Conservationist, scientist, teacher, and writer Aldo Leopold (1887–1948) is most closely associated with the "sand county" landscape—just east of the Driftless—that he and his family worked to restore along the Wisconsin River in Sauk County, Wisconsin. However, Leopold had many opportunities to work in the Driftless landscape. Most prominently, Leopold was an adviser to the restoration program in the Coon Creek watershed in the 1930s—the nation's first watershed conservation project. In this article, first published in *American Forests* magazine, Leopold described the soil erosion calamity that was apparent throughout the Driftless Area and the innovative, community-wide effort to address it at Coon Valley.

There are two ways to apply conservation to land. One is to superimpose some particular practice upon the pre-existing system of land-use, without regard to how it fits or what it does to or for other interests involved.

The other is to reorganize and gear up the farming, forestry, game cropping, erosion control, scenery, or whatever values may be involved so that they collectively comprise a harmonious balanced system of land-use.

Each of our conservation factions has heretofore been so glad to get any action at all on its own special interest that it has been anything but solicitous about what happened to the others. This kind of progress is probably better than none, but it savors too much of the planless exploitation it is intended to supersede.

Lack of mutual cooperation among conservation groups is reflected in laws and appropriations. Whoever gets there first writes the legislative ticket to his own particular destination. We have somehow forgotten that all this unorganized avalanche of laws and dollars must be put in order before it can permanently benefit the land, and that this onerous job, which is evidently too difficult for legislators and propagandists, is being wished upon the farmer and upon the administrator of public properties. The farmer is still trying to make out what it is that the many-voiced public wants him to do. The administrator, who is seldom trained in more than one of the dozen special fields of skill comprising conservation, is growing gray trying to shoulder his new and incredibly varied burdens. The stage, in short, is all set for somebody to show that each of the various public interests in land is better off when all cooperate than when all compete with each other. This principle of integration of land uses has been already carried out to some extent on public properties like the National Forests. But only a fraction of the land, and the poorest fraction at that, is or can ever become public property. The crux of the land problem is to show that integrated use is possible on private farms, and that such integration is mutually advantageous to both the owner and the public.

Such was the intellectual scenery when in 1933 there appeared upon the stage of public affairs a new federal bureau, the United States Soil Erosion Service. Erosion-control is one of those new professions whose

Erosion in the Black River watershed (1935). The steep-sided valleys so characteristic of the Driftless Area, especially those nearer to the Mississippi River, were subject to episodes of catastrophic gully erosion starting in the 1890s. Heavy grazing and intensive cropping exposed the vulnerable loess soils, which then dissolved when intensive rains came. By the early 1930s soil erosion was a nationwide crisis, leading to the establishment in 1933 of the U.S. Soil Erosion Service, renamed and expanded into the Soil Conservation Service in 1935. The Coon Creek Watershed became the nation's first watershed restoration demonstration project, pioneering techniques in private land conservation that would be adopted throughout the country. This image of a deep gully was taken in 1935 just north of Coon Creek in the Black River watershed.

personnel has been recruited by the fortuitous interplay of events. Previous to 1933 its work had been to define and propagate an idea, rather than to execute a task. Public responsibility had never laid its crushing weight on their collective shoulders. Hence the sudden creation of a bureau, with large sums of easy money at its disposal, presented the probability that some one group would prescribe its particular control technique as the panacea for all the ills of the soil. There was, for example, a group that would save land by building concrete check-dams in gullies, another by terracing fields, another by planting alfalfa or clover, another by planting slopes in alternating strips following the contour, another by curbing cows and sheep, another by planting trees.

It is to the lasting credit of the new bureau that it immediately decided to use not one, but all, of these remedial methods. It also perceived from the outset that sound soil conservation implied not merely erosion control, but also the integration of all land crops. Hence, after selecting certain demonstration areas on which to concentrate its work, it offered to each farmer on each area the cooperation of the government in installing on his farm a reorganized system of land-use, in which not only soil conservation and agriculture, but also forestry, game, fish, fur, flood-control, scenery, songbirds, or any other pertinent interest were to be duly integrated. It will probably take another decade before the public appreciates either the novelty of such an attitude by a bureau, or the courage needed to undertake so complex and difficult a task.

The first demonstration area to get under way was the Coon Valley watershed, near La Crosse, in west-central Wisconsin. This paper attempts a thumbnail sketch of what is being done on the Coon Valley Erosion Project. Coon Valley is one of the innumerable little units of the Mississippi Valley which collectively fill the national dinner pail. Its particular contribution is butterfat, tobacco, and scenery.

When the cows which make the butter were first turned out upon the hills which comprise the scenery, everything was all right because there were more hills than cows, and because the soil still retained the humus which the wilderness vegetation through the centuries had built up. The trout streams ran clear, deep, narrow, and full. They seldom overflowed. This is proven by the fact that the first settlers stacked their hay on the creek-banks, a procedure now quite unthinkable. The deep loam of even the steepest fields and pastures showed never a gully, being able to take on any rain as it came, and turn it either upward into crops, or downward into perennial springs. It was a land to please everyone, be he an empire-builder or a poet.

But pastoral poems had no place in the competitive industrialization of pre-war America, least of all in Coon Valley with its thrifty and ambitious Norse farmers. More cows, more silos to feed them, then machines to milk them, and then more pasture to graze them—this is the epic cycle which tells in one sentence the history of the modern Wisconsin dairy farm. More pasture was obtainable only on the steep upper slopes, which were timber to begin with, and should have remained so. But pasture they now are, and gone is the humus of the old prairie which until recently enabled the upland ridges to take on the rains as they came.

Result: Every rain pours off the ridges as from a roof. The ravines of the grazed slopes are the gutters. In their pastured condition they cannot resist the abrasion of the silt-laden torrents. Great gashing gullies are torn out of the hillside. Each gully dumps its load of hillside rocks upon the fields of the creek bottom, and its muddy waters into the already swollen streams. Coon Valley, in short, is one of the thousand farm communities which, through the abuse of its originally rich soil, has not only filled the national dinner pail, but has created the Mississippi flood problem, the navigation problem, the overproduction problem, and the problem of its own future continuity.

The Coon Valley Erosion Project is an attempt to combat these national evils at their source. The "nine-foot channel" and endless building of dykes, levees, dams and harbors on the lower river, are attempts to put a halter on the same bull after he has gone wild.

The Soil Erosion Service says to each individual farmer in Coon Valley: "The government wants to prove that your farm can be brought back. We will furnish you free labor, wire, seed, lime, and planting stock, if you will help us reorganize your cropping system. You are to give the new system a five-year trial." A total of 315 farmers, or nearly half of all the farms in the watershed, have already formally accepted the offer. Hence we now see foregathered at Coon Valley a staff of technicians to figure out what should be done; a C.C.C. camp to perform labor; a nursery, a seed warehouse, a lime quarry, and other needed equipments; a series of contracts with farmers, which, collectively, comprise a "regional plan" for the stabilization of the watershed and of the agricultural community which it supports.

The plan, in a nutshell, proposes to remove all cows and crops from the steep slopes, and to use these slopes for timber and wildlife only. More intensive cultivation of the flat lands is to make up for the retirement of the eroding hillsides. Gently sloping fields are to be terraced or strip-cropped. These changes, plus contour farming, good crop rotations, and the repair of eroding gullies and stream banks, constitute the technique of soil restoration.

The steep slopes now to be used for timber and game have heretofore been largely in pasture. The first visible evidence of the new order on a Coon Valley farm is a C.C.C. crew stringing a new fence along the contour which marks the beginning of forty percent gradients. This new fence commonly cuts off the upper half of the pasture. Part of this upper half still bears timber, the rest is open sod. The timbered part has been grazed clear of undergrowth, but with protection this will come back to brush and young timber and make range for ruffed grouse. The open part is being planted, largely to conifers—white pine, Norway pine, and Norway spruce for north slopes, Scotch pine for south slopes. The dry south slopes present a special problem. In pre-settlement days they carried hazel, sumac, and bluestem rather than timber, the grass furnishing the medium for quick hot fires. Will these hot dry soils, even under protection, allow the planted Scotch pine to thrive? I doubt it. Only the north slopes and coves will develop commercial timber, but all the fenced land can at least be counted upon to produce game and soil cover and cordwood.

Creek banks and gullies, as well as steep slopes, are being fenced and planted. Despite their much smaller aggregate area, these bank plantings will probably add more to the game carrying capacity of the average farm than will the larger solid blocks of plantings on slopes. This prediction is based on their superior dispersion, their higher proportion of deciduous species, and their richer soils. . . .

Forestry and fencing are not the alpha and omega of Coon Valley technique. In odd spots of good land near each of the new game coverts, the observer will see a newly enclosed spot of a half-acre each. Each of these little enclosures is thickly planted to sorghum, kaffir, millet, proso, sunflower. These are the food patches to forestall winter starvation in wild life. The seed and fence were furnished by the government, the cultivation and care by the farmer. There were 337 such patches grown in 1934—the largest food patch system in the United States, save only that found on the Georgia Quail Preserves. There is already friendly rivalry among many farmers as to who has the best food patch, or the most birds using it. This feeding system is, I think, accountable for the fact that the population of quail in 1934–35 was double that of 1933–34, and the pheasant population was quadrupled. Such a feeding system, extended over all the farms of Wisconsin, would, I think, double the crop of farm game in a single year.

This whole effort to rebuild and stabilize a countryside is not without its disappointments and mistakes. A December blizzard flattened out most of the food patches and forced recourse to hopper feeders. The willow cuttings planted on stream banks proved to be the wrong species and refused to grow. Some farmers, by wrong plowing, mutilated the new terraces just built in their fields. The 1934 drouth killed a large part of the plantings of forest and game cover.

What matter, though, these temporary growing pains when one can cast his eyes upon the hills and see hard-boiled farmers who have spent their lives destroying land now carrying water by hand to their new plantations? American lumbermen may have become so steeped in economic determinism as actually to lack the personal desire to grow trees, but not Coon Valley farmers! Their solicitude for the little evergreens is sometimes almost touching. It is interesting to note, however, that no such pride or tenderness is evoked by their new plantings of native hardwoods. What explains this difference in attitude? Does it arise from a latent sentiment for the conifers of the Scandinavian homeland? Or does it merely reflect that universal urge to capture and domesticate the exotic which found its first American expression in the romance of Pocahontas, and its last in the Americanization of the ring-necked pheasant?

Most large undertakings display, even on casual inspection, certain policies or practices which are diagnostic of the mental attitude behind the whole venture. From these one can often draw deeper inferences than from whole volumes of statistics. A diagnostic policy of the Coon Valley staff is its steadfast refusal to straighten streams. To those who know the speech of hills and rivers, straightening a stream is like shipping vagrants—a very successful method of passing trouble from one place to the next. It solves nothing in any collective sense.

Not all the sights of Coon Valley are to be seen by day. No less distinctive is the nightly "bull session" of the technical staff. One may hear a forester expounding to an engineer the basic theory of how organic matter in the soil decreases the percent of run-off; an economist holds forth on tax rebates as a means to get farmers to install their own erosion control. Underneath the facetious conservation one detects a vein of thought—an attitude toward the common enterprise—which is strangely reminiscent of the early days of the Forest Service. Then, too, a staff of technicians, all under thirty, was faced by a common task so large and so long as to stir the imagination of all but dullards.

I suspect that the Soil Erosion Service, perhaps unwittingly, has recreated a spiritual entity which many older conservationists have thought long since dead.

Cows at Taliesin #64, Pedro Guerrero (1940). In 1939 Pedro Guerrero (1917–2012) was twenty-two years old and a recent dropout from the Art Center School in Los Angeles when Frank Lloyd Wright hired him to photograph Taliesin West, then under construction in Scottsdale, Arizona. That engagement began a relationship between the architect and the photographer that would last for the remainder of Wright's life and would launch Guerrero's career as an internationally renowned art and architecture photographer. Guerrero lived in Connecticut but was a regular visitor to Spring Green. The roofline of Taliesin is visible on the horizon in this image.

From *Frank Lloyd Wright: An Autobiography* (1943)

Frank Lloyd Wright

Frank Lloyd Wright (1869–1957) is widely regarded as one of history's most original and influential architects, a legacy that reflects his philosophy of an "organic architecture" that promotes the harmonious integration of the natural and built environments. Wright was born in Richland Center, Wisconsin, and built Taliesin, his landmark home, studio, and

school, along the Wisconsin River in nearby Spring Green. In this passage from his autobiography, Wright explains how his architectural philosophy reflected the influence of his native Driftless landscape.

Taliesin was the name of a Welsh poet, a druid-bard who sang to Wales
the glories of fine art. Many legends cling to that beloved reverend name
in Wales.

Richard Hovey's charming masque, "Taliesin," had just made me
acquainted with his image of the historic bard. Since all my relatives
had Welsh names for their places, why not Taliesin for mine? . . . Literally the Welsh word means "shining brow."

This hill on which Taliesin now stands as "brow" was one of my
favorite places when as a boy looking for pasque flowers I went there
in March sun while snow still streaked the hillsides. When you are on
the low hill-crown you are out in mid-air as though swinging in a plane,
the Valley and two others dropping away from you leaving the tree-tops
standing below all about you. . . .

As a boy I had learned to know the ground-plan of the region in every
line and feature. For me now its elevation is the modeling of the hills,
the weaving and the fabric that clings to them, the look of it all in tender
green or covered with snow or in full glow of summer that bursts into
the glorious blaze of autumn. I still feel myself as much a part of it as
the trees and birds and bees are, and the red barns. Or as the animals
are, for that matter.

When family-life in Oak Park that spring of 1909 conspired against
the freedom to which I had come to feel every soul was entitled, I had
no choice, would I keep my self-respect, but go out a voluntary exile
into the uncharted and unknown. Deprived of legal protection, I got my
back against the wall in this way. I meant to live if I could an uncon-
ventional life. I turned to this hill in the Valley as my Grandfather before
me had turned to America—as a hope and haven. . . .

And architecture by now was quite mine. It had come to me by actual
experience and meant something out of this ground we call America.
Architecture was something in league with the stones of the field, in
sympathy with "the flower that fadeth and the grass that withereth." It
had something of the prayerful consideration for the lilies of the field
that was my gentle grandmother's: something natural to the great
change that was America herself.

It was unthinkable to me, at least unbearable, that any house should be put *on* that beloved hill.

I knew well that no house should ever be *on* a hill or *on* anything. It should be *of* the hill. Belonging to it. Hill and house should live together each the happier for the other. That was the way everything found round about was naturally managed except when man did something. When he added his mite he became imitative and ugly. Why? Was there no natural house? I felt I had proved there was. Now I wanted a *natural* house to live in myself. I scanned the hills of the region where the rock came cropping out in strata to suggest buildings. How quiet and strong the rock-ledge masses looked with the dark red cedars and white birches, there, above the green slopes. They were all part of the countenance of Southern Wisconsin.

I wished to be part of my beloved Southern Wisconsin, too. I did not want to put my small part of it out of countenance. Architecture, after all, I have learned—or before all, I should say—is no less a weaving and a fabric than the trees are. And as anyone might see, a beech tree is a beech tree. It isn't trying to be an oak. Nor is a pine trying to be a birch, although each makes the other more beautiful when seen together.

The world had had appropriate buildings before—why not appropriate buildings now, more so than ever before? There must be some kind of house that would belong to that hill, as trees and the ledges of rock did; as Grandmother and Mother had belonged to it in their sense of it all.

There must be a natural house, not natural as caves and log-cabins were natural, but native in spirit and the making, having itself all that architecture had meant whenever it was alive in times past. Nothing at all I had ever seen would do. This country had changed all that old building into something inappropriate. . . . I couldn't imagine living in any period-houses I had ever seen or the ugly ones around there. Yes, there was a house that hill might marry and live happily with ever after. I fully intended to find it. I even saw for myself what it might be like. And I began to build it as the brow of that hill.

It was still a very young faith that undertook to build that house. It was the same faith, though, that plants twigs for orchards, vineslips for vineyards, and small whips to become beneficent shade trees. And it planted them all about!

I saw the hill-crown back of the house as one mass of apple trees in bloom, perfume drifting down the Valley, later the boughs bending to the ground with red and white and yellow spheres that make the apple tree no less beautiful than the orange tree. I saw plum trees, fragrant drifts of snow-white in the spring, loaded in August with blue and red and yellow plums, scattering them over the ground at a shake of the hand. I saw the rows on rows of berry bushes, necklaces of pink and green gooseberries hanging to the under side of the green branches. I saw thickly pendent clusters of rubies like tassels in the dark leaves of the currant bushes. I remembered the rich odor of black currants and looked forward to them in quantity.

Black cherries? White cherries? Those too.

There were to be strawberry beds, white, scarlet and green over the covering of clean wheat-straw.

And I saw abundant asparagus in rows and a stretch of great sumptuous rhubarb that would always be enough. I saw the vineyard now on the south slope of the hill, opulent vines loaded with purple, green and yellow grapes. Boys and girls coming in with baskets filled to overflowing to set about the rooms, like flowers. Melons lying thick in the trailing green on the hill slope. Bees humming over all, storing up honey in the white rows of hives beside the chicken yard.

And the herd that I would have! The gentle Holsteins and a monarch of a bull—a sleek glittering decoration of the fields and meadows as they moved about, grazing. The sheep grazing too on the upland slopes and hills, the plaintive bleat of little white lambs in spring.

Those grunting sows to turn all waste into solid gold.

I saw the spirited, well-schooled horses, black horses and chestnut mares with glossy coats and splendid strides, being saddled and led to the mounting-block for rides about the place and along the country lanes I loved—the best of companionship alongside. I saw sturdy teams ploughing in the fields. There would be the changing colours of the slopes, from seeding time to harvest. I saw the scarlet comb of the rooster and his hundreds of hens—their white eggs and the ducks upon the pond. Geese, too, and swans floating upon the water in the shadow of the trees.

I looked forward to peacocks Javanese and white on the low roofs of the buildings or calling from the walls of the courts. And from the vegetable gardens I walked into a deep cavern in the hill—modern equivalent of the rootcellar of my grandfather. I saw its wide sand floor planted with celery, piled high with squash and turnips, potatoes, carrots, onions, parsnips. Cabbages wrapped in paper and hanging from the roof. Apples, pears and grapes stored in wooden crates walled the cellar from floor to roof. And cream! All the cream the boy had been denied. Thick—so lifting it in a spoon it would float like an egg on the fragrant morning cup of coffee or ride on the scarlet strawberries.

Yes, Taliesin should be a garden and a farm behind a real workshop and a good home.

I saw it all, and planted it all and laid the foundation of the herd, flocks, stable and fowl as I laid the foundation of the house.

All these items of livelihood came back—improved from boyhood.

And so began a "shining brow" for the hill, the hill rising unbroken above it to crown the exuberance of life in all these rural riches.

There was a stone quarry on another hill a mile away, where the yellow sand-limestone uncovered lay in strata like outcropping ledges in the facades of the hills. The look of it was what I wanted for such masses as would rise from these native slopes. The teams of neighboring farmers soon began hauling the stone over to the hill, doubling the teams to get it to the top. Long cords of this native stone, five hundred or more from first to last, got up there ready to hand, as Father Larson, the old Norse stone mason working in the quarry beyond, blasted and quarried it out in great flakes. The slabs of stone went down for pavements of terraces and courts. Stone was sent along the slopes into great walls. Stone stepped up like ledges on to the hill and flung long arms in any direction that brought the house to the ground. The ground! My grandfather's ground. It was lovingly felt as intimate in all this.

Finally it was not so easy to tell where pavements and walls left off and ground began. Especially on the hill-crown, which became a low-walled garden above the surrounding courts, reached by stone steps walled into the slopes. A clump of fine oaks that grew on the hilltop stood untouched on one side above the court. A great curved stone-walled seat enclosed the space just beneath them, and stone pavement stepped down to a spring or fountain that welled up into a pool at the centre of the circle. Each court had its fountain and the winding stream below had a great dam. A thick stone wall was thrown across it, to make a pond at the very foot of the hill and raise the water in the valley to within sight from Taliesin. The water below the falls thus made was sent by hydraulic ram up to a big stone reservoir built into the higher hill, just behind and above the hilltop garden, to come down again into the fountains and go on down to the vegetable gardens on the slopes below the house.

Taliesin, of course, was to be an architect's workshop, a dwelling as well, for young workers who would come to assist. And it was a farm cottage for the farm help. Around a rear court were to be farm buildings for Taliesin was to be a complete living unit genuine in point of comfort and beauty, yes, from pig to proprietor. The place was to be self-sustaining if not self-sufficient, and with its domain of two hundred acres was to be shelter, food, clothes and even entertainment within itself. It had to be its own light-plant, fuelyard, transportation and water system.

Taliesin was to be recreation ground for my children and their children perhaps for many generations more. This modest human programme in terms of rural Wisconsin arranged itself around the hilltop in a series of four varied courts leading one into the other, the courts all together forming a sort of drive along the hillside flanked by low buildings on one side and by flower gardens against the stone walls that retained the hill-crown on the other.

The hill-crown was thus saved and the buildings became a brow for the hill itself. The strata of fundamental stone-work kept reaching around and on into the four courts, and made them. Then stone, stratified, went into the lower house walls and up from the ground itself into the broad chimneys. This native stone prepared the way for the lighter plastered construction of the upper wood-walls. Taliesin was to be an abstract combination of stone and wood as they naturally met in the aspect of the hills around about. And the lines of the hills were the lines of the roofs, the slopes of the hills their slopes, the plastered surfaces of the light wood-walls, set back into shade beneath broad eaves, were like the flat stretches of sand in the river below and the same in color, for that is where the material that covered them came from. . . .

A house of the North. The whole was low, wide and snug, a broad shelter seeking fellowship with its surroundings. A house that could open to the breezes of summer and become like an open camp if need be. With spring came music on the roofs, for there were few dead roof-spaces overhead, and the broad eaves so sheltered the windows that they were safely left open to the sweeping, soft air of the rain. Taliesin was grateful for care. Took what grooming it got with gratitude and repaid it all with interest.

Taliesin's order was such that when all was clean and in place its countenance beamed, wore a happy smile of well-being and welcome for all.

It was intensely human, I believe.

Letter from the Old Order Amish Churches (1995)

In 1995 widespread public debate broke out over proposals by the Wisconsin Air National Guard to institute low-altitude training flights over the heart of the Driftless Area. Members of the Old Order Amish Churches of Wilton, Hillsboro, La Valle, Loganville, Readstown, Viroqua, Chaseburg, and Cashton, Wisconsin, responded to the proposal with a joint letter—breaking with Amish practice to avoid public controversies.

Dear Lt. Col. Adams,

. . . We are writing to you because we are shocked and saddened to hear that the Air National Guard plans two new air corridors in which, each year, 2,151 training flights will fly at levels as low as 100 feet—over an area in which approximately 5,000 Amish people live. We plead with you to stop this plan because it would be alien and disastrous to our entire, simple, way of life including our religious beliefs, physical safety, and livelihood.

Our religious beliefs are derived from the Old and New Testaments—The Word Of God—and are rooted in a deep reverence for pacifism which would be shattered by the continued presence of military bombers in the skies. Pacifism is at the core of our everyday life and unites us in love for our rural life and in fellowship with one another. Our spiritual life is extremely important to us and to this end we meet throughout the week. We also meet on Sundays when all the communities gather together in different believers' homes to hear the Word of God preached. The Air National Guard's low-flying jets would not only disrupt our peaceful worship with high decibel noise, but also infringe on our Christian religious pacifist beliefs as visual symbols of war rending the heavens overhead us.

Our physical safety would be endangered by low-level flights and all ages of our communities would be at risk. We daily contend with the fact that animals startled by noise often instinctively react in panic to either natural or other sounds—such as those made by motor vehicles. Because we Amish are so often behind horses during our day-to-day rural activities, we cannot stress enough the danger we would be exposed to by the roar of low-flying jets.

Our strict "Old Order" Amish religion prohibits the use of rubber tires and the use of motorized vehicles unless the travel is beyond our community. It also forbids the owning of telephones. This means that most communication inside our community depends on the use of our horse-drawn wooden wheeled buggies. Farming also relies on horse-drawn implements and wagons.

Judging by the accidents caused in our community by the startle effect on animals, we can well imagine the horrors high decibel noise would inflict on us. For instance, just the other day, ice slid off a roof while an Amish farmer was hooking up two big draft-horses. They both bolted and one landed on its back in the ditch. No one is strong enough to hold back an eight-foot-high, ten-foot-long horse, weighing 2,000 pounds!

On another occasion, a dump truck dumped gravel and this noise caused a hitched team of horses to bolt. Such animals remain skittish and untrustworthy for years—while some never get over the shock. A horse pulling a buggy carrying parents with a young daughter sitting between them was startled by the sudden appearance of a car. When the driver of the car honked, the horse reacted instinctively by kicking back at what was behind it—striking the little girl in the head and causing her to bleed to death in her mother's arms. . . .

Many Amish families have about thirty-five cows and heifers totaling approximately 22,000 cows and young stock in the threatened communities. Part of a day's work includes milking by hand, and children from about six years of age and up help with this and many other farm chores. Younger children are also often present in the barns. The physical safety of anyone sitting next to the rear flank of a cow weighing up to 1,500 pounds is in extreme danger should the animal be startled by noise. The cow could kick or trample the milker and anyone else nearby. . . .

We rely on the sale of milk for cheese-making and we have heard of the reduced production of milk by dairy cows in similarly affected areas. High decibel noise would impact the livelihood of all of us. However, jet fumes and fuel spills would be another hazard for those of us who produce organic vegetables and milk for sale.

Loud, low-flying bombers threaten not only our religion and our lives, but also sound a death-knell for our way of life. We are a self-reliant, tax-paying community not taking any government social security, subsidies, set aside programs or aid of any kind. However, we are asking in earnest that the United States Government send a group of people to see how we live and to conduct a scientific survey to answer our concerns.

If we are forced to leave the Kickapoo Valley region, who will buy our farms? Where could we go? Will we be left as prisoners here?

We are very concerned about our situation. We are also very sad about the threat to our farms because our love for our rural way of life is a spiritual value based on Scripture. We believe that the first and second verses, of the second chapter of Paul's Epistle to Timothy, express our hearts' feeling:

"I exhort therefore, that, first of all supplications, prayers, intercessions and giving of thanks, be made for all men;

For Kings and for all that are in authority; that we may lead a quiet and peaceable life in all godliness and honesty. . . ."

The question is what will become of our heart's desire? Also our precious, God-given freedom that we have.

You surely have a home of your own. So, bearing this in mind, you would not want this to interrupt your peace—we are sure. The Golden Rule is, "Do unto others as you would have them do unto you." "Love thy neighbor as thyself."

With this in mind we fervently pray and trust that God will give you heart and feeling to consider our Heartfelt Plea to answer our many questions.

Sincerely,

Signed by over 500 members of the local organizations.

An Ecological Play on a Stage
Known as Dunlap Hollow (1998)

STANLEY TEMPLE

Stanley Temple is the Beers-Bascom Professor Emeritus in Conserva-
tion at the University of Wisconsin–Madison and a Senior Fellow at the
Aldo Leopold Foundation in Baraboo. He lives on ninety-three acres in
Dunlap Hollow, on the eastern edge of the Driftless Area in Dane County,
Wisconsin.

Wisconsin's landscapes rarely remain stable for long; they are dynamic
and inexorably shift in concert with environmental fluctuations. Like
the stage of a long-running play with many acts, a landscape changes as
sets (ecosystems) and characters (plant and animal species) move on
and off stage, responding to the orders of a series of directors who each
leave their unique influence on the plot of the play. The pace of the
action on a landscape stage may be almost imperceptibly slow or terribly swift, but it is inevitable that the scenery and the actors will change,
regardless of how attached some members of the audience may have
become to the previous act.

As members of the audience, individual human beings do not live
long enough to witness many of the long-term twists and turns in the
plot of the ecological play taking place on their favorite landscape stage.
Most will see and appreciate only the few acts that take place during
their brief lifetime. Only with a playbill can they know what has happened in previous acts and what lies ahead. For ecological plays on the
stage of a natural landscape, the most insightful descriptions of past
and future acts are usually written by ecologists who understand the
plot and know how the sets and characters change.

As an ecologist, I have analyzed the plot of the play unfolding on the
landscape stage in which I now live: the seven-square-mile watershed in

northwestern Dane County called Dunlap Hollow. I share the plot with you because it provides a microcosm picture of other ecological plays unfolding on landscape stages throughout the Driftless Region of Wisconsin and because most Wisconsinites, like my neighbors in "the Hollow," have only short-term knowledge of the plot and can easily forget how dynamic the entire play has been in the past and will be in the future.

The curtain rises on the Dunlap Hollow stage some 12,000 years ago, near the end of the Pleistocene glaciation. The edge of a massive sheet of ice is located just at the head of what will eventually become the Hollow. The flora and fauna that comprise the sparse cast are species adapted to cold, wet conditions that exist in the shadow of the huge glacier. The set resembles arctic tundra. The first director of the play is the "Milankovitch cycle," a complex series of oscillations that change the world's climate in predictable ways when the characteristics of the earth's orbit shift. The cycle brought the glaciers to the Hollow's doorstep as the climate cooled, and it then melted them as the climate inevitably warmed again. When the melt began, glacial till and silt-laden water pouring from the slowly retreating glacier washed out a large erosion gully that we now call Dunlap Hollow. This humble debut as an erosion gully at the end of the ice age defined the general topographic features of the landscape and gave the Hollow its sandy soil and eroded bluffs.

But, the plot of the play, under the direction of the Milankovitch cycle, was predictable, and the subsequent changes this director brought were inevitable. As the climate warmed, plants and animals that had retreated to the south during the glacial period began returning to the stage in an orderly progression. The first cast to take center stage in the Hollow was composed of boreal forest plants and animals—spruce and moose and other coniferous forest species. Their act was relatively short, and few characters remained on stage in subsequent acts. Some were eliminated by a new arrival, *Homo sapiens*. Once on stage, this new actor hunted several large mammals, such as mammoths and mastodons, to extinction. Most, however, were displaced by the northward-migrating deciduous forest and its characteristic biota. Many of the characters associated with deciduous forests have remained on stage until the present.

As the Milankovitch cycle progressed with its predictable script, the climate became steadily warmer and drier, allowing a new cast of characters to enter the stage from the south and west. These plants and animals were grassland species, including dry-adapted organisms such as the prickly pear cactus and ornate box turtle. For a time the set in Dunlap Hollow may have looked like a Wisconsin "desert," as a hot, dry climate and sandy, well-drained soils gave the stage a decidedly arid character. This act reached its peak some 7,000 years ago during the so-called "hypsithermal maximum," when average annual temperatures in the Hollow reached a high point and annual precipitation dropped to a low point. Some of the characters from this xeric act have remained on stage, finding refuge on the Hollow's south-facing, sandy slopes where hot, dry conditions still persist today.

Predictably, the climate again began to turn, and increasingly cooler, moister conditions have prevailed ever since. As the climate moderated, a productive mix of prairie and deciduous forest dominated the Hollow's stage, and a new director/actor began to supplant the Milankovitch cycle and dictate the future direction of the ecological play. Native Americans, who had up to this point been minor players on the Dunlap Hollow stage, began to become both dominant actors and directors. By setting frequent fires, they maintained the landscape in a mix of forest, savanna and prairie that produced a supply of preferred game animals, such as elk and white-tailed deer. Their fires temporarily prevented the gradual replacement of prairie by deciduous forest that the Milankovitch cycle had in store for subsequent acts. In fact, for the last 1,500 years, human beings have replaced the Milankovitch cycle as the primary director of the ecological play. But it was not the Native Americans who were to direct the biggest and most rapid changes in the plot; it was the European settlers.

With the arrival of European immigrants in the mid-1800s, the pace of change on the stage quickened as sets and actors began to replace one another more rapidly than ever before. Fortunately, we have a good record of what the stage was like when the new director/actors took over. Descriptions of the original land surveyors paint a revealing picture of Dunlap Hollow in the 1840s.

The survey notes for my property, which includes a Township corner and lies in the very middle of the Hollow, are particularly revealing. Moving north along the Township line, the surveyors found only scattered oak trees in an otherwise prairie-dominated landscape. As they approached the Township corner at the bottom of the valley, they noted that they were in a wet, "low prairie" and that the surrounding hillsides were covered with prairie, scattered oaks and cedars, and a few clumps of low-quality oak forest. Despite the fact that they were within a few feet of the current course of Dunlap Creek, they made no mention of running water, only a few springs that seeped into the wet prairies and fens on the valley's floor. They rolled stones from the hillside to erect a cairn, since there were no nearby "witness" trees to mark the corner.

Soon after this survey, settlers moved in and began altering the landscape dramatically. Both the set and the actors have changed rapidly over the last 150 years. The prairies on the lower slopes of the Hollow were plowed into agricultural fields; the prairies and savannas on steeper ground were converted to pastures; large timber was cut for building material and fuel, and wild fires were suppressed. With the suppression of fire and changes in grazing practices, the pastures on the hillsides were eventually invaded by trees, and young forest replaced savannas and prairies. Today, most of the non-crop land in Dunlap Hollow is forested, with only a few ancient, open-grown oaks embedded within the woods as reminders that not too long ago the area was a savanna. Because the flattest ground on the valley floor was too wet to farm, it was drained by digging a ditch that would eventually be called Dunlap Creek, now a conspicuous feature in the Hollow.

Some characters from previous acts left the stage as their habitats were eliminated. Others took refuge in the remnants that escaped the plow, axe, shovel and livestock. Some native animals, such as the passenger pigeon, timber wolf, bison and elk were hunted out, but the settlers brought in a troupe of new actors, mostly plants and animals from Europe. Quack grass and other Eurasian weeds are now squeezing out remnant prairies; purple loosestrife and reed canary grass have taken over wetlands, and honeysuckle and garlic mustard are invading woodlands. House mice, Norway rats, European starlings and house sparrows abound, and free-ranging domestic cats are now the Hollow's most abundant predators.

Over the last 150 years, the landscape of Dunlap Hollow has changed rapidly, and the cast of characters has changed dramatically, but the play goes on. The script is now being rewritten by new directors who are the current landowners in the Hollow. Many of the new owners have purchased marginal farmland that was taken out of agricultural production over the past thirty years, and they will no longer work the land. According to a recent survey taken by students in one of my conservation courses at the UW–Madison, many of these new owners are interested in making their land more "natural," but they seem to be having some understandable difficulties identifying what natural means in a landscape that has been as dynamic as Dunlap Hollow.

The reactions of some neighbors to the types of ecological restorations that I am undertaking on my property are illustrative. Thinning an overgrown oak savanna on a prominent hillside by logging younger trees and leaving scattered, older oaks was viewed by some as destroying a forest, not recreating a savanna. The burning of the prairie remnant on my property was generally viewed as a positive-if-hazardous activity, but the burning of my fire-starved wetland that was in the terminal stages of degrading from a species-rich mosaic of wet prairies and fens to an overgrown shrub-carr was viewed more suspiciously. Our annual efforts to keep purple loosestrife out of the upstream half of the Hollow's wetlands and the DNR's experiments with biological control were viewed by some as eccentric discrimination against a pretty plant. Our efforts on behalf of some rare wildlife species, such as ornate box turtles and eastern bluebirds, were well received, but our desire to retain a timber rattlesnake population in the Hollow was considered positively daft.

Having seen what's happening on my place, a few of the neighbors are now getting excited about doing ecological restorations on their own property, and I suspect that more will eventually try their hand at being active directors of the ecological play on their land. But a fundamental issue remains to be resolved. What exactly should landowners in Dunlap Hollow do with their land? Their decisions will determine the next act in the play.

Although my crystal ball is murky, I suspect that many will "let nature take its course," which means they'll not take an active role in directing the future of their land. This passive, laissez faire approach to land management has predictable consequences. If today's oak forests are not restored to oak savannas or prairies and burned regularly, they will eventually turn into maple-dominated forests. If prairie remnants are not burned and weeded, they will be taken over by woody vegetation and exotic weeds and eventually take a course towards becoming forests. If wetlands are not burned and weeded, they will be invaded by more woody plants and exotics, resulting in the loss of the most species-rich wetland communities in Dane County. And if we continue to cause global climate change by burning fossil fuels and generating green-house gases, the entire ecological stage of Dunlap Hollow will be shift-ing in a new direction. . . .

From *A Thousand Pieces of Paradise: Landscape and Property in the Kickapoo Valley* (2005)

LYNNE HEASLEY

The valley of the Kickapoo River in Wisconsin became the setting for a painful and controversial episode in land use plans gone awry. Recurrent flooding led to proposals (dating back to the 1930s) to construct a dam on the Kickapoo. Congressional authorization of the project in 1962 led to the acquisition of 140 farms, relocation of the nearby state highway, and initial work on the dam structure. After objections to the environ-mental impacts of the dam were raised, the project was canceled in 1975. It took another twenty years for a citizen-driven process to develop a col-laborative plan to create what is now the Kickapoo Valley Reserve on the former dam site. The story of the dam was part of Lynne Heasley's study of changing communities and land use in the Kickapoo River valley, *A Thousand Pieces of Paradise*. Her prologue is presented here. Heasley is a professor of history and environmental studies at Western Michigan University in Kalamazoo.

Driving due west of Madison, Wisconsin, on U.S. Route 14, you soon leave behind a glaciated landscape of lakes and rolling terrain. You enter a different kind of land, hillier and surely more dramatic if you prefer topographic relief. Unbroken acres of corn and soybeans give way to small fields or pasture on ridges and valley bottoms; mixed hardwood forests lie on the steep slopes in between. A line of white pines appears high up on sandstone outcrops, like a column of weathered soldiers. You have entered the Driftless Area, a region the glaciers never reached. Without glaciers, whose advances and retreats sculpted a lake country across the rest of Wisconsin, the Mississippi River and its tributaries and their tributaries were unimpeded in carving the hills and valleys that characterize the region. One of these tributaries is the Kickapoo River, which glides through the landscape with so many twists and turns that its very name means "one who goes here, then there" in Algonquian. Turn north off 14 to meet one of the twenty-seven thousand people who call the Kickapoo Valley home—perhaps someone who lives on a ridge far above the river—and she will probably tell you that she loves the panorama of fields and forests unfolding like a verdant patchwork quilt. She might add that her neighbors who live down deep in the Valley's hollows enjoy their dark green solitude just as much, but this can be downright claustrophobic to visitors. "Coulee country," they all call it, because of these narrow, haunting valleys. Such sensibilities are not recent either. "No matter in what direction one sets his face a new scene presents itself at each turn of the road and each seems more beautiful than the last," wrote two sisters in 1896 in homage to the Kickapoo Valley.

Still, on a first drive you might not mark this place as one of the most fascinating and important valleys in the Upper Midwest. The Kickapoo Valley is among the poorest parts of Wisconsin, a fact the pretty scenery will not hide. Old cars with For Sale signs by the road, droopy farmhouses with weeds in front and household junk piles around back, abandoned barns lying in charred ruins (used for practice by the fire department when they were no longer safe to keep standing)—these are all part of the view too. Like rural communities around the country, the Valley lost thousands of farmers during the twentieth century. The land did not make it easy to grow a farm there. Short of leveling hills and filling in valleys, Kickapoo Valley farmers could not plant unbroken miles of cash crops, so they could not use large farm machinery at the industrial scale necessary to pay it off. Dairy farming faced the same crisis of scale, dependent on a flimsy pyramid on which the land must sustain the herds necessary for producing larger volumes of milk and the returns per volume (no matter how marginal) must support the capital investment. With a shrinking and aging farm population, and an adjusted gross income only 55 percent of the state average in 1990, economists labeled the Valley "underdeveloped." Others called it Little Appalachia. The Kickapoo Valley could be any hardscrabble place where farmers are having a hard time holding on to land, where teenagers are bored and talk about leaving, and where local officials are praying for economic development.

But stay longer and baffling sights and sounds intrude on first impressions. Even people who have lived in the Valley their whole lives marvel at the shifting scene. For example, just north of a speck of a village called Liberty you will come upon a motocross racetrack. Dusty and filled with motorcyclists bobbing in and out of view, it looks like a strange twist in the proverbial road that goes ever on. How did *that* get way out *here*, you might wonder. And how do the neighbors—or the neighbors' cattle, poor things—feel about all the *noise*? Still, from a cyclist's perspective, this would certainly be an exciting landscape. Not five miles further north, the whining of the machines has ceased and once more the land has morphed into a new vision. As motorized traffic fades away, a clip-clop, clip-clop, clip-clop takes its place. A black horse-drawn buggy sedately rounds a bend in the road. A kind of signature house dominates miles of landscape—large, rectangular, entirely white, a black buggy posted in front. A plain-clad signature person stands out as well. Coulee country, it seems, is also Amish country. All these Amish farms send a pretty strong signal that agriculture is not dead in the Valley (notwithstanding the motocross), but how have the Amish done it? Why do they look so prosperous when other farmers have obviously not prospered?

A mere three-mile detour southeastward and the Rockton Bar provides a pleasant rest stop for a cold Bud, if you want one. The bar appears blessed with its location near the Kickapoo River. Stretching north and south is a vast deciduous forest whose rippling light green surface is smudged and streaked in places with darker stands of white pine. No Amish land this, but an 8,500-acre natural area called the Kickapoo Valley Reserve. If you mused that it must be absolutely gorgeous here when the leaves turn in the fall, you would follow in the reveries of thousands of tourists who came before you. You might even dream for a moment about buying a little piece of land in the area: What a great place to take a family on weekends. In this, too, you would not be the first—to dream or to buy. On the patio of the bar sit picnic tables, slyly inviting you to hang out. This is clearly a place trying to make customers feel at home. And right there with the tables sits a tombstone. (Yes, a granite tombstone.) The rear end of a horse is etched on the tombstone, which reads: "In Memory of Those Who Sold Us Down the Kickapoo River."

A racetrack, an Amish farm, a tombstone at a bar. Together they make no sense. But there they are, in just a fraction of the Valley's 760

Buggy, Carl Homstad (2005). Most members of the Amish communities of the Driftless decline to drive motor-powered vehicles. Instead, horse-drawn buggies are the common form of transportation. Muralist, painter, and woodcut artist Carl Homstad studied at Luther College and lives near Decorah.

square miles. *In memory of those who sold us down the Kickapoo River.* Only a person with absolutely no curiosity could resist asking what this is about. The tombstone expects your questions; it demands them. How did it get here? What stories is it hinting at? With so much happening around every bend, where do you start?

Frac Sand Song (2013)

EMMETT J. DOYLE

Some of the sandstones of the Driftless Area are composed of sand grains with physical properties that are optimal for use in the process of hydraulic fracturing ("fracking"). Starting around 2005, a boom in the mining and processing of "frac sand" took hold in portions of the Drift-less. Although the geological formations of the Driftless landscape had long been mined and quarried, the mining of frac sand has occurred at an unprecedented scale and pace. While researching the causes, economic and environmental impacts, and policy implications of the boom, Minnesota musician Emmett Doyle wrote "Frac Sand Song."

I am nothing but a man, made my life upon the land
West Wisconsin is my home
In a town of farms and mills, high up in the driftless hills
Where as I boy I'd roam
Those sand bluffs would remain, until the company came
To strip the hillside bare
Digging up the sand to frac someone else's land
In some other town somewhere

    And I know it's for the best, I should count myself blessed
    That's what the companies say
    But I'll turn my eyes, hang my head and cry
    'Cause they're haulin' them sand hills away

Well, I know that times are tough, this economy is rough
And we've all seen better days
And when they're mining out the hills, there'll be jobs to be
    filled
For twenty dollar an hour's pay
But the mine don't seem to care if our kids can breathe the air
If the water's there for all
And when the boom is through, those jobs will be gone, too
And they'll leave the countryside raw

Is this the best way, as some people say,
To power our country
Because it seems a damned high cost, when there's so much to be
    lost
And the wind and the sunshine is free
For I think the more I find that it's burning in my mind
It's a damned and shameful sin

To put creation up for bids, and leave nothing for our kids
But ghosts of sand hills in the wind

And I know it's for the best, I should count myself blessed
That's what the companies say
But I'll turn my eyes, hang my head and cry
'Cause they're haulin' them sand hills away
'Cause they're haulin' sand county away

II

COMMUNITIES IN TRANSITION

VER SINCE THE FIRST BANDS OF HUNTERS followed mastodons and
moraines to the edges of the Driftless Area, the region's human
communities have been in flux. The generations of long prehistoric
time may have passed slowly (if intensely), but accelerating change has
marked the last two millennia. The Hopewell trade network, which carried materials to Driftless peoples from as far away as the Rocky Mountains, collapsed suddenly around AD 300 for reasons unknown. The
late archeologist R. Clark Mallam of Luther College described a subsequent four-hundred-year "period of cultural distortion," speculating that
the emergence of the effigy mound tradition "with its attendant symbols and earth-shaping rituals [constituted] a prehistoric revitalization
movement."

That era also lapsed. By around AD 1200 Driftless dwellers ceased
building mounds and concentrated into a handful of larger villages.
These villages, too, moved and migrated—their peoples mingling and
dividing—until the harbingers of European disruption arrived: diseases,
horses, firearms, metal tools, and eastern tribes forced west into the
region. Territorial boundaries continually shifted, as did relationships
among the Spanish, French, British, and American powers. What began
as a trickle with Jean Nicolet's 1634 landing at Green Bay turned into a
flood once lead surfaced in the Driftless.

Then: a progression of immigrations, generations, and departures.
Native peoples banished, moving, returning. Fortunes made—and lost—
in fur, lead, timber, wheat, hops, and tobacco. Horses replaced by tractors, and horses returned to new Amish fields. Telephones and power
lines binding the region, only to be swapped for mobile phones and
distributed electrical generation . . . and even larger powerlines. River

travel abandoned for the railways . . . railways eclipsed by trucks and automobiles . . . automobiles carrying canoes back to Driftless rivers.

Villages have winked in and out across the region. As Ralph Nuzum, a beloved scribe of the Kickapoo Valley, put it in 1955:

> You can't tell much by the looks of a toad. Neither can you tell whether a town will really "go to town" or be abandoned. Almost up to the time of the Civil War, Bell Center was the belle of the Kickapoo. It boasted of having the first Post Office. "Yankeetown" in a pine grove south of Soldiers Grove had the second. Seeleyburg, a little hamlet north of LaFarge, was bustling with logging operations when LaFarge was a wilderness known only as "the corners."
>
> Then look what happened. Seeleyburg folded up like a tent, Yankeetown also gave up its quaint little ghost, and Bell Center lost its big start when Gays Mills blossomed forth with big saw and grist mills.

Some children of the Driftless depart to chase big city dreams, or to escape troubled relationships with home places and people. People from Chicago and Cambodia arrive with dreams of new lives. Just as Norwegian immigrants gained their foothold working Yankee tobacco fields, Hmong and Hispanic people laboring on modern farms find niches for their own enterprises. Some older residents resent the unfamiliar ways of recent immigrants; others welcome the influx of ideas and energy, foods and traditions, children to fill schools, and businesses to enliven quiet main streets.

Change is both hard and hopeful. "I seem to be the only one who swims in the La Crosse [River]," writes literary scholar William Barillas, "except for Hmong children, sons and daughters of recent Southeast Asian immigrants. Perhaps one of those children will grow up to write notable prose about the place."

Driftless Elegy (2013)

Mark Wunderlich

Mark Wunderlich was born in Winona, Minnesota, and grew up near Fountain City, Wisconsin. He has published three collections of poetry and his work has appeared in a wide range of journals, reviews, and anthologies. "Driftless Elegy" was included in Wunderlich's collection *The Earth Avails*. Wunderlich lives in New York's Hudson Valley and teaches at Bennington College in Vermont.

The bridge over the Mississippi is shut,
the traffic diverted to Wabasha

while authorities investigate the undergirding
which is corroded and in danger of collapse.

Work has slowed on both sides of the river
while an enterprising man with a pontoon boat

ferries people from side to side. Fountain City
has long been without a grocery store; Abt's Market

closed when I was a child. The owner whistled,
and the women who worked the front counter

tracked everyone's movements through the town,
gazing out the plate glass windows with awnings

shielding them from the sun. In Minneapolis
the Coast Guard climbs into a Suburban

and makes the trip to Winona to arrest the man
with the boat. What he's doing is illegal, he's told.

"You try to help folks out and all you get is a kick in the ass."
The grocery is gone, the brewery is gone, gone

the house where my father was born,
gone the warehouse where we hung deer in November,

gone the shop with its cigar boxes full of bolts,
hinges, flanges, copper wire, ball bearings, or anything

someone might have saved for projects yet to be imagined.
The cellar where the washtubs bubbled to keep

the baitfish alive—one full of bullheads, one of minnows,
where geraniums overwintered, where the dug bulbs

of tulips were gnawed by muskrats during floods—
that has been filled and paved. A gas pump stands

where the glider rocked, a lit sign where the bridalwreath
once cast its white profusion to the sun.

The sheep are gone from Grandma Haney's pasture.
The last badger was shot from Wiggy Stuber's field.

There's no money in milk anymore, and you marry your herd
anyhow, and who wants to be that bound to anything

that won't love you back? The Gold'n Plump plant expands
in Arcadia, and the owners go to Mexico to recruit.

You know the workers by the angry rash
from fingertip to shoulder, enflamed by chicken water

seeping inside their arm-length plastic gloves.
The bluffs are covered in cedars since no one grazes

anything there anymore.

Who will remember the lodge hall and the good times had there?
Who will remember the handshake for the Rebeccas?

No one visited the museum, so the society put it up for sale.
A millionaire hangs cottages from the bluffs,

rents them to businessmen who drive here from Chicago or
    Milwaukee
to hunt the deer that breed and fatten at the edges of fallow
    fields.

The heads are left with the taxidermist, the meat dropped off at the
    church.
Old houses go vacant, new ones get built—ugly, vaulted
    ceilings,

windows the full two stories of their angular fronts
that jut like glass barge prows from the bluffs.

Hilbert is dead. Mutz is dead. Chester has turned to crumbs in his
   grave.
No one remembers when Babe Schwark died

and Bootie Schmidt is up to the Home for good.
Piggy is long gone, Home his headstone says.

The inveterate drinkers warm barstools at the Golden Frog,
and only those from "away" have anything to do with the Monarch.

Mother's sweater sat unsold in the gift shop
until Papa reclaimed it in a huff.

The property dispute over the mule pasture fence
has finally run its course; no one wins

though the surveyor got struck by lightning and is dead.
The old steamboat dry-docked in Winona

got hauled to the landfill, and someone trained lights
on the outcropping of Sugar Loaf bluff to form, at night,

the jagged outline of a cross.

There are those who claim the DNR
has let loose breeding pairs of mountain lions

in the bluffs around Waumandee. The warden says
that's nonsense, but why would anyone believe him?

Someone burned down the Chicken Valley strip club,
where the girl who won the state cross-country meet

ended up pole dancing, and where her driver's ed teacher
and basketball coach went to watch her on Friday nights.

The Road Dogs host a car shoot to raise money
for a cancerous friend: put a car in neutral,

roll it down a hill, and for $10 you get to shoot the car
as many times as you can. Helps if you're drunk.

A well-meaning ornithologist opened a raptor center
as a local attraction, populated it with the dumb and clumsy—

unlucky birds electrocuted by power lines, shot by moral derelicts
with crossbows, the poisoned, those whose taste for road kill

tangled them with a car. The eagles hop awkwardly around their
     pens,
glare through the wire, their talons like pruning shears

gripping the perches of what will be
their last home.

⇝

I am the end of a genetic line—a family dies with me.
This is hardly a tragedy. We are not an impressive group,

in intellect or physical form. With weak hearts, myopic,
we paddle lazily down the human genome,

pausing to root briefly here on the riverbank
in the shade of these limestone bluffs.

In an early photograph I have, part of the town
goes up in flames—a premonition from the 1880s.

A group of women, corseted, skirts infested with lace,
watch from behind a buckboard as ash flings itself

into the sky. To the right the blur of a girl
rushes away like a ghost. No face. Hardly a form.

Just a hat and a dress, and the news of a fire,
though no one is alive who knows her name.

Lucy Stone historic marker, Robert Clovis Siemon (2016). Suffragist and abolitionist Lucy Stone was a famed orator and activist. She owned land in what was then Bad Axe (now Vernon) County and lived in frontier-era Viroqua in 1856, when she was asked to deliver the Fourth of July address. Her speech drew settlers from throughout the region. This marker in Viroqua's Pioneer Cemetery is inscribed with a tribute by Stone's daughter Alice.

Richland Center, the Cradle of Suffrage in Wisconsin: How Earliest Enthusiasts Led Sisters (1924)

MARY ELIZABETH HUSSONG

Thirty-eight years before the Nineteenth Amendment to the U.S. Constitution was adopted in 1920, activism on behalf of women's suffrage emerged in Richland Center, Wisconsin. Wisconsin became the first state to ratify the amendment in 1919. In 1924 Mary Elizabeth Hussong, then a student at the University of Wisconsin in Madison, reviewed this history in an article published in the *Milwaukee Journal*.

Away down in the southwestern corner of Wisconsin, the little town of Richland Center has been glorified above all towns in the state in that it is the cradle of woman suffrage in Wisconsin.

On an afternoon in June, in 1882, a little band of women met at the home of one of their number, Mrs. Laura B. James, wife of the future Senator James—whose honor it was to carry finally Wisconsin's ratification to Washington—to discuss cautiously and behind drawn blinds the new and fearfully radical subject—woman suffrage.

"Remember," Mrs. Julia Bowen said, "we must be as wise as serpents and as harmless as doves." The idea of a club was approved. But it was decided not to incorporate the word "suffrage" into the name as yet. Instead they organized under the time honored title of "woman's club." Surely this would not offend the most prejudiced husband. Mrs. Julia Bowen was elected president. And thus was formed the first woman's club in the state. . . .

There was nothing militarist about these women, although a few years later the papers were calling them so. They were the wives of the prominent business and professional men of the town. Most of them were mothers and busy housewives. One of them, Mrs. Jennie

Lamberson, whose husband afterwards introduced several suffrage bills in the assembly, said recently: "Although I was deeply interested in suffrage, I had little time to think about it then as I was living on the farm and was busy cooking for hired men and minding twin babies."

Mrs. Laura B. James, at whose home the first meeting was held, was one of the strongest enthusiasts for the cause of suffrage in the state. Mrs. James will long be remembered in Richland Center for her charitable and original mind. She taught in the country schools of Richland County until her marriage when she was twenty-seven. The few remaining charter members of the club are fond of quoting her frequent observation, "For, you know, there's so much good in the worst of us, and so much bad in the best of us." One of the three remaining members who were of that little gathering in June of 1882 paid this early suffrage leader a tribute: "She was a sweet, modest woman—an ideal neighbor."

At a later date, when Richland Center was changed from a village to a city, Mrs. James tried to get a clause into the charter allowing the women of the town to vote. If this strategy had been successful it would have made the little town the one oasis of woman suffrage in the whole United States. Of course the plan was quickly squelched—by the male voters. . . .

One of the early discussions [in the club] was on marriage. Surely there was nothing sweepingly radical about this. But these women, while not "modernists," held opinions on marriage in advance of their day. One of the ideas expressed on this occasion was: "It is a mistake to think that all life is in marriage, the perfection of the individual is as necessary as family training. Girls should not be taught to think that marriage finishes existence."

The first real suffrage speech ever made in Wisconsin was given at a little town near Richland Center as early as 1856. Dr. Henry B. Blackwell, husband of Lucy Stone, settled some land in Wisconsin in 1852. At that time he wrote of Richland Center: "I found a single cabin belonging to Ira Haseltine, where I spent the night." In 1856 when he married Lucy Stone they drove to Viroqua. He wrote: "At a Fourth of July celebration my wife, by invitation, made an anti-slavery and woman's rights address." This was the first woman's rights speech made in the state. . . .

Three months after the formation of the Woman's Club in Richland Center the Wisconsin State Suffrage Association was born in Madison on Sept. 6, 1882. By this time the Woman's Club in Richland Center was bolder and sent fourteen of its members to Madison to help form the state association. . . .

Three years after the formation of the Woman's Club Mrs. Emma C. Bascom of Madison wrote to Mrs. Julia Bowen concerning the work of the Richland Center women: "So I come to you, not ignorant of the abundant liberality the women of the banner town of Richland Center have already manifested for the cause. Throughout the state your little city has become worthily famous for intelligent and progressive senti-ment. With high regard for yourself and co-laborers in the cause of equal right."

From *The Driftless Zone; or, A Novel Concerning the Selective Outmigration from Small Cities* (1997)

RICK HARSCH

Rick Harsch, formerly of La Crosse, now lives and writes in Slovenia. *The Driftless Zone* was his first published novel and, with *Billy Verité* (1998) and *The Sleep of Aborigines* (2002), form his Driftless Trilogy.

Years ago I visited our courtroom to see what kind of people went there. I saw a man in a blue jumpsuit, jail-issue, a big man with an unrepli-cable nose, long wild hair, thick frontiersman's beard, standing before the judge. If I had to call him something I would probably say "trapper." The prosecutor called him "pedestrian on the interstate." The big man nodded. It was true. The judge considered that a moment, then asked him where he came from. "Out West," he said. The judge asked what he was doing here, why he had "come East." Without hesitating, the man said, "I came to see the Driftless Zone." And the judge sentenced him to the night he'd already spent in jail.

I told this to a friend of mine, a demographer, who was visiting from Chicago. I wanted to make too much of the Driftless Zone, I suppose; I wanted the refusal of the glaciers to visit our region to have a meaning that resisted the ravages of time and civilization and I thought I spotted that meaning in the high incidence of odd behavior in La Crosse, a common denominator of what I saw as rugged schizophrenia, which perhaps I glorified as the last vestiges of the primal human spirit perversified by its struggle to break free of the confines of its own deadening strictures. I would've put it better back then, before the onset of these convolutions. Still, no matter how well I put it I was talking to a demographer. He told me that I was witnessing the result of a process common to all small cities. This is pretty much what he said: "A city is defined as much by who has left as by who remains. What you see in small cities—rather, what you don't see—are the beautiful and the talented, those whose virtues are better rewarded elsewhere. For instance, let's say you are an ambitious and capable young man—you're going to want to go to a big city where you can make some money. Let's say you're beautiful—then you go to Hollywood, or latch on to someone with talent, someone who will take you to a big city. If you understand this, you'll see why your leading citizens here always seem grotesque. Those who rise to the top are filling vacancies left by those more fit for those roles. It even extends to your bar queens—your vamps or vixens, if you will. Even your few prostitutes. If you take the average prostitute from Chicago and walk her down the street here, I'll bet nine out of ten people would think she was an actress. I'm sure you can see how broad the implications are—they extend even to the arts: where do you go if you make beautiful music? Where are the symphonies? New York, Chicago, Philadelphia. What all this comes down to is nothing more or less than my specialty—proportion. In proportion, the small city lacks talent, beauty, smarts, the can-do spirit, lovely music. . . . What you do have is a high percentage of misfits, fools, various mediocrities, ineptitude, a shabby sort of grandiosity, an enlarged capacity for botching ill-conceived projects. In proportion you'll have more of everything you don't clearly lack, more flashers, peeping toms, dim-witted substitute teachers, petty thieves (the pettiest thieves), vandals—I could go on and on. And from the other end you have the farmers, the replacements. These are the only ones who still have values, only their values no longer apply. As long as they're able to remain on their farms they're all right. But they come here uprooted; their traditions no longer make any sense. They're lost. And as long as people are stuck here, or stick themselves here, farmers or otherwise, they lack vision. They live entirely within this little city and don't see outside it. On the surface there would seem to be equilibrium, but that's not the case. People are too big for the small city—they're overflowing with humanity, with human yearnings, human desires. They don't see out, though, so they compensate inwards and a sort of implosion occurs, which in this case equals perversion. Whenever a life is in this way misapplied, directed entirely the wrong way, it becomes perverse; all the grandiosity of human society is played out on too small a stage. It's like raising an alligator in a terrarium. See any polar bear at the zoo, the way it paces or slumbers larger than life—that's what's happening to the human characteristics in this town; big wild emotions are pacing restlessly in too small environs; or they're sleeping, ostentatiously, or ominously, or pathetically. If you shrink your world to an area of, say, twenty square blocks, you're going to be grievously wrong about everything. Because the world is, simply, the world—Earth, which is floating in space. You forget that, you shrink it down to a size you mistakenly think you can manage, and your vision becomes grotesque. Imagine the map in the mind of the man of your city. Very detailed for a mile in each direction, and then a vague sector called 'Further out in La Crosse' or 'North La Crosse' or 'Past the hospitals'; beyond that—wilderness, infinite wilderness. For the rest of us the infinite wilderness doesn't begin till somewhere past the moon. So for these people a great many real things that have real bearing on their lives go uncharted. If you had an Einstein here and you gave him one of these La Crosse maps to start with, he'd at least make it to Chicago—he'd be curious, he'd explore. He wouldn't settle for the map. So then you wouldn't any longer have an Einstein here. You'd have another Billy Verité to take his place, though, someone who doesn't have the wherewithal to make it across the river. So again it comes down to leaving and staying; it's this selective outmigration that defines the small city. It's not just La Crosse, it's all small cities—and small towns, too."

I wouldn't say I disagree with him. I would say . . . I agree with him. But sometimes I remember the good old days, the days I knew were going to be called the good old days even as they happened—which is what real good old days are. I was in a position I'm in no position to describe in detail, in which the money, though it wasn't much, came easy—it wasn't much, but it was enough to pay a cheap rent, to eat at Sabatino's or the Lunch Encounter whenever I wanted, enough for cigarettes and coffee. I slept as late as I wanted, took long walks, and knew a woman who let me lean back into her in the bath tub while I smoked. I was only obliged to be someplace for one hour a day, and only three days a week. I knew then they were the good old days—and they happened here.

From *Driftless* (2008)

DAVID RHODES

David Rhodes is the author of five novels. Rhodes grew up near Des Moines, Iowa, and in 1971 earned a Master in Fine Arts degree through the Iowa Writer's Workshop. *Driftless* (2008), from which this chapter ("Hiring Help") is excerpted, marked Rhodes's return to writing after a thirty-year hiatus. In 2013 he published a sequel, *Jewelweed*.

July Montgomery and his twenty-eight-year-old neighbor Wade Armbuster sat at a round metal table on the front deck of July's house. They were drinking coffee and eating the last of a peach pie. Despite the cool morning air, a cloudless sky permitted an uncommonly brilliant sun to heat up everything it could reach into, and their clothes and the brick front of the farmhouse were saturated with warm comfort.

Wade wanted to borrow July's block and tackle to pull the engine out of a car he was fixing up.

July wanted help with his third crop of hay.

The negotiations were complicated. Wade worked at the cheese plant, and his schedule was inflexible yet erratic. He had the strength of two ordinary men and would be good help, but July wasn't sure he would bring the hoist back.

July forked another piece of pie into his mouth, contemplated the texture with his tongue, and gazed into the shrubs growing along the edge of the house.

"How long you need the hoist?"

"Long enough to trick out the motor—pistons, rings, stroker crank, roller cam, and three-way valves."

"Sounds expensive."

"Power costs money," said Wade.

"Young people get hurt in cars like that."

"People get hurt doing lots of things," said Wade, his face thin and intense. The sunlight reflected from the jewelry in his ear and nose. "How much hay you got?"

"Two full days, maybe four. Can't pay you much."

"If I can use your shop—here—I'll work for nothing. You've got good tools."

"Here?"

"That way the folks won't be nagging me."

"You still on probation?"

"I guess so."

"Sounded like a bad deal to me—what I heard," said July. "Wasn't entirely your fault. Someone backed you into a corner and you came out of it."

Wade looked away, following a sound on the road. He admired July but didn't care for him to know it. The older man lived alone and made his own rules. No one told him what to do and something in his eyes said two things at once: I like you but I don't compromise on anything important.

Over the eastern horizon, Rusty Smith's dual-wheeled pickup came toward them, eventually turning like a bloated silver fish into the narrow tributary of the driveway. He stopped at the edge of the yard, then drove another thirty yards to the open machine shed, where he climbed from the cab and stood waiting for July to speak with him in private. "Here's the deal," said July. "You can use my shop, but I don't want any of my tools disappearing and I've got to talk to your parents first. I know you're old enough to do whatever you want, but that's just the way it is. I don't want any trouble with your folks. And I don't mind if you occasionally drink around here, but I can't tolerate drunks."

Wade left.

July swallowed the bottom half of his coffee and joined Rusty in the machine shed. They discussed the weather for several minutes, milk prices and road construction.

"Those Amish," muttered Rusty. "When you hire them, how do they get back and forth from work—in buggies?"

"That's right," said July. "If you want them quicker, pick them up."

"I've got a lot of work to get done. How do you call them?"

"You don't call them, Rusty. They don't have phones. You go over. It's the old way of doing business."

"I'm not saying I'm going to."

"Going to what?"

"Hire them." Rusty spit on the ground in an almost friendly manner, climbed back in his pickup, and drove away.

Fifteen minutes later, he turned into Eli Yoder's barnyard. A dozen or more chickens, geese, and guinea hens performed a clamorous and feathery retreat. A black and white dog barked anxiously from a safe distance away. Stepping from the truck, Rusty looked for signs of human life among the shabby collection of wood-framed buildings, sheep pen, cement silo, and an overturned cart. Chestnut draft horses grazed beyond the barn and a curl of smoke rose from the tiny, unpainted house.

Hoping to find someone outdoors, Rusty walked to the barn. Road-hoppers flew out of his path, their papered wings rasping. A barefoot child—perhaps four or five years old—darted from a nearby shed carrying a pail. She glanced fearfully at him from beneath her white head scarf and continued running along a dirt path to the house, where she closed the door behind her.

Finding no one in the barn, Rusty followed the dirt path to the house and knocked on a windowless door. It opened and a large woman stood directly inside, holding a broom, her head covered with a coarse dark-blue bonnet with strands of gray hair poking out around the edges. A full-length dress of matching blue provided a shapeless background for the untied apron falling from her neck. Her bare feet seemed surprisingly large, imposing and immanently functional, as though two normal-sized feet were protectively hidden inside them. She did not speak but continued staring at the floor, gripping the broom with red-knuckled hands. Three children under school age stared wide-eyed from a darkened corner of the room. Rusty shifted his weight inside his cowboy boots and pulled his right ear lobe with his left hand. "I'm looking for Eli."

No response.

"He here?"

"Nope," said the woman without looking up or offering another explanation.

It seemed an unusually masculine reply, putting Rusty partly at ease, and he continued, "You know where I can find him?" He took a cigarette from his jacket pocket and inserted it into his mouth.

"Fillin' silo over to Bontrager's."

The three children cautiously moved out of the darkened corner and were now about halfway across the little room, keeping the woman between them and the door. The boy—the youngest of the three—continued to stare at Rusty with extreme anxiety, as though Rusty were someone he had been specifically warned about. The only light in the room came through a single window, partly obscured by curtains, and the smell of kerosene lay heavy on the air. The smell lodged something loose in Rusty, a memory he held for a moment then let fall.

"Where's that?" he asked.

"Three places over," she said, jerking the broom handle to indicate north. "Pumpkin patch by the road."

Rusty lit his cigarette and blew out smoke. "I'll be going over there, then."

Rusty found the farm. Six buggies parked in front of the house—some with horses still in harness. Amish men were filling silo next to the barn. Several stood on a wagon piled with bundled cornstalks, feeding them into a gasoline-powered chopper. Other horse-drawn wagons could be seen in a nearby field, where more Amish loaded more cornstalks. All wore straw hats, blue coats, and black boots. The older men had beards without mustaches; the youngest were clean-shaven.

As Rusty approached, the operator of the chopper walked out to meet him. "I am Levi Bontrager," he said in slightly broken English over the roaring sound of the chopper. "Can I be of help to you?"

"Looking for Eli Yoder," said Rusty. He reached for a cigarette and then decided against it. Levi Bontrager turned and shouted in German to the workers unloading the wagon. A tall, thin man with a narrow black beard jumped to the ground and came forward. Bontrager returned to his position beside the chopper.

"July Montgomery said you do carpenter work. I need work on my house."

"Jha," replied Eli, looking out from under his hat like a badger looking out of its burrow. "What kind of work?" It was impossible for Rusty to judge his age, not only because his clothes, hair, and facial grooming did not communicate the usual signals, but also because of his general comportment. He might be a young man unusually mature, or an older man unusually immature. His teeth, for instance, were in deplorable condition, but his posture was markedly erect; while it seemed inconceivable for a young man to have such rotten teeth, it seemed equally inconceivable for an older man to stand so straight. His eyes were proud, even vain, but not arrogant. The teeth again captured Rusty's attention. You just didn't see bad teeth anymore, not like you used to. Rusty's father had bad teeth—real bad—and he quickly forced the memory away from him.

"Roof work, windows and trim, and humps in the bedroom floor," said Rusty. "Shouldn't take longer than a week or two."

"When you need this done?" Eli asked, absently brushing curls of dried corn leaves from his sleeves.

"Need it done right now."

"You say you know July Montgomery?"

"Yup. I'm Russell Smith, and my farm's not too far from here."

"People call you Rusty?"

"Some do," Rusty replied, disturbed at being identified by someone he knew nothing about.

"I should take a look at what you have."

"When can you come?"

"Right now."

"All right. I've got my truck here, I mean I suppose it's okay for you folks to ride in a truck, I mean if it isn't . . ."

"It's okay," said Eli. He walked straight to the truck, climbed in, and closed the door.

Rusty hadn't anticipated this. He was unaccustomed to sharing the interior of his truck with anyone and could count on one hand the number of times a passenger other than his wife had sat beside him. He lit a cigarette before settling behind the wheel and noticed a strong smell of human sweat mixed with corn silage.

On the road, he could think of nothing to say. Every topic seemed likely to violate some religious sensibility or unnecessarily accentuate the many obvious differences between them. But while the silence gnawed at Rusty as if it were a rat imprisoned in a wooden box, Eli Yoder appeared unperturbed. He gazed at the passing landscape from beneath his hat, occupying his place on the seat with an indifferent ease.

"Hope the smoke doesn't bother you," said Rusty, nearing the end of his cigarette.

"It don't."

Rusty lit another and they continued until they reached the state highway.

"If you don't mind, I'd like to stop at the convenience store," said Eli. "If you have the time."

Rusty parked on the lower side of Kwik Trip, where posters announced cheap cigarettes, beer, lottery tickets, bananas, and frozen pizza. Eli went in. Rusty remained in the truck, wondering what business an Amish could have here. Even Rusty disliked going inside, where teenagers abounded, middle-aged women talked in shrill voices, and everyone seemed to move in a fluorescent world of forced humor and snacks wrapped in plastic. Beneath advertisements for a video featuring a blond girl beneath a man with a knife in his teeth and a sale on toilet paper, Rusty could see the top of Eli's hat. Five minutes later he came out and climbed in the truck carrying a plastic mug of coffee and a pastry filled with raspberry jam.

"Thanks," he said, sipping from the mug. "I needed to make a telephone call and they had free doughnuts with a cup of coffee. I didn't get any breakfast."

Rusty backed out of the lot. "Didn't think you people used phones," he said.

"Try not to," said Eli. "But you got to make a living."

They went the rest of the way in silence.

At Rusty's home, Eli looked up at the roof and learned that twenty-five years had passed since the asphalt shingles had been replaced.

"Fifteen years is usually the end of shingles," said Eli. "But that steep slope I suppose added to their life. You got good surface underneath?"

"Got the old shingles underneath," said Rusty.

"Should tear them out, put in new plywood."

"Plywood's blamed expensive," said Rusty. "No sense in fixing something isn't broke. Another set of shingles will outlast me no matter what's under 'em."

They walked all the way around the house, looking at the siding and paint. "Rotten boards here," said Eli and poked a finger into a hole beneath a window frame. "But the boards could be replaced, I suppose, without replacing it all."

"It's a matter of time," explained Rusty. "This has to be done—all of it—in a month. Wife's mother and sister are coming. Has to be done."

Eli nodded. He understood the need as well as the deadline.

They went inside to inspect the floor in the downstairs bedroom, where Rusty explained that some minor flattening was in order. Eli began tugging his beard at the sight of the hump along the outside wall. "Don't like this," he said.

His fears were confirmed in the basement. "Your joists rotted off as the house settled," he announced. "Water running down the side of the house rotted away the plate, and over here you can see all the way through to outside."

"What we talking here in the way of time?" asked Rusty.

"Can't tell until we get in there—new plate, break out all this old cement, hard to tell."

Rusty felt a coiled cinch tighten around his neck. "Can you still be finished by the end of the month?"

"I should think so," replied Eli.

"Does that mean yes or no?"

"God willing." And he smiled a smile from which his beard seemed to be expressing more than his actual face—the kind of smile, Rusty feared, that could also be employed when everything was not finished on time.

"When can you start?"

"End of the week or beginning of next, I suspect."

"Sooner the better. Do you have tools?"

"We have hand tools. The work would go faster with electric, but it makes no difference to us. My sons and I are familiar with either."

"I have power tools," said Rusty. "You can use them. How much do you and your boys charge?"

"Fifteen for myself, seven for my youngest and eight for the oldest."

They were both distracted by the sound of footsteps on the basement stairs. "Russell? Russell, are you down here? Is everything all right?"

"Everything is fine. Go back upstairs."

"What are you doing down here?"

"We're almost through. Go back upstairs, Maxine."

"Is there some problem down here?"

"No. Go back upstairs."

"Hello, I'm Maxine, Russell's wife," she announced after discovering Eli standing beside her husband.

Eli looked at the cement floor in greeting. He was unaccustomed to talking with women, at least English women.

"What's your name?" she asked.

"Yoder."

"Are you here about the repair work?"

"Jha."

"Where do you live?"

Eli turned partly around so as not to be facing her directly, but not so far as to actually turn his back to her. "Over Bundy Hollow."

"Close to the Williams' farm?"

"Three places south."

"Oh, I know where you live. You have all those ducks and chickens that come out to the road. It's a nice spot. How long have you lived there?"

"Three years in November."

"Where did you come from before that?"

"Pennsylvania."

"Do you have a family? That's a small house."

"It's large enough for us."

"How many do you have in your family?"

"My wife and I have seven children, and my mother-in-law lives with us."

"Didn't a barn burn down near you?"

"The Millers—lost half their cows last year."

"I heard you put the roof on the new building."

"Along with my boys."

"I thought that was you. Eva Miller comes into the library regular. She said you did excellent work. How old are your children?"

"Isaac is seventeen and Abraham is sixteen. The younger ones are younger."

"Do you have any daughters?"

"Three."

"Russell and I have two married daughters. Only two grandchildren, though—a newborn girl and a toddler. His name is Brian. Do you have any grandchildren?

"No."

"Is it true that your children don't go to school past the eighth grade?"

"It's our way."

"Russell doesn't even have a seventh grade education, but that was more usual in his day. It kind of limits a person's opportunities— I mean in the modern world. You don't have any problem with your knees, do you?"

"No."

"That's good. Russell can hardly walk, I'm afraid. Can I get you something to eat or drink?"

"No."

"Well, I'll leave you two men alone to do your work. It's been nice meeting you, Mr. Yoder. I suppose Russell explained that the old wood shingles will have to be taken off the roof and new plywood put down. My sister says that's absolutely essential, and she's in real estate. And we need roof vents."

Maxine labored with thick steps up the creaking staircase.

Rusty and Eli did not look at each other and continued discussing the rotted joists. On the way back to Eli's house, Rusty was surprised when his passenger asked—without the slightest embarrassment—if there was time to stop at the feed mill for a bag of ground corn, a roll of fencing, and a pair of sheep shears. The sheep shears had apparently been left by another Amish living on the other side of the county and waited to be picked up. Yes, there was time, Rusty said, *my time.*

When they arrived at Eli's little house, the frowning older woman appeared again in the doorway—still barefoot and still clutching her broom—and three little children bolted past her, rushing into the yard in wild anticipation. Ignoring Rusty as if he did not exist, they seemed delighted with the arrival of the items from the feed mill. Only the little boy shot him a quick, fearful glance. Eli lifted the chicken feed and wire out of the back and placed them in the children's eager arms, and they staggered off happily toward the rickety outbuildings. Rusty did not get out of his cab.

On the way home, he stopped at the lumberyard to order the needed materials.

"I hear you're hiring Amish," said the lumberyard owner.

"Who told you that?"

"July Montgomery was in here a while ago and said you were going to hire Eli Yoder."

"Something wrong with that?"

Restoration on Shake Rag Street, Mineral Point (c. 1940). By the 1930s many of the cabins and related structures built decades before by the Cornish miners of Mineral Point were in a state of disrepair and were being taken down. Mineral Point residents Robert Neal and Edgar Hellum began to acquire and restore several buildings on Shake Rag Street, including the Polperro House (pictured here in the 1940s). In 1970 the restored buildings were transferred to the Wisconsin Historical Society. They are now part of the Pendarvis Historic Site.

"Not a thing."

"Make sure these materials are delivered before Thursday," said Rusty. "And put a tarp over them when you drop them off. I don't want them rained on."

Postville: Iowa's Entry into the Post-Modern (2009)

Robert Wolf

The communities of the Driftless Area remain in flux, subject to national and global trends involving immigration, labor, economic disparity, and cultural and demographic change. These forces came into sharp focus during a 2008 incident when Mexican and Guatemalan workers in Postville, Iowa, were the target of a federal enforcement action. As part of his commitment to giving voice to change and opportunity in the Driftless, artist, writer, and publisher Robert Wolf of Decorah, Iowa, documented the episode in his book *Heartland Portrait: Stories from the Rural Midwest*.

On May 12, 2008, the Department of Homeland Security conducted the largest immigration raid in U.S. history at Agriprocessors' slaughterhouse in Postville, Iowa. At that time Agriprocessors was the country's largest kosher processing plant. Located in the heart of northeast Iowa, Postville was once what one of its residents described as Mayberry, an ideal American small town. Now she and her husband want to leave Postville, but they doubt anyone will buy their house after the raid, which swept up nearly 400 illegal Guatemalans and Mexicans and has left the town economically depressed and bitterly factionalized. "We can't get anything out of our house [now]. Because we can't afford to buy a house elsewhere, we are thinking of moving it elsewhere."

Only ten years ago, with its population of Caucasians, Hispanics, American and Russian Jews, Postville hosted its first annual "Taste of Postville" that featured foods from each of the town's cultures. "They haven't had it [Taste of Postville] now for three or four years," the resident said. "The people who put their heart and soul into it got sick of the town and left. The Jewish people offered Israeli salad and samples of their kosher meats. The Russian people would make their soups, like borscht, and the dairy people would have an ice cream stand. We loved it." She remembers with affection the quiet lull before the tourists would arrive for the festival. "It was just like walking through a peaceful neighborhood back then."

Beneath appearances, realities were far different. Agriprocessors was owned by the Rubashkin family from Crown Heights, Brooklyn, an enclave of conservative and ultraconservative Jews. The Rubashkins are Lubavichers, an ultraconservative sect that believes that the messiah, Menachem Mendel Schneerson, died in 1994. On Saturday, the Jewish Sabbath, Lubavich rabbis wear square fur hats that sit like boxes atop their heads. They wear the white and black checked prayer shawls. All mature Lubavich males are bearded and dress in black seven days a week.

When the Lubavichers arrived in Postville in 1987 to assume operation of the processing plant, local residents received a shock. With the arrival of the plant's Hispanic workers and their families, they received another. Rural Iowans had never experienced either culture. In fact, at that time many rural Iowans may not have even seen black people in the flesh, just in photographs or movies, or on television. But in recent years nonwhites have been slowly moving into the Driftless region and cultural horizons have widened considerably. But back in 1987. . . .

What happened to Postville since then is what happens worldwide when an unworldly culture is confronted by the ruthless exploitative force of urban money. This is not to say that rural Iowans have not experienced some of their own wealthier people pushing their weight around, getting their way with town councils and county supervisors. But the Rubashkin family is big money, and made big contributions to the Iowa Republican Party and to powerful Iowa Republicans, including U.S. Senator Charles Grassley and U.S. Representative Tom Latham. Some of this money came from Shalom Rubashkin, former CEO of Agriprocessors, and some from his close relatives.

The Rubashkins were no strangers to the inside of a federal courtroom. . . . As of this writing, the *Des Moines Register* reports that a "new, 163-count indictment adds nine mail-fraud charges to the allegations against [Shalom] Rubashkin, and 14 counts of wire fraud. . . . Each new charge carries a maximum 30-year prison sentence and a $1 million fine if Rubashkin is convicted." Among other charges, Rubashkin and Agri-processor managers have been cited for knowingly providing false social security numbers to the illegal Guatemalan and Mexican workers. . . .

Three months before the raid the *Des Moines Register* reported that "Agriprocessors Inc. has a history of noncompliance with state and federal regulations related to food safety, pollution and workplace safety at its Postville facility, government records show." The article then went on to list numerous violations, including the lack of worker respiratory protection, the discharge of pollutants into Postville's water treatment system, the exposure of workers to hazardous chemicals, the presence of fecal matter on processed chickens, and the presence of fecal matter sprayed around three work areas.

On May 18, six days after the raid, I interviewed then-eighteen-year-old Postville High School senior, Santiago Cordero. Cordero came to this country with his uncle at age fourteen. In high school he was a member of the soccer team, which included Hispanics, Jews, and Postville-born youngsters. It was a tight-knit group.

For a time Santiago worked at the plant, checking the line of chickens. The supervisors, he said, were "always yelling at the people. Like if the machine breaks, they yell at the people." As for working there: "It's not really safe. The floor was dirty. Sometimes the water just accumulated—the water they use to wash the chickens. If there was a lot of water we would have to get permission to stop the line. I would tell them [the supervisors]. They would stop the line and would get someone to wash the floor so it would be safe to the people to walk along."

Besides that, he said, "The chemical they use is bad for people, I think. It burned my eyes. They probably used too much. [They use it] to disinfect the chickens."

Santiago's mother, a small Mexican woman who was caught in the raid and wore a GPS anklet, spoke to me through her son. (Santiago's father was working at the school and was not picked up.) His mother said that the plant's working conditions were "poor. It wasn't safe. The floor—most of the time—it was slippery."

I asked her if the people who did the hiring know that many of the workers were illegal. "They did know. Some of the people inside the Agriprocessors gave them their I.D.s."

The raid was conducted by Immigration and Customs Enforcement (ICE), an agency within Homeland Security. She described the raid. "I

got scared because when we were working they just came in and everybody tried to escape. But they just pointed the guns at people. And then
also they had cattle prods. They [ICE] say: 'Turn around. We will hand-
cuff you like you were rats.'

"They got everybody in one place and they grabbed some of the
women from their hair. They couldn't even go to the bathroom. They
[ICE] said, 'Just wait.' They yelled to the men, 'You sons-of-bitches, you
will not escape.' And they just kept laughing at the people. And some
of the people were hit for no reason, men and women.

"They like handcuffed the men. They would like set them down and
pull them up by the handcuffs. And if some of the men told officials
the handcuffs were too tight and they asked them to remove them, the
officials made them even tighter. When they were searching the people,
some of the women were searched by men, even where they're not supposed to be searched.

"They [the workers] say: 'Why this necessary to hit the people? They
were sitting still.'

"Why they do that? Why the immigration pointing guns at the
people? They just yell at them and then many workers got handcuffed.
Why they didn't do this ten years before when there was only men? Now
that there is entire families some of the fathers are away [arrested] and
how's the mothers going to work and take care of the children? They're
just taking families apart.

"They videotaped the people outside [the plant after the raid] but why
didn't they videotape how they were treating the people?"

About 900 ICE agents had participated in the raid and about 400
immigrants had been arrested and were held for a time at the National
Cattle Congress in Waterloo, Iowa. . . .

Back in Postville, Catholic clergy and volunteers set up a food pantry
at St. Bridget's Church where many had taken sanctuary in the days following the raid. Food donations and other needed items began arriving from nearby towns. Volunteers and staff alike were desperately
overworked.

The treatment the immigrants received from Homeland Security
was brutal, but so was their treatment by their Agriprocessor supervisors. At the time of the raid, Mary Klauke was Rural Life Director for
the Dubuque Archdiocese. She spent over one year with the immigrants, trying to help the women and children left in Postville following

their husbands' arrests. Exactly one month following the raid, Mary drove a young Hispanic boy and his father to La Crosse, Wisconsin, for a medical appointment. On the drive the father showed Mary one of his arms.

She wrote in her diary: "He shows me a scar on his arm—a long welt that looks to me like a bad burn scar. In fact it sends shudders through my whole body, even after thirty-three years since having experienced a bad burn myself.

"'No,' he says, 'no burn.' As he clasped his hands together and swung them down in front of him, he said, 'Club. Supervisor hit.'"

Klauke asks: "How could anyone be hit so hard with a club that it would cause a scar so deep, so thick and so long?"

Two months after the Postville raid, Mary suggested that I conduct a workshop to gather stories on the raid's aftermath. She and Jeff Abbas and Linda Szabo were among the five workshop attendees. Jeff, who commutes daily to Postville, is manager of KPVL Postville Community Radio, kept the town aware daily of the ongoing tribulations. He was also a major source of background and updates for the national media while singlehandedly keeping KPVL on the air. This excerpt from his story, "Hometown to the World," gives a needed piece of the larger picture:

"'Postville—Hometown to the world.' The sign welcomes the traveler on Highway 18. And it welcomes me every day on my way to work. Over the course of the last two years, I have seen it, read it and thought about it every day. And, for a while, I believed it. To say all the people of Postville truly lived that motto would be a stretch. More accurately, it should read 'Postville—Hometown to the World—We say that because it sounds good.'"

For years Jeff lived in California. When he returned to northeast Iowa and began working in Postville, he welcomed the town's multiculturalism and began befriending Hispanics and Jews. But this, he wrote, came with "a hidden price. The people with whom I share an ancestry and cultural tradition began to perceive me as a bit of an oddball."

The outsider passing through town and seeing on the same sidewalk a Mexican man with a wide brimmed hat, a farmer in coveralls, and a bearded Jew dressed in black would think what a wonderful town! But, wrote Abbas, "Sadly, [the sign outside Postville] was little more than frosting on a burned cake. The average, lifelong resident who graduated from Postville High, played football and basketball and married Mary

Jane because they went together in high school had no more interest in embracing cultural diversity than he had in rereading *Moby Dick.*"

Abbas soon had problems with his board, a simple outcome of his violation of the small town dicta: "Go along to get along" and "Don't rock the boat." Abbas, like any genuine human being, was outraged by the entire string of events, and so would not let the city or the nation forget it for one day. For that he garnered the resentment of his board. He was letting northeast Iowa and the world know that Postville was not Mayberry. . . .

Linda Szabo is willing to say as much too. In fact, she is the only Postville resident besides the town's Catholic clergy who has had the courage to speak her mind on this issue. The silence of the majority is a testimony to the unspoken code of small towns that Jeff Abbas violated. . . . Linda writes:

A menorah above the meat-processing plant in Postville, Carol Highsmith (2016). The Agri-Star meat-processing plant in Postville, Iowa, features a large menorah, lit during the eight-day Jewish celebration of Hanukkah. After the 2008 raid on the kosher plant by U.S. immigration agents, hundreds of its workers were deported and the owner of the plant, Aaron Rubashkin, was arrested, convicted, and imprisoned. The plant was rescued from bankruptcy and reopened by another Orthodox Jew, Hershey Friedman of Montreal, Canada.

"Who am I? I am a lifelong citizen of Postville. I have been a resident of this community for nearly fifty years. . . .

"As I reflect on the past months since the immigration raid, the day that crippled this community, devastating the lives of the people who live here; I realize how long, the many years it has taken, for the stifled emotions I presently harbor to have escalated. Unleashing and letting go of the expected secrecy characteristic of conforming has not and will not be easy. . . .

"Post-raid, my family has endured the agonizing 'good-byes' to countless dear friends, family by family—Hispanic, Arab and Jewish. . . . I say 'countless' because in all the chaos post-raid, it is almost impossible to determine who is still here and who has gone amongst the Hispanic population of Postville. I can only predict the families will continue to depart for quite some time. I am certain none of the families will return once they leave. Postville is a source of horrific memories for them. It is very heartbreaking for me as well.

"It has been a challenging year. Postville has been tested each passing day since the May ICE raid. Sadly, I harbor bitter feelings toward others who accuse the 'whole town' of being 'guilty' of what transpired in Postville. I look back on what has happened; and I see the irreparable damage that passive acceptance has caused this community. The years when community leaders 'reveal' only what they deem necessary for the public to know, those years must come to an end. I will no longer sit back and wait for someone else to decide what is best for Postville. I will no longer think of Postville as the Christian community, the Jewish community or the Hispanic community. I believe when you separate groups, you are asking for trouble. There is a much higher likelihood of corruption. This is how we ended up where we are today. Passive acceptance finally caught up to us.—What happened in Postville, happened slowly over time . . . twenty years." . . .

Postville is not an anomaly. Given the same ingredients—poverty, a sudden influx of urban money, and radically different cultures—divisions within a town will intensify, not only between the groups but within them.

The relative poverty across much of the Driftless region should alert us to the fact that the Postville experience could happen elsewhere here. One obvious source of the problem is material—a lack of capital that results in a shortage of business and employment. Another source is a decline of spirit, that which enabled this region's settlers to build towns, industry and agriculture and is needed now to rebuild the same. We cannot stand much more rescuing by individuals and companies that build processing plants, factory farms and manufacturing plants, get tax breaks, and leave us, or that stay and send the profits elsewhere. Habitual reliance on outside capital and spirit results in negligible self-reliance and eventual self-depletion.

Prosperity goes a long way to salving old sores. The rebuilding of a vibrant culture will demand more, but for a start it will suffice.

Things I Love About Where I Am (2012)

KATHE DAVIS

Kathe Davis moved to the Kickapoo Valley in Wisconsin after retiring from teaching literature at Kent State University in Ohio.

> Township of Kickapoo, WI
> on the Kickapoo River
> in the Ocooch Mountains
> in the county formerly known as Bad Axe

> The goat at the bottom of the hill.
> The ruined farmhouse with
> a mini-Stonehenge in front
> and solar panels in back.

> The sudden willow
> at the T-intersection,
> manifesting voluminous
> and perfect as on
> a Chinese porcelain, but
> yellow, yellow . . .

> The fake deer on the bluff
> who changes clothes for each holiday.

The town I live in, population 395.
Its library, corner Wisconsin & Railroad,
with its 83-year-old librarian, who
not only shushes no one, but talks
herself, constantly and
at the top of her voice.

The post office, corner of 4th & Elmo,
open Saturdays 8:45 to 9:30,
where the mailman posts his photos,
8 × 10 glossies of the town white squirrel,
close-ups of the tree-nursery eagles
feeding their young,
details of the holiday-clad fake deer.

The real deer path across
the corner of my yard,
four kinds of woodpeckers
gobbling suet,
wild turkeys in the snow.

All the long-haired men.

12

Futures

THROUGHOUT HISTORY, PEOPLE HAVE IMAGINED many futures for the Driftless. In the landscape we inhabit now, we wonder what its future may hold.

Will suburban and exurban development out of the Twin Cities, Madison, Rochester, Eau Claire, La Crosse, and Dubuque swallow farmland and natural areas? Or will these communities, and their smaller neighbors, turn around and revitalize themselves from within? Will communities fray amid change or cohere through shared values and identities?

Will ancient cultures and older traditions be reclaimed, revived, reinvented?

Will eroding support for public education leave young people disadvantaged relative to their cousins in wealthier areas? Will the children of the Driftless remain? Will they leave for opportunities elsewhere? Will those who leave return?

From where in the world, and with what worldviews, will people arrive in the Driftless? How will they be welcomed?

Will the Driftless, where it is far from interstate highways or international airports or broadband access, stagnate as a cultural and economic backwater? Will a renaissance in regional food, art, and culture provide a model for rural areas across the country?

What will drive demand for land? Who will own it and how will they care for it? Will water follow fur, lead, lumber, and sand as another commodity for export out of the Driftless?

Will Driftless forests degrade under neglect and irresponsible management? How will Driftless prairies and savannas and wetlands fare? Will abandoned pastures become permanent thickets of buckthorn, honeysuckle, and Russian olive? Will goats be deployed with surgical precision to restore health to lands overcome by exotic brush? Will feral hogs expand their range?

Can wild elk and bison return to the Driftless? How about black bear, cougar, and timber wolf? Will climate change drive kudzu and the red swamp crayfish into the Driftless and chase sugar maples and brook trout out? What will become of the whippoorwill, red-headed woodpecker, and cerulean warbler? Butterflies, bees, and other pollinators? Will beaver return in abundance and create floodplain wetlands? Will fire return as a shaper of landscapes?

What will Driftless farms of the future look like? Will agricultural production be the work of many independent farms or consolidated into operations driven by ever-expanding economies of scale? Will King Corn and Queen Soybean reign over ever-expanding swaths of land? Will food entrepreneurs thrive as they supply Driftless products to millions in Chicago, Milwaukee, and the Twin Cities? Will organic agriculture continue to flourish, or will organic farmers face market upheavals like those that undercut wheat, hops, tobacco, and milk in the past? Will farmers of perennial crops earn profits from carbon reabsorbed into their soils, grasslands, wetlands, and trees?

Will localized energy markets create a demand for renewable sources and drive innovations in transportation, infrastructure, architecture, and technology?

How will a changing climate disrupt the people, animals, plants, waters, and soils of the Driftless?

Will glaciers *ever* get here?

The Driftless Area will never again be what it was, but the history and potential of the land, its people, and their relationships will unfold in its forever becoming. Ages of waters shaped these Driftless hills and valleys. We are now, as always, coming around the next bend in the river.

Broken Gates (2012)

KEN McCULLOUGH

Poet Ken McCullough was born in Staten Island, New York, and has lived and drawn inspiration in landscapes from Newfoundland to the

mountains of Montana and Wyoming to Minnesota's blufflands, where
he lives on a farm outside of Winona. He has published nine books of
poetry and served as Winona's poet laureate.

> Enter into his gates with thanksgiving
> and into his courts with praise:
> be thankful unto him and bless his name.
>> Psalm 100:4

> Make a joyful noise unto the Lord, all the earth:
> make a loud noise, and rejoice, and sing praise.
>> Psalm 98:4

When I came to live here, fifty years into my life
in this valley cut by the river
all I knew was wandering, but this
the Driftless Region, is what I breathe and drink now.
Today, in bleak midwinter, the earth glazed
and dreaming of the long light, my days grow short.
I recall the taste of sunflower, prickly pear
and chokecherry. Mint, wild licorice, and grape.
The rank tastes of flood and choking wildfire.

A thousand years ago, the taste of water here,
the honey in the trees, the flowers and the grasses,
how the air tasted, the morning dew
favored by the deer, fog on the skin,
a blackcap bursting on the tongue.
The flesh of goat, of deer, of bear and elk,
when we were still on speaking terms
with the crow, the rattler and the coyote.

Bones of our horses and dogs are buried here.
We shovel the droppings from the barn
and mix it with compost from our table—
it takes our time, our blood, and feeds us.
I know the taste of okra from the garden,
sweet corn, tomatoes and arugula,
Brussels sprouts and blue Italian beans

and these stunted carrots—the soil not right—
pale orange gnomes from Peer Gynt's wildest nightmares.
I know apples, rhubarb, pears and little plums.

Today, I bless the fences fallen into disrepair,
Bless the rainwater in the cistern,
Bless the long throat of the well, 500 feet.
Bless these twisted implements turned to rust,
old Irv's sweat transmuted into apples.
Bless the flicker, nuthatch and the chickadee.

And bless you and you and you tonight,
and most of all bless you, my son.
Do not subdue and do not have dominion.
You are husband to this land, and steward;
enter these broken gates with thanksgiving.
We have brought you the old songs tonight,
if your friends and you would listen. Sing
most of them the same way, come up with
new tunes for the others. Just keep them breathing.

In autumn, when flocks are passing overhead,
take the river, and greet them with a joyful noise.

for Orion, at the Winter Solstice, 2009

From *Way Station* (1963)

CLIFFORD D. SIMAK

Clifford Simak (1904–1988) imagined a different Driftless future. The unofficial master of pastoral science fiction, he wrote prolifically and received numerous awards and distinctions. Born in Millville, Wisconsin, he often brought country characters and the rural setting of his youth into contact with alien civilizations from across time and space. In *Way Station*, a farm house tucked in a narrow Driftless valley is chosen as a secret stopover by space travelers intent on learning if humankind can overcome its warring ways and join the intergalactic community. In this excerpt, the farmer, a Civil War veteran named Enoch Wallace, meets his alien recruiter Ulysses.

He was sitting on the steps and it was late afternoon. He was watching the great white thunderheads that were piling up across the river beyond the Iowa hills. The day was hot and sultry and there was not a breath of moving air. Out in the barnyard a half a dozen bedraggled chickens scratched listlessly, for the sake, it seemed, of going through the motions rather than from any hope of finding food. The sound of the sparrows' wings, as they flew between the gable of the barn and the hedge of honeysuckle that bordered the field beyond the road, was a harsh, dry sound, as if the feathers of their wings had grown stiff with heat.

And here he sat, he thought, staring at the thunderheads when there was work to do—corn to be plowed and hay to be gotten in and wheat to reap and shock.

For despite whatever might have happened, a man still had a life to live, days to be gotten through the best that one could manage. It was a lesson, he reminded himself, that he should have learned in all its fullness in the last few years. But war, somehow, was different from what had happened here. In war you knew it and expected it and were ready when it happened, but this was not the war. This was the peace to which he had returned. A man had a right to expect that in the world of peace there really would be peace fencing out the violence and the horror.

Now he was alone, as he'd never been alone before. Now, if ever, could be a new beginning; now, perhaps, there had to be a new beginning. But whether it was here, on the homestead acres, or in some other place, it still would be a beginning of bitterness and anguish.

He sat on the steps, with his wrists resting on his knees, and watched the thunderheads piling in the west. It might mean rain and the land could use the rain—or it might be nothing, for above the merging river valleys the air currents were erratic and there was no way a man could tell where those clouds might flow.

He did not see the traveler until he turned in at the gate. He was a tall and gangling one and his clothes were dusty and from the appearance of him he had walked a far way. He came up the path and Enoch sat waiting for him, watching him, but not stirring from the steps.

"Good day, sir," Enoch finally said. "It's a hot day to be walking. Why don't you sit a while."

"Quite willingly," said the stranger. "But first, I wonder, could I have a drink of water?"

Enoch got up to his feet. "Come along," he said. "I'll pump a fresh one for you."

He went down across the barnyard until he reached the pump. He unhooked the dipper from where it hung upon a bolt and handed it to the man. He grasped the handle of the pump and worked it up and down.

"Let it run a while," he said. "It takes a time for it to get real cool."

The water splashed out of the spout, running on the boards that formed the cover of the well. It came in spurts as Enoch worked the handle.

"Do you think," the stranger asked, "that it is about to rain?"

"A man can't tell," said Enoch. "We have to wait and see."

There was something about this traveler that disturbed him. Nothing, actually, that one could put a finger on, but a certain strangeness that was vaguely disquieting. He watched him narrowly as he pumped and decided that probably this stranger's ears were just a bit too pointed at the top, but put it down to his imagination, for when he looked again they seemed to be all right.

"I think," said Enoch, "that the water should be cold by now."

The traveler put down the dipper and waited for it to fill. He offered it to Enoch. Enoch shook his head.

"You first. You need it worse than I do."

The stranger drank greedily and with much slobbering.

"Another one?" asked Enoch.

"No, thank you," said the stranger. "But I'll catch another dipperful for you if you wish me to."

Enoch pumped, and when the dipper was full the stranger handed it to him. The water was cold and Enoch, realizing for the first time that he had been thirsty, drank it almost to the bottom.

He hung the dipper back on its bolt and said to the man, "Now, let's get in that sitting."

The stranger grinned. "I could do with some of it," he said. Enoch pulled a red bandanna from his pocket and mopped his face. "The air gets close," he said, "just before a rain."

And as he mopped his face, quite suddenly he knew what it was that had disturbed him about the traveler. Despite his bedraggled clothes and his dusty shoes, which attested to long walking, despite the heat of this time-before-a-rain, the stranger was not sweating. He appeared as fresh and cool as if he had been lying at his ease beneath a tree in springtime.

Enoch put the bandanna back into his pocket and they walked back to the steps and sat there, side by side.

"You've traveled a far way," said Enoch, gently prying.

"Very far, indeed," the stranger told him. "I'm a right smart piece from home."

"And you have a far way yet to go?"

"No," the stranger said, "I believe that I have gotten to the place where I am going."

"You mean . . ." asked Enoch, and left the question hanging. "I mean right here," said the stranger, "sitting on these steps. I have been looking for a man and I think that man is you. I did not know his name nor where to look for him, but yet I knew that one day I would find him."

"But me," Enoch said, astonished. "Why should you look for me?"

"I was looking for a man of many different parts. One of the things about him was that he must have looked up at the stars and wondered what they were."

"Yes," said Enoch, "that is something I have done. On many nights, camping in the field, I have lain in my blankets and looked up at the sky, looking at the stars and wondering what they were and how they'd been put up there and, most important of all, why they had been put up there. I have heard some say that each of them is another sun like the sun that shines on Earth, but I don't know about that. I guess there is no one who knows too much about them."

"There are some," the stranger said, "who know a deal about them."

"You, perhaps," said Enoch, mocking just a little, for the stranger did not look like a man who'd know much of anything.

"Yes, I," the stranger said. "Although I do not know as much as many others do."

"I've sometimes wondered," Enoch said, "if the stars are other suns, might there not be other planets and other people, too."

He remembered sitting around the campfire of a night, jawing with the other fellows to pass away the time. And once he'd mentioned this idea of maybe other people on other planets circling other suns and the fellows all had jeered him and for days afterward had made fun of him, so he had never mentioned it again. Not that it mattered much, for he had no real belief in it himself; it had never been more than campfire speculation.

And now he'd mentioned it again and to an utter stranger. He wondered why he had.

"You believe that?" asked the stranger.

Enoch said, "It was just an idle notion."

"Not so idle," said the stranger. "There are other planets and there are other people. I am one of them."

"But you . . ." cried Enoch, then was stricken into silence.

For the stranger's face had split and began to fall away and beneath it he caught the glimpse of another face that was not a human face.

And even as the false human face sloughed off that other face, a great sheet of lightning went crackling across the sky and the heavy crash of thunder seemed to shake the land and from far off he heard the rushing rain as it charged across the hills.

From *Going Driftless: Life Lessons from the Heartland for Unraveling Times* (2015)

STEPHEN J. LYONS

The soil conservation, organic farming, perennial agriculture, and local food movements all have important roots among the farms and communities of the Driftless Area. All continue to evolve in new ways, bolstering local economies and drawing increasing attention from beyond the region. In his book *Going Driftless*, author Stephen Lyons explored this vision of farming's potential to restore the natural and human communities of the Driftless.

Intrigued by the idea of a distinctive Driftless taste, I visit the Hoch Orchard & Gardens near La Crescent in southeastern Minnesota. On a chilly afternoon in April—the season of mud—I meet owners Jackie and Harry Hoch (pronounced *Hoke*). The endless winter was beating a slow retreat. Thick, jagged ice still clung to the steep hillsides above

Rendering of the La Farge dam project (c. 1950). One future that has not come to pass in the Driftless is a dam on the Kickapoo River at La Farge, shown here as an artist's rendition. The dam was originally conceived in the 1930s for flood control, and work was finally begun in the 1960s. One hundred and forty farms were purchased, many unwillingly, for expanded plans to fill the valley above the dam with a large lake for recreation. An environmental impact assessment raised concerns that the dam would result in water quality issues, and federal analyses concluded that projected costs would exceed benefits. The dam was abandoned, half-built. The community was left deeply fractured over lost farms, divided families, and broken promises. The property languished in limbo for decades until citizen groups pushed for its new incarnation as a nature reserve, managed by a board of state, local, and Ho-Chunk Nation representatives.

Highway 61 along the Mississippi River, and up on top there were still tenacious scoops of worn-out snow on a few north-facing slopes.

The Hochs own ninety-five ridge-top acres. A tall fence attempts to repel browsing deer. A good-natured rivalry exists between valley farmers and ridge-top farmers. As Jackie jokes, "We farm the washed-out, rock-filled ridge tops. The valley farmers have the deep rich soil that used to be ours."

For an orchard, higher elevations make for more ideal growing conditions than lowlands. Harry says that the fruit favors hilltops that have good air drainage and longer hours of sunlight. Hillside orchardists also tend to have fewer issues with disease and moisture. Forty of the Hochs' ninety-five acres are in fruit production, twenty-four acres devoted to apples, about half the size of the average U.S. commercial orchard.

The Hochs' farm is a certified organic operation. They grow more than fifty varieties of apples. Honeycrisp, a popular winter-hardy apple developed by the University of Minnesota specifically for the Driftless region, is their biggest crop. The U.S. Apple Association describes its taste as "a honeyed, mild flavor and a crispness deemed explosive."

The Hochs sell about 8 percent of their harvest to food cooperatives in the Twin Cities. The rest of their apples are sold on their farm and at local farmers' markets. Apples that don't pass the grade for quality become cider. Apples below the cider grade become animal feed. The orchard also produces apricots, plums, sweet cherries, raspberries, strawberries, and grapes. A hard cider and winery business is in the works, and the Hochs also maintain sheep, pigs, and poultry.

The Hochs do not waste any apples, and they control their own packaging and distribution instead of turning over those decisions to a commercial packinghouse. Jackie says, "Our farm is kind of unique, because Harry figured out a system where we utilize all of the crop. So many times orchards go out and pick the highest quality fruit because if they pick less than the highest quality and send it to a packinghouse, they will lose money per bushel because of the payment to the packinghouse. We do our own picking, our own packing, and our own delivery. We do it all."

Annual production over the past five years has ranged from four to eight thousand bushels. A bushel is around forty-two to forty-eight pounds. Harry says, "There are a lot of young trees on this farm, so the production should increase to twelve or fourteen thousand bushels."

Wholesale Honeycrisp prices run around two dollars a pound for the highest grade. Specialty varieties such as the newer variety called SweeTango sell for even more.

When you talk with the Hochs, you realize that they are savvy business people. Harry has a master's in communication and sustainable agriculture; Jackie has a master's degree in business and experience managing 300 employees at a medical lab in the Twin Cities. They also manage several interns on their farm and pay them a fair wage, at least $1,000 a month plus room and board, during the several months that they work at the orchard. (Jackie cooks most of the evening suppers.) The internships are organized through a partnership with two programs: the Minnesota Agricultural Student Trainee and the Multicultural Exchange for Sustainable Agriculture.

"There are a lot of programs that people have for interns where they're only being paid a little bit," Jackie says. "What we feel is that they should be getting at least minimum wage, because this is a business and while this is an education for them, they are still providing us with service. I can teach them the importance of weeding strawberries, but they still have to weed all the strawberries." On the day that I visited, there were interns from France, Ecuador, Massachusetts, and Brazil. A man from the Republic of Georgia was due to arrive in July. "We get to travel the world without leaving the farm," Jackie says.

The orchard was purchased as a hobby farm for Harry's father in the 1950s. Andy, a World War II veteran, was a bachelor at the time, living and working in nearby La Crosse. In a twenty-year period, Andy planted 3,000 apple trees on sixty acres. Only a handful of those trees exist today. He married in the mid-1960s and started a family of three children that included Harry. The kids were raised in La Crosse but would visit the farm on the weekends, summers, and holidays. Andy's wife, also named Jackie, would have loved to move to the farm permanently, but Andy resisted. Andy passed away in 1983; Jackie passed away in 2013.

Harry always had a dream of running the orchard, so he bought out his two siblings. He and Jackie made an initial attempt to run the orchard in the 1980s, but the changing apple industry and an outdated farm with outdated varieties worked against them. Harry recalls, "Consumers were going from a handful of varieties—Red Delicious, Golden Delicious, Granny Smith—to all specialty varieties. We had an old orchard of standard-sized trees that my father had planted and that we had to renovate." . . .

The Hochs moved to the Twin Cities to pursue their education and careers. "We left the farm with the intention of coming back. We just didn't know whether it would be a retirement project or whether it would be when the kids were still young." For the next eight years, they commuted back and forth from the Twin Cities to the Driftless ridge-top farm to replant the orchard and rebuild the infrastructure. Jackie says, "We were planting trees that were either dwarf or semi-dwarf so the intent was to have trees that were in production when we moved back."

They returned with their two young daughters, Missy and Angie, in 1997. By then the apple industry had changed and adapted to consumers' demands for new varieties. The University of Minnesota had developed varieties such as Honeycrisp and Zestar that grew especially well in the Driftless soils. The young trees that the Hochs had planted began bearing fruit, and the demand for organics increased.

"We planted our orchard to sell to the food coops. Customers at the coops are more apt to buy a lot of varieties instead of just the main two or three varieties they like," Harry says. "When we market to these coops they're always asking if there is another variety. That is a completely different attitude from the conventional industry that wants to use their valuable shelf space for the proven varieties."

In Madison, Michelle Miller [of the University of Wisconsin] had referred to Harry as the IPM (integrated pest management) king. She told me that other Driftless orchardists who were not certified organic, but wanted to be, would come to Harry for advice as to how to make the shift to producing *eco-apples*. Harry said their overall mission was "to develop a truly sustainable system that creates a more independent farm with minimal off-farm inputs."

He began to put into place state-of-the-art IPM techniques he had learned at the University of Minnesota. These techniques called for fewer pesticides on the environment while utilizing, he said, "weather data recorders, pheromone trapping, population monitoring of insects, and action thresholds." That led to the use of "softer" organic products that have less impact on the environment.

"I studied a little more about soil ecology and the difference between a prairie soil and a forest floor, and which one is more fungal dominated. I started to learn about the animals' impact on the soil and how the soil evolves to match the plants in the system. To get to be a truly sustainable system you need to have animals and plants working together in a cyclical system. So our goal now is to see if we can rotate animals through a perennial food system.

"I have taken my education mostly from horticulture and sustainable agriculture and broadened it toward more ecological ideals."

To prepare for this permaculture environment, the Hochs have begun to take fields out of fruit production and grow the grains that will overwinter their animals.

La Crosse River, Memorial Park to County Highway J, Michael Lind (2014). This is one of a series of paintings by Michael Lind interpreting the landscapes of different Driftless rivers he paddled in 2014. Lind is a farmer at Driftless Organics and Big River Beef in rural Soldiers Grove, Wisconsin.

The Hochs' plan of creating a self-contained agricultural cycle was inspiring to me. With a renewed interest by consumers in where and how their foods are produced and grown, it seems that the Hochs are embracing the future, using good science and a practical business model. I thought back to Jackie's pride in being "ridge people." Similar to watching the approaching weather come across the horizon, the Hochs had also sensed a future that was free of confinement animal production and GMO-laden foods. A permaculture future is a return to an agrarian past. Modern science such as IPM practices are utilized, but permaculture adheres to the notion that every input or action is not an end in itself to a particular problem, but part of a continuum of living in which sustainability and environmental health are of paramount importance. This is hard to understand if you live detached from the roots of where your food is produced.

In the Driftless region, the Hochs' mission is becoming part of the norm, no matter if one farms in the valleys or on the ridge tops. Harry said that one of the commonalities of the Driftless residents, no matter where they live, is a love of the region's diversity. "You've got deciduous trees, you've got woodlands, coniferous woodlots, meadows, prairies, bottomlands, blufflands—all of this diversity within a five-minute drive in any direction. So the people who like that diversity are probably the ones who are going to stay, and that's probably what the Driftless culture is."

From *Jerusalem Creek: Journeys into Driftless Country* (2002)

TED LEESON

As many of the Driftless Area's watersheds and streams have recovered from past degradation, trout populations have thrived—as has interest throughout the region in trout fishing. In *Jerusalem Creek*, Ted Leeson, an author and emeritus professor of English at Oregon State University, explored the trout streams of the Driftless Area. In his pursuit of trout, Leeson reflects on the connections between our inner and exterior landscapes, between the wild and the human, and between the past and the future.

The driftless area, like most landscapes on earth, is damaged goods, proof again, were any needed, that we live in a fallen world, and by looks of it, fallen from a rather great height. The first loss is always innocence. There is no gainsaying the fact that we have buggered the thing, badly.

But in the quest to preserve what wilderness still remains on earth, it is easy to forget or overlook or, worst of all, dismiss the driftless area and the places like it, the landscapes of home. There is a disturbing voice in modern environmental thinking that regards these tamed lands as already lost, nature's shock troops fallen before human advance, the dead and wounded and missing in action, valuable primarily as grim examples of what must not be allowed to happen elsewhere; they are the potential fate of the real environment that is left. Behind this attitude lies the troubling assumption that the only natural worlds of authentic value, ecologically and spiritually, exist in places untouched and exotic, in the Alaskan wilderness or South American rain forests or Pacific reefs. . . .

There is a possibility of place that lies between the wilds of the upper Amazon and the concrete wasteland of a shopping mall, of land that is used but not used up, domesticated but not enslaved, where valleys and streams have not been forced completely into human disguise. I say this, of course, in part from the perspective of a trout fisherman, which is always myopic, and even as I am fully aware that there is no such thing anymore as a nonpolitical trout. Each one exists by sufferance, by virtue of a land-restriction, a stream-saving deal, a lawsuit, court injunction, state or federal land designation, a regulation or statute or someone's goodwill. Every fish is one that easily might not have been. To see even these fish as the dominant feature of the landscape may well be valuing them far out of proportion to their actual significance, as occupants of a biological niche or as an indicator species. To regard a place with wild trout as having some measure of environmental integrity may just be another form of self-delusion, but in the end I am a trout fisherman and cannot help but believe that trout express something about the land. There is a narrow line between indifferent resignation to a diminished world and appreciating what gifts still remain. . . .

At one edge of the driftless area, off a bit by itself, lies Lapp's Branch, a lovely spring creek in a very green place. The stream would run through the center of Lapp's Cove were this tiny hamlet big enough to have a center to flow through. It is little more than a short row of houses bounded by a ridge on one side and by the stream on the other. That it has a name at all, I suspect, owes to a need for something to call the baseball team. In this part of the country, having a baseball team is almost a civic obligation, and considering that almost everyone participates, it doesn't take a town of much size to field nine players. There are local leagues for fast-pitch and slow-pitch, for men and women and children, as well as the informal pickup contests and family rivalries that are settled in the evenings after work or on a Saturday morning. Almost every town that has a team also has a field. The diamond at Lapp's Cove is a pleasant park, not large but well kept. Picnic tables are spread beneath the shade of rows of oaks that flank the first and third baselines. The infield points toward the creek; the distance from home plate to the stream bank is perhaps twenty-five feet, and between them is a high chain-link fence that probably paid for itself long ago in lost baseballs.

The section of Lapp's Branch that meanders up to the edge of the park is pretty fair water. But like all anglers, I prefer whenever possible to fish beyond the sight and sound of people, away from barns and buildings and the noise of passing traffic. If I cannot find actual solitude, I will seek out a place on the stream where tall or wooded banks screen out the houses and highways, where I can indulge the illusion of being off alone. Fly fishing is filled with small deceptions of just this sort, about water and fish, flies and techniques. They are little adjustments that the mind works on itself, ways of orchestrating enjoyment to conform with the circumstances at hand. I don't need to know that I am fishing in the middle of nowhere, but I like it to seem that way as much as possible. So from time to time, if it was the middle of the week and quiet and no one was around, I would spend a few hours fishing the stretch of stream that runs behind the baseball diamond.

On one of these occasions, not so long ago, I found myself on the water when a game was going on, though I wasn't aware of it at the time; it must have started after I put in and began wading upstream. As I got closer, I could hear the voices of the people watching the game; the shouts of the players; once in a while, the dull metallic thunk of an aluminum bat meeting a softball; the yelling and laughter of kids horsing around—ordinary sounds that are ordinarily not disagreeable. But when I'm fishing, that level of ambient commotion brings out in me a kind of prickliness and irritation that I know even at the time is entirely unjust. I imagine myself imposed upon, that half the reason I came fishing—to enjoy the intimacy of place—is now gone; the other half—catching a fish—still remains, but under the circumstances it feels like a lot less than half. The general activity, the noise drifting overhead as I fished, the simple awareness of other people so close by, all were impossible to ignore, and most days I would have packed up my tackle, corralled my various indignations, and retreated to more private water.

But for reasons I cannot explain, I didn't leave and continued working my way upstream until I was just behind home plate. With the high banks and thick vegetation, I couldn't see anything, and was certain that the people in the park had no idea I was there, though a keen eye might have detected the switch of a rod tip back and forth just above the tops of the tall grass. It struck me then that there was a kind of intimacy in this too. It would not have been my first choice of arrangements for fishing, and still would not be, and it by no means produced some gush

Farmed Frame, David Wells (2012). David Wells is a Madison-based artist, teacher, and art curator and director of the Edgewood College Gallery. Wells used worn and rusted farm machinery parts to create *Farmed Frame* for the inaugural "Art D'Tour" in Sauk County, Wisconsin, in 2012. The photograph by Katrin Talbot appeared in the *Milwaukee Journal Sentinel* on September 7, 2012.

of expansive sympathy for the universal brotherhood of man. But I was drawn into it in some odd way. We were all in a place we liked, doing something that we enjoyed, staying out of each other's way, observing a kind of compromise unwittingly drawn among strangers in the small place we all occupied. I was fishing on the edge of town. People lived there. The trout were still rising. It wasn't ideal, but it felt strangely like enough.

The terrain of every life, of a landscape or a community or a person, is a series of negotiated settlements, a set of boundaries that always enclose a space of loss. Remembering the past is not the same as returning to it, and moving forward not the same as abandoning it. In negotiating, the question is not to hold on to or reclaim innocence—that is not possible—but the nature of the bargain struck. It is a prerogative of youth, and one of the great values, to regard compromise as defeat. Later, though, you see it more in the light of victory, because if you have lived at all, you've seen real defeat, and it looks a good deal different.

From *The Driftless Land: Spirit of Place in the Upper Mississippi Valley* (2010)

KEVIN KOCH

Kevin Koch is a native of Dubuque, where he is a professor of English at Loras College. In 2010 he published *The Driftless Land*, a collection of essays on the natural, cultural, and spiritual geography of the Driftless landscape. Its last chapter, excerpted here, is "Where the Earth Breathes: A Vow of Stability."

I am gazing out my office window. I have a fifth-floor office in a century-old building at Loras College, on a bluff, facing east. Before and beneath me lie the streets of Dubuque, Iowa, dusted last night with a fresh four-inch snowfall. Steep hills descend to the river valley nested with Victorian homes, church steeples, and an eclectic clutter of nineteenth-century downtown facades. A bit further lies a frozen stretch of Mississippi River, the U.S. 151 bridge crawling with steady but not crowded traffic, a slow-moving train on the opposite shore, and steep-sided Wisconsin bluffs in a wintry mosaic of brown and white. The view is, in short, a fine diversion from grading papers.

This place is home.

Having said that, I've left the word "this" intentionally vague. By home, I could be referring to Loras College, where I have taught for more than twenty-five years. I could be referring to the 1906-constructed house where I live and where we still ponder whether the limestone-walled basement corner room may have been a summer kitchen or a horse barn. I could be referring to Dubuque, which has been my home for fifty years, and my family's since the 1880s. I could be referring to the Driftless Land, to North America, or to the world. For all of these are my home.

But in another sense, I can't know or care for the world without first knowing and caring for my local home, without first developing a sense of place.

And how is any of that that the slightest bit meaningful to my students, who have come from other places and will graduate and move again? Or to my children, who love the faraway mountains more than the river, and who, like most Americans, will move, on average, every seven years and change careers just as often? To a culture in which one city looks like another with its replicated box-store giants, or which finds its strongest allegiances to virtual, electronic communities? Have I, at mid-life, simply settled into anachronistic beliefs?

After reading Scott Russell Sanders' *Staying Put: Making a Home in a Restless World* with my Nonfiction Writing class, I asked my students to write briefly about the ways in which they are "wanderers" and the ways in which they are "rooted." There was, of course, a tug and pull between these two. The same students who "want to see the world" and "have new experiences" are simultaneously "rooted" in family and faith, for example. It is healthy to be both rooted and wanderer.

Sanders reminded us, as we travelled through his essays, that although American culture did not invent "wandering," we certainly have perfected it. Native Americans found their way to the Americas more than 12,000 years ago across icy lands of the Bering Strait made passable by the retreat of the oceans during the last Ice Age. They dispersed across North, Central, and South America. The climate warmed, the ice retreated, and the oceans rebounded. Soon enough the wanderers were cut off from their Asian origins. The rest of our ancestors, of course, arrived at various times within the last four hundred years, coming to the Americas for gold, for land, for jobs, for religious freedom, as punishment, to escape starvation, as draft evaders, or were transported against their will as slaves.

Nothing new in that civics lesson, except that we haven't stopped moving ever since: westward expansion, plowing the plains, the Underground Railroad, and California migration, where, as Joan Didion writes, we'd better get it right because we've run out of continent. Now the migration is to the South, where Americans take refuge from the (ironically ever-milder) Northern winters.

But wandering, as Sanders points out, is pretty much a human genetic trait, along with speaking and story-telling, a trait that signifies what it means to be human. The peoples of the "old world" of Europe and Asia wandered to their present locations out of Africa, and even indigenous peoples are often nomadic. We learn to scope out the neighborhood and wonder what lies over the mountain. And much good has come from our human wanderings: the enrichment of cultures and literatures, the spread and expansion of knowledge and trade, the sharing of foods and agricultural practices.

Of course, the modern world has brought wandering to new heights, with the automobile, jet, internet, and a sense of ourselves in a "virtual world" that is often not rooted in physical locale at all.

But there is a downside to our wandering, and, especially, to our loss of the sense of place. . . . Even those of us not on the move may lose our connection to and understanding of the land. In my home state of Iowa, we have plowed or paved nearly every available acre. Iowa rates nearly last in the country for the amount of land set aside for parks and wildlife refuges. Agricultural and commercial water-runoff courses through the state's streams, bowls into the Mississippi River, and feeds a Dead Zone in the Gulf of Mexico where nothing grows or lives for hundreds of miles past the great river's mouth.

These things happen when we lose touch with the land, resist rooting down in the place where we live, or fail to understand how our place connects inch by inch, acre by acre, to the next place, and to the whole ecosystem of earth.

Since 1849, Trappist monks have lived at New Melleray Abbey, fifteen miles west of my home in Dubuque, deeply connected to their own corner of the prairie. They were invited here by Dubuque's first Catholic Bishop, Matthias Loras, from their home at Mount Melleray Abbey in Ireland, where, like the rest of their countrymen, they were starving through the potato famine. About thirty monks still live at New Melleray, many of them aged. Many have lived their entire adult lives at the abbey, their vows dating as far back as 1942, although a handful of monks have taken vows in the past ten years.

There are many kinds of monks, St. Benedict reminds his readers in the opening to his sixth-century Rule for monastics. Among others, there are hermits, like the Desert Fathers, the earliest Christian monks who favored the caves of the Egyptian desert. There are wandering monks, "who keep going their whole life long from one province to another, staying three or four days at a time in different cells as guests. Always roving and never settled." But Benedict writes for the Cenobites, those who live in community and who vow, among other things, a life of "stability." They will remain, the rest of their lives forward, at this abbey alone, and will likewise be buried within.

At New Melleray Abbey, rows of simple iron crosses in an interior courtyard mark the graves of the monks, who are buried in simplicity, with no casket, just a thin shroud separating them, for a while, from the soil.

The vow of stability, for monks, means a pledge to remain at the abbey, to persevere in the liturgies of the day, to work humbly, to own nothing and to regard the tools, implements, and vessels of the abbey as sacred. Inevitably, this attachment to the abbey translates into a deep connection to the land on which it sits. Thomas Merton, a twentieth-century Trappist from Gethsemane Abbey in Kentucky, explains: "How necessary it is for monks to work in the fields, in the rain, in the sun, in the mud, in the clay, in the wind: these are our spiritual directors and our novice-masters. They form our contemplation. They instill us with virtue. They make us as stable as the land we live in."

Stability for the rest of us does not mean—should not mean and cannot mean—vowing to stay put in the same locale where we've been born or landed our first job. We do live in the real world, where mobility is the rule of life. But stability is a call to be in the fields, in the rain, the mud, and the clay no matter where we're at, no matter for how long. Our dirty hands, wet faces and backs, and sore feet are testimony to our contact and connectedness to the earth that birthed us and will receive us back again.

I light out on a winter's hike toward the preserve near my house. Today it's hard going, though. Repeated cycles of ice and snow and thaws have left the wooded bottomland with a thick and icy crust that I sink into about every third step.

It's a long way back into the woods to where I'd intended to go, past fifty-foot rock outcroppings and 100-foot bluffs, past century-old lead mine pits, past a limestone tower formation called the Twin Sisters, past the railroad tracks, past an overlook of the Catfish Creek valley. Can't say I'm up to crunching through the ice crust all the way back to the far reaches of the preserve, so I decide instead to use the crusty snow to my advantage and climb a steeply wooded hillside, using a hiking stick and digging the edges of my boots down into the snow.

I've been up through these woods and on the top-land clearing before, but not for a couple of years. The lead mine pits are more numerous up here. A scraggly woods has grown in around them in the 150 years since they were last mined, but here and there a burr oak with great lateral branches attests that these hills were once savannas thinly forested with the massive trees that had leisurely spread their branches above the prairie.

The lead mine pits are, for the most part, easy to spot. They dot the upper third of the hillside (although there are others in the bottom lands as well) with deep circular scoops and tell-tale rock-strewn edges. Most stretch about six feet across, although they can be as wide as twenty. In some cases they were the entry points to lead mine shafts, but the older pits merely scratched along a surface vein, so it's not uncommon to find four or five in a row—usually east to west—where someone had scored a hit along a backbone.

If this were Ireland—and these miners *were* Irish immigrants, by and large—and if my ancestors had come upon these rounded pits with no prior knowledge of their making, no doubt we'd attribute them to fairies.

Sometimes, however, in a rocky terrain like this it is hard to tell which is lead mine and which is cave. I find the latter at an indentation in the hill I'd spied on my climb up. Instead of a shallow scooped-out pit, I find a vertical shaft walled with bedrock limestone sinking away beneath the forest floor. The mouth of the cave is about twice my girth and ominously ringed with sloping ice. My stomach crawls at the mere thought of what a slip could do, as there would be no way to climb back out and—judging by the lack of footprints in the snow—one ought not to count on a passerby. Curiosity doesn't even tempt this cat, except to find a stone to toss inside, to hear how long it takes to clatter to the cave floor. It takes . . . long enough.

Switching tactics, I grab a handful of powdery snow and sprinkle it above the opening, and the light puff of warm air escaping from the depths scatters the powder as if it were confetti.

This yawning of the earth intrigues me! I could tell you about the consistency of cave temperatures, cool against summer air and warm against the winter, could tell you how the warmer air will rise out of a vertical shaft in winter. But if it's all the same to you, I must tell you instead that the earth itself is breathing, and its mouth—one of many I am sure—is located on a hillside near my home.

You will find it if you venture out across the snow in the Driftless Land, if you know which valley to enter and which hillside to climb, if you can locate the vertical cave shaft in the overgrown woods.

I won't guarantee that I will find it back when I go there next. I'm notoriously bad with directions. Or maybe, like fairy rings in Ireland, it will simply pick up and move.

But for a moment, I was in contact with the bedrock of my home. I felt its breath.

Along with the bleak stories of those who have abused the land are the stories of connection, of those who have learned the Benedictine quality of stability, of those who have rooted down in a particular place for the while they are here. A professor I know brings his students to the Mines of Spain to collect prairie seed for new plantings. Citizens in Dubuque fight to save the river bluffs from overdevelopment. A wildlife refuge is procured by the County Conservation Board. Students and their teachers haul away brushy trees and restore an oak savanna. . . .

My college students will be graduating in a few weeks. One will go off to study in Ireland. Several are returning home to Chicago. Their flight patterns from past years have been varied, landing them for work or study in Seattle and Denver, Texas and Michigan and Washington, D.C. One of my former students taught in the Peace Corps in Eastern Europe, wrote for a computer magazine in Egypt, and then found himself back in the states in Milwaukee and then Rochester, working for nonprofit organizations.

The vow of stability does not mean living life in one place, going back to one's hometown and staying there forever. In fact, rooting down and connecting to place is more of a frame of mind than a matter of time lived in a single place. Some people, like me, *have* lived most of their lives in one place, but you can root down just as certainly when you move from place to place.

I am invited to speak to a small gathering of graduating seniors. When you move to a new place, I tell them, look around. Find out what brought the people here, learn how the land was formed. Understand what grows here, and why, and what creatures live here, and *have lived* here before. Pause and think before you turn a spade of ground, whether for a new house, a new shopping center, or a new shed in the back yard. That is not to say *don't build* that house, supermarket, or shed. But *pause and think* before you begin: Is this what is best for this place, not just now, but for the long run? Sometimes the answer will be yes, sometimes it will be no. But it is important to ask the question.

I tell them, I don't know how much you have explored *this* place that is right now still your home in the Driftless Land. At the Mines of Spain south of town, the area's first lead miners scraped out small conical ore pits, and today the weathered indentations lie silent and recaptured in the woods. Go there, find them. Near the Little Maquoketa River north of town, a brisk hike up more than one hundred railroad-tie steps will bring you face to face with the Native American past in the form of burial mounds. Go *there*. At Swiss Valley you will find rock outcroppings that puncture the soil like the great bone of earth piercing through skin. Here and there are prairie remnants. And even if you've rarely left campus, surely you've seen, across the river, that mound on the horizon, Sinsinawa, but did you know that it was holy ground, not just to the Dominicans who have called it home for 150 years, but to the Native

Americans before them, who called the region "Manitoumie," Where the Great Spirit Dwells? Go there, too.

The monks take their vow of stability.

How well they must know, over time, the sounds their footsteps make in the cloister, the smells of food in the refectory, the slant of light in the chapel at Vespers. The tactile physicality is the contact point leading inward to the spirit, much like the corpus Christi leads to the eternal.

You and I may live in a different world than the monks. But a vow of stability—of looking and seeing and touching that which is right here before us—may help us find that place in the hillside where the earth opens its mouth and breathes.

That ice flows like slow-motion liquid
might be news to some,
inscribed as it is in drumlins and moraines the ancient glaciers left
    behind.

Slowly, repeatedly, the glaciers awakened
and crept down from the north,
scoured the plains,
and slid around, beside, behind
the Driftless Land.

An island in a sea
of creeping floes,
a rugged boat
with rocky masts
that prick the ice pack,
adrift
in some polar vertigo.

But it is the ice that floats,
not you,
secured to bedrock
in the Driftless Land.

Sources and Further Readings

Sources of quotations and selected texts are listed below in the order of their appearance. Additional works cited in the preface and section introductions are also included, as well as further readings related to the section themes.

GENERAL SOURCES

Boudreau, R. *The Literary Heritage of Wisconsin.* Vol. 1, *Beginnings to 1925.* La Crosse, WI: Juniper Press, 1986.

Boudreau, R. *The Literary Heritage of Wisconsin.* Vol. 2, Part A, *1925–1960.* La Crosse, WI: Juniper Press, 1995.

Flanagan, J. T. "The Middle Western Historical Novel." *Journal of the Illinois State Historical Society* (1944): 7–47.

Greasley, P. A., ed. *Dictionary of Midwestern Literature.* Vol. 1, *The Authors.* Bloomington: Indiana University Press, 2001.

Hedin, R., ed. *Where One Voice Ends Another Begins: 150 Years of Minnesota Poetry.* St. Paul: Minnesota Historical Society, 2007.

Leary, J. P. *Wisconsin Folklore.* Madison: University of Wisconsin Press, 1998.

Nesbit, R. C. *Wisconsin: A History,* second edition revised and updated by W. F. Thompson. Madison: University of Wisconsin Press, 1989.

Rounds, C. R. *Wisconsin Authors and Their Works.* Madison: Parker Education, 1918.

Stephens, J., and M. Lefebvre, eds. *The Journey Home: The Literature of Wisconsin through Four Centuries.* Madison: North Country Press, 1989.

Ostergren, R. C., and T. R. Vale, eds. *Wisconsin Land and Life.* Madison: University of Wisconsin Press, 1997.

Wisconsin Cartographers' Guild. *Wisconsin's Past and Present: A Historical Atlas.* Madison: University of Wisconsin Press, 2002.

EPIGRAPH

Thomas C. Chamberlin, chapter 15 ("Quaternary Age") of *Geology of Wisconsin, Survey of 1873–1879* (Madison: Commissioners of Public Printing, 1883), 1:269.

Ben Logan, *The Land Remembers: The Story of a Farm and Its People* (Madison: University of Wisconsin Press, 2017; originally published 1975), 5.

Jim Funmaker, in the film *Gather Like the Waters* (Lone Rock, WI: Ootek Productions, 1994), by Dave Erickson and Michael J. Mossman. See *Wisconsin Indian Literature: Anthology of Native Voices*, edited by Kathleen Tigerman (Madison: University of Wisconsin Press, 2006), 88.

PREFACE

Marcel Proust's full quotation appears in *The Prisoner*, volume 5 of *Remembrance of Things Past* (first published in French in 1923 and translated into English in 1929): "The only true voyage of discovery, the only fountain of Eternal Youth, would be not to visit strange lands but to possess other eyes, to behold the universe through the eyes of another, of a hundred others, to behold the hundred universes that each of them beholds, that each of them is."

Gary Snyder's statement on common ground can be found in his book *A Place in Space: Ethics, Aesthetics, and Watersheds* (Washington, DC: Counterpoint Press: 1995), 235.

Wallace Stegner referenced Wendell Berry's statement, without citation, in his essay "A Sense of Place," in *Where the Bluebird Sings to the Lemonade Springs: Living and Writing in the West* (New York: Random House, 1992), 199.

1. GEOLOGIC ORIGINS

Lawrence Martin's *The Physical Geography of Wisconsin* was first published as Wisconsin Geological and Natural History Survey Bulletin No. XXXVI (1916) and was later reprinted in 1932 and 1965 editions by the University of Wisconsin Press. Quotations are from pages 103 and 105.

Patricia Monaghan's "Getting to Black Earth" was published in the Black Earth Institute's online *About Place Journal* 2, no. 2 (August 2013).

Robert H. Dott Jr. and John W. Attig, *Roadside Geology of Wisconsin* (Missoula, MT: Mountain Press Publishing Company, 2004), 21–22, 119–20.

Gwen M. Schultz, *Wisconsin's Foundations: A Review of the State's Geology and Its Influence on Geography and Human Activity* (Madison: University of Wisconsin Press, 2004), 181–82.

Thomas C. Chamberlin and Rollin Salisbury, "Preliminary Paper on the Driftless Area of the Upper Mississippi Valley," in *Sixth Annual Report of the United States Geological Survey to the Secretary of the Interior, 1884–1885*, edited by John Wesley Powell (Washington, DC: Government Printing Office, 1885), 205–6, 210–11, 315–16, 318–19, 322.

W J McGee, "The Pleistocene History of Northeastern Iowa," in *11th Annual Report of the Director of the U.S. Geological Survey, 1889–90, Part I* (Washington, DC: U.S. Government Printing Office, 1891), 367–70, 371–72, 374–76, 377–78.

Katherine Mead's "Watch for Fallen Rock" appeared in *Verse Wisconsin* 109 (July 2012): 13.

Further Readings

Anderson, W. I. *Iowa's Geological Past*. Iowa City: University of Iowa Press, 1998.

Brick, G. A. *Iowa Underground: A Guide to the State's Subterranean Treasures*. Black Earth, WI: Big Earth Publishing, 2004.

Daniels, E., J. G. Percival, and J. Hall. *First Annual Report on the Geological Survey of the State of Wisconsin*. Madison: David Atwood, 1854.

Hall, J., and J. D. Whitney. *Report on the Geological Survey of the State of Wisconsin*. Madison: Legislature of Wisconsin, 1862.

Hobbs, H. "Origin of the Driftless Area by Subglacial Drainage—A New Hypothesis." In *Glacial Processes Past and Present*, edited by D. M. Mickelson and J. W. Attig, 93–102. Geological Society of America Special Paper 337, 1999.

Hodge, J. T. "On the Wisconsin and Missouri Lead Region." *American Journal of Science and Arts* 43 (1842): 35–72.

Hole, F. D. "Soils of the 'Driftless Area.'" *Wisconsin Academy Review* 6 (1959): 8–9.

Iannicelli, M. "Evolution of the Driftless Area and Contiguous Regions of Midwestern USA through Pleistocene Periglacial Processes." *Open Geology Journal* 4 (2010): 35–54.

Irving, R. D. "The Quaternary Deposits of Central Wisconsin." *Geology of Wisconsin*, vol. 2, 608–36. Madison: David Atwood, 1877.

Keating, W. H. *Narrative of an Expedition to the Source of St. Peter's River, Lake Winnepeck, Lake of the Woods, &c. &c*. Philadelphia: H. C. Carey & I. Lea, 1824.

Knox, J. C. *Quaternary History of the Driftless Area*. Madison: Geological and Natural History Survey, University of Wisconsin–Extension, 1982.

Mickelson, D. M., J. C. Knox, and L. Clayton. "Glaciation of the Driftless Area: An Evaluation of the Evidence." In *Quaternary History of the Driftless Area*, 155–69. Madison: Wisconsin Geological and Natural History Survey, University of Wisconsin–Extension, 1982.

Owen, D. D., J. Leidy, J. G. Norwood, C. C. Parry, H. Pratten, B. F. Shumard, and C. Whittlesey. *Report of a Geological Survey of Wisconsin, Iowa, and Minnesota: and Incidentally of a Portion of Nebraska Territory*. Philadelphia: Lippincott, Grambo & Company, 1852.

Reinertsen, D. L. *Guide to the Geology of the Galena Area*. Champaign: Illinois State Geological Survey, 1992.

Trewartha, G. T., and G.-H. Smith. "Surface Configuration of the Driftless Cuestaform Hill Land." *Annals of the Association of American Geographers* 31, no. 1 (1941): 25–45.

Trowbridge, A. C. *Glacial Drift in the "Driftless Area" of Northeast Iowa.* Iowa City: Iowa Geological Survey, 1966.
Winchell, N. H. *The Geological and Natural History Survey of Minnesota. The Fifth Annual Report for the Year 1876.* St. Paul: Minnesota Geological Survey, 1877.

2. ANCIENT PEOPLE

Patty Loew's comment on the time horizons of ancient and modern Native peoples is from *Indian Nations of Wisconsin: Histories of Endurance and Renewal* (Madison: Wisconsin Historical Society Press, 2001), 2.
Edna Meudt, "Wisconsin Mounds," *Wisconsin Academy Review* 9, no. 3 (Summer 1962): 104.
James L. Theler and Robert F. Boszhart, *Twelve Millennia: Archaeology of the Upper Mississippi River Valley* (Iowa City: University of Iowa Press, 2003), 189–92.
Patty Loew, *Indian Nations of Wisconsin: Histories of Endurance and Renewal*, 1–2, 5, 6, 11.
Richard C. Taylor, "Notes Respecting Certain Indian Mounds and Earthworks, in the Form of Animal Effigies, Chiefly in the Wisconsin Territory, U.S.," *American Journal of Science and Arts* 34 (July 1838): 90–91, 92, 93, 94–95, 104.
Laurie Hovell McMillin, *Buried Indians: Digging Up the Past in a Midwestern Town* (Madison: University of Wisconsin Press, 2006), 121–26.
David S. Faldet, *Oneota Flow: The Upper Iowa River and Its People* (Iowa City: University of Iowa Press, 2009), 51–55, 56–57, 58–59.
E. Barrie Kavasch, "Wisconsin's Cave of Wonders," *Ancestral Threads: Weaving Remembrance in Poetry and Essays and Family Folklore* (Lincoln, NE: iUniverse, 2003), 41.

Further Readings

Arzigian, C. "The Emergence of Horticultural Economies in Southwestern Wisconsin." In *Emergent Horticultural Economies of the Eastern Woodlands*, edited by W. F. Keegan, 217–42. Carbondale: Southern Illinois University, 1987.
Gale, G. *Upper Mississippi: Or, Historical Sketches of the Mound-builders, the Indian Tribes, and the Progress of Civilization in the North-west; from AD 1600 to the Present Time.* Chicago: Clarke and Company, 1867.
Gartner, W. G. "Late Woodland Landscapes of Wisconsin: Ridged Fields, Effigy Mounds, and Territoriality." *Antiquity* 73, no. 281 (1999): 671–83.
Lapham, I. A. *The Antiquities of Wisconsin as Surveyed and Described.* Washington, DC: Smithsonian Institution, 1855; republished by University of Wisconsin Press, 2000.

Lewis, T. H. "Effigy Mounds in Iowa." *Science* 146 (1885): 453–54.

Mallam, R. C. "Iowa's Endangered Cultural Heritage." *Annals of Iowa* 46, no. 5 (1982): 355–72.

Peet, S. D. *The Mound Builders: Their Works and Relics.* Chicago: Office of the American Antiquarian, 1892.

Salzer, R. J. "The Gottschall Site: 3,500 Years of Ideological Continuity and Change." *Ontario Archaeology* 79/80 (2005): 109–14.

Schrab, G., and R. F. Boszhardt. *Hidden Thunder: Rock Art of the Upper Midwest.* Madison: Wisconsin Historical Society Press, 2016.

Shetrone, H. C. *The Mound-Builders.* Tuscaloosa: University of Alabama Press, 2004; originally published 1930.

Stiles-Hanson, C. "Petroglyphs and Pictographs of the Coulee Region." *Wisconsin Archaeologist* 68, no. 4 (1987): 287–340.

Taylor, S. "Description of Ancient Remains, Animal Mounds, and Embankments, Principally in the Counties of Grant, Iowa, and Richland, in Wisconsin Territory." *American Journal of Science* 44 (1842): 21–40.

Theler, J. L. *Woodland Tradition Economic Strategies: Animal Resource Utilization in Southwestern Wisconsin and Northeastern Iowa.* Iowa City: University of Iowa Office of State, 1987.

3. HISTORICAL ECOLOGIES

Laura Sherry, "Meditations," *Old Prairie du Chien* (Paris: Edward W. Titus, 1931), 73.

Henry David Thoreau's notes from his 1861 trip to Minnesota are transcribed and annotated in *Thoreau's Minnesota Journey: Two Documents: Thoreau's Notes on the Journey West and The Letters of Horace Mann, Jr.*, edited by Walter Harding (Geneseo, NY: The Thoreau Society, 1962), 3–5 .

Carol Ryrie Brink, *Caddie Woodlawn* (New York: Simon & Schuster Children's Publishing, 1936), 27–36.

Herman S. Pepoon, "An Ecological Survey of the Driftless Area of Illinois and Wisconsin," *School Science and Mathematics* 9, no. 5 (May 1909): 441–46; 9, no. 6 (June 1909): 441, 445, 446, 522, 523–25, 526–27.

John T. Curtis, *The Vegetation of Wisconsin: An Ordination of Plant Communities* (Madison: University of Wisconsin Press, 1959), 12–14.

Monika E. Shea, Lisa A. Schulte, and Brian J. Palik, "Reconstructing Vegetation Past: Pre-Euro-American Vegetation for the Midwest Driftless Area, USA," *Ecological Restoration* 32, no. 4 (2014): 422, 425, 429–30.

"Changes in Wildlife Over Time" is drawn from "Western Coulees and Ridges Ecological Landscape," chapter 22 in *Ecological Landscapes of Wisconsin: An Assessment of Ecological Resources and a Guide to Planning Sustainable Management*, Wisconsin Department of Natural Resources, PUB-SS-1131 (Madison: Wisconsin Department of Natural Resources, 2012), 32–37.

Cecile Houghton Stury, "Desoto Hills," *Sun Across Wisconsin* (publisher not identified; 1951), 61.

Further Readings

Dinsmore, J. J. *A Country So Full of Game: The Story of Wildlife in Iowa.* Iowa City: University of Iowa Press, 1994.

Fritz, G. J. "Native Farming Systems and Ecosystems in the Mississippi River Valley." In *Imperfect Balance: Landscape Transformations in the Pre-Columbian Americas*, edited by D. Lentz, 225–50. New York: Columbia University Press, 2000.

Hansen, H. P. "Postglacial Vegetation of the Driftless Area of Wisconsin." *American Midland Naturalist* 21, no. 3 (1939): 752–62.

Hartley, T. G. "The Flora of the 'Driftless Area.'" *University of Iowa Studies in Natural History* 21, no. 1 (1966).

Kline, V. M., and G. Cottam. "Response to Climate and Fire in the Driftless Area of Wisconsin." *Ecology* 60, no. 5 (1979): 861–68.

Norwick, R., J. Janvrin, S. Zigler, and R. Kratt, *Habits and Habitats of Fishes in the Upper Mississippi River.* La Crosse, WI: Upper Mississippi River Conservation Committee, U.S. Fish and Wildlife Service, 2011.

Philippon, D. J. "Thoreau's Notes on the Journey West: Nature Writing or Environmental History?" *American Transcendental Quarterly* 18, no. 2 (2004): 105–18.

Pielou, E. C. *After the Ice Age: The Return of Life to Glaciated North America.* Chicago: University of Chicago Press, 2008.

Pusateri, W. P., Roosa, D. M., and D. R. Farrar. "Habitat and Distribution of Plants Special to Iowa's Driftless Area." *Journal of Iowa Academy of Science* 100, no. 2 (1993): 29–53.

Ritterbusch, C., ed. *H. S. Pepoon: Pioneer Conservationist of Northwest Illinois (Essays on Ecology 1904–1933).* Galena, IL: Prairie Works, 2011.

Scott, W. E., ed. *Silent Wings: A Memorial to the Passenger Pigeon.* Madison: Wisconsin Society for Ornithology, 1947; reprinted in 2014 with a foreword by S. Temple.

4. Native Voices

The descriptions of Native place names are drawn from: Virgil J. Vogel, *Indian Names on Wisconsin's Map* (Madison: University of Wisconsin Press, 1991); Warren Upham, *Minnesota Geographic Names: Their Origin and Historic Significance* (St. Paul: Minnesota Historical Society, 1920); Virgil J. Vogel, *Iowa Place Names of Indian Origin* (Iowa City: University of Iowa Press, 1983); Edward Callary, *Place Names of Illinois* (Champaign: University of Illinois Press, 2008); and Edward Callary, *Place Names of Wisconsin* (Madison: University of Wisconsin Press, 2016).

Ulysses S. White's "The Story of Devils Lake" appeared in the *Hocak Worak Newspaper* (Black River Falls, WI), January 27, 2012, p. 8.

The statement of Hoowaneka/Hųwąnįka (Little Elk) was reported by Caleb Atwater in *Remarks Made on a Tour to Prairie du Chien Thence to Washington City, in 1829* (Columbus, OH: I. N. Whiting, 1831; reprint, New York: Arno Press, 1975), 121–22.

The full title of Black Hawk's autobiography is *Life of Black Hawk or Mà-Ka-Tai-Me-She-Kià-Kiàk: Embracing the tradition of his nation; Indian wars in which he has been engaged; cause of joining the British in their late war with America, and its history; description of the Rock River village; manners and customs; encroachments by the whites, contrary to treaty; removal from his village in 1831: with an account of the cause and general history of the late war; his surrender and confinement at Jefferson barracks and travels throughout the United States*. The original edition, edited by John Barton Patterson, was published in Cincinnati in 1833. The selected reading appears on 130–37, 138.

George William Featherstonhaugh, *A Canoe Voyage Up the Minnay Sotor; with an Account of the Lead and Copper Deposits in Wisconsin; of the Gold Region in the Cherokee Country; and Sketches of Popular Manners; &c. &c. &c* (London: R. Bentley, 1847), 229–37.

Reuben Gold Thwaites, "Narrative of Spoon Decorah," *Collections of the State Historical Society of Wisconsin* 13 (1895): 458–59, 461–62.

Mountain Wolf Woman and Nancy Oestreich Lurie, *Mountain Wolf Woman, Sister of Crashing Thunder: The Autobiography of a Winnebago Indian* (Ann Arbor: University of Michigan Press, 1966), 1, 2–5, 6–7.

Further Readings

Bieder, R. E. *Native American Communities in Wisconsin, 1600–1960: A Study of Tradition and Change*. Madison: University of Wisconsin Press, 1995.

Blowsnake, S., and P. Radin. *Crashing Thunder: The Autobiography of an American Indian*. Ann Arbor: University of Michigan Press, 1999; originally published 1926.

Catlin, G. "Letter—No. 52, Camp Des Moines." In *Letters and Notes on the Manners, Customs, and Condition of the North American Indians: Written During Eight Years' Travel in 1832–1839*, vol. 2, 141–50. New York: Wiley and Putnam, 1842.

Green, W. "Description of the 1837 Ioway Map." In *An Atlas of Early Maps of the American Midwest, Part II*, edited by W. R. Wood, 14–17. Springfield: Illinois State Museum, 2000.

Hagan, W. T. *The Sac and Fox Indians*. Norman: University of Oklahoma Press, 1958.

Kappler, C. J., ed. *Indian Affairs: Laws and Treaties*. Vol. 2, *Treaties*. Washington, DC: Government Printing Office, 1904.

Loew, P. *Indian Nations of Wisconsin: Histories of Endurance and Renewal*. Madison: Wisconsin Historical Society Press, 2001.

Lewis, J. O. *The Aboriginal Port-folio: A Collection of Portraits of the Most Celebrated Chiefs of the North American Indians*. Philadelphia: J. O. Lewis, 1835.

Nichols, R. L. *Black Hawk and the Warrior's Path*. Hoboken, NJ: Wiley-Blackwell, 1992.

Radin, P. *The Winnebago Tribe*. Lincoln: University of Nebraska Press, 1990; originally published 1923.

Smith, D. L. *Folklore of the Winnebago Tribe*. Norman: University of Oklahoma Press, 1997.

Tigerman, K. *Wisconsin Indian Literature: Anthology of Native Voices*. Madison: University of Wisconsin Press, 2006.

Trask, K. A. *Black Hawk: The Battle for the Heart of America*. New York: Macmillan, 2006.

5. EXPLORATIONS

William Eberhart's "La Crosse at Ninety Miles an Hour" first appeared in *The Hudson Review* 6, no. 2 (Summer 1953). Reprinted in *Collected Poems, 1930–1976* (New York: Oxford University Press, 1976), 237.

Jacques Marquette, *Le Premier Voÿage qu'a Fait Le P. Marquette Vers le Nouveau Mexique & Comment s'en est Formé le Defsein* [*Of the First Voyage Made by Father Marquette toward New Mexico, and How the Idea Thereof was Conceived*]. Available in various editions. This passage is drawn from *The Jesuit Relations and Allied Documents*, vol. 59, edited by Reuben Gold Thwaites (Cleveland: The Burrows Brothers Company, 1898), 105–7.

Zebulon Montgomery Pike, *The Expeditions of Zebulon Montgomery Pike to Headwaters of the Mississippi River, through Louisiana Territory, and in New Spain, during the Years 1805-6-7*, edited by Elliott Coues (New York: Francis and Harper, 1895; first published 1810), 28–35, 39, 41–42, 43–45, 46–47–50, 53–55, 56–65, 66–69, 72–73.

Henry R. Schoolcraft, *Narrative Journal of Travels through the Northwestern Regions of the United States: Extending from Detroit through the Great Chain of American Lakes to the Sources of the Mississippi River, Performed as a Member of the Expedition under Governor Cass in the Year 1820* (Albany: E. & E. Hosford, 1821), 323–25, 327–29, 330–31, 337–38, 358–61.

John Muir's letters to Emily Pelton are held in the Wisconsin Historical Society Archives, Collections SC185, SC1676, and Neb Mss A, in Madison, Wisconsin.

William Cronon, "Landscape and Home: Environmental Traditions in Wisconsin," *Wisconsin Magazine of History* 74, no. 2 (1990): 82–85, 90–91.

Robin Wall Kimmerer, "Kickapoo," in *Gathering Moss: A Natural and Cultural History of Mosses* (Corvallis: Oregon State University Press, 2003), 62–68.

August Derleth, "Old Man Fishing," in *West of Morning* (Francestown, NH: Golden Quill Press, 1960), 29–31.

Further Readings

Atwater, C. *Remarks Made on a Tour to Prairie du Chien Thence to Washington City, in 1829.* Columbus, OH: I. N. Whiting, 1831; reprint New York: Arno Press, 1975.

Burke, W. J. *The Upper Mississippi Valley: How the Landscape Shaped Our Heritage.* Waukon, IA: Mississippi Valley Press, 2000.

Carver, J. *Travels through the Interior Parts of North America in the Years 1766, 1767, and 1768.* London: Printed for C. Dilly, H. Payne, and J. Phillips, 1781.

Hubach, R. R. *Early Midwestern Travel Narratives: An Annotated Bibliography, 1634–1850.* Detroit: Wayne State University Press, 1998.

Kellogg, L. P., ed. *Early Narratives of the Northwest, 1634–1699.* New York: Charles Scribner's Sons, 1917.

Lanman, C. *A Summer in the Wilderness Embracing a Canoe Voyage up the Mississippi and around Lake Superior.* New York: D. Appleton, 1847.

Legler, H. E. "Narratives of Early Wisconsin Travellers, Prior to 1800." In *Proceedings of the State Historical Society of Wisconsin,* 157–93. Madison: State Historical Society of Wisconsin, 1906.

Thwaites, R. G., ed. *The Jesuit Relations and Allied Documents: Travels and Explorations of the Jesuit Missionaries in New France, 1610–1791,* vols. 1–71. Cleveland: The Burrows Brothers Company, 1898.

6. Early Economies

William Cronon's comment appears in *Nature's Metropolis: Chicago and the Great West* (New York: WW Norton, 1992), 29.

Alice D'Alessio's "Diggings" appeared in *Verse Wisconsin* 107 (November 2011), at http://www.versewisconsin.org/Issue107/poems/dalessio.html.

Henry E. Legler, "Life in the Diggings," *Leading Events of Wisconsin History: The Story of the State* (Milwaukee: Sentinel Company, 1898), 165–68.

"Public Land Sale" appeared in the June 5, 1847, edition of the (Lancaster) *Wisconsin Herald* and was apparently penned by its editor, James M. Goodhue. It was included in Joseph Schafer, *The Wisconsin Lead Region* (Madison: State Historical Society of Wisconsin, 1932), 137–38.

Antoine Grignon, "Recollections of Antoine Grignon," *Proceedings of the State Historical Society of Wisconsin* (Madison: State Historical Society of Wisconsin, 1914), 110–11, 113, 124–26.

Walter A. Blair, *A Raft Pilot's Log: A History of the Great Rafting Industry on the Upper Mississippi, 1840–1915* (Cleveland: Arthur H. Clark Company, 1930), 29–31, 33, 34, 35, 25, 35–36. Blair's obituary appeared in the *Davenport Democrat,* December 24, 1939, p. 1.

Agnes M. Larson, *History of the White Pine Industry in Minnesota* (Minneapolis: University of Minnesota Press, 1949), 39–40, 43, 45–46.

Hildegard Binder Johnson, *Order Upon the Land: The U.S. Rectangular Land Survey and the Upper Mississippi Country* (New York: Oxford University Press, 1976), 85–87.

Laura Sherry, "Dreamers," in *Old Prairie du Chien* (Paris: Edward W. Titus, 1931), 53.

Further Readings

Conzen, M. P. "The European Settling and Transformation of the Upper Mississippi Valley Lead Region." In *Wisconsin Land and Life*, edited by R. C. Ostergren and T. R. Vale, 163–96. Madison: University of Wisconsin Press, 1997.

Derleth, A. *Land of Gray Gold: Lead Mining in Wisconsin.* New York: Aladdin Books, 1954.

Gilman, R. R. "The Fur Trade in the Upper Mississippi Valley, 1630–1850." *Wisconsin Magazine of History* 58, no. 1 (1974): 2–18.

Keyes, C. R. "Spanish Mines: An Episode in Primitive American Lead-mining." *Annals of Iowa* 10 (1912): 539–46.

Murphy L. E. *A Gathering of Rivers: Indians, Métis, and Mining in the Western Great Lakes, 1737–1832.* Lincoln: University of Nebraska Press, 2004.

Robinson, E. V. D. *Early Economic Conditions and the Development of Agriculture in Minnesota.* Minneapolis: University of Minnesota, 1915.

Russell, C. E. *A Rafting on the Mississip'.* Minneapolis: University of Minnesota Press, 1928; reissued 2001.

Trewartha, G. T. "French Settlement in the Driftless Hill Land." *Annals of the Association of American Geographers* 28, no. 3 (1938): 179–200.

Trewartha, G. T. "A Second Epoch of Destructive Occupance in the Driftless Hill Land: (1760–1832: Period of British, Spanish and Early American Control)." *Annals of the Association of American Geographers* 30, no. 2 (1940): 109–42.

Walthall, J. H. *Galena and Aboriginal Trade in Eastern North America.* Springfield: Illinois State Museum, 1981.

Wyman, M. *The Wisconsin Frontier.* Bloomington: Indiana University Press, 1998.

7. Settler Stories

Thomas R. Smith's "Sesquicentennial Song" is from his chapbook *Kinnickinnic* (Madison: Parallel Press, 2008), 19.

Juliette Augusta Magill Kinzie, *Wau-Bun: The Early Day in the Northwest* (Philadelphia: J. B. Lippincott, 1873), 113–18, 119–23. Originally published in 1856 and reprinted in many editions since.

Fabu, "Macaja Revels Camped at a Stream of Water," in *Echolocations: Poets Map Madison*, edited by Sarah Busse and Wendy Vardaman (Middleton, WI: Cowfeather Press, 2013), 153.

Chauncey H. Cooke, "A Badger Boy in Blue: The Letters of Chauncey H. Cooke," *Wisconsin Magazine of History* 4, no. 1 (1920): 89, 90, 91, 92–93, 94, 96–98; 4, no. 2 (1920): 208–9. Cooke's letters have been compiled and published as *A Badger Boy in Blue: The Civil War Letters of Chauncey H. Cooke*, with an introduction by William Mulligan Jr. (Detroit: Wayne State University Press, 2007).

Gertrude Frazier and Rose B. Poff, *The Kickapoo Valley: The Gem of Wisconsin* (La Crosse, WI: Brookhaven Press, 1896), 4–5, 7–8, 94–99.

Pearl Swiggum's untitled article from her "Stump Ridge Farm" column originally appeared in the *Crawford County Independent*, October 4, 1990, p. 2.

Jacqueline West, "Yanys," in *Cherma* (Madison, WI: Parallel Press, 2010), 9.

Further Readings

Andrzejewski, A., A. R. Alanen, and S. F. Scarlett, eds. *Field Guide to Southwestern Wisconsin*. A guidebook produced for the 2012 meeting of the Vernacular Architecture Forum. Madison: UW–Madison Departments of Art History and Landscape Architecture, 2012.

Cooper, Z. L. *Black Settlers in Rural Wisconsin*. Madison: State Historical Society of Wisconsin, 1977.

Gould, W. "Early Black Settlers in Rural Wisconsin Left a Proud Legacy" and "Descendant Proud of Rich Family History: Her Story Reveals Complex Tapestry of Vernon County Pioneers." *Milwaukee Journal Sentinel*, January 6, 1997, pp. 1A, 6A.

Hudson, J. C. "The Creation of Towns in Wisconsin." In *Wisconsin Land and Life*, edited by R. C. Ostergren and T. R. Vale, 197–220. Madison: University of Wisconsin Press, 1997.

McDermott, J. F. "Minnesota 100 Years Ago." *Minnesota History* 33, no. 3 (1952): 112–25.

Nelson, D. T., ed. *The Diary of Elisabeth Koren, 1853–1855*. Northfield, MN: Norwegian-American Historical Association, 1955; 7th printing, 2015.

Reps, J. W. *Views and Viewmakers of Urban America: Lithographs of Towns and Cities in the United States and Canada, Notes on the Artists and Publishers, and a Union Catalog of Their Work, 1825–1925*. Columbia: University of Missouri Press, 1984.

Sheldon, T. H. "Narrative of a Pioneer of Wisconsin and Pike's Peak." *Wisconsin Magazine of History* 12, no. 4 (1929): 403–23.

Trewartha. G. T. "French Settlement in the Driftless Hill Land." *Annals of the Association of American Geographers* 28, no. 3 (1938): 179–200.

8. Farming Lives

Laura Sherry, "Me and My Man," in *Old Prairie du Chien* (Paris: Edward W. Titus, 1931), 8–9.

William Rudolph Smith, *Incidents of a Journey from Pennsylvania to Wisconsin Territory, in 1837, Being the Journal of Gen. William Rudolph Smith, U.S. Commissioner for Treaty with the Chippewa Indians of the Upper Mississippi* (Chicago: Wright Howes, 1927), 65–67.

Hamlin Garland, *A Son of the Middle Border* (New York: Macmillan Company, 1917), 1–5, 12–13, 27, 36–39, 42–43.

Laura Ingalls Wilder, *Little House in the Big Woods* (New York and Evanston: Harper & Row, 1932), 199–211.

Ben Logan, *The Land Remembers: The Story of a Farm and Its People* (Madison: University of Wisconsin Press, 2017; originally published 1975), 6–12.

Lynne Burgess, "It Is Natural," *Wisconsin People & Ideas* 52, no. 3 (Summer 2006): 20.

Further Readings

Apps, J. W. *Wisconsin Agriculture: A History.* Madison: Wisconsin Historical Society Press, 2015.

Cates, R. L. *Voices from the Heart of the Land: Rural Stories That Inspire Community.* Madison: University of Wisconsin Press, 2008.

Gallagher, J. P., R. F. Boszhardt, R. F. Sasso, and K. Stevenson. "Oneota Ridged Field Agriculture in Southwestern Wisconsin." *American Antiquity* 50, no. 3 (1985): 605–12.

Gard, R. E., and D. O'Brien. *Down in the Valleys: Wisconsin Back Country Lore and Humor.* Madison: Wisconsin House, 1971.

Hildebrand, John. *Mapping the Farm: The Chronicle of a Family.* New York, Alfred A. Knopf, 1995.

Lieberman, A. *Neighbors: A Forty-Year Portrait of an American Farm Community.* San Francisco: Collins Publishers, 1993.

Pine, C., and C. Spengler. *CROPP Cooperative Roots: The First 25 Years.* La Farge, WI: CROPP Cooperative, 2013.

Shepard, M. *Restoration Agriculture: Real World Permaculture for Farmers.* (Austin, TX: Acres USA, 2013).

Wolf, R. *Heartland Portrait: Stories from the Rural Midwest.* Decorah, IA: Free River Pres, 2009.

9. Waterways

Kevin Koch writes of the Mississippi River in *The Driftless Land: Spirit of Place in the Upper Mississippi Valley* (Cape Girardeau: Southeast Missouri State University Press, 2010), 34.

"The Pinery Boy" was included by Franz Rickaby in *Ballads and Songs of the Shanty-Boy* (Cambridge: Harvard University Press, 1926), which was expanded and reprinted as *Pinery Boys: Songs and Songcatching in the Lumberjack Era*, edited by Franz Rickaby with Gretchen Dykstra and James P. Leary (Madison: University of Wisconsin Press, 2017), 187–89. Alan Lomax included the song in *Folk Songs of North America in the English Language* (Garden City, NY: Doubleday, 1960).

Mark Twain, *Life on the Mississippi* (Boston: James R. Osgood and Company, 1883), 564–65, 567–70, 571–79.

Wallace Stegner, from "The River," in *American Places*, edited by Elliot Porter, W. Stegner and Page Stegner, and John Macrae III (New York: Dutton, 1981), 59–60, 67–69.

Catherine Young, "Water Song," *About Place Journal* 2, no. 3 (2013), at http://aboutplacejournal.org/the-future-of-water/catherine-young-ii-iii.

Lynne Diebel, *Crossing the Driftless: A Canoe Trip through a Midwestern Landscape* (Madison: University of Wisconsin Press, 2015), 87–89, 90–92.

Joseph Langland, "War," in *Selected Poems* (Amherst: University of Massachusetts Press, 1991), 52.

Further Readings

Anfinson, J. O. *The River We Have Wrought: A History of the Upper Mississippi.* Minneapolis: University of Minnesota Press, 2003.

Carson, E. C., and J. E. Rawling III. *Late Cenozoic Evolution of the Lower Wisconsin River Valley: Evidence for the Reversal of the River.* Wisconsin Geological and Natural History Survey Open-File Report 2015–02. Madison: University of Wisconsin–Extension, 2015.

Derleth, A. W. *The Wisconsin: River of a Thousand Isles.* Madison: University of Wisconsin Press, 1942.

Durbin, R. D. *The Wisconsin River: An Odyssey through Time and Space.* Cross Plains, WI: Spring Freshet Press, 1997.

Fremling, C. R. *Immortal River: The Upper Mississippi in Ancient and Modern Times.* Madison: University of Wisconsin Press, 2005.

Juckem, P. F., R. J. Hunt, M. P. Anderson, and D. M. Robertson. "Effects of Climate and Land Management Change on Streamflow in the Driftless Area of Wisconsin." *Journal of Hydrology* 355, no. 1 (2008): 123–30.

Knox, J. C. "Human Impacts on Wisconsin Stream Channels." *Annals of the Association of American Geographers* 67, no. 3 (1977): 323–42.

Merrick, G. B. *Old Times on the Upper Mississippi: The Recollections of a Steamboat Pilot from 1854 to 1863.* Cleveland: A. H. Clark, 1909.

Metcoff, J. *Along the Wisconsin Riverway.* Madison: University of Wisconsin Press, 1997.

Motoviloff, J. *Driftless Stories: Outdoors in Southwest Wisconsin*. Madison: Prairie Oak Press, 2001.

Oates, T. *Lower Wisconsin River: Images*. Madison: University of Wisconsin–Extension, 1994.

Salwey, K. *The Old-Time River Rats: Tales of Bygone Days on the Wild Mississippi*. Minneapolis, MN: Voyageur Press, 2009.

Skeate, J. *Familiar World: Notes of a Driftless Fly Fisher*. Decorah: Sattre Press, 2009.

Thwaites, R. G. *Historic Waterways: Six Hundred Miles of Canoeing down the Rock, Fox, and Wisconsin Rivers*. Chicago: A. C. McClurg, 1888.

10. Conserving Lands

Aldo Leopold's most fully developed discussion of the "land community" is in his essay "The Land Ethic" in *A Sand County Almanac and Sketches Here and There* (New York: Oxford University Press, 1949).

Robert Gard's unnamed poem appeared in *Wisconsin Sketches* (Madison: Wisconsin House, 1973), a book that Gard and artist Aaron Bohrod collaborated on, edited by Mark Lefebvre.

Aldo Leopold, "Coon Valley: An Adventure in Cooperative Conservation," *American Forests* 41, no. 5 (May 1935): 205–8.

Frank Lloyd Wright, *Frank Lloyd Wright: An Autobiography* (New York: Duell, Sloane, and Pearce, 1943), 167–71, 174.

The "Letter from the Old Order Amish Churches" was submitted as public testimony and appeared in *A Place to Which We Belong: Wisconsin Writers on Wisconsin Landscapes*, edited by Dennis Boyer and Justin Isherwood (Madison: 1000 Friends of Wisconsin, 1998), 110–12.

An edited version of Stanley Temple's "An Ecological Play on a Stage Known as Dunlap Hollow" was included in *A Place to Which We Belong: Wisconsin Writers on Wisconsin Landscapes*, edited by Dennis Boyer and Justin Isherwood (Madison: 1000 Friends of Wisconsin, 1998), 95–97.

Lynne Heasley, *A Thousand Pieces of Paradise: Landscape and Property in the Kickapoo Valley* (Madison: University of Wisconsin Press, 2005), 16–18.

Emmet J. Doyle's "Frac Sand Song" was composed in 2013 and is licensed by Creative Commons.

Further Readings

Anderson, R. "Coon Valley Days." *Wisconsin Academy Review* 48, no. 2 (2002): 42–48.

Apfelbaum, S. I. *Nature's Second Chance: Restoring the Ecology of Stone Prairie Farm*. Boston: Beacon Press, 2009.

Green, W. "The Great River Refuge." In *Flyways: Pioneering Waterfowl Management in North America*, edited by A. Hawkins, R. Hanson, H. Nelson, and H. Reeves, 431–39. Washington, DC: U.S. Fish and Wildlife Service, 1984.

Hawkins, A. S. "Return to Coon Valley." In *The Farm as Natural Habitat: Reconnecting Food Systems with Ecosystems*, edited by D. L. Jackson and L. L. Jackson, 57–70. Covelo, CA: Island Press, 2002.

Helms, J. D., G. A. Pavelis, S. Argabright, R. G. Cronshey, and H. R. Sinclair. "National Soil Conservation Policies: A Historical Case Study of the Driftless Area." *Agricultural History* 70, no. 2 (1996): 377–94.

Hoxmeier, R. J. H., D. J. Dieterman, and L. M. Miller. "Brook Trout Distribution, Genetics, and Population Characteristics in the Driftless Area of Minnesota." *North American Journal of Fisheries Management* 35, no. 4 (2015): 632–48.

Imlay, M. J. "A Case for Protecting the Driftless Area of the Upper Midwest." *Malacological Review* 6, no. 1 (1973): 64–65.

Luhning, J. "Birth of a Conservation Movement: Contour Farming in Wisconsin." *Edible Madison* 14 (Fall 2013): 34–42.

Pearson, T. W. *Frac Sand Mining and the Struggle for Place, Community, and Democracy.* Minneapolis: University of Minnesota Press, 2017.

Pearson, T. "Frac Sand Mining in Wisconsin: Understanding Emerging Conflicts and Community Organizing." *Culture, Agriculture, Food and Environment* 35, no. 1 (2013): 30–40.

Steingraber, S. "Sand County, the Sequel." *Orion Magazine* 31, no. 3 (May–June 2012): 10–11.

Steinmetz, B. *That Dam History: The Story of the La Farge Dam Project.* La Farge, WI: Kickapoogian Press, 2011.

Sterling, B., ed. *The People Remember: An Oral History of the Kickapoo La Farge Dam Project.* Sparta, WI: Prell Books, 2004.

Trimble, S. W. *Historical Agriculture and Soil Erosion in the Upper Mississippi Valley Hill Country.* Boca Raton, FL: CRC Press, 2012.

11. COMMUNITIES IN TRANSITION

R. Clark Mallam, "Some Views on the Archaeology of the Driftless Area in Iowa," *Proceedings of the Iowa Academy of Science* 91 (1984): 16–21.

Ralph Nuzum, *Here on the Kickapoo* (Viroqua, WI: Nuzum, 1955), 9. Reprinted by the Friends of the Kickapoo Valley Reserve in 2008.

William Barillas, *The Midwestern Pastoral: Place and Landscape in Literature of the American Heartland* (Columbus: Ohio University Press, 2006), xiv.

Mark Wunderlich's "Driftless Elegy" first appeared in *The Literary Review* 56, no. 3 (2013) and was included in *The Earth Avails* (Minneapolis, MN: Graywolf Press, 2014), 12–16.

Mary Elizabeth Hussong, "Richland Center, the Cradle of Suffrage in Wisconsin: How Earliest Enthusiasts Led Sisters," *Milwaukee Journal*, December 21, 1924, part 4, p. 1.

Rick Harsch, *The Driftless Zone; or, A Novel Concerning the Selective Outmigration from Small Cities* (South Royalton, VT: Steerforth Press, 1997), 50–53.

David Rhodes, *Driftless* (Minneapolis: Milkweed Editions, 2008), 88–97.
Robert Wolf, "Postville: Iowa's Entry into the Post-Modern," *Heartland Portrait: Stories from the Rural Midwest* (Decorah, IA: Free River Pres, 2009), 269–76.
Kathe Davis's "Things I Love About Where I Am" appeared in *Verse Wisconsin* 109 (July 2012), at http://www.versewisconsin.org/Issue109/poems/davis.html.

Further Readings

Fellows, W. "Dana Duppler." In *A Passion to Preserve: Gay Men as Keepers of Culture*, 204–10. Madison: University of Wisconsin Press, 2004.
Hoelscher, S. D. *Picturing Indians: Photographic Encounters and Tourist Fantasies in H. H. Bennett's Wisconsin Dells.* Madison: University of Wisconsin Press, 2008.
Lemley, C. K., and J. Feyen. *Back to the Land Oral History Project*, https://sound cloud.com/wdrt-news/tamara-dean-back-to-the-land?in=wdrt-news/sets/individual-stories-for-1.
Loew, P. *Seventh Generation Earth Ethics: Native Voices of Wisconsin.* Madison: Wisconsin Historical Society Press, 2014.
MacGregor, L. *Habits of the Heartland: Small-Town Life in Modern America.* Ithaca, NY: Cornell University Press, 2010.
Mattison, Wendy, Laotou Lo, and Thomas Scarseth, eds. *Hmong Lives: From Laos to La Crosse, Stories of Eight Hmong Elders.* La Crosse, WI: Pump House Regional Center for the Arts, 1994.
McBride, G. G., ed. *Women's Wisconsin: From Native Matriarchies to the New Millennium.* Madison: Wisconsin Historical Society Press, 2005.
Mouser, B. L. *For Labor, Race, and Liberty: George Edwin Taylor, His Historic Run for the White House, and the Making of Independent Black Politics.* Madison: University of Wisconsin Press, 2011.
Pederson, J. M. *Between Memory and Reality: Family and Community in Rural Wisconsin, 1870–1970.* Madison: University of Wisconsin Press.
Teatro Indocumentado. "Historia de nuestras vidas." *The Postville Project*, at http://postvilleproject.org/stories/items/show/54.

12. FUTURES

Ken McCullough's "Broken Gates" provided the title for his poetry collection *Broken Gates* (Red Wing, MN: Red Dragonfly Press, 2012), 40–41.
Clifford D. Simak, *Way Station* (New York: Doubleday, 1963), 24–28.
Stephen J. Lyons, "Near La Crescent, Minnesota," in *Going Driftless: Life Lessons from the Heartland for Unraveling Times* (Guilford, CT: Rowman & Littlefield, 2015), 69–74.
Ted Leeson, *Jerusalem Creek: Journeys into Driftless Country* (Guilford, CT: Lyons Press/Globe Pequot Press, 2002), 215–21.

Kevin Koch, *The Driftless Land: Spirit of Place in the Upper Mississippi Valley* (Cape Girardeau: Southeast Missouri State University Press, 2010), 196–204.

Further Readings

Bowen, S., and K. De Master. "Wisconsin's 'Happy Cows'? Articulating Heritage and Territory as New Dimensions of Locality." *Agriculture and Human Values* 31, no. 4 (2014): 549–62.

Johnson, R. "Forging a Driftless Culture." *Big River Magazine* (July–August 2015): 24–27.

Knoot, T. G., M. E. Shea, L. A. Schulte, J. C. Tyndall, M. D. Nelson, C. H. Perry, and B. J. Palik. "Forest Change in the Driftless Area of the Midwest: From a Preferred to Undesirable Future." *Forest Ecology and Management* 341 (2015): 110–20.

Knox, J. C. "Large Increases in Flood Magnitude in Response to Modest Changes in Climate." *Nature* 361, no. 6411 (1993): 430–32.

Lyons, J., J. S. Stewart, and M. Mitro. "Predicted Effects of Climate Warming on the Distribution of 50 Stream Fishes in Wisconsin, USA." *Journal of Fish Biology* 77, no. 8 (2010): 1867–98.

Matuszak, S. "The Driftless Manifesto." *Roads & Kingdoms*, posted September 22, 2015, at http://roadsandkingdoms.com/2015/the-driftless-manifesto.

Sanders, S. R. *Staying Put: Making a Home in a Restless World*. Boston: Beacon Press, 1993.

Schulte, L. A., M. Rickenbach, and L. C. Merrick. "Ecological and Economic Benefits of Cross-Boundary Coordination among Private Forest Landowners." *Landscape Ecology* 23, no. 4 (2008): 481–96.

Walsh, P. "Many Sand Counties." *Landscape Architecture Magazine* (March 2015), at https://landscapearchitecturemagazine.org/2015/03/23/many-sand-counties.

Wisconsin Initiative on Climate Change Impacts. *Wisconsin's Changing Climate: Impacts and Adaptation*. Madison: Nelson Institute for Environmental Studies, University of Wisconsin–Madison, and the Wisconsin Department of Natural Resources, 2011.

Index

Page numbers for illustrations and captions are in italics.